D0026179

PUBLICATION DESIGN FOR EDITORS

ROBERT BOHLE

Virginia Commonwealth University

PRENTICE HALL, Englewood Cliffs, New Jersey 07632

Bohle, Robert H.
Publication design for editors / Robert Bohle.
p. cm.
Includes bibliographical references.
ISBN 0-13-737537-9 :
1. Printing, Practical--Layout. 2. Newspaper layout and typography. 3. Magazine design. 4. Newsletters. 5. Editing.
I. Title.
Z246.B635 1990
808'.06607--dc20 89-37549
CIP

Editorial/production supervision
and interior design: Colleen Brosnan
Cover design: Miriam Recio
Manufacturing buyer: Carol Bystrom and Ed O'Dougherty

A Division of Simon & Schuster
Englewood Cliffs, New Jersey 07632

Printed in the United States of America

10 9 8 7 6 5 4 3 2 1

ISBN 0-13-737537-9

Prentice-Hall International (UK) Limited, *London*
Prentice-Hall of Australia Pty. Limited, *Sydney*
Prentice-Hall Canada Inc., *Toronto*
Prentice-Hall of India Private Limited, *New Delhi*
Prentice-Hall Hispanoamericana, S.A., *Mexico*
Prentice-Hall of Japan, Inc., *Tokyo*
Simon & Schuster Asia Pte. Ltd., *Singapore*
Editora Prentice-Hall do Brasil, Ltda., *Rio de Janeiro*

For Sharon, Cameron, and Christopher

CONTENTS

PREFACE

In some ways this is a philosophy book.

In some ways it is less about editing and design as the generally accepted terms are used—fixing words and sentences, and placing those in ink on paper—than it is about a certain way of looking at words and pictures.

Philosophy is defined as, among other things, a system of general principles underlying thought or activity. My overarching purpose in writing this book is to espouse my philosophy of editing and design.

I wanted to use the word "edesign" in the book's title (and Prentice-Hall's Steve Dalphin is probably right in nixing the idea) to underline how important is the integration of editing/design: only a new word truly catches the tone.

The concepts behind *edesign* are not new, and they are certainly not *my* ideas alone. This approach to editing and design is, unfortunately, not widespread, but its time has come.

The most basic function of editing is to present information in an understandable form, to take tons of raw information and turn it into pounds of news. Mass communication is never perfect; an editor's job is to lift the level of communication to its highest level.

Design, itself, communicates. It can add meaning to content, enhancing what a writer has done. Because design communicates, it *must* be considered part of the editing process. It is as important a part of editing as are grammar and style. Design should not be merely a cosmetic touch added almost as an afterthought when the editing of the words has been completed.

In this book, when I speak of design, I mean *journalistic design,* as opposed to *artistic design.* Journalistic design is concerned with the communication of information. Therefore it is functional design. Artistic design is concerned first with looking good, not necessarily communicating. I think publication design ought to be journalistic design.

Integrated editing, a term I use to mean editing that includes concern for (journalistic) design at every step of the process, should be considered a redundancy. Good editing *should* be "integrated"; it *should* consider the presentation of the information as the words are pared and sharpened. Unfortunately, this is rarely the case.

Mary K. Baumann, while art director of *Geo* magazine, observed:

> A lot of designers don't get along very well because they can't think in terms of words and also, on the other side, there are a lot of editors who can't think in terms of pictures. Really, the perfect marriage is between people who can think about both of them in terms of their function. If you can start that process back when the story starts to happen, it's even more exciting and that's where it's got to start. You've got to deal with the information you want to impart to your reader.[1]

I've got that quote on a poster above my desk, and you should too.

Too many editors, and too many books about editing, tend to focus on the words and ignore design until the end of the process, when it is often too late to achieve the best presentation for communication. Many editing books have only a chapter or two on design and page layout. These rarely discuss *how* to present information optimally.

This book, however, approaches design as an integral part of the editing process. Its aim is to be a general overview and introduction to the "edesign" process, not the last word on either design or editing. Word editing is only touched upon in a brief appendix. Other fine books, listed in the extensive bibliography, cover these topics individually quite well.

This book is meant to be the bridge between books about words and books about design. It is aimed mostly at "wordsmith" editors, or those who think of editing as strictly fixing the writer's work. My goal is to make word people more comfortable with and better at designing their publications.

To use the language of computers, I want to make design more "user-friendly." I once thought design and layout skills were birthrights of the talented, that somehow you either had *it* or you didn't. Then I learned the principles of visual perception and communication. The more thoroughly I came to understand these principles and how the brain—not the eye—sees, the better I understood how to design the shape of my printed communication.

This book is meant to be the book I wish I had when I got started. I hope to show you that good design can be created by anyone (yes, I said *anyone*) who can understand and follow some basic principles. (Now *great* design *is* something else. When I understand *that,* I'll write another book!)

The text is general enough to be used by a wide variety of communications classes, such as publications design, beginning newspaper design, business communications, public relations, among others; as well as by communications professionals, such as newspaper editors, newsletter editors, and corporate publication editors.

This is not a book for beginners. I assume that you already have at least a rudimentary understanding of writing and editing for mass communication.

The structure is meant to take you through the important phases of understanding journalistic design: basic design concepts, design applied (or layout), typography, and then discussions on how to use photos, art, graphics, and color in an effective design.

The three chapters on the production end of publication design—typesetting and printing, paste-up, andpaper—are admittedly minimal. Detailed discussions of print production really lie beyond the scope of this book. I want you

[1]In J.N. Black, "Magazine Design: The Evolution," *Folio* (November 1983), p. 87.

to understand how to talk to a printer, but not necessarily how to do something yourself. You should refer to Wendell Crow's fine book *Communication Graphics* (Prentice-Hall, 1986) or *Pocket Pal* (International Paper Company), or one of the other books listed in the Bibliography for more complete information.

The last three chapters run through the process lightly for newsletters and brochures, for magazine-size publications, and for newspapers, both full size and tabloid. Case studies included in these chapters show you practical design decisions at work.

Each chapter ends with a Checklist meant to summarize the important points in that chapter as well assome major points from previous chapters. Reading the Checklist alone should tell you pretty much what you need to know *and understand* at that point in the process

Many chapters have a list of projects, explorations, discoveries—whatever you think they should be called. The object is to give you a chance to try your hand at putting the principles into practice.

The back of the book consists of a Glossary, a Selected Bibliography, and an appendix that outlines some editing tips.

The goal of this book is to make editors more visually literate. We live in an increasingly visual world, and if print communicators wish to keep pace, they too must become more visual. This does not mean that design becomes all, that form now overrides content.

It does mean, however, that design must take its rightful place as an integral part of a complete, or perhaps"compleat," editing process.

ACKNOWLEDGMENTS

This is where authors always thank those who have been particularly helpful in putting together the massive effort that is a book. Were I to thank all of the people who helped, inspired, cajoled, gave me free time, or taught me—with great patience—the best of what they know, this section would expand beyond all reason. I have tried my best to distill all that I have gained into this presentation of ideas. I simply must mention the most crucial helpers.

Naturally, I would like to thank all those (listed below) who allowed me to use samples of their work to illustrate points. I would like especially to thank Dave Doucette, Jim Belcher, John Howze, and Susan Darr for spending time with me on the telephone for the case studies in the last three chapters. Thanks, too, need to go to Suzanne Egan, who helped with proofing and the index.

My students and colleagues guided me through the fine-tuning process of some of these ideas and exercises. Steve Dalphin at Prentice Hall was accurate with his suggestions, and he was understanding as I missed deadlines. Steve and Colleen Brosnan, the production manager, were both wonderful to work with. Thanks.

I have learned much, first through books and then through many wonderful personal encounters, from Edmund C. Arnold, Mario Garcia, and Roy Paul Nelson. These gentlemen have opened my eyes to see the world of art, type, color, and ink on paper in a different way. A week with Nigel Holmes, Robert Lockwood, Ed Miller, and David Gray helped me to see that information needs to be displayed in its best form: either in words or visuals.

Although it may seem trite to dip into family and friends at this point as well, without certain gifts of love and/or time from those close to you, projects like these simply don't occur. My children and my wife gave up many weekends and evenings with me to help on this project. My sons continued to give their time as we went through the production process. Without their help, this book would simply have ended as a manuscript in rough form on a shelf.

What is good about this book is in no small part because of these people. What is weak or wrong with the book is solely my responsibility, my inability to take what has been given to me and to do something good with it. If you do find flaws, or points you'd like to argue, please let me know. I'm looking forward to learning from all of you.

Appreciation is also due to the following reviewers for their careful review and helpful comments: George C. Brown, Southern Illinois University; William Korbus, University of Texas at Austin; and Sandra Moriarty, University of Colorado, Boulder.

Permission to use examples came from Jim Belcher, Central Fidelity Bank; Craig Bernhardt, Bernhardt Fudyma Design Group; Dorothy Bland, *USA Today*; Susan Darr and Carol Crosthwaite, Southwestern Bell Corporation; Dave Doucette, Salinas Californian; Leah Dunaief, *The Village Times;* Pat Durkin, Dominion Newspapers; Leatrice Eiseman, The Pantone Color Institute; Tom Engleman, Dow Jones Newspaper Fund, Inc.; Michael F. Foley, *St. Petersburg Times*; Ira Gamm, FIGGIE International; Ed Henninger, *Dayton Daily News;* Paul Hogan, *Tampa Tribune;* John Howze, Hawthorne/Wolfe Design Consultants; Nigel Holmes, *Time* Magazine; Donald A. Howarth, Ernst & Whinney; Joan Kufrin, Leo Burnette Company, Inc.; Calvin Lowery, Gannon/Hartley Ltd.—PMM; Charles W. Maynes, *Foreign Policy;* Dan Perkes, Associated Press; Beth Quartarolo, Transamerica Corp.; Jim Raper, *Virginian-Pilot and Ledger Star;* Don W. Robinson, *The Register-Guard;* Charles Rowe, *The Free Lance-Star;* Guido H. Stempel III, *Journalism Quarterly;* Ferdinand C. Teubner, *Editor & Pub*lisher Magazine; Juliet Travison, *U&lc, The International Journal of Typographics*; Donald Traynor, Rockport Publishers; and Mike Vogl, Poudre Valley Hospital.

Robert Bohle
Richmond, Virginia

CHAPTER

1

INTEGRATED EDITING

The Process Overview

Although editors usually are thought of as working toward the end of the turning-information-into-news process, they really are involved throughout. Editors discuss the direction of a publication, set coverage limits, and decide on what will be included—and excluded—in a particular issue.

Thus, before reporters make their first attempts to scan the environment for information valuable to their readers, editors have had input. Rarely, however, in this process do editors consider design, or *how* the printed communication will be presented to readers.

This is a fundamental error in editing because *design communicates.* This concern is not about making stories look good. Design can help the reader understand the material better. And that, quite simply, is what editing is all about.

Because design does communicate meaning, it becomes a tool that can be used to enhance a story or publication by initially attracting the reader's attention and/or by supporting content. Given that effective mass communication is so difficult anyway, ignoring a tool that may aid in communicating is done only at great risk.

Integrated editing, or considering design throughout the process of creating a message in print, is a method by which communicators use design to help focus the work of reporters, artists, photographers, and word editors. By considering the rough shape of the final form of the message, even from the conception of the story, everyone in the process can do the job more effectively.

Editors who use integrated techniques are *visually literate.* In general, this means that how the information will be presented is important. It is important not only during production but also during the gathering of information. Visually literate editors train their reporters also to be visually literate. If reporters and writers gather the proper material for both visual and word presentation of the information, the job of the editor is made easier. And communication is improved.

NEWSGATHERING

Reporters for any publication, whether a newspaper, a company magazine, or an organizational newsletter, must gather news prior to the final processing by editors. Many publications, and all newspapers, gather news by the *beat system.* A beat is a person or office that reporters call on regularly to check for news.

Sometimes editors also make assignments to reporters, or reporters gather news on their own initiative. Whatever the newsgathering process, it must go on before editing begins.

This scanning of the environment for information worthy of being turned into "news" is the first part of the newsgathering process. Information then must travel through the gatekeeping sequence to become news. At each point in the sequence, a gatekeeper—we're talking about an "editor" here—accepts or rejects information. A complete story can be accepted or rejected, or just a small part. The point is, however, that both the final form and the content of the information are being decided well before the final page layout stage. This is why visual communication decisions must be made from the beginning and then continued throughout the newsgathering process.

How these news judgments are made, or how they should be made, by the reporters and gatekeepers is beyond the scope of this discussion. Briefly, it has to do with the traditional "news values" of consequence, proximity, timeliness, human interest, etc. Many other factors, however, influence what reporters and editors see as news and, for that matter, what recipients of information see as news.

For the purposes of our discussion it is important for reporters and editors to ask themselves a question or two during each stop in the gatekeeping sequence:

What is the best way to communicate this information? Is it visual?

or

Is there a visual element that can enhance this information?

Both questions contain the word *visual.* These questions are asked about copy (or text) by visually literate communicators because they lead to the *best presentation of the information,* not just to the best story. The best presentation is not always limited to the best and fewest words.

This attention to the presentation of the information from the beginning is like a reporter searching for an angle on a story. "What is this all about?" is a

Figure 1-1 This Southwestern Bell Corporation company publication exhibits all the proper attributes of integrated editing: good type contrast, interesting artwork, and, inside, a solid basic grid for displaying the information. (Courtesy of Southwestern Bell Corporation)

The Free Lance-Star
FREDERICKSBURG, VIRGINIA

TUESDAY, JULY 26, 1988 15

AREA/STATE

Pageant: Jitters turn into smiles

Sewage transfer ban is dilemma

When the points were added up, Robyn Beth Jolliffe of Spotsylvania was chosen to receive the winner's crown at last night's Miss Fredericksburg Fair pageant.

Family of girl killed by bus gets $150,000 settlement

Tami Crisman gets some help backstage taking off her riding boots, which were part of her casual wear outfit.

Posner elected mayor during lively session

Herbert Posner

Oyster catch outlook bleak

Higher salinity in Potomac spreads shellfish disease

Figure 1-2 Even newspapers, which long ignored the design imperative, now try to use large photos, white space, interesting typography, and a grid system of design. (©The Free Lance-Star)

GRACESCOPE

Business perspectives for managers of GRACE — *March/April 1984*

What's Next? Ceramics and Composites

Grace is building a position in technical ceramics and composites—materials that are tied to the kite strings of electronics, communications, energy saving, the military and other high flyers.

Ceramics and composites (reinforced plastics) do jobs cheaper and better, offer good strength-to-weight ratios and supplant certain metals.

According to Jack Rimmer, the just-retired Grace executive vice president and group executive, Industrial Chemicals, "We are phasing in ceramics and composites as some of our major businesses mature."

Adds Charles H. Ehlers, a Grace vice president and Dewey and Almy's president: "We are early enough to become a significant factor in these materials. This is not catch-up."

Terrence D. Daniels, a Grace executive vice president and group executive, General Development, concurs. "While we're not pioneers, we are at the start of the development cycle," he holds. "We'll grow with these industries at an attractive profit margin and establish market share without getting into a cutthroat ball game. Because the two industries are highly fragmented, we can find niches for specialties."

Grace has forged beyond its stake in Emerson & Cuming (1978) and Amicon (1983) to acquire Diamonite Products (1983), Composite Technologies Corporation (1983) and Metaramics Inc. (1984)—with more to come.

Emerson & Cuming has brought to Dewey and Almy, its parent division, know-how in microwave absorbers, electromagnetic interference (EMI) shielding, and fire-resistant and flotation materials. Amicon has delivered to ICG its savvy in conductive epoxies for electronics, among many strengths.

Mr. Daniels says Grace acquired *Diamonite* to gain a firm hold on ceramics and to draw on this company's manufacturing ability. Operating almost 45 years, Diamonite is the largest U.S. maker of technical ceramics by injection molding. It serves 800 customers and is in "attractive businesses" such as energy, Mr. Daniels stresses.

Based in Shreve, Ohio, with 250 employees, Diamonite forms and fires products of technical ceramics. They are at least 85% aluminum oxide—

(Cont. on p. 2)

Figure 1-3 Many corporate publications do not have the benefit of large staffs or color or other special effects. *Gracescope,* designed by an outside consultant, is a fine example of a well-designed corporate publication. (Courtesy of the Bernhardt Fudyma Design Group)

good question to ask, no matter where you sit in the gatekeeping process. Knowing approximately where you will end up or what you want to say makes writing the story much easier. Thinking about the presentation of the raw information—visual or words or both?—and deciding on the optimum method makes communication more effective.

Much information is better presented in a form other than the narrative. Such raw statistical data as sports summaries, stock market reports, and even weather forecasts are better communicated in tabular form. Some events are better communicated by photograph or artwork. Maps, bar charts, "fever-line" charts, and pie charts are just different ways to present information that may communicate better in a visual mode.

Newspaper sports sections have known this for years. Statistical data are relegated to box scores and other *agate*-type presentations. The reporter can then be freed to concentrate on what needs to be in narrative form: the events, the color, and the quotes.

Editors who assign a definite "story" to information before a visually literate reporter has decided whether that mode is the best way to report it may

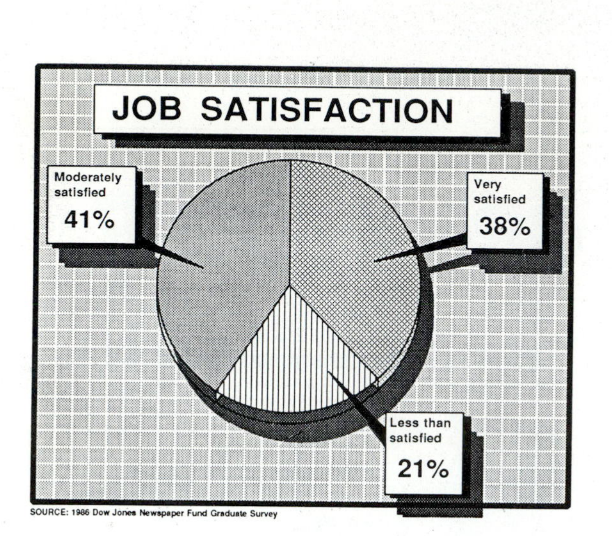

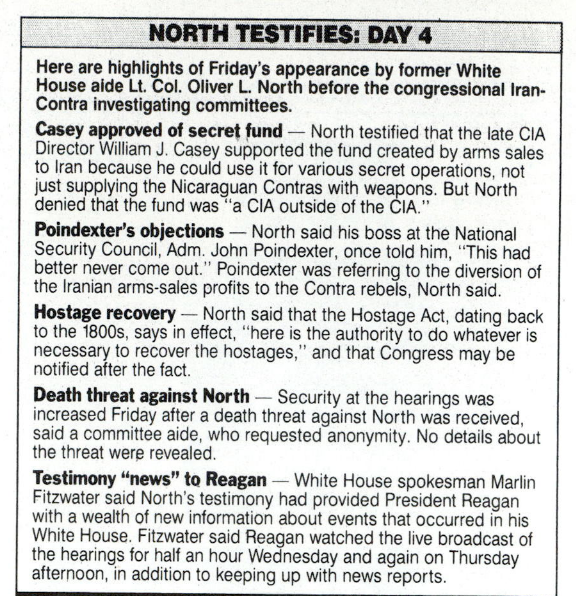
NORTH TESTIFIES: DAY 4

Here are highlights of Friday's appearance by former White House aide Lt. Col. Oliver L. North before the congressional Iran-Contra investigating committees.

Casey approved of secret fund — North testified that the late CIA Director William J. Casey supported the fund created by arms sales to Iran because he could use it for various secret operations, not just supplying the Nicaraguan Contras with weapons. But North denied that the fund was "a CIA outside of the CIA."

Poindexter's objections — North said his boss at the National Security Council, Adm. John Poindexter, once told him, "This had better never come out." Poindexter was referring to the diversion of the Iranian arms-sales profits to the Contra rebels, North said.

Hostage recovery — North said that the Hostage Act, dating back to the 1800s, says in effect, "here is the authority to do whatever is necessary to recover the hostages," and that Congress may be notified after the fact.

Death threat against North — Security at the hearings was increased Friday after a death threat against North was received, said a committee aide, who requested anonymity. No details about the threat were revealed.

Testimony "news" to Reagan — White House spokesman Marlin Fitzwater said North's testimony had provided President Reagan with a wealth of new information about events that occurred in his White House. Fitzwater said Reagan watched the live broadcast of the hearings for half an hour Wednesday and again on Thursday afternoon, in addition to keeping up with news reports.

Figure 1-4 An informative visual can range from the typical pie chart (left) to an "info box," which simply presents information in quickly and easily digestible bits. These graphics are stronger visual magnets and can grab the attention of scanners. (L, Courtesy of The Dow Jones Newspaper Fund, Inc.; R, © Dayton Daily News)

be hindering rather than helping the communication process. This is why it is crucial to understand and use "integrated" editing principles as early as the planning meeting for an issue. You may, for instance, decide to send an artist instead of a writer to cover an event.

The second question that needs to be asked of information is more common. Some, but not all, information is best told as stories, but that does not preclude visuals.

Studies have shown that readers tend to read more newspaper articles that contain an art element than stories without, and they tend to read deeper into a newspaper article with a large photo than one with a small photo. Thus, a visual with a story is not "wasted space." It increases the chances a story will be read. Also, because the visual display of information acts as a graphic magnet on the page, some readers may be drawn to the story who otherwise would have missed it.

Most publications have two kinds of readers: full-time readers, or those who tend to read everything in each issue either out of habit or because they just like your publication; and "scanners," or those who allow their eyes to drift over each page only as long as it takes their fingers to turn to the next.

If something reaches out and grabs them, they'll stop; if not, they'll fan the pages right to the back of the book and move on to something more interesting.

Informative visuals added to stories serve both kinds of readers, but they are especially important to the scanners in your audience. They need to be stopped and made interested enough in the information to quit fanning the pages and read your content. One way to do this is to present the information graphically. (Fig. 1–4).

Another aspect of this, especially for newspaper editors, is that today most nonreaders of newspapers are that way because, they say, they don't have enough time. This is in part because most newspapers—and *USA Today* is the notable exception—continue to ignore the scanners and feed blocks of gray type to their habitual readers.

Scanners see that gray, decide that even if something of interest is hiding there, they do not have time to search for it, and move on. Or worse yet, they cancel their subscription. Corporate communicators are in much the same situation. In fact, readers of corporate publications probably have even *less* time to read or dig for information than do newspaper readers.

So an informed editor should be deciding not so much whether a visual should be used, but what kind should be used.

THE TOOLS

Those two important questions again are:

What is the best way to communicate this information? Is it visual?

or

Is there a visual element that can enhance this information?

The first question, usually asked during the assigning process, not during hands-on editing, leads to the consideration of a number of visuals:

Photographs. An obvious choice, for some events are simply better handled by a photographer.

Tables. If you wish to compare a series of numbers, a table usually is best. Listing numbers and words in columns allows readers to make quick comparisons.

Charts. If the numbers you wish to compare are very different (tables are better when the numbers are so close to one another that visual differences would be hard to illustrate) or if you want to show relationships, or if you want to show changes over time, charts are often better. Charts are covered more completely in Chapter 8.

Fever-line charts are good when changes over time are described. The visual rise and fall of the line of data on the chart can portray certain kinds of information better than can several paragraphs in a story.

Bar charts are good when you want to compare individual quantities, not necessarily how those quantities change over time. Bar charts can have vertical or horizontal bars.

Pie charts are useful when you want to compare the relationships among parts of a whole, say parts of an organization's budget, or number of people working in each division of a company.

Art graphics. These are basically pictures of two or more items you wish to compare in some way (and informative words are almost secondary to the art). They are another way to tell a story visually instead of with words.

Maps. Although maps are more frequently used as a visual accompanying a story, they may well be stand-alone elements on a page, if the information is brief and geographical.

"The various marketing and branch expansion programs are in place and working, and based upon our outlook for the balance of the year, 1988 should represent our fourteenth year of consecutive earnings growth."

—Lewis N. Miller, Jr.

Figure 1-5 Pulling out and printing a quote in larger type is a simple and effective way to add graphic information to a page.

KEY PERFORMERS

The five $100 winners during the first quarter in our Investor Referral Program were:

- **ED HARRELL,** Emporia
- **NANCY HARRISON,** Richmond
- **MARIE HARPER,** Brookneal
- **PAT HOLLORAN,** Peakland
- **LEWIS JOHNSON,** Amelia

Figure 1-6 Because scanners appreciate quick bites of information, pulling out the top news from a story is a way to turn scanners into readers.

The second question posed above, about visuals to go with a story, is the more usual question, and it is the one to be asked *during* the editing process. Some visuals are time-consuming. It is frequently too late to create a good visual when you are facing a deadline.

But even during the editing process, attention can be given to a number of devices that are both visual and information-providing.

Pullouts. The most common bit of information pulled from a story is a direct quote from a main source. Sometimes these are called *quoteouts* or *call quotes.* Placed properly near the beginning of a story, these can sometimes act as visual magnets and draw a scanner into a story (Fig. 1–5).

Naturally, a pullout is not as good as a chart; it does not add *new* information; it merely repeats something from the story, no matter how interesting that something may be. Nonetheless, it is a visual device worth considering, especially on deadline.

Some pullouts are not quotes, but just something of interest from the story. In a sense these are like *blurbs* in a magazine. Blurbs are those little paragraphs (or *grafs*) in display type at the beginning of a story used to tell you a little more about the content than the title does. These are most useful on a newspaper jump page, or on ensuing pages in a magazine spread when no good quotable material is available.

At-a-glance box. Readers who scan your pages for a quick fix of information appreciate quick summaries. Placing these summaries in a special box with easy-to-read organization gives you another visual for your page (Fig. 1–6).

At-a-glance boxes can be simple summaries or highlights or:

- checklists
- chronologies
- key players
- or a number of other options, open to your creativity

The popularity of lists has been shown several times by *The Book of Lists* by Irving Wallace and his family. Checklists often can be stand-alone graphics.

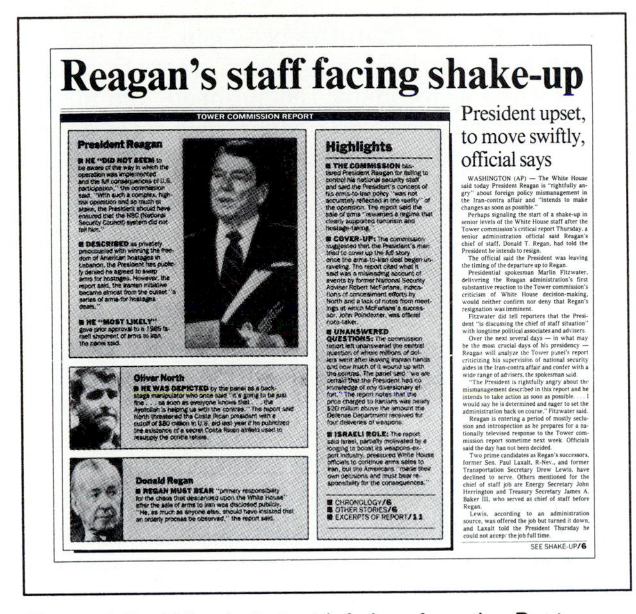

Reagan's staff facing shake-up

TOWER COMMISSION REPORT

President Reagan

■ **HE "DID NOT SEEM** to be aware of the way in which the operation was implemented and the full consequences of U.S. participation," the commission said. "With such a complex, high-risk operation and so much at stake, the President should have ensured that the NSC (National Security Council) system did not fail him."

■ **DESCRIBED** as privately preoccupied with winning the freedom of American hostages in Lebanon, the President has publicly denied he agreed to swap arms for hostages. However, the report said, the Iranian initiative became almost from the outset "a series of arms-for hostages deals."

■ **HE "MOST LIKELY"** gave prior approval to a 1985 Israeli shipment of arms to Iran, the panel said.

Oliver North

■ **HE WAS DEPICTED** by the panel as a backstage manipulator who once said "it's going to be just fine . . . as soon as everyone knows that . . . the Ayatollah is helping us with the contras." The report said North threatened the Costa Rican president with a cutoff of $80 million in U.S. aid last year if he publicized the existence of a secret Costa Rican airfield used to resupply the contra rebels.

Donald Regan

■ **REGAN MUST BEAR** "primary responsibility for the chaos that descended upon the White House" after the sale of arms to Iran was disclosed publicly. "He, as much as anyone else, should have insisted that an orderly process be observed," the report said.

Highlights

■ **THE COMMISSION** blistered President Reagan for failing to control his national security staff and said the President's concept of his arms-to-Iran policy "was not accurately reflected in the reality" of the operation. The report said the sale of arms "rewarded a regime that clearly supported terrorism and hostage-taking."

■ **COVER-UP:** The commission suggested that the President's men tried to cover up the full story once the arms-to-Iran deal began unraveling. The report cited what it said was a misleading account of events by former National Security Adviser Robert McFarlane, indications of concealment efforts by North and a lack of notes from meetings at which McFarlane's successor, John Poindexter, was official note-taker.

■ **UNANSWERED QUESTIONS:** The commission report left unanswered the central question of where millions of dollars went after leaving Iranian hands and how much of it wound up with the contras. The panel said "we are certain that the President had no knowledge of any diversionary effort." The report notes that the price charged to Iranians was nearly $20 million above the amount the Defense Department received for four deliveries of weapons.

■ **ISRAELI ROLE:** The report said Israel, partially motivated by a longing to boost its weapons-export industry, pressured White House officials to continue arms sales to Iran, but the Americans "made their own decisions and must bear responsibility for the consequences."

■ CHRONOLOGY/6
■ OTHER STORIES/6
■ EXCERPTS OF REPORT/11

President upset, to move swiftly, official says

WASHINGTON (AP) — The White House said today President Reagan is "rightfully angry" about foreign policy mismanagement in the Iran-contra affair and "intends to make changes as soon as possible."

Perhaps signaling the start of a shake-up in senior levels of the White House staff after the Tower commission's critical report Thursday, a senior administration official said Reagan's chief of staff, Donald T. Regan, had told the President he intends to resign.

The official said the President was leaving the timing of the departure up to Regan.

Presidential spokesman Marlin Fitzwater, delivering the Reagan administration's first substantive reaction to the Tower commission's criticism of White House decision-making, would neither confirm nor deny that Regan's resignation was imminent.

Fitzwater did tell reporters that the President "is discussing the chief of staff situation" with longtime political associates and advisers.

Over the next several days — in what may be the most crucial days of his presidency — Reagan will analyze the Tower panel's report criticizing his supervision of national security aides in the Iran-contra affair and confer with a wide range of advisers, the spokesman said.

"The President is rightfully angry about the mismanagement described in this report and he intends to take action as soon as possible. . . . I would say he is determined and eager to set the administration back on course," Fitzwater said.

Reagan is entering a period of mostly seclusion and introspection as he prepares for a nationally televised response to the Tower commission report sometime next week. Officials said the day had not been decided.

Two prime candidates as Regan's successors, former Sen. Paul Laxalt, R-Nev., and former Transportation Secretary Drew Lewis, have declined to serve. Others mentioned for the chief of staff job are Energy Secretary John Herrington and Treasury Secretary James A. Baker III, who served as chief of staff before Regan.

Lewis, according to an administration source, was offered the job but turned it down, and Laxalt told the President Thursday he could not accept the job full time.

SEE SHAKE-UP/6

Figure 1-7 This photo/text info box from the *Dayton Daily News* is an example of work from a visually literate editor. It summarizes the Tower Commission Report with interesting segments (well separated by gray screen boxes) of information. The use of photos and type helps to add visual interest. The end point of the graphic—the bottom right-hand corner—teases the reader inside to three related stories. (© Dayton Daily News)

Mr. Saine also announced our Board of Directors voted to increase the quarterly cash dividend 7.4% to $.29 per share for a new annual rate of $1.16 per share. That increase reflects the confidence in our company's continued long-term success.

Retail sales emphasized

Our future growth will most likely depend on our ability to take advantage of the many retail banking opportunities available to us, Mr. Saine indicated.

Constantly improving our already outstanding customer service, fully developing our retail sales force and expanding our distribution network are critical factors within our retail banking framework.

Our supermarket banking project plays a major role in retail expansion. The arrangement with Farm Fresh to participate in this unique, exciting venture was one of our most significant decisions during the last year.

Figure 1-8 Subheads should be bold enough to attract attention. A bold sans serif typeface can do this well. Leave white space above the subhead.

Chronologies often help clarify complex situations by showing the order in which events occurred. Chronologies also can give your new readers a feeling for "how-did-we-get-here-from-there?"

Listing and describing the "key" players in a story can provide a helpful reference. Some novelists have provided family trees for their complex plots.

Nearly any of these options for a visual can be used with a photograph or illustration (Fig. 1–7). If you used any of these as a stand-alone graphic, a photo or illustration is probably called for. It is better to use the art off to one side, not under the information.

Design in publications is just like design in fashion: Tastes come in and out of style. For many years recently, the subhead has been "out," especially in most newspapers. Subheads, however, can be very useful to the visual editor if used properly. Subheads can help break up a long story in more palatable chunks, and they can be graphic elements (Fig. 1–8).

Writers must first write stories in segments, in more easily digested subsections. These segments are keyed by true subheads; that is, they act as headlines for what follows; they are not merely graphic elements inserted to break up the gray, as they were in the old days.

If writers don't first provide copy written this way, it is often too difficult for an editor to fix it. This action shouldn't be difficult for writers to do. It just means a rethinking of how stories are written, a rethinking with *presentation* of the material in mind, which is the point of this book.

In fact, writers probably should provide the editor with suggested subheads with each subsection. Then the editor can attend to those along with the rest of the story.

The subhead should be set in larger type than the body copy, not just in boldface type. A good rule of thumb is to set them two points larger than the body type and have an extra line of white space above the subhead. You might even consider using the headline typeface since it is, in a sense, part of the headline schedule.

PLANNING AND MANAGEMENT

Good editing really begins with the conception of the story and with the discussion during a planning meeting. Present at this meeting should be your top visual people—the art director, graphics director or photo editor—as well as your word people.

Content ideas can and should be generated by anyone, and departmental lines should not get in the way of creative thinking. For instance, an art director can have a terrific idea for a story, and a writer can have one for an illustration or information graphic.

If staff members are given the opportunity to think in terms of content and the best way to present it, instead of trying to guard their own content turf, your publication will be greatly improved.

It is during this planning session when the questions posed earlier in this chapter should be asked: (1) What's the best way to present this information? and (2) Are there any visuals to go with it?

With enough advance planning, assignments can be made for that special map, photo, illustration, or story to make the best possible package of information available to your readers.

For instance, let's take a story about the new interchange on an interstate highway near you. The usual and easy solution is to write a story and discuss the progress being made: the clearing of the land, the grading of the on-and-off ramps, the pilings for the bridge over the interstate, etc. Maybe you could get a photo.

Without advance planning that's about all you would have time for anyway.

But if you had discussed the story possibilities—no, let's say *information* possibilities—early enough, you could come up with all sorts of visual opportunities that not only would look good, but would also provide valuable information.

Most of your readers are curious, whether you publish a general-interest magazine, a newspaper, or an in-house publication. They like to know *how* things work, or *why* something is done this way and not that way. When you tie in the spending of their own tax dollars—in this case the cost of the new interchange—you've got even more interest!

As to the new bridge, what is the weight of those girders your readers see every day on their way to and from work? And how securely are they fastened? For that matter, how are they fastened at all? How much weight can they carry? How much is that weight in something they can understand? Just because these aren't the questions that people stop one another in the street to ask doesn't mean they wouldn't be interested in knowing.

And how about that incredible cloverleaf? How did the engineers know where to put it so it would line up with existing streets that will eventually connect? How does that kind of planning and surveying take place? And how did they work out the grading of the dirt so that long sloping-off ramp actually lines up properly with the overpass?

This kind of information can best be presented with illustrations, perhaps in combination with photographs. Either a writer or an artist—or better yet a staff research person—can gather the necessary data, which can then be shared.

What you end up with is much more interesting than your standard story or aerial photograph. And it is much more than interesting; it is educational. Looked at this way, integrated editing is really nothing more than a more heavily researched presentation of information with a bent toward visuals.

Another example would be a story about one of your writers getting a chance to go up in the trainer version of a highly advanced jet fighter at a nearby military base. The local company that supplies many of the materials for the jet and the military have offered to show you how well it works.

Why just write a story, or take a shot of a jet taking off a runway? These rarely give the reader the kind of necessary context to make the information more meaningful and interesting.

For instance, how big is the jet, compared to things we all know? How fast can it go? Let's put it in terms we know, such as how long it would take it to travel from Main Street out to the West End. And how quickly does it accelerate and take off compared to a DC-9 or Boeing 737? How much did it cost, compared to a DC-9 or a 737? How many "miles per gallon" of fuel does it get?

Much of this information can be handled better in a visual: either an illustration or a series of well-thought-out photographs, or even simple charts, if you're worried about having to go out and hire a staff artist.

The point is that the visual can quite simply help get information through to the reader in a memorable way that words alone simply cannot manage. This is good journalism, good communication, period.

Visually literate reporters, who are arguably more important than visually literate editors because they have to gather the information in the first place, always must ask about accompanying visuals. Gathering relevant maps, charts, and other visual information when on-site is as important as taking notes. Then the decision-makers at the publication have more raw data to choose from as they decide how to present the information.

Some visuals are basically word visuals—such as subheads and quote pullouts—and the reporter can create and present these when turning in the story. The decision to use, however, must lie with the editor.

To sum up, integrated editing is:

1. A process that considers the visual presentation of information at every step of editing.
2. A process based on reader research: Readers are attracted to the visuals on a page, and they often become interested in reading a story because of the visual.
3. A process that includes reporters, artists, illustrators, photographers, and the copy desk, as well as editors.
4. A process that creates "user-friendly" publications by making the information easy to find and easy to read, as well as informative and interesting.

This kind of approach works only if you have the management plan set up to accommodate integrated editing.

A good management plan includes

- written goals and guidelines for the publication, including a typography and design stylebook;

- written job descriptions, which can include the point that story ideas can be generated from anyone;
- one person in charge of the overall design of the publication with a clear and direct line of authority; and
- a commitment from the top of the organizational chart to the bottom on quality design and quality reproduction of that design.

Integrated editing techniques, or how to edit with design in mind, will be covered more specifically in the last three chapters of this book, once you've learned a little more about the individual tools available to you.

CHECKLIST

1. Approach information with an open mind. Is the visual a better way to present to readers what they need to know? What they want to know? Is there a good visual than can help attract readers and then help them understand the information?
2. Does your idea-generating process include your visual people from the very beginning? They need to be able to suggest ideas as well. There is no reason to limit your planning meetings to the word people and then expect the visual people to plug holes in the typographical presentation with their best "guesses" for what the word people want or need.
3. Use *all* the tools available to you—words as well as visuals as well as laying out the other two in a coherent package—to maximize your communication.
4. During your initial read-through of a story—the one you do without putting pencil to paper or moving the cursor—is a good time to look for visuals to go with a story (assuming your reporter has left you without them). Also, look for parts of the story that would be better off in a table or chart.
5. Some ideas are simply missed by word people because they just don't think of information in visual terms. Be sure to get some visual people involved in your publication planning. Or better yet, **you** *get visual!*

Also:

1. Look over your management chart or even how you produce your own publication or story. How and where can you fit attention to the visual in there?
2. Design a management chart that you think would best utilize design at every step of the way. If you do not work for a publication, create a chart for a local newspaper or magazine. You will probably have to get a copy of that publication's chart or interview the editor.
3. Write the editors of publications that you think are well designed. How do the editors integrate their word people and visual people?
4. Much of good integrated editing has to do with planning, communication, strategies, etc. This sounds very much like problems solved by studying *management* techniques. Go to a good management book or, better yet, to someone you know who is good in management. Find out ways that sound management principles can be applied to getting visual people into the planning/editing process.

CHAPTER

2

FORMATS AND TYPOGRAPHIC CONSTANTS

Every publication has a set format—or, very simply put, size and grid structure—and a number of repeating features that use certain typographical and design styles for headings. The standard format and typographical "constants" act as familiar guideposts to help the reader through the publication. Before any attention can be paid to placing photos and stories on the pages themselves, the format and constants need to be made firm. These are the framework on which the design succeeds or fails.

As the saying goes, "First freeze the pond, then let the skaters dance."

Choosing a page size for a newspaper is easy: You publish what management wants you to, either broadsheet or tabloid (although tabloid publications come in varying sizes depending on the press web). To a certain extent, magazine editors also have to deal with the size requested by management.

But creators of one-shot publications, or editors of publications just starting out, have the opportunity to decide the size and visual "tone" of the publication, or whether it will be avant-garde or traditional.

For these persons, both the size and the style of the publication are important considerations before work can begin. For those "stuck" with a certain size publication, these issues also are important as they try to wring the most from their format.

PAGE SIZE

Newspapers

Newspapers use two basic sizes. *Broadsheet,* or full-size, papers are generally 13-by-21-1/2 inches. Tabloid papers are generally half that size, 10-3/4-by-13 inches, but the depth varies. Some tabloid pages are as deep as 17 inches.

Profile

LaSpina whittles with X-acto and coping saw

by LESLIE BRIDSON

Arm in arm the elderly couple stand. She is wearing a dress, spotted with flowers. In the pocket of his dark jacket a white flower sits. He stands, supported by a cane. This is a wood carving by Jack La Spina.

A self-taught wood carver, LaSpina is a native of Brooklyn. He attended New York City Community College, where he majored in industrial art teaching.

About four years ago, LaSpina began carving wood as a hobby. "I had an interest in it and I just picked up a piece of wood one day, and just started whittling at it."

Prior to this, he had never really had an interest in art. "I had art classes through schools but I never had any kinds of classes in like sculpture work or stuff like that."

LaSpina estimates that it took him "a good year of a lot of scraps" to learn how to carve. "Every once in a while I still have some that come out good and some that wind up in the fireplace," he laughs.

LaSpina explains how he learned how to sculpt wood. "Well, I had seen it done at various fairs and stuff and I had bought a few books on wood carving. So from reading and a little imagination I started doing some carving of my own."

He carves caricatures, "various things, cowboys and Indians, farmers, train conductors." LaSpina chose caricatures "for no particular reason. I just found them to be interesting. You can do what you want with it, as opposed to doing, say, a life figure and trying to get it as perfect as the person. You've got a lot more leeway with caricatures."

LaSpina's wood carvings, roughly six inches high, are made with a sparse number of tools. "I do everything by hand (painting included). I only use a coping saw and an X-acto knife or pen knife, whatever is available."

Most of his works are made from pine, but he also uses poplar and locust. "Pine is easy to get a hold of and the poplar is good. It has a lot of different color grains. And the locust is a very good grain. Cross-cutting it doesn't split on you."

He is displaying his carvings in the Bank of New York in Setauket. "It's the first time I've ever displayed anywhere in public."

Says LaSpina, "I called the bank. I knew someone had some stuff in there, some art figures. So I asked if I could display my stuff. They said that when it was empty I was more than welcome to use it." His caricatures, previously displayed there, are back on display—this time for "a couple of weeks."

LaSpina is uncertain as to whether he will display his carvings again. "I'll see how the public takes it, if there's anyone interested in them. I'll take it from there." His work is for sale, but, he explains, not the originals. "I will make the comparable figures. They won't be exact because as I said, they're all hand carved, so nothing will be exact. But they will be very similar."

What LaSpina enjoys the most about his hobby is that it is relaxing. "It gives you the freedom to do what you want with it. It's something that keeps [you] busy, calms your nerves."

LaSpina, a resident of Setauket for several years, used to work in New York City doing display work for a plastics company, and would commute on the Long Island Rail Road. "Commuting back and forth to the city, I would carve once in a while on the train, just to pass some of the time."

According to LaSpina he has not thought about turning his hobby into a profession. "It's a hobby. I don't know if I'd ever do it for a living. I may someday. I'd like to open up, maybe, a little shop during the summer and teach little kids in the neighborhood to do some carving. I have my son doing soap carvings."

LaSpina's nine-year-old son, Robert, has been working on soap carvings for about three months now. "He enjoys it. He spends an hour or two at night carving. If I'm doing some carving, he'll sit next to me and do some soap."

LaSpina married two-and-a-half years ago. Widowed, Donna had a son, Robert. The couple has a daughter, Melissa, 10 months old.

LaSpina carves "mostly whenever I have a free hour here and there." He laughs and says, "But we also have a baby so that's 90 percent of my time."

'I just found them to be interesting. You can do what you want with it, as opposed to doing, say, a life figure and trying to get it as perfect as the person. You've got a lot more leeway with caricatures.'

LASPINA WHITTLES AWAY with some attentive help from Robert. *Photo by Maxine Hicks*

LASPINA CARVED this couple with the simplest of tools. *Photo by Maxine Hicks*

November 20, 1986 The Village Times/Beacon Page L3

GOOD MORNING
Figure of speech: when you only talk about dieting

The Virginian-Pilot AND The Ledger-Star

WEATHER
Mostly sunny with high in the 90s, low in the 70s. Complete weather/A4

SATURDAY
JULY 11, 1987

10th Year, No. 82 — SERVING SOUTHEASTERN VIRGINIA AND NORTHEASTERN NORTH CAROLINA — © The Virginian-Pilot and The Ledger-Star

North: Covert fund was Casey's idea

Americans believe North, poll shows

By E.J. DIONNE Jr.
New York Times News Service

By an overwhelming margin, the American people say they believe that Lt. Col. Oliver L. North is telling the truth about the Iran-Contra affair, the latest New York Times-CBS News Poll has found.

The survey also showed that most say President Reagan is lying.

The poll, conducted Thursday, found that North has etched a remarkably favorable personal image on the minds of Americans. They view him as a patriot, and believe that he acted with the president's knowledge and approval.

The poll also offered a portrait of a public rendering complex judgments. For example, the apparent fondness for North registered in the survey did not prevent a majority from saying that he had been wrong to flout the law. And only 18 percent rated the colonel "a national hero."

Moreover, the telephone survey of 658 Americans 18 years or older found that the Democratic-led select committees interrogating North are receiving high marks from the American people. This finding flies in the face of angry complaints Friday by several Republican members that some questioning of the

Please see POLL, Page A3

Lt. Col. Oliver L. North
Listening to a question Friday

Iran money financed secret agenda

By CHARLES GREEN and R.A. ZALDIVAR
Knight-Ridder News Service

WASHINGTON — The late CIA Director William J. Casey seized upon the Iran arms dealings as a way to create a secret contingency fund to finance a wide range of covert operations outside regular government channels, Lt. Col. Oliver L. North told Congress on Friday.

Sen. Daniel K. Inouye, D-Hawaii, termed the scheme a "secret government within our government," and Sen. William S. Cohen, R-Maine, said the disclosure was "perhaps the most serious revelation" of the 2-month-old hearings into the Iran-Contra affair.

North, testifying for a fourth day before congressional Iran-Contra investigative committees, said Casey wanted to use the profits from the weapons shipments to conduct top-secret overseas operations that would not bear the imprint of the CIA.

The former White House aide said one such operation was the purchase for $350,000 of the Danish ship Erria, used to beam radio signals into a hostile country — identified by sources as Libya — in May 1986.

The signals reportedly broadcast disinformation aimed at removing Libyan leader Moammar Gadhafi from power. North said he

Please see NORTH, Page A3

Standoff ends in tragedy

3 Michigan officers slain by captors

By SUSAN AGER
Knight-Ridder News Service

INKSTER, Mich. — Just before dawn Friday it became sickeningly clear that even the experts had been fooled, by a 69-year-old woman accustomed to big, fast talk.

Through the long muggy night there was hope, even optimism. But inside rooms 105 and 106 of the Bungalow Motel, three Inkster police officers lay dead on the floor, riddled by dozens of bullets. One without a face. One without an arm.

"Liars," spit out John Anthony of the FBI at 3:40 a.m., moments after Alberta Easter and her three adult sons surrendered and police entered the motel rooms. They expected, after the 10-hour siege, to untie their colleagues and hug them.

Instead, they found ammunition shells littering the floor like peanut shells, enough guns "to take on the Contras," according to one who saw the weapons, and three police officers dead, long dead, dead probably since just minutes after they arrived about 5:15 Thursday afternoon to arrest Easter and one son.

The charge: writing a rubber check for $286 to rent an 8-year-old Ford station wagon.

Never in the state's history have three police officers been slain in a single incident. Never in the 60-year history of the Inkster Police Department had an officer been killed in the line of duty.

Dead are Officer Daniel Dubiel, 36, who has a pregnant wife and four children; Officer Clay Hoover, 24, who was engaged to be married; and Sgt. Ira Parker, 41, married and the father of four children, who responded to a calm call for help from Dubiel and Hoover.

Parker's son, Ira Parker Jr., 18, would watch the scene at the motel for several hours without knowing his father was inside.

Arrested and expected to be arraigned on murder charges today are Alberta Easter, 69, and her

Please see SLAIN, Page A2

AP photo

An unidentified police officer of Inkster, Mich., waits Thursday night while three of his fellow officers were thought to be held as hostages. The three were found dead early Friday morning.

Calif. shipyard accident kills 5

By BARRY M. HORSTMAN
Los Angeles Times News Service

SAN DIEGO — Five civilian shipyard workers were killed and seven others injured when a crane-operated steel basket plunged nearly 30 feet onto the deck of a U.S. Navy ship Friday.

The accident, the worst in the history of the National Steel & Shipbuilding Co., occurred as workers secured the combat support ship Sacramento, undergoing basic overhaul, to a pier after it had been moved from dry dock, according to Fred Hallett, the company's vice president.

The 175-foot crane was transferring the basket holding the 12 men from a berthing barge next to the ship to the dock when the basket came loose and fell about 30 feet to the ship's third deck, Hallett said. After glancing off an upper deck, the basket came to rest on the next deck, on top of at least one worker, witnesses said.

"It was a real mess ... one of those sights you hope you never have to see," said rigger John Farinsky, who chatted with the victims as they climbed into the basket. "I was talking to them one minute and then as I turned around I heard this loud crash. When I looked in the air, all I saw was the crane with the wires hanging down, and I knew what had happened."

One survivor, 37-year-old Ford Pulley, said he "felt a tug on the line" just before the basket dropped.

Please see CRANE, Page A2

Who wrote the Bible?

Scholar-sleuth's 10-year search for answers is bound to offend

By JANNY SCOTT
Los Angeles Times News Service

SAN DIEGO — Richard E. Friedman likes a good thriller. He's a Raymond Chandler aficionado — like many other Bible scholars, it just so happens. So when he sat down after 10 years of looking into who wrote the Bible, he thought of writing his book in the style of Alfred Hitchcock.

After all, there was a fundamental mystery: Whodunit? There was a large body of clues to be examined and sorted through. The sleuth-hero could have been modeled on a renowned Bible scholar — say, Friedman's former professor of Bible at Harvard University.

Friedman ended up scuttling the detective-fiction idea. But he adopted the pace and tone of a detective on a case. "Because that's how I feel about scholarship," the 41-year-old University of California, San Diego, professor said recently. "That's how I feel when I'm doing it."

Friedman has reached some rather startling conclusions about the Old Testament, conclusions that some scholars may share but that run counter to popular notions. Among people of fundamentalist and orthodox views, his forthcoming book on the subject may ruffle feathers.

He concludes that certain stories are purely inventions of the authors,

Please see BIBLE, Page A2

Anonymous AIDS testing will be offered at Beach

By DEBBIE MESSINA
Staff writer

VIRGINIA BEACH — Fearing that potential AIDS victims may shun medical attention for fear of being identified, the state Department of Health plans to conduct anonymous testing.

A clinic expected to open in two weeks at Little Neck Road and Virginia Beach Boulevard will provide free AIDS testing and counseling — no questions asked.

"Our experience in other parts of the country is that not all people are willing to go to private physicians or local health departments," said Betty Rouse, epidemiologist for the eastern region of the state Health Department.

Physicians and public health departments offer confidential testing, but they still require a name and address.

"Many people are still reluctant to be tested in that environment," Rouse said.

At the Virginia Beach clinic, clients will be identified only by a numbered code.

The clinic will be the fourth anonymous testing site in the state. Others are in Northern Virginia, Roanoke and Richmond.

AIDS — acquired immune deficiency syndrome — suppresses the body's immune system and is al-

Please see AIDS, Page A2

DEVELOPING MBAs: Real estate, business grads find a need for each other/**D1**

SHE CHOOSES LIFE: Thalidomide victim rejects any notion that she's disabled/**E1**

GARBAGE BARGE: Islip's infamous cargo is coming home as 400 tons of ash/**A5**

Dream come true: Busch leader Tim Simpson credits nocturnal message/**C1**

Figure 2-1 Weekly newspapers are often tabloid size (left), about one-half the size of full-sized or broadsheet, newspapers (right). (L, Courtesy of The Village Times; R, Courtesy of The Virginian-Pilot and The Ledger-Star)

Most newspapers in this country are broadsheet. The tabloid-size page has an undeserved negative connotation attached to it because so many tabloid publications are filled with sex, crime, and an-alien-fathered-my-child-that-Elvis-delivered stories.

Still, some fine newspapers, including Long Island's *Newsday* and the *Christian Science Monitor,* are in tabloid format. This format offers better opportunities for advertising sales (it's easier to sell full-page ads) and for magazine-style design (you often end with having to place only one story per page, giving you more freedom). (See Fig. 2–1.)

Readers also like tabloid-size publications because they are easier to hold and read, especially if they are commuting or in a busy location. The pages of a tabloid are simply easier to turn than are the awkward broadsheet pages.

Tabloids are not as good, however, in creating sections for differing content. With a broadsheet, having separate sections for local news, sports, business, lifestyles, etc., is easily done. This way, the paper can be shared with other readers as well.

GIVING PITCHERS A HAND

Rawlings' Rollie Latina deprives batters

"I began understanding (my father) when my own dreams of playing pro ball were abruptly ended by a broken ankle."

HOW GLOVES ARE MADE

Baseball gloves are made in seven major steps.

- **A specialist** in leather tracks young calves with the perfect skin type through their early years.
- **The adult** cow is harvested at the right moment, and the processing takes place to turn it into the finest in Corinthian leather.
- **The leather** is sent to the Rawlings baseball glove facility for cutting and shaping.
- **Trained personnel** take designs created by Rollie Latina and cut the leather into the roper shapes.
- **The pieces** are taken to the sewing department where robots use rawhide to attach the pieces.
- **The pieces** are shaped and pressed into the proper configurement. Coloring takes place at this step.

Rollie Latina has carried on the family tradition of designing baseball gloves for Rawlings Sporting Goods. He and his late father, Harry, are responsible for more than 30 patents during their 40 years with Rawlings.

Figure 2-2 This page from *Craftsman,* FIGGIE Corporation, shows that news-oriented company publications can still break away from the newspaper look. Note the use of a quoteout, a summary box, and initial letters. (Courtesy of FIGGIE International, Inc.)

A tabloid, because of press limitations, is usually one section. Parts of it cannot be shared. Some tabloids have gone to a center section that can be pulled out or several small tabloids folded into one. Neither is very successful. The center pullout creates odd page numbering, and the center section still takes a little searching for. With several tabloid sections, the back sections are difficult to deal with as one opens and reads the first section.

Still, because it offers such excellent design opportunities, the tabloid is a format worth considering for special sections, weekend magazines, or a new newsprint publication in a market. The different format for a special section, for instance, helps to separate it from your normal content.

Broadsheet papers are the standard and familiar format for newspaper readers around the country. Although the broadsheet's size makes it difficult to design and read, the habits of both readers and industry make changes hard to imagine. Broadsheet newspapers will be with us for many years.

Broadsheets probably have little application outside the newspaper industry. They simply are not convenient enough, for either reading or mailing, for any corporation to consider as a publication.

Even if a more newsy approach is desired for a corporate publication, the tabloid format will work fine. Because most company publications are in the common 8-1/2-by-11-inch format, a tabloid format will be enough to set apart the content of a news oriented publication (Fig. 2–2).

Magazines

Nonnewspaper publications such as magazines can use nearly any page size, but the most common are 8-1/2-by-11 inches and 10-1/2-by-13 inches. Many publications use a smaller format. *Reader's Digest*, for instance, uses a 5-1/2-by-7-1/2-inch size. *TV Guide* is another high-circulation small magazine. Others have even more unusual page sizes (Fig. 2–3).

The 8-1/2-by-11-inch format is by far the most widely used, although it is really harder to design than is the 10-1/2-by-13-inch format, which is used by *Life* magazine. The larger format gives designers more opportunities for the design of special spreads with stories and multiple photos. It is certainly better for play of large, single photographs as well.

FOREIGN POLICY

NUMBER 64 FALL 1986 $5.25

Editor
Charles William Maynes

Associate Editor
Alan Tonelson

Circulation Director
Peggy Jarvis

Copy Editor
Joan Berne

Production Manager
Patricia Sheehan-Burns

Advertising Manager
L. Maxine Fowler

Editorial Assistants
Sarah Geithner, Jane Y. Junn

Editorial Board
Thomas L. Hughes (*Chairman*)
Seweryn Bialer
Ralph C. Bryant
Albert Fishlow
Frances FitzGerald
Morton H. Halperin
Stanley Hoffmann
Robert D. Hormats
Karl Kaiser
Jan M. Lodal
Donald F. McHenry
Thierry de Montbrial
Joseph S. Nye, Jr.
John E. Rielly
William D. Rogers
Helmut Sonnenfeldt
Tad Szulc
Richard H. Ullman
David Watt

Staff Assistants
Cynthia L. Dowdell, Kevin P. O'Prey

Founded in 1970
by Warren Demian Manshel
and Samuel P. Huntington

Designed by Samuel Antupit

© 1986 by the Carnegie Endowment for International Peace. All rights reserved. No part of this publication may be reproduced in any form without permission in writing from the publisher.

(a)

A WORD ABOUT WHO WE ARE . . .

It's likely you parked your car this morning on a part of the hospital campus where cattle, hogs, chickens and corn once thrived: the 40-acre pasture of the Larimer County Hospital and Poor Farm. Back in 1903, when the area's first hospital opened near the present site, dairy products, meat, fruits and vegetables were grown on the grounds to feed the tiny hospital's 40 patients—less than are now cared for on one floor. People with contagious diseases were isolated in a small building called the Pest House, and doctors rode horse-drawn buggies to visit patients in their homes. Today, the Pest House is a profitable thrift store and the little brick hospital is a sprawling, 217-bed regional medical center whose patients often come and go in helicopters.

In 1962, county officials transferred ownership of the hospital to a special hospital district, Colorado's first, and *Poudre Valley Hospital* was born. The district spans 2200 square-miles of Larimer County's mountains and plains, bounded roughly by Wyoming, Weld County and the Continental Divide. It's governed by a five-member board of directors elected by district residents, who are assessed a small property tax each year.

More than 1000 employees and almost 200 physicians staff Poudre Valley Hospital; they are people who fashion their care with quality, people who believe in progress and make it happen. PVH consistently has influenced patterns of health care in northern Colorado and will continue to do so by providing comprehensive services for inpatients, outpatients, and nonpatients (who participate in programs that help healthy people stay healthy).

We think you'll enjoy being part of this rich heritage of innovation and service!

(b)

(c)

Figure 2-3 (a) *Foreign Policy* is printed on 4.25-by-10-inch paper, (b) the *Poudre Valley Hospital's Employee Handbook* on 7-by-8.5-inch paper, (c) the *Burnettwork* on 11-by-17 white stock. All are effective formats for the information they impart. (a, Reprinted with permission from *Foreign Policy* [No. 64, Fall 1986]. Copyright 1986 by the Carnegie Endowment for International Peace; b, Courtesy of Mike Vogl, Poudre Valley Hospital; c, © Leo Burnett Company, Inc., 1983. Printed in U.S.A. Used with permission of Leo Burnett Co., Inc.)

The 8-1/2-by-11-inch format has less space for special spreads. This does not mean that the only approach the designer can take is to lay out column after column of type and try not to goof it up. The excellent designs in such magazines as *Sports Illustrated* are proof that the format is not limiting.

Smaller pages are acceptable for certain publications, providing the size fits the need. For instance, *TV Guide* would be much less convenient at any larger size. For certain academic journals, such as *Journalism Quarterly,* the small format is fine because (1) it must be mailed and (2) it is a heavily text-oriented publication. Also, because it will be kept on bookshelves—and not coffee tables—it needs to be sized and shaped more like a book (Fig. 2–4).

The bottom line is that the size of the publication should fit the needs of the content and of the audience. Analyze your readers' needs, your content, and how you intend to circulate your publication (U.S. Postal Service regulations may affect your decision).

If the publication will be heavily oriented toward photos, then a larger format makes more sense. If the content consists of mostly type alone, then a smaller format is acceptable.

If the publication will tend to be left on desks or tables, then a large format is fine. If your readers will want to save your publication as a reference, then a book-sized publication will be better.

A final factor may be the number of pages you will be running. If you will have a small amount of content, and thus few pages, you may want to opt for a smaller format. This would give the publication more pages and a thicker feel. Readers would get the impression they are getting a lot for their money and/or time.

By J. David Kennamer

Gender Differences in Attitude Strength, Role of News Media and Cognitions

Media attention predicts strength of attitude about economic issues for men, but not for women.

► Public opinion researchers have long noted the importance of the difference between a shouted and a whispered response to an opinion survey.[1] The strength with which attitudes are held can help identify what has been called "effective public opinion," which, as Wilhoit and Weaver have pointed out, can be important in predicting political and social activism.[2] It seems, therefore, that the study of the antecedents and correlates of the strength with which attitudes are held should be an important part of the study of attitudes, and thus of public opinion.

While the study of attitudes has declined somewhat in mass communications research in favor of cognitive variables,[3] this trend should not be taken too far, especially if we accept Allport's conclusion that attitude is "the most distinctive and indispensable concept of contemporary American social psychology."[4] The recent emphasis on such variables as agenda setting, learning of political information and the creation of social and political "realities" need not be seen as an abandonment of attitude as a dependent variable if one also realizes the artificiality of the distinction between attitude and cognition.

Best[5] has listed two components of an attitude: awareness of an attitude object and an evaluation of that attitude object. Awareness is a form of knowledge, and the formation of a positive or negative evaluation requires that the individual see the attitude object as being salient, at least in a minimal way. Issue salience has been at the heart of agenda setting research, and Weaver notes the increased salience of an issue "is likely to invoke a mixture of cognitions and feelings linked to that issue. And this mixture is likely to have direct impact on public opinion regarding not only that issue, but also those persons and institutions associated with that issue."[6]

Knowing that an attitude exists, feeling the need to evaluate it and the strength of

► The author is assistant professor in the School of Mass Communications at Virginia Commonwealth University, in Richmond. A previous draft of this paper was presented at the meeting of the Association for Education in Journalism and Mass Communication, Memphis, Tenn., August, 1985.

[1] Charles W. Roll and Albert H. Cantril, *Polls: Their Uses and Misuses in Politics* (Cabin John, Md.: Seven Locks Press, 1980).

[2] G. Cleveland Wilhoit and David H. Weaver, *Newsroom Guide to Polls and Surveys* (Washington, D.C. American Newspaper Publishers Association, 1980).

[3] Lee B. Becker, Maxwell E. McCombs and Jack M. McLeod, "The Development of Political Cognitions," in Steven H. Chaffee, ed., *Political Communication* (Sage Publications, 1975); Steven H. Chaffee, "Mass Media Effects: New Research Perspectives," in Daniel Lerner and Lyle Nelson, eds., *Communication Research: A Half-Century Appraisal* (Honolulu: University Press of Hawaii, 1977); Steven H. Chaffee, L. Scott Ward and Leonard P. Tipton, "Mass Communication and Political Socialization," *Journalism Quarterly*, 47:647-659,666 (Winter, 1970).

[4] Gordon W. Allport, "The Historical Background of Modern Social Psychology," in Gardner Lindzey and Elliot Aronson, eds., *The Handbook of Social Psychology*, 2nd Ed., (Reading, Mass.: Addison-Wesley Publishing Company, 1968).

[5] James J. Best, *Public Opinion: Micro and Macro* (Homewood, Ill.: Dorsey Press, 1973).

[6] David Weaver, "Media Agenda-Setting and Public Opinion: Is There a Link?" in Robert N. Bostrom, ed., *Communication Yearbook 8* (Beverly Hills: Sage Publications, 1984), p. 690.

782

Figure 2-4 Even an academic journal can benefit from the use of typographical contrast and ample white space. (© Journalism Quarterly, Association for Education in Journalism and Mass Communications)

COLUMN GRID

The foundation, the invisible underlying structure for any publication, is its *column grid.* The grid delimits widths of columns of type, photos, and any other element placed upon it. All elements on a page should—normally—fall on a multiple of one column (or your basic unit of width).

The concept of architecture is a good one to use when facing the design of pages. In a sense, your page is a two-dimensional space that must be constructed functionally (it won't "collapse" or interfere with movement within the structure) and attractively (no one wants to look at an ugly building—or an ugly page).

Your column grid and basic spacing guidelines are the foundation, the framework upon which you build your design. Thus, just as the framing of a building must be able to support the siding, your column grid must be appropriate for your content and layout strategies.

Most publications have standard column grids. Broadsheet newspapers, for instance, usually use a six-column format, although some papers use eight

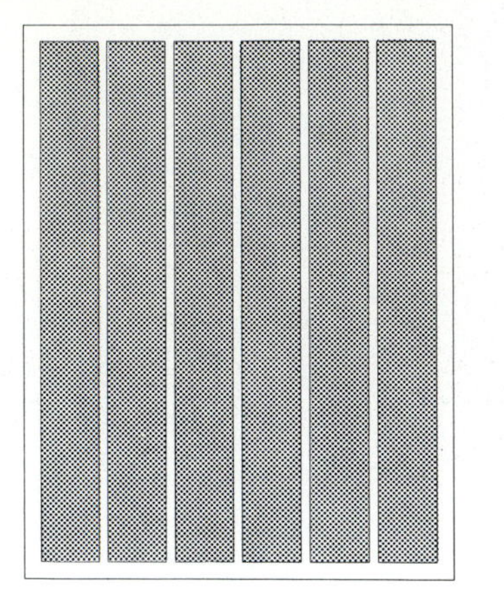

(a)

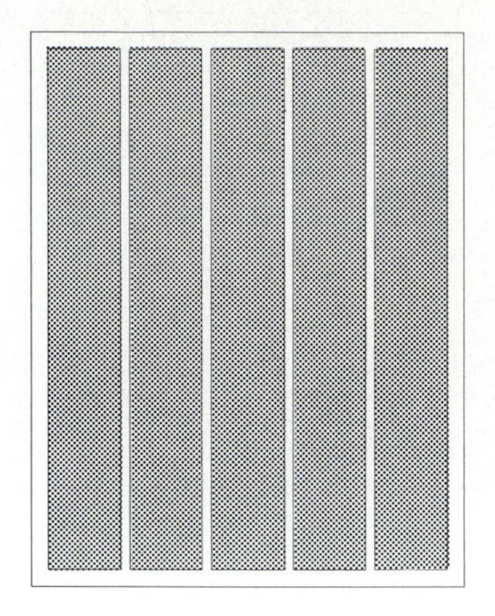

(b)

(c)

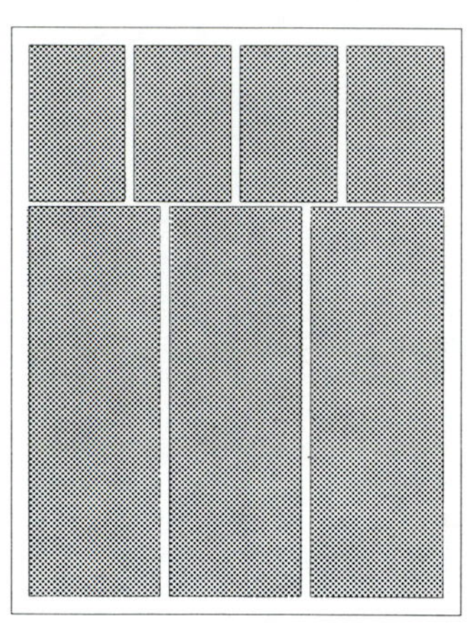

(d)

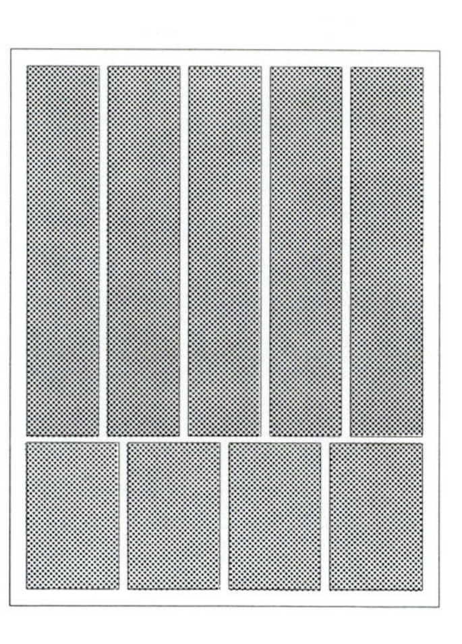

(e)

Above: Southwestern Bell Telephone's Lynn Sauer heads for an FCC meeting in Washington. Below: Robert A. Dickemper, Southwestern Bell Telephone's vice president-federal relations.

ules or allowed expenses, the rulings can be equitably determined.

2. Regulating the airwaves The FCC's jurisdiction over the radio spectrum means it gets involved, for example, with Southwestern Bell Mobile Systems and Southwestern Bell Telephone. Because cellular mobile phone service uses radio frequencies, the agency has the authority to grant operating licenses to SBMS for its cellular systems. And the Telephone Company still offers conventional mobile phone service, which also uses radio technology to carry conversations.

3. Structuring the company Through its Computer Inquiry II decision, the FCC determines for the telecommunications industry which services are basic and which are enhanced.

The Telephone Company may offer basic services, but terminal equipment or enhanced services must be offered, if at all, through a structurally separated entity. The agency monitors regional holding companies to make sure these requirements are being met.

"Because the FCC has so much authority over our business, it's crucial that we maintain good working relationships with the agency," says Jim Barone, assistant vice president-revenue requirements for Southwestern Bell Telephone. "Now that we're out from under the old Bell System, we have to chart our own destiny.

"We're better able to do this if we represent ourselves well before the FCC, explaining our views on how its policy decisions could further or hinder our operations and the public interest."

Southwestern Bell Telephone is, of course, no newcomer to representing itself before regulators. It has done so for years in state regulatory matters. There are, however, several differences between the state and the federal regulatory process.

"Perhaps the biggest difference is that when we file a state rate request, we're on center stage," says Robert A. Dickemper, vice president-federal relations based in Washington for Southwestern Bell Telephone.

"In a commission proceeding, we're only one of many players. Our viewpoint certainly receives consideration, but it's only one of many that will finally shape the FCC commissioners' rulings. Nevertheless, it's important that we take every opportunity we can to speak to issues before the commission that have an effect on us. It's the only way we have available to us to influence the outcome of a ruling."

22 Enterprise / No. 3, 1984

(f)

Figure 2-5 The underlying grid of a page sets the guidelines on which the design works. The samples (a-e) show the many ways column grids can be set up and even mixed on a page. You should vary column widths occasionally. The *Enterprise* page (f) shows its underlying 3-and-1 column grid. A floating half-column, which can appear in various positions on a page, can be used for captions, as well as quotes or just simply extra white space. (d, Courtesy of Southwestern Bell Corporation)

columns. The front page and section fronts of *USA Today* use a seven-column format. Tabloid newspapers use either a four- or a five-column grid (Fig. 2–5). Most 8-1/2-by-11-inch magazines use a three-column format. Smaller book-size publications will use one or, at most, two columns.

The grid should be set up for optimum readability of the body type, but in fact, the optimum size for selling ads often sets the size. Your publication should strive for its "optimum" format based on its size.

The optimum format is one that allows columns of the proper size for type legibility (discussed in Chapter 4) yet gives the advertising sales staff reasonable sizes to work with. Six columns is the generally accepted optimum format for broadsheet newspapers, four columns for tabloids, and three columns for 8-1/2-by-11-inch publications.

Once the grid is set up, it must be followed closely. The size of the space between columns of type—the *gutter*—should be used as the basic spacing element for all other elements on a page.

For instance, on a photo spread, the horizontal spacing between photos should be the same as the gutters. Spacing and designing with your particular grid will be covered in greater detail in Chapter 3.

Sticking to your grid does not mean that you cannot run type wider than the one-column measure in your publication. In fact, the opposite is true. Changing the line measure occasionally is an effective and easy-to-use design tool. As with all other design tools, however, use it carefully.

You could, for instance, run two legs of type in three columns. But if you do, remember to have the outside edges of your columns fit precisely on the grid, and the gutters should still be exactly the same width.

Another way to use the grid, oddly enough, is to ignore it. If you do this only on special pages or packages, then those gain the additional emphasis you want. Readers notice when something is different from the normal. Use this to your advantage.

In fact, a good way to approach the grid is to follow it faithfully on all the standard items and break it on the special ones. You can do this by using larger gutters between legs of type and/or making columns wider. (The following chapters cover type and the recommendations for column measures.)

As we will look at in the next chapter, breaking the "rules" of your publication format is only one way to emphasize a design element on your pages. Because the grid is so important, you should break it infrequently and with good reason.

THE SWISS GRID

A more specialized approach on grids is the *Swiss grid.* This is a much more precise structure for pages, with set horizontal spaces—alleys—as well as the standard vertical spaces—gutters. The Swiss grid system is based on the gestalt principles (discussed in Chapter 3) that people like their visual information very clearly organized and aligned.

The following discussion is a brief introduction to the concept. It does not cover the system in detail. For more information, check the bibliography at the end of this book.

A Swiss grid is built upon a basic spacing unit for all elements. Every element on a page is either one or a multiple of one spacing unit in size. The size of that unit is the *leading* (line spacing) figure for your body type. Spacing between elements is also a multiple of your basic unit.

Thus, if you will be using 9-point type with 10 points of line spacing, spacing between elements on your pages must be a multiple of 10 points. The other major way in which the Swiss grid differs from simple page grids is in the creation of modules on the page for content.

A Swiss grid approach adds logic and regularity to the placement of elements, quickly and easily organizes elements, and can help solve design problems in less time and cost (after initial setup) than wide open page formats. It can be used for both simple and complex design problems.

Setting Up

The hardest part of working with a Swiss grid is in first setting up the grid's parameters. After that, placing your elements on the page is fairly easy, and certainly more fun.

Because the basic spacing unit is a line of body type (including the extra point(s) of space for leading), you must have an exact number of lines of body

Figure 2-6 The Swiss grid system spacing is based on the leading of your body type. This way the baseline of a line of type will always fall on the bottom line of a grid module. The alley spacing is based on the leading figure as well—that is, it's the same as one line of type (including leading). Type can, however, end in the middle of a module. New type should always begin at the top edge of a module. The example on the right shows a basic six-column grid.

type that fit in a column or module. After basic margins are set up, the top/bottom margins may have to be adjusted slightly to accommodate a certain exact number of lines.

Then you need to decide how many columns you will need. The guiding principle here is to select a size narrow enough to accommodate your smallest element easily. Often this is a small head-shot photo (or mug shot) of someone. For instance, if you are working on an 8-1/2-by-11-inch newsletter, you can't use a two-column format and use tightly cropped mug shots as well. The columns are simply too wide. Because type, photos, and other elements can always cover multiple columns in width, be sure your basic grid unit is sized small (Fig. 2–6).

A good guideline is to halve the width of your basic type column (less, actually, with the necessary additional gutter) as your basic unit. Then your former "half-column" material, such as mug shots or column logos, fits into a definite grid position with definite spacing around them. You can use this narrower basic size for the head shots, cutlines, quotes, etc. With more basic choices for planned placement of elements, your spreads can look more creative, though based on a recognizable and logical grid. Even special spreads can look different by using the various columns in a new way.

Once you have your margins and columns set up, you need to decide upon the size of the horizontal spaces, the *alleys.* Each alley is one or more lines of type in depth. Usually an alley is one or two spaces deep, and approximately the same size as the gutter. The depths of the modules also should be set up to accommodate your smallest photo size. Lines of type can be cut off nearly anywhere: Photos such as small mug shots need certain sizes to be useful.

Because each module will hold a precise number of lines of type, as will each alley, you may need to make some adjustments again to your margins, or even to your leading figure, to get everything to come out even.

Again, this is the tough part of setting up a Swiss grid system for your publication. You must go back and forth and make adjustments until the spacing and units come out just right. But remember: Once your Swiss grid is set up, you will never have to wrestle with it again!

Placing Elements

Following gestalt principles, the rules for placing elements on a Swiss grid are based on precision, regularity, and alignment. In a sense, your Swiss grid is a system of precise coordinates for the placement of elements.

The rules are simple:

- Photos and illustrations must (in general—there are always exceptions!) fill an exact number of modules.
- Type must begin at a corner, usually the upper left, of any module. Headlines may be aligned left or right and bottom on a module over body type, however.
- Don't fill your pages to the brim. A good rule of thumb is to leave approximately one-third of a page's modules empty.
- You may bleed photos beyond the grid.
- Headlines covering multiple columns should cover at least half of the last grid module.
- Oddly shaped units may be placed on a grid as long as they cover a reasonable number of grid modules.
- Don't fiddle with type parameters (say, adjusting the leading of a multiline headline to fit a grid module). The beauty of the Swiss grid is the *design* flexibility based on very precise measurements and placement rules, including the type itself.
- Grids can be angled on a page to create further visual interest. Don't slant your grids too much, however, because the type then becomes too hard to read.
- With long columns of type, the alleys between modules will have type going through them. You also may place a thin column rule in the center of the vertical gutters.

The Swiss grid is not the answer to the beginner's design problems. In fact, the Swiss grid in the hands of a rookie can lead to some boring and even unattractive designs. But with some care, it can be a good way to organize very different content into a coherent package. Readers appreciate that.

TYPOGRAPHICAL CONSTANTS

Every publication has certain elements that appear in each issue. Newspapers have the nameplate, the masthead, section flags, logos for columnists, and so on. Magazine-type publications have similar constants, plus a table of contents.

Although newspapers, and to a lesser extent magazines, have "constant" typography in body type, captions, headline schedule, and such, this discussion will center on the typography and design of other constants.

he Free Lance-Star

Tonight
Simmer
TOMORROW +
Steambath
(Weather on Page 2)

)3, NO. 127 FREDERICKSBURG, VIRGINIA, SATURDAY, MAY 30, 1987 25 CENTS

Figure 2-7 Avoid cluttering the nameplate of a newspaper. Here, weather is presented haphazardly in an "ear." (© The Free Lance-Star)

Newspapers

The most obvious example of a constant in a newspaper is its nameplate or *flag*. This, by the way, is *not,* repeat, *not* the masthead, despite the large number of people who call it that. The masthead is the listing on the editorial page of the top executives at the paper.

The nameplate of a newspaper tells the reader a lot about the content and the approach to that content. The nameplate contains the name of the paper, the date, the volume and number of the issue, the city and state of publication, the cost, and perhaps a slogan or graphic.

A newspaper may also use teasers above the nameplate or in one or both of the "ears," but these should not be considered part of the nameplate proper (Fig. 2–7). Any content in the ears tends to create clutter. And some evidence exists that tease boxes above the nameplate are of minimal value and perhaps not worth the clutter.

Traditional newspapers tend to use text or black letter type (often mistakenly called "Old English," which is the family name for one particular kind of type) (see Fig. 2–7). A more modern typeface in the nameplate should indicate a more modern and open approach to the news inside: *USA Today* is not *The Wall Street Journal. Smithsonian* magazine is not *Rolling Stone.*

Changing the typography in the nameplate should be done cautiously. Readers of any publication are very much creatures of habit. If you decide to go with the drastic plastic surgery of changing the type, readers may complain bitterly that "their" publication just isn't the same old friend any more.

Section flags should follow the basic flavor of the nameplate. Traditional newspapers should have traditional flags and keep as much of the nameplate typography as possible continuing throughout the paper. Because using a black letter for anything but the name of the paper is not recommended, the type for all the other contents is usually another typeface.

Still, if the nameplate uses a graphic device, such as a rising sun, or a ship, the section flags should continue that device somehow inside. This helps give the publication a feeling of order and continuity. Readers become familiar and comfortable with the continuing reminder of the publication's personality.

Column logos, used with a mug shot of the columnist and/or without, need to continue the basic typography and design flavor. This use of "standard" typography and design for all "standard" features of the newspaper serves as familiar guideposts as the reader scans the content (Fig. 2–8).

This is yet another way in which design helps content. Readers have said that they *like* the grouping of content in certain related sections as identified by a familiar standing logo. It has been compared to the labeling of aisles in a grocery store: The signs tell you right where to go for certain items.

The informed editor will create sections and subsections for certain related stories and photos, anchor those in the paper, and identify them with clear and attractive logos. This is possibly the best example of the integrated approach to setting up a format for your publication.

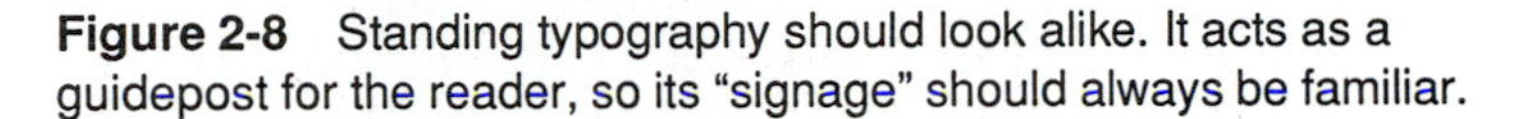

Figure 2-8 Standing typography should look alike. It acts as a guidepost for the reader, so its "signage" should always be familiar.

Folios—the name of the paper, date, and page number, which are used as much for proof to advertisers that an ad truly ran as they are devices for readers—must also follow the general flavor of the other constants.

Newspaper folios are usually at the top of the page, with the page number always at the outside corner. The page is so large that readers nearly always start at the top and work down, so it is the most convenient place. Some tabloid newspapers, however, have used folios successfully at the bottom outside corner and even running sideways up or down the outside corner.

The typographical continuity should continue even to the classified ad section. Naturally, the section flag should be like the others, but even the categorical subsections in the classifieds can continue the typography of other standing features.

The wise newspaper designer finds ways to organize and tie together all the content in the paper. By creating a plan for all standing features, the designer not only creates an attractive publication but also provides a service to the editor who is trying to organize and present the content in the best way possible.

The designer and the editor must always work together to create the best package. Of course, the best possible combination is to have *truly* integrated editing by having both skills in the same person!

Magazines

Most of the above discussion goes for magazines as well. The cover and logo (the name of the publication) of a magazine can tell you a lot about what you will find inside. I know that the old saw is "you can't tell a book by its cover." But you can't tell me that you expect to find the same thing in *Rolling Stone* as you would in *Smithsonian* magazine!

Magazine logos have less information than do newspaper nameplates. Usually they consist of the name of the publication, the date, and the price of the magazine. The address and other information is included in the masthead inside (Fig. 2–9).

Magazines should also develop a typographical consistency for all standing features. These are most evident in the table of contents (often including the masthead) and what is often called simply "back-of-the-book" material: columns, briefs, and shorter bits of information grouped categorically under standing column logos. These should be related in tone to the magazine's content and be familiar guideposts for your readers. Again, the aim of design and type consistency is to use visuals to guide your readers to and then help them through your content.

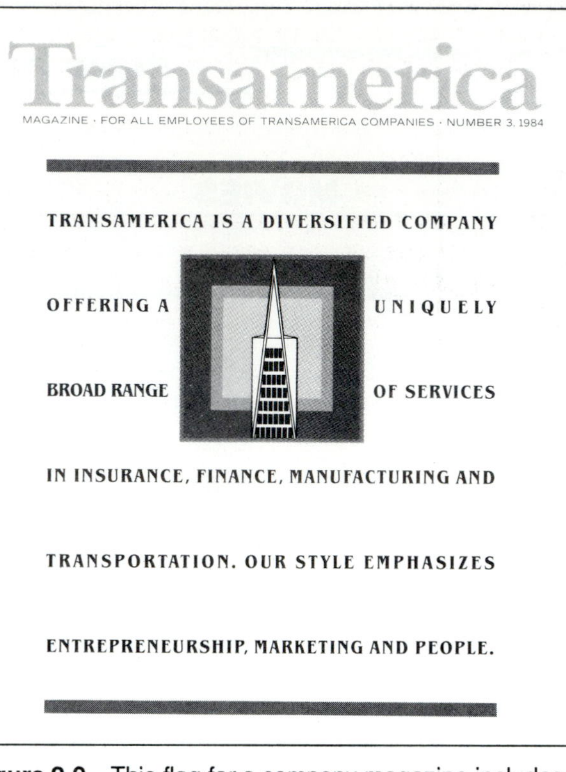

Figure 2-9 This flag for a company magazine includes the company name and the date. (Courtesy of Transamerica Corp.)

Table of Contents

The table of contents (T of C) is an extremely important part of your publication. Its function is not only to show readers where they can find certain items but also to "sell" the content. It is a teaser for the inside as well as a simple listing.

Tables of contents most often include the titles of articles and features and the masthead. Also, they may include a note from the publisher or editor and a credit/explanation for a cover photograph or illustration (Fig. 2–10).

The most important function of the table of contents is to give information to readers quickly. You will need a brief description of feature material and merely a title and/or name for continuing features, such as columns or tips columns.

Because readers are interested in information first and where it is located second, it makes no sense to list page numbers first. Yet many publications will use a huge, boldface page number to draw the eye, as if page **9** was more important than the content.

It is logical to sell the content and then quickly and quietly tell readers where that content can be located. Put the page number to the right of the information, either immediately or connected with rules, or leaders, if you must (ugh!).

You should also find a way typographically to show the difference between regular content and new features in that particular issue. You can use typographical contrasts (to be discussed in Chapter 4), such as **bold** vs. light, CAPS vs. U&lc, roman vs. *italics,* and so on. Along with that you could use indentations, such as used in common outlines, to show the different content. Or you can use different columns within a table.

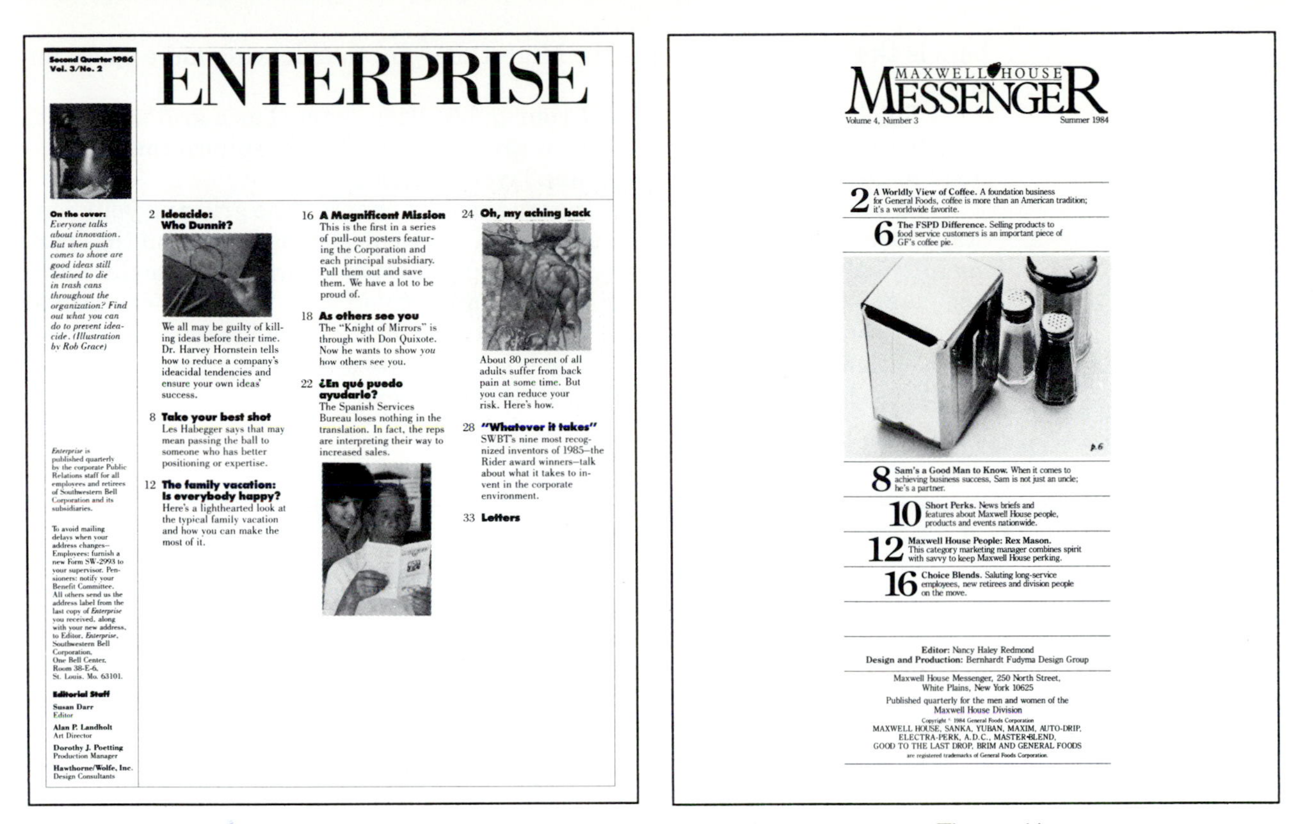

Second Quarter 1986
Vol. 3/No. 2

ENTERPRISE

On the cover: *Everyone talks about innovation. But when push comes to shove are good ideas still destined to die in trash cans throughout the organization? Find out what you can do to prevent ideacide. (Illustration by Rob Grace)*

2 **Ideacide: Who Dunnit?**
We all may be guilty of killing ideas before their time. Dr. Harvey Hornstein tells how to reduce a company's ideacidal tendencies and ensure your own ideas' success.

8 **Take your best shot**
Les Habegger says that may mean passing the ball to someone who has better positioning or expertise.

12 **The family vacation: Is everybody happy?**
Here's a lighthearted look at the typical family vacation and how you can make the most of it.

16 **A Magnificent Mission**
This is the first in a series of pull-out posters featuring the Corporation and each principal subsidiary. Pull them out and save them. We have a lot to be proud of.

18 **As others see you**
The "Knight of Mirrors" is through with Don Quixote. Now he wants to show *you* how others see you.

22 **¿En qué puedo ayudarle?**
The Spanish Services Bureau loses nothing in the translation. In fact, the reps are interpreting their way to increased sales.

24 **Oh, my aching back**
About 80 percent of all adults suffer from back pain at some time. But you can reduce your risk. Here's how.

28 **"Whatever it takes"**
SWBT's nine most recognized inventors of 1985–the Rider award winners–talk about what it takes to invent in the corporate environment.

33 **Letters**

Enterprise is published quarterly by the corporate Public Relations staff for all employees and retirees of Southwestern Bell Corporation and its subsidiaries.

To avoid mailing delays when your address changes– Employees: furnish a new Form SW-2993 to your supervisor. Pensioners: notify your Benefit Committee. All others send us the address label from the last copy of *Enterprise* you received, along with your new address, to Editor, *Enterprise*, Southwestern Bell Corporation, One Bell Center, Room 38-E-6, St. Louis, Mo. 63101.

Editorial Staff

Susan Darr
Editor

Alan P. Landholt
Art Director

Dorothy J. Poetting
Production Manager

Hawthorne/Wolfe, Inc.
Design Consultants

MAXWELL HOUSE
MESSENGER
Volume 4, Number 3 Summer 1984

2 **A Worldly View of Coffee.** A foundation business for General Foods, coffee is more than an American tradition; it's a worldwide favorite.

6 **The FSPD Difference.** Selling products to food service customers is an important piece of GF's coffee pie.

p.6

8 **Sam's a Good Man to Know.** When it comes to achieving business success, Sam is not just an uncle; he's a partner.

10 **Short Perks.** News briefs and features about Maxwell House people, products and events nationwide.

12 **Maxwell House People: Rex Mason.** This category marketing manager combines spirit with savvy to keep Maxwell House perking.

16 **Choice Blends.** Saluting long-service employees, new retirees and division people on the move.

Editor: Nancy Haley Redmond
Design and Production: Bernhardt Fudyma Design Group

Maxwell House Messenger, 250 North Street, White Plains, New York 10625

Published quarterly for the men and women of the Maxwell House Division

Copyright © 1984 General Foods Corporation
MAXWELL HOUSE, SANKA, YUBAN, MAXIM, AUTO-DRIP, ELECTRA-PERK, A.D.C., MASTER-BLEND, GOOD TO THE LAST DROP, BRIM AND GENERAL FOODS are registered trademarks of General Foods Corporation.

Figure 2-10 Table of contents pages can be done many ways. The goal is to make the information accessible as well as attractive. The *Enterprise* magazine T of C includes a masthead (a). The extra bold article titles are strong eye grabbers. The Maxwell House *Messenger* page draws attention to the small typography by leaving ample white space. The logo and page numbers are in a warm light brown, helping to keep the over-large numbers from dominating. (a, Courtesy of Southwestern Bell Corporation; b, Courtesy of the Bernhardt Fudyma Design Group)

The masthead fulfills basically a business function, but that doesn't mean it has to be ugly. It, too, should follow the type and design guidelines set up for all standing features, whether it runs on the T of C page or elsewhere.

In general, most mastheads include a reduced version of the logo; the addresses for editorial content and, if appropriate, the national ad agency handling accounts; the volume and issue number; the important people in the organization, such as board of directors, publisher, top editorial people, and sometimes everyone on the staff; and subscription/circulation information.

If your publication qualifies for second-class postage, the ISSN (International Standard Serial Number) is placed there. If you copyright your publication or if you want to include a disclaimer about your connection with some or all of the content, the masthead is the place.

Regardless of whether you place the masthead, which can often take an entire column, with the T of C or elsewhere, anchor it in one place, either very early in the publication, or in the case of small newsletters, on the back cover. Make it easy to find.

Folios in a magazine are not stuck with the top of the page, as with most newspapers. In fact, many magazines seem to prefer the foot margin. Whichever place you decide is best for your folios, place them outside your type page in the margins. One of the reasons the foot margin is preferred for folios or page numbers is that the foot margin is the largest margin, thus leaving more space for them.

The basic building blocks of your publication—your basic grid structure, whether it is a simple grid or a Swiss grid, and your typographical constants—need to be in place before design and layout can begin.

In a sense, as explained further in the next chapter, the grid and your constants *are* part of your overall design plan. Those decisions impact on the "personality" of your publication, as expressed in its basic format, nameplate and logo, and basic typography. Still, the grid must come first. Then you can decide how to "hang" elements logically and creatively on that publication framework.

With a few further decisions, you lock in an overall design plan and begin to express that plan in the day-to-day layout of your pages.

CHECKLIST

1. Set up an attractive and functional basic grid before you do anything with your publication.
2. A good column grid structure should be at once flexible and rigid: flexible to allow a creative designer some opportunities for variation, yet rigid enough to provide that air of familiarity for the reader.
3. The format you choose should reflect the needs of your content and of your readers. The format should show off the content in the best possible light.
4. The Swiss grid is difficult to set up, but with practice it can be an effective solution to some of your design problems. However, don't take it for granted. It is still possible to design an unattractive publication using a Swiss grid. Follow the rules. Then experiment to discover your tastes and allow them to mature. With practice, you will make occasional mistakes, but you will become better. Without practice, nothing will ever happen.
5. Take your favorite publication and try to "strip" it down to its "skeletal" grid structure. Measure the type page/margins, the columns, gutters, etc. Is it a Swiss grid publication? (That is, can you fill the spaces between elements with even numbers of lines?) Can you see a pattern for breaking the grid with wider or narrower columns? See if you can write a set of rules for that publication based on what you discover. Then write that publication, request its style manual, and see how well you did.
7. Set up a practice Swiss grid with modules, gutters, and alleys. Then design six or seven (or more if you're having fun!) different pages for a publication of your choice. All the pages should have a consistent look to them. Try a number of different approaches to the placement of art and type: tight, wide, etc.
7. Have you found anything so far that smacks of "creativity," that is, a fuzzy ability that some people just "have" and some people don't? Of course not. As I explained in the introduction, much of good visual presentation of information has to do with *logic, planning,* and *math.* Even you left-brain people out there should be able to design pages well!

CHAPTER

3

DESIGN

The word "design" conjures up a host of unfavorable impressions for most editors. It smacks of "art" and art smacks of an inborn talent beyond the reach of anyone worth a subjunctive mood or nonrestrictive clause. And anyway, artists don't edit.

But an understanding of the underlying principles of design will help the editor lay out pages. I am a firm believer that if you understand *how* or *why* something works, you will be able to work with that something much more effectively. This is important. Better laid out pages lead to better communication with the reader. Design, in a sense, is a lubricant for information.

This chapter provides that foundation of knowledge in how we see things and how the brain deals with what we see and how it organizes visual information. After this knowledge is acquired, understanding some of the basics of page design and layout becomes easier and more logical.

ATTENTION AND GESTALT

The eyes process much visual information that the brain never deals with on an active level. When we aim our eyes in a direction, we *see* a lot more than we can *look at.* The focus area is only about 3 degrees of the approximately 180 degrees we can see.

For instance, as you see these pages, you can only "look" at a certain portion at a time. As you read these words, you can see the other words on the page, but you can't read them because your attention area is limited. It is rather like trying to read a barn-sized sign in the black of night with a small-beam flashlight: You have to run the beam over the sign bit by bit to understand the entire message.

Attention is sometimes an active process: You choose where your eyes want to point when you read. But it is also often a passive process: Your eyes are drawn—outside your will, if not actually against it—to certain areas of a visual field. This is visual attraction. Attention is *more* than attraction because it involves meaning. When you try to extract meaning from something, you must pay attention to it.

For instance, when the average reader looks at a newspaper page, he or she is drawn first to the photographs, then to spot-color elements, and then to headlines. A research project by The Poynter Institute for Media Studies in 1985 showed this. Generally speaking, this eye movement is true of all readers: The eyes are attracted to certain kinds of visual elements. Continuing research in eye movement done by The Gallup Organization should continue to better-inform those who present information.

The first-seen elements on a page tend to be larger or bolder or irregularly shaped or in color. Although these are important, content can draw the eye as well. Try putting a large, bold, irregular splotch of color next to an equally large, black-and-white photo of a naked person and you'll see what I mean. After stopping at these points, the eyes become much more under the active control of the reader, and returns can be made to the most interesting points, either in terms of the visual stimulation or of the content.

Attention also tends to be given to the familiar and to patterns. The attention span is limited, so the most easily "excitable" portions of the memory area of the brain seek matches from the visual stimuli the eye is sending along.

The most easily excitable portions of the memory tend to be those most frequently excited in the past. The power of this tendency to match with familiar patterns is so strong that it is almost impossible to see a new pattern as "new" if it looks like something familiar.

For instance, look at the following shape. It is a unique shape, but because it *looks like* an O and an E, that's how we see it. The brain wants desperately to make sense out of the universe, to force the unknown into previously known patterns, or into the "known," in whatever way it can.

Or look at the following:

to get her

Some readers probably saw "to get her" and others saw "together": The spacing was set purposefully so that the meaning (as defined by the space) was ambiguous. Depending on what you wanted to see or what you expected to see, the brain decided to "see." The way you display your type and other design elements can work in the same way. You can either make communication easy and clear or you can make it ambiguous.

There are two major theories on how the brain deals with visual information from the eyes. The first says that the brain compares the new stimuli with previously stored patterns or *templates*. If the brain finds a match with a familiar pattern, even if it has to stretch a bit to make the match, the new stimuli are identified.

Figure 3-1 In the top diagram, your brain organizes by shape: You see the three circles, three squares, and three triangles as sets. In the bottom diagram, the brain notes the tone faster than the shapes, and so organizes the three darker shapes into a set.

The second theory says that the brain analyzes new stimuli as combinations of elemental features. For instance, letters of the alphabet are combinations of horizontal, vertical, diagonal, and/or curved lines.

Given the right combination of features, no matter how oddly they may be combined, the brain can identify a letter. The template-matching theory would require many templates to identify letters because of all the possible forms for any given letter. The features-analysis theory says that as long as the elements are aligned in the correct basic structure, the letter can be identified.

Regardless of which theory is correct, you can see that perception relies on certain structures made up of lines and shapes. Publication design is little more than paying attention to these basic shapes and using them in such a way as to not confuse the reader. Although "creativity" certainly plays a part, it is not strictly necessary in order to become a competent page designer.

Another helpful set of principles for the inexperienced designer is the gestalt principles of perceptual organization, named after gestalt psychologists.

In essence, the main gestalt principle says that the whole is greater than the sum of its parts, that the pattern is more important than the individual element. In fact, there is some evidence that we see the pattern much more quickly and more accurately than we see the individual units.

Here again, we have the brain sifting through visual information looking for the familiar and for patterns.

The gestalt principles, according to John R. Anderson[1], are:

Similarity. Objects that look alike tend to be grouped together (Fig. 3–1). This involves shape, color, size, position (and attitude or angle), and texture. A relationship is implied when elements are similar, as with the uniforms of an athletic team, or the same color and shape corporate logo. Therefore, on a pub-

[1]John R. Anderson, *Cognitive Psychology and Its Implications,* 2nd ed. (New York: W.H. Freeman and Co., 1985).

Figure 3-2 The eye tends to group elements that seem to be clustered, even if they are not meant to be. In the top row, all the dots are equally spaced. All dots are seen separately. On the bottom row, the one dot on the left stands out alone because of just a little extra space between it and the others.

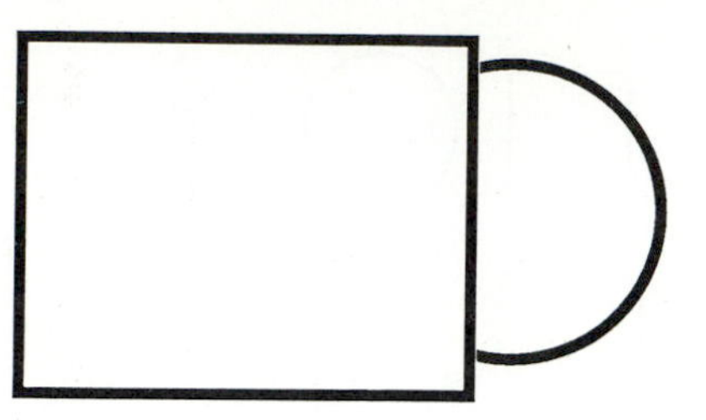

Figure 3-3 Here we "see" a rectangle occluding a circle, although it could just as easily be a part circle attached directly to the side of the rectangle. But we want to "continue" the line to create the circle.

Figure 3-4 Not only do we "see" the triangle in the middle, which is at best only implied by the notched circles, we "see" that the triangle is a bit lighter than the white of the page outside the triangle. The brain has "seen" a difference that simply is not there.

lication page, similar shapes and colors, etc., imply that the content is related. Unfortunately, this principle is frequently ignored, adding unnecessary confusion.

Proximity. Similar elements closely grouped will be seen as a unit and not as individuals. (Fig. 3–2). Tightly spaced elements have an almost magnetic attraction to each other. If a pattern is evident, the grouping of elements may be loose.

Good Continuation. Segments of shapes or lines are put together in their easiest and most pleasing configuration. (Fig. 3–3).

Good Form and Closure. If an incomplete shape would become a familiar shape by mentally completing it, that is what the brain does. Again, this is an effort by the brain to make the unfamiliar familiar. Even completely novel shapes are divided into units. (Fig. 3–4).

What does this have to do with laying out decent-looking pages?

If you can understand and then control the eye movement, from the initial entry point, through the other stopping-off points, to the departure point for a page, then you can make the information-gathering process easy. This is what good functional design is all about.

You can move your readers' eyes around the page in a calm and coherent manner, making the information-gathering process easy and pleasurable. Or you can ignore what we have learned about how people both see and look and create random design, leaving poor readers to wander aimlessly on the page (Fig. 3–5).

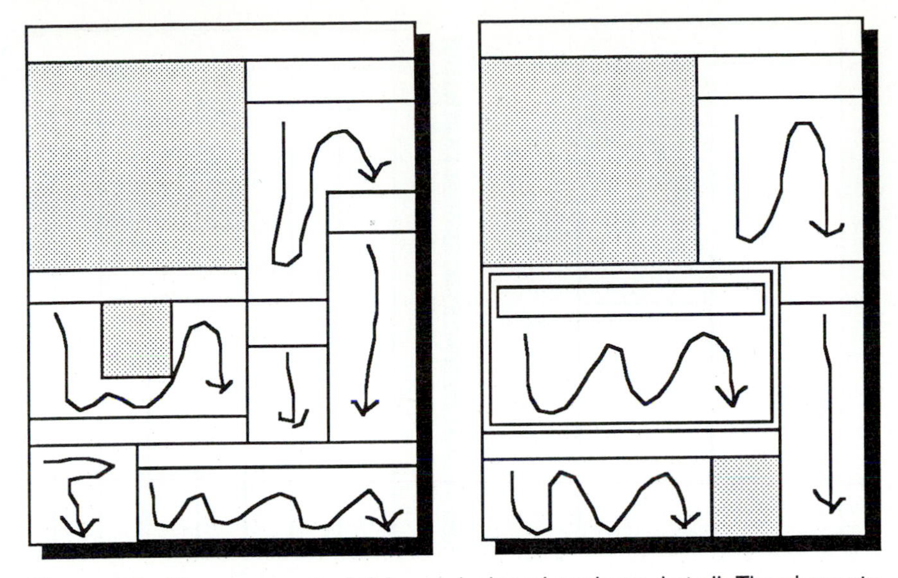

Figure 3-5 The page on the left is not designed or planned at all. The elements seem to be placed at random. The other page gives you a clear idea of where each story begins and ends.

Readers like their information quick and easy. It's not enough to give them information: the getting of that information must be easy and pleasurable. One communications theorist (William Stephenson) has gone so far as to say that media use is an act of "play" by readers.

DESIGN TOOLS OF THE TRADE

After understanding the above general principles on *how* we look and see, editors next need to understand the more specific available tools. It is through the use of these visual tools that the principles can be put into practical use on your pages.

Basically, anything on your pages is made up of line, shape, tone, and (visual) texture. With these, you can manipulate reader response to your presentation.

Line

Lines can be classified into horizontal, vertical, diagonal, and curved. Each has a connotative, or second-level, meaning that can add to or detract from your message.

Horizontal lines are restful and at peace with their surroundings. Horizontal lines, then, should not be used as part of a design on highly active content, such as football games, county fairs, etc.

This concept carries over into the width of columns of type on your page. Wide columns of type (though it depends on the size of your page, let's say 24 picas or more) say "quiet" and "bookish." The wide lines of type emphasize the horizontal (Fig. 3–6).

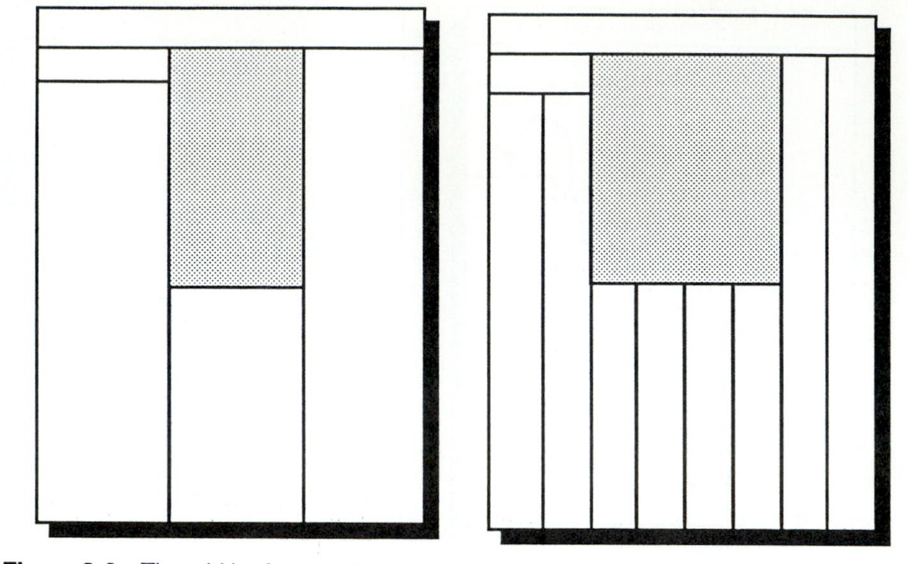

Figure 3-6 The width of your columns can say either quiet or "bookish" (L) or be more active.

If you want to add action and excitement to a spread, you would use narrower columns of type. Don't go so narrow, however, that readability of the type is hampered.

Vertical lines are dignified and strong, like the columns in classical architecture. The very columns of type in your publication represent vertical lines. They add order and stability to the content. They also show potential for movement (Fig. 3–7).

Column rules represent simple vertical lines that help balance the horizontals of the headlines and flags. Vertical lines create up and down movement. On a tall page, such as a broadsheet newspaper page, or even a "tall" tabloid, vertical lines in a layout can help the reader see the layout as one unit.

Diagonal lines show the most movement and action. Diagonal lines can very easily lead the eye through a layout. You would use diagonal content elements in "avant-garde" spreads as well because they break the rules of the format grid that the rest of your publication follows. The very breaking of a rule adds power to the diagonal.

Curved lines are sensuous and classy. Curved lines also show motion, but they are more controlled than is a diagonal: Diagonal lines are rocket launchings; curved lines are figure skaters doing a spiral on ice.

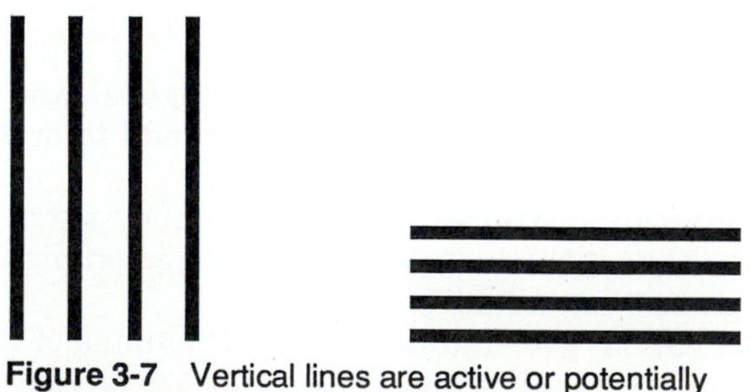

Figure 3-7 Vertical lines are active or potentially so. Horizontal lines emphasize the passive. You can use these visual impressions to enhance the meanings of your words.

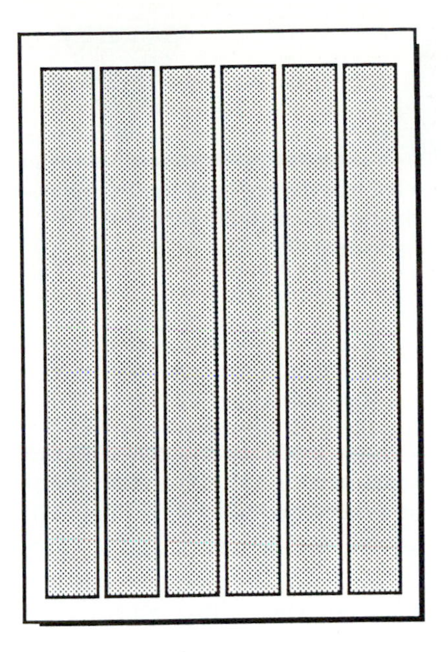

The Free Lance-Star
FREDERICKSBURG, VIRGINIA

Lifestyle

THURSDAY, JULY 21, 1988 41

Trouble brings families together

By MARTY MORRISON

Irene and Okie Folsom hold the Mitts twins, Lynn and Johnathan. They're seated in the living room of the Mitts home in Spotsylvania.

Empty nest syndrome hits hard

ERMA BOMBECK

Career woman discovers family is what matters

ANN LANDERS

VCR manufacturers to raise prices

Love is...

Figure 3-8 Real and imaginary lines are formed by columns of type. On the sample on the left, the columns line up in obvious chunks of space. This is because the eye is continuing lines along tops and bottoms of columns of type to create enclosed rectangles. This works too with real columns of type in a publication (right). The gestalt of similar size and shape of the columns, along with the connecting imaginary lines at top and bottom, helps to create visual units for the information. (R, © The Free Lance-Star)

In design, lines are both real and imaginary. Real lines are made up of the alignment of the tops of several columns of type, or the columns of type themselves, which end up being long, thick (though gray) lines (Fig. 3–8).

As will be discussed in Chapter 7, imaginary lines are also part of the content of many photographs and illustrations. These lines can continue through and across the rest of your design and create motion, etc.

Because any of these real or imaginary lines can cause the eye to move, a good designer will use them to get the eye to travel to other important parts of the design, such as the story or the body copy in an ad.

Shape

Because type is set in columns of type, graphic design ends up being mostly horizontal and vertical lines. Thus, the most frequent shapes on a page are rectangles and squares. But triangles and circles also are useful shapes to consider in design.

The basic page size of your publication is the most obvious rectangle. Your columns of type and photographs on a page also are rectangles. Because of the plethora of rectangles in any publication design, the occasional use of a triangle or a circle can add emphasis to that element.

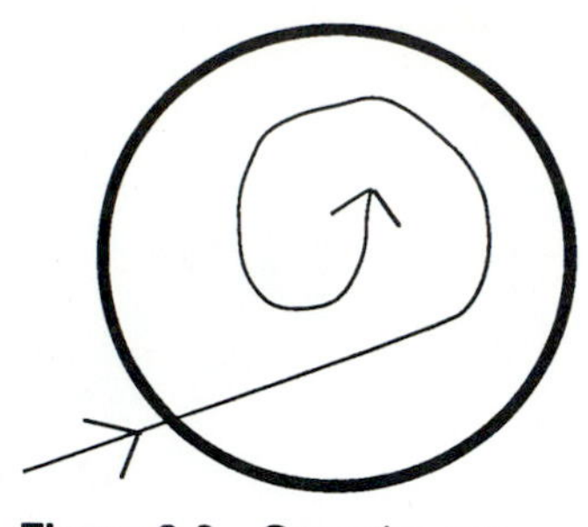

Figure 3-9 Once the eye enters a circular shape, it tends to stay there.

Figure 3-10 The left triangle appears stable, unmovable. The one on the right is unstable and could tip anytime. Which shape might you use for an exciting and active layout?

Circles are especially good as parts of nameplates or column logos, the constants in any publication. Circles are good for logos because the eye movement stays within the shape. And again, because most everything else on a page will be a rectangle, using circles with your constants can add a special flavor (Fig. 3–9).

Triangles are either solid—with the point up—or they show potential to tip over—point down. Either way, triangles have good eye movement around the three points (Fig. 3–10). Squares, on the other hand, show little movement around the four corners. Thus, the triangle is a good shape to keep in mind for a layout, especially an ad layout. The use of three focal points in a design creates visual interest in the design by forcing the eyes in a restless move around the three points.

This is where an understanding of perception and gestalt comes in. The eye naturally looks for patterns, as we have learned, and having three points enhances the pressure to search your design. A four-point design is much too stable to stimulate good eye movement.

Tone

It is tone and shape that give our eyes something to see. Tone is the relative darkness or lightness of an object. In a sense, tone is the black-and-white equivalent of color in design (Fig. 3–11).

Color helps us to differentiate objects and, in a black-and-white design, it is the tone that does this: pure black, through various shades of gray, to pure white, or at least as white as the paper stock allows us to get!

Tone in a design is usually achieved with *halftone* screens. Screens consist of dots of various sizes and proximity to one another. Light-gray tones are made up of small dots relatively far apart. With dark-gray screens, the dots have gotten so large that the screen appears to be a black background with white dots. The eye mixes the combination of black and white—as you might mix black and white paint—to create the impression of gray.

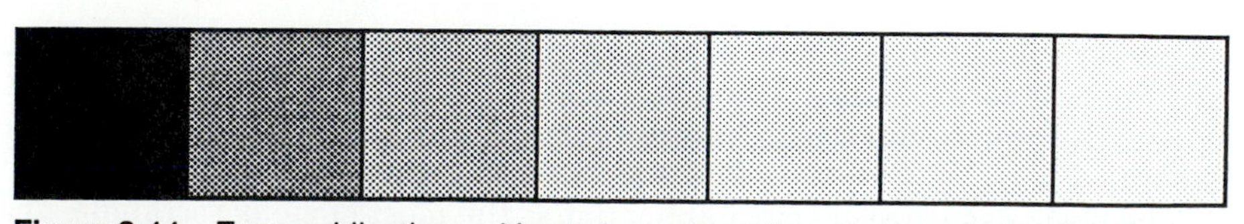

Figure 3-11 Even publications without chromatic color can use achromatic color: black, white, and various shades of gray. Desktop publishing software is making the use of screens easier all the time.

Just ten years ago, readers of print media in the Richmond metropolitan area had few choices: the daily Richmond Newspapers, the weekly Afro-American, and the monthly Richmond Lifestyle. Richmond was known more as a publishing graveyard rather than a vigorious marketplace. By 1988, though the environment for print media had changed significantly. From a potent mass circulation weekly and several emerging suburban weeklies, to a handful of alternative monthly publications, to a statewide business magazine based in the city, Richmond is witnessing a renaissance of print media that is interwoven with the city's economy.

Just ten years ago, readers of print media in the Richmond metropolitan area had few choices: the daily Richmond Newspapers, the weekly Afro-American, and the monthly Richmond Lifestyle. Richmond was known more as a publishing graveyard rather than a vigorious marketplace. By 1988, though the environment for print media had changed significantly. From a potent mass circulation weekly and several emerging suburban weeklies, to a handful of alternative monthly publications, to a statewide business magazine based in the city, Richmond is witnessing a renaissance of print media that is interwoven with the city's economy.

Just ten years ago, readers of print media in the Richmond metropolitan area had few choices: the daily Richmond Newspapers, the weekly Afro-American, and the monthly Richmond Lifestyle. Richmond was known more as a publishing graveyard rather than a vigorious marketplace. By 1988, though the environment for print media had changed significantly. From a potent mass circulation weekly and several emerging suburban weeklies, to a handful of alternative monthly publications, to a statewide business magazine based in the city, Richmond is witnessing a renaissance of print media that is interwoven with the city's economy.

Figure 3-12 Depending on the typeface itself and the leading, blocks of body type can appear darker or lighter. All the type is 10 points. The type on the left is 10 on 10 points of leading, the middle is 10 on 12, and the right is 10 on 15.

The tone of a screen is called for by using the percentage of an area that is filled with dots. For instance, a light-gray screen would be a 10 percent or 20 percent screen because only that portion would be covered by the dots.

Sometimes screens are used over type, and sometimes simply as background to an entire design. When using screens with type, be very careful not to make the screen so dark that the type becomes hard to read. Use either bigger or bolder type under a screen.

An aspect of tone that is not often considered by designers is the tone of the type itself on the page. Especially from a distance, the line after line of body type adds tone to a design. The type you choose, the size, the line width, and the leading all affect how dark or light your columns of type appear (Fig. 3–12).

The more leading you add to a block of type, for instance, the lighter it appears. The principle is the same as that of a halftone screen: The more white paper that shows between the little dots of black, the lighter the element will appear. Control the tone of your type by making typographical decisions on a sample page, not just on the drawing board. A column logo that may look great by itself may be lost on a page with heavy type.

Texture

Anything you see gives you an impression of what it would feel like were you to touch it. This is true in graphic design. Usually a graphic designer adds texture to a design through the use of specialty screens. Besides the pure grays of halftone screens, designers can use screens that simulate a variety of textures, such as mezzotint or steel etching. Certain typefaces also can appear "soft" or "hard," masculine or feminine (Fig. 3–13).

Typography

Typography

Figure 3-13 The top typeface gives you a different "feel" from the bottom sample.

DESIGN PRINCIPLES IN PUBLICATION LAYOUT

Once these elements are considered and controlled, the editor is faced with placing elements in an attractive and coherent package on a piece of paper. Luckily, other principles regarding how individual elements should be related are also available. According to Roy Paul Nelson, these are *balance, proportion, contrast* or *emphasis, sequence, unity,* and *simplicity.*

Balance

Elements on your page have a visual or optical "weight." The more a reader is attracted to an element, the more "weight" it is considered to have. A good design has elements with visual weights in balance. In general, large objects are visually "heavier" than small objects, color elements heavier than black and white (B&W), irregular shapes heavier than common shapes (circle, square, etc.), and so on. In fact, if white space on a page is sufficiently large, it can have quite a "heavy" visual weight. The page designer's job is to use these attributes to create a balanced design.

The simplest way to achieve balance in a design is to center everything: symmetrical or formal balance. However, centering is used to a fault in many smaller newspaper ads. It is the easiest but often not the best way to achieve balance.

Symmetrical balance is boring, just as the square is probably the least interesting shape because of its ho-hum regularity of four even sides. Symmetrical balance is great for formal occasions, but it does not surprise and/or please the reader as much as asymmetrical design.

For instance, two photos don't have to be the same size and played in mirror-image column positions to achieve balance. Play a large photo near the center line and play a smaller photo at the edge of the spread; that is, farther from the visual fulcrum point (Fig. 3–14). This puts the two photos in visual balance.

In general, designs should balance side to side—or across pages in a magazine—top-to-bottom, and even diagonally, especially on a broadsheet newspaper page.

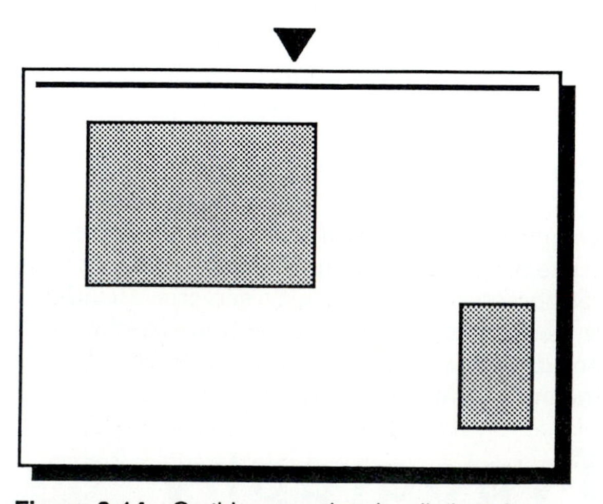

Figure 3-14 On this page, the visually heavier element is nearer the center of balance, and thus doesn't overpower the smaller element in the corner. This type of balance is called *informal* or *asymmetrical* balance.

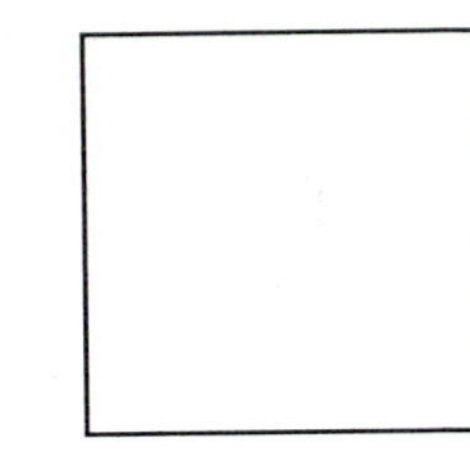

Figure 3-15 On the left, a golden rectangle; on the right, a dull, boring square.

Figure 3-16 Because the optical center is higher on a page than the actual center, the bottom margin on a flat piece should be larger than the others.

Understanding balance and using it properly come with practice. After a while you will just "feel" what is right and what isn't, without having to think so hard to do it. Patience and practice are called for.

Proportion

Visual communicators and artists have known for centuries that certain relationships between elements—certain distances, shapes, etc.—are more visually pleasing than others.

The "golden proportion," approximately 0.62 to 1 or about 3 to 5, provides a relationship between the sides of a rectangle that is more interesting than the obvious 1-to-1 ratio of a square. We can see the relationship between the sides of a square immediately. It is routine, even boring (Fig. 3–15).

With a "golden rectangle," however, the relationship between the sides is not so obvious. The eyes/brain have to spend a little more time checking out each side to look for the pattern, the gestalt. Thus, it is more visually interesting.

Another accepted formula is the "root-2 rectangle," a little closer to a square. The root-2 rectangle is formed by taking the diagonal of a square as the radius of a arc. Where the arc crosses the baseline is the proper width for the long side of the rectangle. A golden rectangle can be made in similar fashion. After dividing a square in half and drawing the diagonal of a half, an arc is swung down to the baseline again to locate the proper distance for the rectangle.

These shapes can be used in graphic design for the shapes of pages themselves, the shapes of photos and drawings within those pages, the depth of type blocks, and so on. This is not to say that you need to try to fit everything into these shapes. But you should remember that symmetry and total precision and similarity are not visually interesting.

For instance, margins around the page of a flier or magazine should not be equal. At the very least, the bottom margin should be somewhat larger than the other margins (Fig. 3–16).

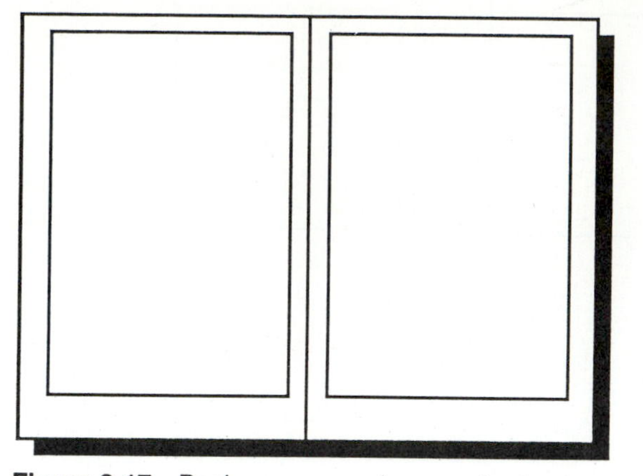

Figure 3-17 Book or progressive margins have differently sized margins on all four sides of the type page, where your information will appear.

For a magazine or book, the margins along the gutter should be small, the top margin a bit larger, the side margin larger still, and the bottom margin largest of all. These are called *progressive* or *book margins* (Fig. 3–17). Remember, however, to leave large enough inside margin space to read the type without having to force the pages wider than the binding would normally allow.

The point is that the spatial relationships within the two-dimensional objects on the page, the page itself, and the margins and other areas of white space on the page look better when they have pleasing proportions.

This approach is really two-dimensional architecture. Your design, when "built" during paste-up, should be both pleasing to the eye and functional. A beautiful building is useless if it can't be used; a beautiful page is useless if it can't be read because of dysfunctional elements.

Contrast or Emphasis

A good design has a starting point or focal point. Mario Garcia calls this the *center of visual impact* (CVI). The CVI is where the reader enters the page, an action that the designer must control (Fig. 3–18). Without a CVI, a page is a mass confusion of elements competing for attention. Readers may simply go elsewhere.

The CVI is given *emphasis* by making it *contrast* with the other elements on the page. The attributes listed under "Balance" above work here as well: The CVI gains emphasis by its placement (high), its size (large), its tone (bold or in color), its shape (unusual), or even white space (surround the element with a much larger amount). Elements that break a margin or any other visual "rule" on your page gain emphasis as well.

Typographical contrast also is an important point to remember. Your message is delivered in type, but in various kinds of type: headlines or titles, blurbs or subheads, body type, captions, large quotes pulled from a story, or in maps and graphics.

These different parts of your message should not look the same. Captions, for instance, should *look* very different from body type. Readers should be able to identify immediately what they are reading.

MONDAY
JULY 18, 1988

The Virginian-Pilot

SECTION B

■ YOUR HOROSCOPE/B6
■ ANN LANDERS/B6

The Daily Break

Gov. Michael Dukakis and his wife, Kitty, wave to supporters. Married 25 years, she's still the most important person in his life.

AP photo

KITTY, KITTY

Dukakis' lively wife may be catalyst of merriment in White House

Diane McLellan is Washington editor of Washingtonian magazine, where this article first appeared.

By Diana McLellan

AFTER ALMOST EIGHT years of Ron and Nancy Reagan's Hollywood-on-the-Potomac, Washington D.C. is bracing for the winds of change again. Some of the brisker gusts will, as always, be fanned by a new first lady.

Even the term "first lady" blows in and out. Concocted in the 1870s by a woman journalist to flatter Lucy Webb Hayes, it was banned from the Kennedy White House. ("It sounds like a saddle horse," moaned Jackie.) But it was decreed the sole correct term for the missus by the Reagans.

Nomenclature aside, think for a moment of each wife's prevailing zephyrs. Jackie's French food and fashion and lighthearted dancing parties; Lady Bird's Texas barbecue and wildflower fever; Rosalynn's down-home eats and homemade duds; Nancy's California flash and Adolfo dash.

Right now, the future's fickle finger points to Barbara Bush or Kitty Dukakis — "Class vs. brass," says an old Washington lawyer.

Barbara Bush embodies the old, cave-dwelling Washingtonian's idea of class: well-mannered, calm, contented, with the cozy, low-key interest of her caste and age — tennis, gardening, needlepoint, grandchildren, walking and tossing sticks for Millie, the family's English springer spaniel. Barbara Bush's White House, friends predict, would be much like her vice-presidential residence, pretty, informal, teeming with nieces and nephews, resounding with the clink of ice cubes, the clank of horseshoes, the crackle of barbecues, the muted crinkling of old money.

Is Kitty Dukakis brass? Even now, temporarily sidelined while recovering from surgery, she is, says a close friend, "a caution." Kitty is slim, dark, dynamic, Jewish, sexy, chic — warm-hearted but wired and so outspoken that her husband's campaign has quietly assigned a "Kitty Litter Patrol" to mop up misunderstandings in her wake.

After Michael Dukakis walks away with the nomination from this week's Democratic convention in Atlanta, and if he wins in November, his wife will be the fourth divorced woman to occupy the White House — Rachel Jackson, wife of Andrew, in the 1820s; Florence Harding, wife of Warren in the 1920s, and Betty Ford, wife of Gerald in the 1970s, preceded her. And she'll be the first lady whose husband, Ronald Reagan notwithstanding, is probably crazier about his wife than any president in history.

Says a Boston journalist: "After 25 years of marriage, the guy is besotted with her. She's Michael's closest confidante and friend, the most important person in his life. She offers everything in the world he feels he hasn't got: romance, glamour, mystery, sex appeal."

An astonished audience got a bracing

Please see **KITTY**, *Page* **B3**

The Dukakises shortly after Kitty's neck surgery. She's known to be outspoken and "a caution."

TRIBUTE

Curly's daughter sticks up for stamp to honor the Three Stooges

By Neil A. Grauer
Special to The Baltimore Sun

SOMEHOW THE IDEA of a United States postage stamp honoring the Three Stooges makes people laugh.

And that is just fine with Janie Howard Hanky of Westminster, Md. Her father, Jerome "Curly" Howard, spent his life making people laugh as the shaved-headed, roly-poly member of the famed knockabout trio. So it seems appropriate that the thought of a stamp honoring him, his black-banged older brother Moe Howard, and frizzy-haired partner Larry Fine should inspire grins and chuckles.

"Yes, he did make people happy," said Hanky, 40, who was just 3½ years old when her father died in 1952, following six years of ill health. "He brought joy and happiness to generations of Americans, especially during tough times, such as the Depression and World War II."

"And sometimes laughter is what helps keep people going on."

At least one high-ranking government official is not snickering at the prospect of a proposed Stooge stamp. Charles Wick, director of the United States Information Agency — and a former Hollywood producer who once worked with the Stooges — thinks "they would be highly eligible" for the honor.

When a person or persons is honored by the issuance of a commemorative stamp, it is "a tribute to the standards they represent, which are admirable, or indicates that those who are honored have become part of the fabric of American life," said Wick, who produced the most elaborate, but least profitable, feature-length Stooge epic, "Snow White and the Three Stooges," in 1961.

Please see **STOOGES**, *Page* **B3**

From top, Stooges Joe Besser, Moe Howard and Larry Fine

ON THE AIR

In TV world that lacks taste, tact, 'Nite' dawns like an innocent oasis

By Tom Shales

CABLE CAN TAKE much of the blame for sleazing up television, but even it has its moments of decency. Each evening on the Nickelodeon Channel, there's "Nick at Nite," a collection of sitcoms from TV's childhood-from back before its terminal puberty began.

Programs like "My Three Sons" and "Mr. Ed" and "The Ann Sothern Show" were ridiculed in their day for being innocuous and silly. You're darn right they're innocuous and silly! And that is just what makes them so appealing now. They don't deal with sexual politics and nobody talks dirty in them.

Nickelodeon also shows condensed versions of "Rowan and Martin's Laugh In," which was considered trailblazingly risque when it played on NBC from 1968 to 1973. Yesterday's naughty, however, is today's quaint. Dick Martin saying "You bet your sweet bippy" is preferable to what would be said now.

Sweet bippies are out. The explicit has replaced the innuendo.

Not all the "Nick at Nite" shows are soothingly tame. "Make Room for Daddy," with braying moose Danny Thomas, is as objectionable now as it was then. Thomas is loud and boorish; only the two kids on the show were really funny. The program slips frequently into lachrymose schmaltz.

But mostly "Nick at Nite" is an innocent oasis. Really old reruns seem preferable to last year's reruns, which the networks are showing, and shrieky reruns from the late '70s and early '80s, which local stations are showing. If you go back far enough, you can find television minding its manners and being nice.

Please see **TV**, *Page* **B3**

FILM REVIEW

Eastwood's 'Pool' may be dead end for Dirty Harry

By Mal Vincent
Film critic

WE KEEP WAITING for him to grit his teeth and mutter "Make my day!"

In this case, perhaps he should, rather, have demanded that someone "make my movie." "The Dead Pool," the fifth in the "Dirty Harry" series since the tough, never-by-the-rules cop first blew away a psychopathic killer in 1971, is the least of the bunch. The problem here is lack of plot.

Harry Callahan, who once was pretty tough and down to earth, seems to have been elevated to something of a mythic cult figure. The present script has everyone bowing to Dirty Harry as if he were a movie star, not a scruffy cop. The bureaucratic bosses threaten, again, to throw him off the force because he's crashed a few cars. (No police department in the world could have afforded the car-crash budget of Harry's five movies.) Harry needs a little grit. Dirty him up a bit and send him back on the streets and perhaps he might show some signs of life.

The plot is nothing more than a series of random killings. A group of

Please see **POOL**, *Page* **B4**

Clint Eastwood brings back Dirty Harry in "The Dead Pool."

Figure 3-18 All pages should have an entry point, or a *center of visual impact*. This is where readers should enter the page. On this page it is clearly the main photo. Then the eye travels to the other photos. (Courtesy of The Virginian-Pilot, Norfolk, Va.)

This is done by contrasting all caps with uppercase and lowercase letters, roman with italic, bold with light, serif type with sans serif, large with smaller, etc. This not only helps communicate the information more quickly but it makes your page look more interesting and attractive.

Sequence

After the reader has been attracted to your CVI, you want to walk that reader through your page(s) in a pleasurable and interesting fashion. This means that the sequence of stops after the CVI must be clear.

Generally, readers start any page or spread in the upper left corner, sort of a default CVI. By thoughtfully using proper emphasis, however, you can induce readers to start nearly anywhere on a page, even the lower right-hand corner, the traditional departure point for the page. Be aware, however, that asking readers to fight gravity by starting at the bottom of a page, or by asking them return to the top after a trip down page is usually asking too much. Readers simply don't like to defy reading gravity.

Proper sequence is achieved a number of ways. The most obvious way would be to start at the top and number or letter photos or elements in the sequence you wish. But that would quickly get boring or tiresome.

Another way is to use the "imaginary" line created by the content of a photo or illustration or by the edges of artwork or columns of type. By aligning elements, the designer creates movement by forcing the eye to follow the imaginary line.

This action is a result of the gestalt principles, which explain that the brain likes to look for patterns in a visual field.

Another design manipulation is to use the concepts introduced under contrast and emphasis. If a reader will look at a large item first, then that reader will move to a smaller element next.

For instance, if you play a large photo, a medium-sized photo, and then a small photo on a page, that is exactly the order readers will follow as they look over the page. Sequence is created with large-to-small, color-to-B & W, irregular-to-normal shape, etc.

Consider CVI and a diminishing sequence of visual impact and you get a coherent design. Ignore them and you get random design, a potpourri of placement principles. The idea is to use design to increase reader traffic on your page. Attract readers, intrigue them to pay attention, and then let your sparkling content take over.

Designer Robert G. Scott says to "keep the eye moving within the format until attention is exhausted. There must be no leaks where the eye is allowed to escape from the pattern by accident."

Unity

As I hope I'm being ridiculously redundant about, design is a function of content. Therefore it must support the content by giving serious matters serious display, and less serious content "fun" display.

In the same way, the typeface, design style, color, and layout must fit together in a unified package to truly help communicate the content.

If you have an illustration with bold, thick lines, the type you use should also use bold, thick lines, such as a bold Helvetica. If your artwork is made up of delicate lines, a heavy Helvetica would look out of place (Fig. 3–19). The same goes for border tapes. Bold type and bold tape go together, bold type and thin tape may not, unless the unusual contrast is what you want.

In a simpler sense, unity also refers to keeping some things constant throughout your publication. As mentioned in the previous chapter, all stand-

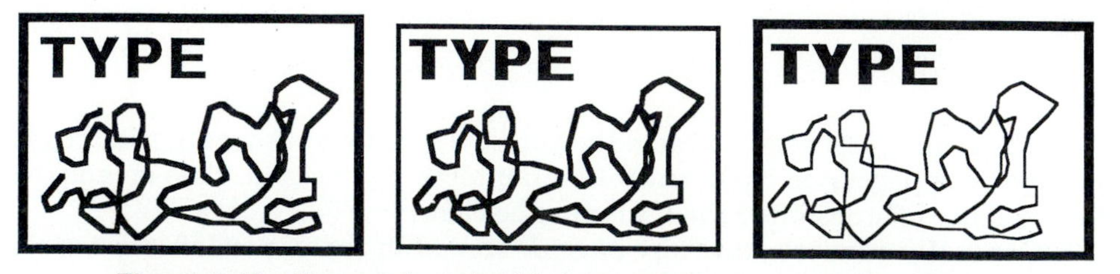

Figure 3-19 Type and art should show contrast on a page, to add to the visual interest of the content. Either make the art/type combination the same (L) or have lots of contrast (R). Don't make both medium weights.

ing headlines or column logos should be in the same typeface. The design should be similar, if not exactly the same.

In a newspaper, the headline typography for all but special pages is the same. In a magazine, more freedom is given to article titles, but other typographical consistency in section logos and folios hold the overall design package together.

Some people argue that contrast and unity are opposing principles. How can you have both?

The overarching principle is unity, but it is the unity of *constants* in your publication, not boring unity of layout. The unity comes in the framework, in the design plan. Contrast and emphasis enter in how you lay out individual pages.

Again, a good way to look at this idea is in architecture and construction. Unity is the foundation, the framework of the house. Contrast is the outer skin, the architectural design that allows the same basic structure to take on a unique look.

The design plan is set up and solidified well before any individual publication begins, or at least it should be. The layout of individual pages, following the principles of the overall design plan, comes later. First freeze the pond, then let the skaters dance.

Simplicity

The best designs, the best layouts, are simple ones. Even complex page designs that at first blush appear complex turn out to be mere embellishments of a simple plan

Tastes in any kind of design change in cyclical patterns: Ties get wider and narrower; skirts get longer and shorter. Tastes in graphic design also change and go in cycles. But simple, functional design is one of those universal principles that will work anywhere, anytime.

Keep your designs simple. A simple design helps communicate the information at hand: just what you are trying to do. A flashy design calls attention to itself, not to the content. People pick up publications to get the content, not to admire a wonderful design. If that wonderful design attracts readers to the content and then makes that visit easy and rewarding, then great! The design worked.

The old KISS formula is worth remembering, but let's defuse it a bit. Instead if "Keep It Simple, Stupid!" write this above your work station:

KEEPING IT SIMPLE = SUCCESS

Simplicity in design means:

- few elements instead of many
- more white space, instead of crowding in many elements
- grouping similar elements for easy reading
- few typographical changes.

A good test to use on any design element is: remove it. If the design falls apart and becomes confusing, then you've gone too far in your editing. Yes, design can and must be edited too. If nothing happens when you remove it, then leave it out and congratulations! You have just made your design simpler. And better.

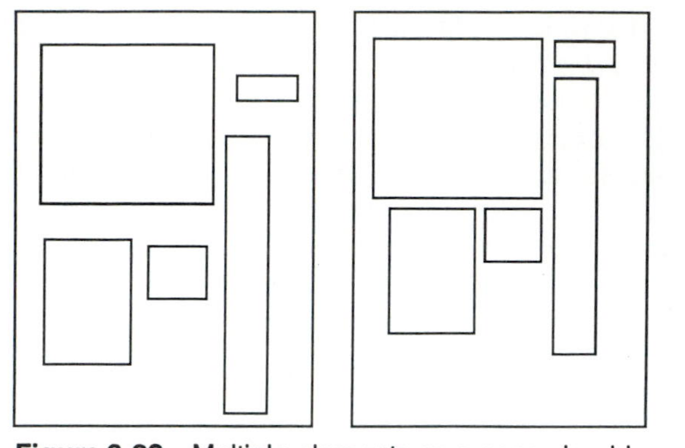

Figure 3-20 Multiple elements on a page should be grouped together (R). Use the gestalt principle of tighter spacing between elements than surrounding elements. The left example shows how different gutter sizes lead to a chaotic design.

WHITE SPACE

Nothing matters.

That's not the statement of a depressed person: It's the statement of someone who understands how white space, the "nothing" part of a page design, can help hold it together. Punctuation marks in a sentence act as separators; white space is used as punctuation in a design. Both are necessary for meaning.

The first basic rule of using white space is to keep the larger portion of it outside your design. The white space between elements should be minimal and smaller than your margins.

For most publications, the basic margins and the white space between the columns of type are set up already. Thus, the only white space under your control is on the page itself, as you place elements on your grid.

A good, simple design has elements concentrated closely together with larger and differing amounts of white space surrounding them (Fig. 3–20). The space between elements should be no less than the basic spacing element on your page: your gutter width. If the gutters between legs of type are one pica, then strive for one pica between photos in a photo spread, for instance.

Another use of white space is to add visual interest and emphasis to a layout. However, you should remember two useful tricks about white space.

First, you should leave one corner of your page or spread white (Fig. 3–21). This forces your layout into asymmetrical balance, a more visually appealing approach than having it centered. Sometimes this can be achieved by simply going back to a layout you have done that doesn't "sing" and removing something from one of the corners. Voila! The design is improved.

Second, set up an area of white space and then violate that "rule" by placing an element there or by allowing an element to hang in that space. The element gains emphasis just because it breaks a rule. And the design gains visual interest.

Follow these three rules about using white space:

- Use more white space surrounding the design than inside it.
- Allow one corner of a design to remain empty.

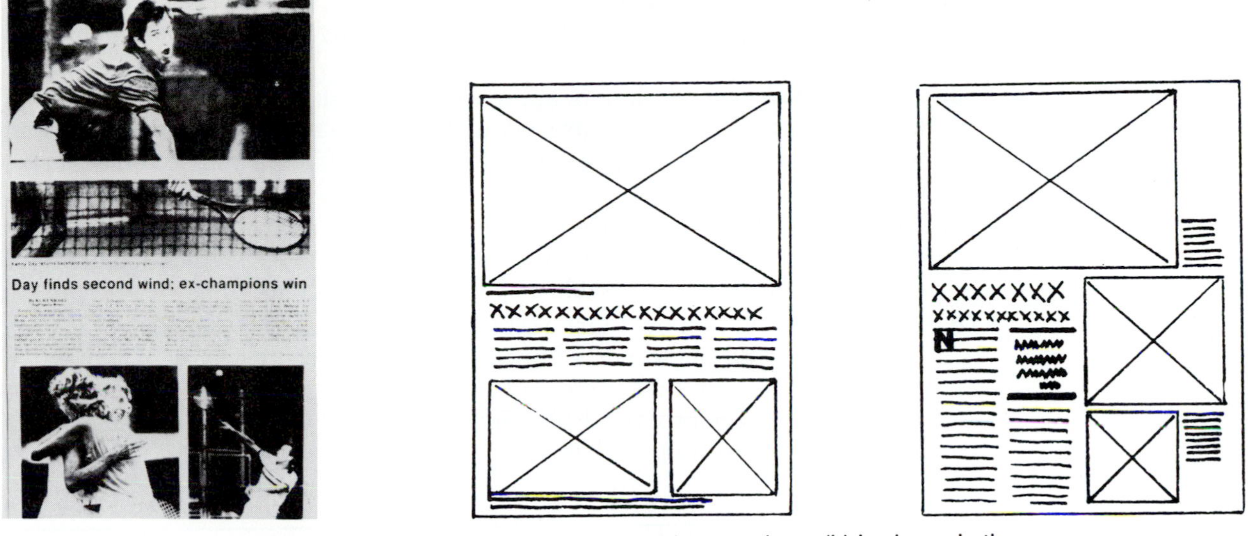

Figure 3-21 The design of the story/photo package (L) is shown in the dummy in the center. It is too tight. By adding white space to one corner, and by adding other graphic elements, the package can be presented with more excitement (R). (© The Free Lance-Star, Fredericksburg, Va).

- Set up an area of white space—a larger margin, for instance—and then violate it with an element you want to draw attention to. By doing so, you can go a long way toward making your designs more visually appealing.

This discussion was meant to demystify the process of page design somewhat. As I think you can see, designing a publication or laying out a page can be a much easier process if you understand a little about how human beings perceive visual displays. After that, to quote Paul Hornung, "It's just practice, practice, practice."

These principles will be referred to frequently in the chapters about laying out pages and designing specific publications.

CHECKLIST

1. Understanding a number of relatively simple visual principles—gestalt, proportion, balance, etc.—will demystify the act of laying out a page. A good, solid page layout can be made by someone who is not an artist, if these principles are followed.
2. A good layout is not one that wins design contests, but one that interests readers and helps communicate the content.
3. Word editors worry about syntax. How about designers? Might not the rules about the order of scanning a page layout be, in essence, a visual syntax, a set of rules for putting visual elements together?
4. White space is an important part of design. It creates a pleasing framework for your content (margins), and it can be used to add emphasis to certain parts of your design.

5. Speaking of framework, how does your page grid, or even the Swiss grid, fit into this discussion of design? How can you apply the principles of balance, unity, contrast, etc., in a Swiss grid format?
6. Find out how page designers approach their tasks. Write or call designers and discover how they prepare, what they think about as they are deciding what goes where on the page, where the art will be played, and how large, etc.
7. Draw up five different horizontal and five vertical shapes for rectangles. Try different proportions between the long and short sides. Which look better? Are any of those shapes usable on your present column grid?
8. Draw a number of 2-by-3-inch rectangles on a sheet of paper. Better yet, do up a master and photocopy a bunch of them for practice work. Then divide each rectangle into first three and then four smaller rectangles of pleasing shapes. Which combination looks most pleasing? Why? Your finished product should look something like this:

9. Play with shapes and colors, and type to learn more about the gestalt principles. For instance, using similar shapes (as in Fig. 3–1 or Fig. 3–2), place elements at various distances and see how the eye tends to group similar ones. Try it with type: How far apart can you pull letters before the word falls apart? Take a galley of body type and cut into two parts. Place a headline above the bottom half. Slide it up until it looks as if it goes with the body type above. Then move it around and notice where it looks the best. That position should be just noticeably closer to the type below.

CHAPTER 4

TYPOGRAPHY

Regardless of the particular kind of print publication, communication must take place through type. Knowing about and understanding the use of type is crucial for the modern editor. Type comes into play in both the word editing and the design and layout functions of the editor. A word editor is concerned with getting the best words in the best order. Type, which can be hard or easy to read, plays a part in that process. A poor selection of typefaces can interfere with the message.

Type naturally plays a part in design as well. Some typefaces are classic and elegant; some are modern and jazzy. A good designer must understand type, how to discuss it and how to use it. All other design decisions, except for the basic "personality" of the publication, must follow decisions about type.

HISTORY

Our alphabet today is based on the Latin alphabet. The Romans, as in other aspects of their culture, borrowed heavily from the alphabet of the Greeks, who had based their alphabet on the Phoenician version.

The first alphabets were constructed about 1500 B.C. The Phoenicians, traders who sailed all across the Mediterranean Sea, created their alphabet as a quicker way to keep track of the cargoes.

The Greek alphabet of 24 letters, all capitals, improved on the Phoenician version. The Romans took the Greek alphabet and added U, V and W. The J was added during the medieval period, as monks copying the Bible wanted to add something special to the bottom of the first letter of Jesus' name, which at the time was an I.

In America, during the early 1800s, the use of a long *s,* a letter that looked like a lowercase *f* without the crossbar, faded and the letter was removed from the alphabet. Since then the Latin alphabet has remained the same.

TERMINOLOGY

As with most technical areas of expertise, typography has its own vocabulary. Anyone who needs to work with typesetters and/or printers needs to be able to use and understand this special language.

Races or Groups

Typefaces are divided into major *races* that are separated by general characteristics of the letterform. The general rule always has been not to mix races of type on the same job, but this rule, like most others, has many exceptions. The rule is a good one for beginners, however.

Roman type is divided into old roman, transitional roman, and modern roman. All roman typefaces have *serifs:* small, usually horizontal, finishing strokes, and each letter is comprised of thick and thin lines. Old roman type has bracketed serifs, or serifs that round into the main stroke of the letter, and little difference between the thick and thin strokes.

Modern roman typefaces have very thin serifs with no brackets and a large difference between the thick and thin portions of the letter. Transitional typefaces, as you might guess, fall somewhere in between.

Most roman faces also have *italic* versions as well. True italic typefaces are different "cuts" of the typeface that share the same basic characteristics as the roman version. However, they often look very different (Fig. 4–1). Many so-called italic faces, especially in the sans serif, are just the roman version made to lean to the right. These are more rightly referred to as *oblique,* not italic.

Sans serif typefaces have no serifs (*sans* is the French word for "without"). Some typographers divide this race further into the true sans serifs, which have precisely uniform strokes, and "gothics," with slight narrowing or "pinching" of certain strokes, such as the bowl of the *p* where it attaches to the stem.

Script and cursive typefaces simulate handwriting. Cursive letters, which have scriptlike finishing strokes, do not actually connect, though they sometimes appear to. Many italic typefaces look like cursive faces, so care in identification is important here.

Text or black letter faces are often mistakenly called "Old English," which

Typography

Figure 4–1 True italics are a totally different cut of the letter. The type at the top is just slanted or obliqued roman type. Underneath is true italic.

Figure 4–2 Black letter or text type is often used in newspaper nameplates. Here, the bottom example exhibits tool lines.

Figure 4–3 Type terminology.

is the name of a particular family of text type. Text type resembles the hand-drawn letters of medieval scribes (Fig. 4–2).

Novelty and ornamented typefaces are used infrequently and only for special purposes. Novelty faces may look like neon signs or even people. Ornamented faces have lines, stars, or other devices added to the letter.

Certain terms concerning letters themselves come up frequently in discussions with print shops. These include ascender, descender, counter, bowl, x-height, cap height, arms, stems, bars, loops, stress, and so on (Fig. 4–3).

Measurement

Type is measured using the *point system,* based on a system developed by Pierre Fournier in 1737. The size of type, how wide it is set on the page, and the amount of space between letters, words, and lines are all measured with this system. Before this system was developed, type sizes were assigned names. For instance, 8-point type was called brevier, 24-point type was double pica, and 51/2-point type was agate.

The larger spaces are measured in picas, that is, 1/6 of an inch. The smaller spaces are measured in points: 1/72 of an inch. Thus, there are 12 points to a pica. The easy way to work out calculations using this system is to think of feet and inches. Just as certain distances must be stated in both feet and inches—for example, 12 feet, 6 inches—certain spaces in type must use both picas and points; for example, 12 picas, 6 points.

Smaller spaces and type itself are measured in points. Although there are 72 points to an inch, a 72-point H, for instance, is not one inch high. This is because type is measured from the top of a capital letter to the bottom of a small fraction of white space below the descender (e.g., the "tail" of the p). A capital letter ends up being approximately two-thirds of the point size in height.

TYPE LEGIBILITY

Type has two functions on a page. First and foremost it is the deliverer of the communication. People have to be able to *read* the type easily and quickly if your communication is to be delivered to them. Second, it has a design function: Type can be a graphic element on the page that either adds to or detracts from the visual appeal of your package.

Hence, the first type decision concerns how easily it can be read. Research on the legibility of type—how easily letters and words are recognized—and the readability—the writing style—has been conducted for many years. In general, it has been found that

- readers prefer a roman typeface for body type because they are most used to seeing that race.
- roman type may well also be more readable than sans serif faces because the serifs help connect the letters to form the word shape that we see when we read.
- the wider the line setting of type, the more line spacing is needed.
- the optimum line length is difficult to agree upon. A workable rule of thumb is that the line should be 150 to 200 percent of the point size in picas. Thus, the optimum length for 10-point type would likely be between 15 and 20 picas.
- letters should be medium weight for text type.
- all capital letter words should be avoided in large blocks of type.
- frequent paragraphing helps legibility.[1]

These are rules for body type. Display type is usually so brief that some of the rules can be safely broken. Setting short headlines or titles in all caps, for instance, is acceptable.

Type Spacing

Just as both sound and silence are important elements in music, so too both the letterform itself and the white space surrounding it are important in type. The white space around and within a word set in type can affect legibility and/or meaning. Remember the exercise we did earlier with the word "together"? There, ambiguous interword spacing created a different meaning.

White space and type are usually discussed in terms of letterspacing, word spacing, line spacing, and margins.

When type is designed, the spacing between letters is considered. But because of the nature of typesetting, this spacing is often an average space. The space between some pairs of letters is thus too much, and with others, not enough (Fig. 4–4).

For this reason, a number of special spacing rules are included. Called "kerning pairs," these special combinations of letters have less than the usual amount of space between them. *Kerning* is a term that means reducing the space between any pair of letters.

For instance, the capital *T* leaves a lot of white space beneath its outstretched "arms" or crossbar. Beginning the next letter where it should leaves too much white space between the letters, and they appear to be disconnected. So the typesetting computer is told to allow less than the usual amount of space between a T and a *y*. The *y* then tucks in beneath the arm of the T and the spacing "looks" right, though technically there is an overlap (see Fig. 4–4).

The key here is "looks" right: adjust the letters so that the spacing looks even. Gregg Berryman suggests that you imagine pouring an equal volume of sand between the letters. The spacing should be such that the "volume" of the "sand" between letters is always the same.

[1]Rolf Rehe, *Type and How to Make It Most Legible* (Carmel, Indiana: Design Research International, 1972).

Type

word spacing
x

Figure 4–5 Word spacing should be proportional to letterspacing. Tight kerning calls for tight word spacing, and loose letterspacing calls for loose word spacing.

Type

Figure 4–4 Kerning allows letters to sit together more tightly and with more appeal. Here, the bottom example is kerned. Note that the *y* is tucked in under the arm of the *T*.

Bengt Jägerholm is general manager of Rexolin Europe and managing director of two corporate units: Rexolin Chemicals AB and W. R. Grace AB. With headquarters in Helsingborg, Sweden, Rexolin makes and markets mainly HCN (hydrogen cyanide)-based products including chelated micronutrients for plant growth, and piperazines, or deworming agents, for animals and humans. He supervises two factories, in Helsingborg and Teeside, U. K., and about 300 employees there and in sales offices in London and Worms, West Germany.

Mr. Jägerholm holds an M. B. A. degree from the University of Göteborg, Sweden. He has always worked for companies that are partially American-owned. Before joining Grace in 1980, he was director of marketing for Unifos Kemi, a plastics raw materials producer, then 50%-owned by Union Carbide.

Figure 4–6 Here line spacing is too tight for typeface and for boldness. The paragraph is very difficult to read.

Word spacing should be proportional to the letterspacing: Tight letterspacing calls for tight word spacing and loose letterspacing calls for loose word spacing.

Take care with word spacing, however, when you have decided on tight letterspacing. Many times the tight letters look good, but the word spacing is so sparse that the type is hard to read. Be sure that each word can be seen alone. In general, the space of the width of a lowercase letter in that particular type style and size is a good rule of thumb (Fig. 4–5).

Line spacing is one of the more important typographical factors under your control. Select a tight line spacing—or “leading” in hot type terminology—and your type melts into a hard-to-read gray mass. Make it too loose and it looks almost like a child’s book, and is equally hard to read.

The accepted rules of thumb are:

- For body type, an additional point or two is good. For instance, 10-point type would require 11 or 12 points of line spacing (or +1 or +2 points, if your printer uses that method).
- The wider the line the more line spacing. The extra white space between the lines helps readers in their empty sweeps from the end of one line to the beginning of the next.
- As type gets larger, more line spacing is needed. Display type requires more than just one or two additional points if it's above 36- or 42-point.

Type as a Design Element

Type can be used as a design tool. This will be covered more specifically in later chapters, but a few words now would be appropriate. As a design element, type can

- guide the reader to the beginning of a story or graphic,
- visually separate distinct stories or elements on a page,
- add typographical contrast or "color" to otherwise gray type.

Learning how to use type this way is the first step. Using type in a design must come later.

Guidance

Display type (for example, headlines in newspapers and titles in magazines and other publications) cues the reader to the beginning of stories. Its size and boldness against the white of the paper creates visual interest. Remember that readers are drawn to elements that are bigger or bolder, etc. Headlines automatically attract readers before body type does. Reader habit, or the fact that we are now simply used to looking at a head and then beneath for the story, also guides readers' eyes.

Separation

Type also should be used to separate unlike or unrelated elements on a page. For instance, pullouts and cutlines should be set in a different typeface from the body type. Remember that one of the goals of design is to make communication easier. Type is one of the easiest tools to use in doing this. Learn how to use type in this way, and the rest of designing and laying out pages becomes easier. The type characteristics that can be used are:

- CAPS vs. U & lc
- differing line measures
- justified vs. ragged
- roman vs. sans serif
- differing weights

Using these characteristics of type to help the reader separate components of a page into discrete elements is better than relying on the reader to do it alone or on such artificial methods as boxes.

Contrast

Finally, type can make a page visually interesting by creating contrast. The eye prefers contrasts to monotones, just as your ear would prefer to hear a professor's lecture delivered with vocal inflections to one intoned with a sonorous and somnolent one-note hum. Contrast can be designed into a page, but it is best to work in typographical contrast first. Design contrast should follow.

Type contrast can be achieved best by using CAPS vs. lowercase and by using bold vs. medium and/or light weights in the same typeface. Use bold caps to gain attention and to show the reader where to start, and then switch to lighter lowercase type to deliver the message (see Fig. 4–7).

Any mass of type (for example, a column of text type, a multiline headline, etc.) is a visual element as well. Type columns, for instance, can present different levels of gray to the eye. Depending on the typeface itself, the letterspacing, the leading, etc., the lightness or darkness of the tone of your body type will change. It is important to be aware of this "tone" of your masses of body type because the rest of your typography should match or clearly contrast.

For instance, a rather bold body type—or one that gives the impression of a comparatively dark gray tone—calls for bold headlines and extra white space. Conversely, a relatively light body type would look out of place with the same bold head letter. Your message always should be written in a readable style and printed in the most legible typeface. The type masses should be attractive as well. In general, select your body type first and then make your selections for headlines and typographical constants.

For instance, *unjustified* or *ragged* type looks better when the line-ending indentations are neither too big or too little. A large block of boldface type is too hard to look at, much less read. This is because when letters are made bold, the extra black is added to the *inside* of the letter, thus making counters and bowls smaller and harder to see quickly. As a result, the eye has to work harder to differentiate letters and word shapes. Worse yet is a paragraph in all caps. Words in uppercase and lowercase are simply easier to read. Save words in all caps for short bursts of display type. Size will help here.

Most of a publication is made up of the text or body type and the display type, or headlines/titles. There remains, however, a few elements in type that fit neither category: such things as section flags, column logos, folios or page numbers, cutlines, etc. These are often referred to as "typographical constants," and were discussed earlier in this book.

SLOW GROWTH FOR NEWSPRINT CAPACITY

NEWSPRINT PRODUCTION CAPACITY IN the U.S. will rise by an average of 1.3 per cent a year from 1984 to 1986 compared with 4.2 per cent from 1968 to 1983, according to a recent survey of 250 companies by the American Paper Institute. A total of 231,000 tonnes of capacity will be added during the 1984-86 period. From 1979 to 1983, U.S. mills increased their total newsprint capacity by 1.66 million tonnes, or 40 per cent.

Canadian mills are expected to continue providing about 57 per cent of U.S. newsprint needs, the institute says. Canadian newsprint mills are forecast

Figure 4–7 Bold caps for the headline help draw the eye to this brief.

Another area for differing type comes with the pullouts mentioned earlier as well, such elements as at-a-glance boxes, maps, quoteouts, etc.

Following the idea of contrast, these constants and "accessories" should be in a different but compatible typeface with your head letter. One option is to use the headline typeface (for newspapers) or an attractive sans serif (for both newspapers and magazines) for the accessory or secondary typeface. The headline face and the type used for constants, however, should not be the same. Generally, you would want to use differing groups of type here.

The next step after understanding how to use type functionally as a way to communicate your message is to investigate its design possibilities.

Type *is* art.

> Overall, typographic design is a special art, which requires considerable training—training that encompasses not only the letters themselves, but also study of the dimensional arts. On one level, typography performs the task of conveying ideas. Yet by themselves, unincorporated into words, letters are beautiful abstract shapes.
>
> *Martin Solomon*

Body type is so small that its artistic value, aside from its tone and texture when it is displayed in a mass, is minimal. Display type, however, has great visual appeal. Manipulated properly, type can make a page with no other art element attractive, airy, and pleasurable to read.

Type design deals with the same basics mentioned in the previous chapter: line, space, contrast, and tone.

Line is almost too obvious to mention, but the letterforms themselves consist largely of lines. Then you have the lines of type themselves. The lines, as in design, can be vertical and bold, or curved, italic, and classy.

Certain individual letters, because of their lines, have almost lines of force within them, just as can be found within some photos or artistic compositions. Capital A, for instance, with its pointed top and widely spread base, is a solid letter (Fig. 4–8). No one can move an A that doesn't want to be moved.

On the other hand, V is in a precarious position. Will it tip over? Which way will it go? The V has potential motion; the A will not move. The letter K seems pinched in the middle. The motion is inward, toward the squeeze point in midletter. The "pinch" in a B doesn't work quite this way; a B tends to move the eye to the right.

What good are these ideas to the designer? Well, at first blush, this is dipping into the "artsy" aspect of design and away from the journalistic. But let's be openminded here. Knowing the almost subliminal feelings that readers *receive* (whether you meant to send them is not in question) from certain letters or typefaces can help you be a better communicator. Worrying about such fine points of typography may seem pointless. But any tool, no matter how subtle, that helps you communicate is worth considering.

A V K B

Figure 4–8 Letters themselves are graphic elements that add a "feeling" to what the reader is seeing. These letters have certain shapes that add to their symbolic meaning. Compare the solid *A* to the precariously balanced *V* with the triangle shapes in Fig. 3–10.

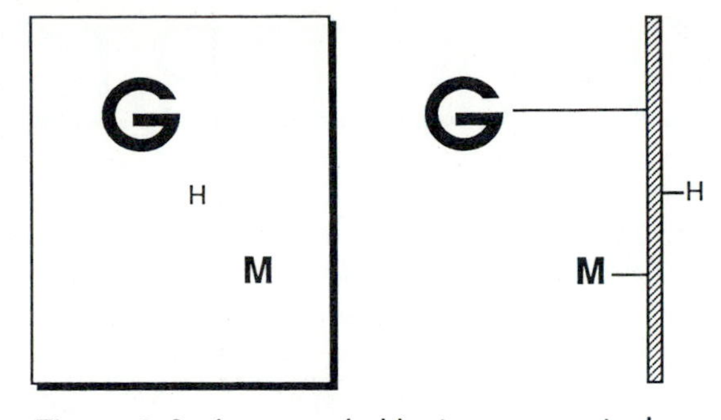

Figure 4–9 Larger or bolder type seems to rise at the viewer from the plane of the page; smaller, thinner typefaces seem to recede. This "third dimension" effect can be used to make a page more visually interesting.

Space between letters, words, and lines has already been touched upon. Spaces here change the way we see words, and they change the "look" or tonal value of masses of type. Certain typefaces need more space surrounding them than do others, either for optimum legibility or for optimum attractiveness or both.

Another interesting bit of space in typography is that "within" the letters. The counters and bowls are the obvious examples. The space surrounding letterforms is nearly as interesting visually as the letterforms themselves. Interesting visual studies can be made by creating not letters themselves but the shapes of the space between letter pairs.

Contrast has also been mentioned, but another aspect of contrast needs to be mentioned here. Bold typefaces have more mass and have larger strokes than do light typefaces. That fact alone creates a visual contrast.

Bolder typefaces also seem closer to the reader than do lighter typefaces. This creates an almost three-dimensional effect. This third dimension on a page, as mentioned in the design chapter, is an excellent way to add visual interest to your pages.

With type, imagine that a medium-weight letter lies exactly on the plane of this page. A boldface letter then seems to be closer to you, to be "above" the page, and lightfaces seem to be beyond or "below" it (Fig. 4–9). Also, larger sizes advance toward the reader, while smaller sizes recede. Large vs. small is just another example of contrast. (This is the same effect that happens with advancing "warm" colors—red, orange, yellow—and receding "cool" colors—blue, green, violet.)

Creating interesting visual experiences for the readers of your communication cannot be forgotten as we discuss "functional" design. Yes, functional design is important. Using the most legible type and typographical parameters for a given job is crucial.

At the same time, however, a well-designed communicative piece can be pleasing to the eye; it can be an art piece as well as a communication. Readers will spend more time with your message if the time they spend there is visually pleasing.

Archibald MacLeish has said that "a poem should not mean, but be." In a sense, we can say that good typography and design, should "mean" (functional, journalistic design) as well as "be" (artistic design) whenever possible. If you know enough about type and design to do both, then you've really accomplished something special.

ITC AMERICAN

LIGHT

Either because of our classless society, or in spite
of it, Americans have always been smitten by roy
alty. So there was universal approval when we fin
ally found a family we could crown "The Royal Fa
mily of the American Theatre." The Barrymores
deserved the title. Grandfather John Drew Sr. wa
s a famous Irish actor. Grandmother Louisa Lane
Drew was one of the most revered actresses and t
heatre managers of the 19th century. Both their
children, John Jr. and Georgina went on stage. A
nd after Georgina married the English actor, Ma
urice Barrymore (stage name, Herbert Blythe) th
ey became the parents of Lionel, Ethel and John
Because the Barrymores were perpetually on tou
r, the children grew up in their grandmother's ho
use. Their lives were clouded early on by Georgin
a's untimely death, and later, by Maurice's menta
l deterioration. So it was almost exclusively throu
gh their grandmother's influence that they foun

MEDIUM

Either because of our classless society, or in spi
te of it, Americans have always been smitten b
y royalty. So there was universal approval whe
n we finally found a family we could crown "Th
e Royal Family of the American Theatre." The B
arrymores deserved the title. Grandfather Joh
n Drew Sr. was a famous Irish actor. Grandmot
her Louisa Lane Drew was one of the most reve
red actresses and theatre managers of the 19t
h century. Both their children, John Jr. and Ge
orgina went on stage. And after Georgina mar
ried the English actor, Maurice Barrymore (st
age name, Herbert Blythe) they became the pa
rents of Lionel, Ethel and John. Because the Ba
rrymores were perpetually on tour, the childre
n grew up in their grandmother's house. Their
lives were clouded early on by Georgina's unti
mely death, and later, by Maurice's mental dete
rioration. So it was almost exclusively throug

LIGHT CONDENSED

Either because of our classless society, or in spite of it, America
ns have always been smitten by royalty. So there was universal
approval when we finally found a family we could crown "The
Royal Family of the American Theatre." The Barrymores deser
ved the title. Grandfather John Drew Sr. was a famous Irish act
or. Grandmother Louisa Lane Drew was one of the most revere
d actresses and theatre managers of the 19th century. Both the
ir children, John Jr. and Georgina went on stage. And after Geo
rgina married the English actor, Maurice Barrymore (stage na
me, Herbert Blythe) they became the parents of Lionel, Ethel a
nd John. Because the Barrymores were perpetually on tour, th
e children grew up in their grandmother's house. Their lives w
ere clouded early on by Georgina's untimely death, and later, b
y Maurice's mental deterioration. So it was almost exclusively t
hrough their grandmother's influence that they found stabilit
y and direction. Though none of the Barrymore children want
ed to act, out of necessity and their grandmother's connection
s they were eventually drawn to the theatre. Lionel (1878–195
4) hoped to be an artist. As a teenager, he occasionally played s

MEDIUM CONDENSED

Either because of our classless society, or in spite of it, Amer
icans have always been smitten by royalty. So there was uni
versal approval when we finally found a family we could cro
wn "The Royal Family of the American Theatre." The Barry
mores deserved the title. Grandfather John Drew Sr. was a f
amous Irish actor. Grandmother Louisa Lane Drew was one
of the most revered actresses and theatre managers of the 1
9th century. Both their children, John Jr. and Georgina wen
t on stage. And after Georgina married the English actor, Ma
urice Barrymore (stage name, Herbert Blythe) they became
the parents of Lionel, Ethel and John. Because the Barrymo
res were perpetually on tour, the children grew up in their g
randmother's house. Their lives were clouded early on by Ge
orgina's untimely death, and later, by Maurice's mental dete
rioration. So it was almost exclusively through their grandm
other's influence that they found stability and direction. Tho
ugh none of the Barrymore children wanted to act, out of ne
cessity and their grandmother's connections they were eve
ntually drawn to the theatre. Lionel (1878–1954) hoped to b

Figure 4–10 These samples from the International Typeface Corporation show weight variations of one of the many typefaces available to the creative designer. By using different weights, visual interest is added. Better yet, differing content can be set apart visually, thus helping the reader understand the content more easily. (Reprinted with permission of U&lc, International Journal of Typographics)

CHECKLIST

1. Type deserves attention by visually literate editors. It is primarily a communicative tool, but it also is a design tool. Use it to communicate first. Always.
2. For body type, use roman. For display type, use either major group.
3. In general, caps and lowercase letters are more readable than all caps. The latter, however, are fine for logos and headlines.

TYPEWRITER

BOLD

**Either because of our classless society, o
r in spite of it, Americans have always b
een smitten by royalty. So there was uni
versal approval when we finally found a
family we could crown "The Royal Famil
y of the American Theatre." The Barrym
ores deserved the title. Grandfather Joh
n Drew Sr. was a famous Irish actor. Gra
ndmother Louisa Lane Drew was one of t
he most revered actresses and theatre m
anagers of the 19th century. Both their c
hildren, John Jr. and Georgina went on s
tage. And after Georgina married the En
glish actor, Maurice Barrymore (stage n
ame, Herbert Blythe) they became the p
arents of Lionel, Ethel and John. Becaus
e the Barrymores were perpetually on to
ur, the children grew up in their grandm
other's house. Their lives were clouded e**

BOLD CONDENSED

**Either because of our classless society, or in spite of it, A
mericans have always been smitten by royalty. So there w
as universal approval when we finally found a family we c
ould crown "The Royal Family of the American Theatre."
The Barrymores deserved the title. Grandfather John Dre
w Sr. was a famous Irish actor. Grandmother Louisa Lane
Drew was one of the most revered actresses and theatre m
anagers of the 19th century. Both their children, John Jr.
and Georgina went on stage. And after Georgina married t
he English actor, Maurice Barrymore (stage name, Herbe
rt Blythe) they became the parents of Lionel, Ethel and J
ohn. Because the Barrymores were perpetually on tour, th
e children grew up in their grandmother's house. Their li
ves were clouded early on by Georgina's untimely death, a
nd later, by Maurice's mental deterioration. So it was alm
ost exclusively through their grandmother's influence th
at they found stability and direction. Though none of the
Barrymore children wanted to act, out of necessity and th
eir grandmother's connections they were eventually draw**

abcdefghijklmnopqrstuvwxyz
ABCDEFGHIJKLMNOPQRSTUVWXYZ
1234567890!$%¢&*( )
ÇØÆŒßçøæœ

abcdefghijklmnopqrstuvwxyz
ABCDEFGHIJKLMNOPQRSTUVWXYZ
1234567890!$%¢&*( )
ÇØÆŒßçøæœ

Figure 4–10 (Continued)

4. Even if you have no art at all on your pages, type can be used to add visual interest by using typographical contrast. This means use bold and light, caps and U & lc, etc., to create visual differences between parts of your message.
5. Go through a type specimen book (if you don't have one, buy one). Look over the wide variety of typefaces. Which ones are easy to read? Which ones difficult? Can you see the difference that size, line spacing, and weight make on easy readability?
6. Go to a well-designed publication. Ignore color, art, and everything else but the type. Check out the body type. Can you identify what kind it is? What size and leading? How is type used for nonbody type and nonheadline or title uses, that is, folios, bylines, cutlines, jump line, etc.? Are caps used anywhere? Based on what you discover, try to write down the typographical style rules of the publication. Then write that publication and ask for a copy of its style manual.

7. Create your own style manual based in part on the manual you got from your favorite publication. Don't simply copy the rules, but use theirs to create your own.
8. Start a swipe file of creative uses of headline typography. Use an idea when it is appropriate in your own publication.
9. Copy or trace lines of display type from your type specimen book. Make sure that you select the type you are presently using for flags and column logos and headlines. What typefaces look good together? What ones look unattractive together? Is there a set principle of typography that you can apply here—that is, what is it about two typefaces that make them look good/bad together?
10. Using what you found out from No. 9, create new typographical constants and/or headline or title schedule for your publication.
11. Just for fun, come up with a sound in the English language now made by a combination of two letters, say *ph* or *th*. Using a sheet of graph paper to gain precision, design a 27th letter for our alphabet to represent that sound.
12. Go all the way and design a new alphabet. Perhaps your publication has a special flavor or tone that no other typeface seems to capture. Design your own constants with this new typeface.

CHAPTER

5

LAYOUT STRATEGIES

Now that we've talked about type and basic design principles, we need to face one of the most frightening activities of the editor/designer: the responsibility of the blank page. While the page is blank, perfection is still possible. This chapter expands the discussion of basic design in the previous chapters.

As soon as you begin to place elements, you make a commitment to a certain layout of elements that is meant to enhance content. Looking at it from the pessimist's point of view, every time you put something on a page, you've taken a negative move: Because a "perfect" page does not exist, everything you do takes away from the perfection of the blank page.

But let's be optimistic and go over some ways to minimize your fall from editing grace.

BASIC GOALS

Every page layout, whether it's for a newspaper or a smaller-sized publication, has a number of goals—all centering on enhancing communication. It should do the following:

1. Attract readers first to the page, and then to every element on that page.
2. Surprise readers so they stop their quick scan of the page and say, "Gee whiz!"
3. Hold readers long enough for your very interesting content (assuming your writing and editing are in proper order) to take over and hold them on that page.
4. Visually connect elements on the page that have related content.
5. Visually separate elements on the page that have unrelated content.

Attraction

Attraction to the page can be accomplished by using elements that fill the bill in terms of the visual principles introduced in Chapter 3: large elements, bold, colorful, oddly shaped, etc.

The other point to remember is that research has shown that readers also tend to look at photographs first, even when color elements are competing. So, for the most part, the designer knows that readers will be attracted to a page with one or more photos and that readers will look at the photos first.

Thus, if you have photographs with every page or element, you know they will be seen and that readers will at least enter the page. But what if you don't have any photos for a page?

You still have several tools you can use. One is to box a story with tape. If you do that you must remember to set the type narrower so that the letters don't get jammed against the box. Another strategy is to use a gray screen, either on a graphic of some kind or, if necessary, over type itself (Fig. 5–1). The gray of the screen will attract just as strongly as if it were color. In effect, screens are "color" in black and white. Use a gray screen only when the spread has no art. If art is present, just box.

Other tools you can use as visual magnets to attract the readers to a story are: an initial cap at the beginning of the story, a drop or readout headline, a

■ Commercial loan success / See pages 4-5

Central Fidelity News

VOL. 5, NO. 2 / FEBRUARY, 1987

'Banking on a higher standard'

New 1987 ads promote theme

"Banking on a higher standard" will be our Bank's new positioning statement for 1987.

"All of our 1987 advertising will use 'banking on a higher standard' as a common thread," explains Jean Segner, manager of the Marketing Communications Department. "It's a natural evolution from our prior theme, 'We're out to set the standard in banking,' and provides us with an umbrella under which our quality service image and all our products will comfortably fit."

We promote quality service by our everyday actions with our customers, prospects and fellow employees. Our products also deliver a quality message, and we've tied tangible consumer benefits to the "banking on a higher standard" line.

Again sponsoring ACC

For the third year, we're bringing televised Atlantic Coast Conference basketball to Virginia by helping sponsor the telecasts—a service in itself to the state's many college basketball fans. Our three new television commercials carry that theme much further. Two of them promote timely and important products—IRAs and ATMs—while the third draws closer attention to the relationship between our Bank and ACC basketball. All three spots deliver an unmistakable message linking Central Fidelity and quality.

You should be very familiar with each of the three commercials which began in early January. They will continue running through the ACC season.

The IRA ad features a mountain climber who scales a difficult peak, symbolizing our top-of-the-line IRA products. The commercial also provides a hook to our versatile Self-Directed IRA and superior Best Rate IRA with its guaranteed minimum rate.

We have already received many favorable comments concerning our new "Night and Day" commercial because of its quality theme, classy imagery and the convenience of our service, highlighted by our 24 Hour Banking machines and affiliation with the MOST network.

AT A GLANCE

The "banking on a higher standard" positioning statement accomplishes three very important purposes:

- Positions all our products and services in a quality manner
- Stresses products with tangible benefits
- Directs advertising toward consumers making bank selection decisions

A woman singing Cole Porter's "Night and Day" spotlights our 24 Hour Banking machines and our affiliation with the MOST network.

The third spot highlights our ACC Sweepstakes in which we are giving away seven trips for two to the ACC tournament held March 6-8 at the Capital Centre in Landover, Md. The commercial features a basketball setting in which a customer in one of our branches uses a "bank" shot to deposit an entry form into a basket for such items.

A point-of-purchase display draws attention to the ACC Sweepstakes in all of our 145 branches statewide. We also have copies of *The Central Fidelity Bank Book* and University of Virginia basketball schedule cards at the display. Anyone can enter this sweepstakes. In addition to the ACC tickets, every branch will hold a special drawing, with the winner in each branch receiving a mini-television.

In other advertising, we began a Self-Directed IRA newspaper campaign in January for the Richmond and Hampton Roads markets. From March through April 15, we will conduct a statewide newspaper ad

□ See **New theme**, page 2

New look enhances publications

Beginning with this issue of *Central Fidelity News*, our entire internal communications program will have a new look. And a new publication!

This new look represents only a slight redesign from our previous *Central Fidelity News* format. But it will present a more comfortable, attractive and consistent image for all of our internal publications—*Central Fidelity News*, *Update* and the new *Performers*.

Central Fidelity News will continue keeping you abreast monthly of the overall themes and messages, important events and outstanding salespeople in all regions throughout the company.

Update will still keep you updated in a timely manner each week on the important events about which you need to know.

Performers will highlight those staff members who have achieved outstanding sales and service levels and have been recognized for their outstanding work. This new publication will be printed monthly.

All of our internal communications will continue providing the quality type of image and service with which each of you provide our customers, prospects and fellow employees every day.

Bank Marketing Director Debbie Brooks (left) and Marketing Communications Manager Jean Segner (right) discuss what props should be used for our new ACC Sweepstakes spot.

Members of the prodution crew begin assembling the set and adjusting their equipment for our dramatic ACC Sweepstakes commercial, which was shot in Charlotte, N.C.

Figure 5–1 A gray tint block surprinted over type can enhance a pullout or a special story or brief. (Courtesy of Central Fidelity Bank)

Suppose you owned a grocery store. Chances are you'd buy your family's food there, right? The reason is obvious. By shopping your own store, you'd be contributing to the economic health of your business. That's the idea behind a new principle you'll be hearing a lot about during the next few months: "Buy SBC."

"We're encouraging the various subsidiaries within Southwestern Bell Corporation to think of their sister companies whenever they need a product or service," explains Ray Mashburn, division manager-strategic planning for SBC and chairman of the Corporate Business Council (CBC). The council, a collection of representatives from SBC subsidiaries, is devoted to finding new opportunities for the various companies to do business with one another.

"In 1984, Southwestern Bell companies spent $1.2 billion with outside vendors," Mashburn says. "Only $77 million—6.4 percent of the $1.2 billion—changed hands among the subsidiaries. The more we increase that amount, the better we'll serve our shareowners by keeping more money within the corporation.

"Since divestiture, we've been extremely cautious about this idea. In our new environment, most of us thought that strict separation of the various subsidiaries was the best policy.

"But now we realize the various subsidiaries *can* do business with each other in many areas—as long as the proper procedures are followed."

Specifically, the proper procedures may include taking bids and being sure that necessary contracts are in place.

A principle, not a rule

"Keep this in mind: We're not mandating that the subs do business with one another," Mashburn says. "But if one subsidiary offers a product or service needed by another, we'd like to see the company have a chance to get the business.

"We don't believe any subsidiary should do business with another if the requirements of competitive pricing, quality and service—as well as legal require-▶

Enterprise / No. 1, 1986 **31**

Figure 5–2 Initial letters can be used to attract attention and break up the gray. Be sure that the first initial letter is bigger than all the others by about 20 percent. (Courtesy of Southwestern Bell Corporation)

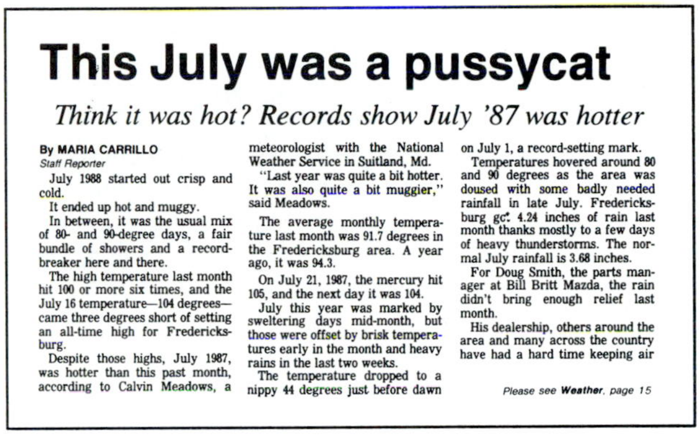

This July was a pussycat

Think it was hot? Records show July '87 was hotter

By MARIA CARRILLO
Staff Reporter

July 1988 started out crisp and cold.

It ended up hot and muggy.

In between, it was the usual mix of 80- and 90-degree days, a fair bundle of showers and a record-breaker here and there.

The high temperature last month hit 100 or more six times, and the July 16 temperature—104 degrees—came three degrees short of setting an all-time high for Fredericksburg.

Despite those highs, July 1987, was hotter than this past month, according to Calvin Meadows, a meteorologist with the National Weather Service in Suitland, Md.

"Last year was quite a bit hotter. It was also quite a bit muggier," said Meadows.

The average monthly temperature last month was 91.7 degrees in the Fredericksburg area. A year ago, it was 94.3.

On July 21, 1987, the mercury hit 105, and the next day it was 104.

July this year was marked by sweltering days mid-month, but those were offset by brisk temperatures early in the month and heavy rains in the last two weeks.

The temperature dropped to a nippy 44 degrees just before dawn on July 1, a record-setting mark.

Temperatures hovered around 80 and 90 degrees as the area was doused with some badly needed rainfall in late July. Fredericksburg gc: 4.24 inches of rain last month thanks mostly to a few days of heavy thunderstorms. The normal July rainfall is 3.68 inches.

For Doug Smith, the parts manager at Bill Britt Mazda, the rain didn't bring enough relief last month.

His dealership, others around the area and many across the country have had a hard time keeping air

Please see ***Weather****, page 15*

Figure 5-3 A second-deck headline adds information and visual interest to the page. Scanners, who are constantly in a hurry, like them because they find out what *not* to read. (© The Free Lance-Star, Fredericksburg, Va.)

quoteout or other pullout from the story, or a map or information graphic.

The point of adding literally "attractive" visual elements is to increase the chances that a reader will stop off at a story. If you have only a headline, or a headline and a photo, you haven't given yourself many chances to stop that reader.

If you give readers several visually attractive and/or informative appetizers throughout the page, you have a better chance they will stay for an entree or two: your stories.

If you use initial caps, you may drop them into the body type, or let them ride above. Notice, however, that not dropping them in allows a lot of white space between your headline and your first line of type. You could continue to use large caps throughout your longer stories, but if you do, make further letters smaller than your first one (Fig. 5–2).

Readout or drop heads are becoming more popular with newspapers because, in part, they add more display type to attract readers as well as give them more information about the story. These heads, about half the size of the main head and underneath it, are usually set in a contrasting type face (Fig. 5–3).

In the magazine world, blurbs perform the same function. Blurbs either precede or follow the title and explain the story in some way. Because they are set in display type, 14 points or larger, they have a visual pull. Better yet, they also contain information that may pull that recalcitrant scanner into the story.

Another handy device is to pull something interesting from the story—these, naturally, are called pullouts—and run it in display type with some tape or graphic. It is visually interesting and it contains information about the story.

"I can remember dreaming about this when I was a kid. It happens once in a lifetime. The main thing for me would be being selected out of the thousands of players in the country, and wearing the United States' colors. That feeling would be hard to describe."

J.R. Reid

None of these articles mentioned the various fluids and solids that come into the world with the New Life

Figure 5-4 A quote pulled from a story and displayed in larger type is a good way to draw readers into the lead paragraph. Quoteouts can be typographically unique (L) or just bold type. The point is that, although they are information items, they act as graphic attention-getters on a page.

Because readers like to feel as if they are there with the reporter, "quoteouts," or direct quotes pulled from the story and run in display type, are highly useful visual elements to add to a story.

Generally, quoteouts are run a bit narrower than the normal line measure and in 18 to 24 points with ample leading. Giant quotation marks can add a nice touch, as long as they don't overwhelm the quote itself (Fig. 5–4). The purpose of any additional graphic device is to draw attention, but it needs to let go then and allow the reader to get the content.

Graphic devices that are too loud and garish, such as a headline in color, often act as a bothersome light shining in the face of readers as they try to read the content. The presence simply makes reading difficult.

Quoteouts do not have to be placed near the location of the actual quote in the story. The quoteout *should*, however, be found in the story. If you have selected a good quote that teases the reader into the body type, the reader will want to reread the quote in context.

In general, quoteouts—and anything else inserted in a leg of type—should be placed at the *top* of the leg: the type should wrap under it. If the type legs get very long and gray, say seven inches or more, then quoteouts may be placed at the optical center, or about three-fifths of the way up the leg (Fig. 5–5). In a page full of type in a magazine format, this would be the proper placement, although the top of a page is acceptable.

In a newspaper, a good rule of thumb is to place the quote—or other pullout from your story—at the top of the second leg (Fig. 5–6). This position gets it close to the beginning of the story, where you want readers to be anyway. If the story is a five- or six-column story, however, placement in the middle column or column three would be more visually pleasing. Designers and typographers are in disagreement whether to place an element in the middle of a leg of type at the end of a paragraph or in the middle of a paragraph. (The easy way to dodge this argument is to place the pullout at the top of the leg.)

Placing the pullout at the end of a paragraph may lead the reader to stop there and search the top of the next column to find where the story continues.

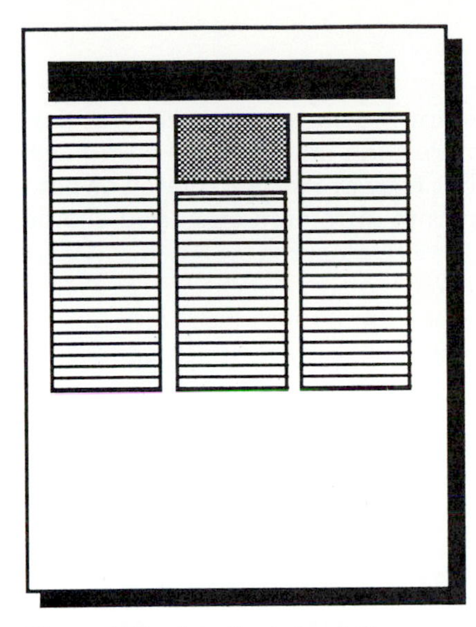

Figure 5-5 A pullout should be placed either at the top of a leg of type, or in the case of a deep vertical play, at just above the center of the type legs.

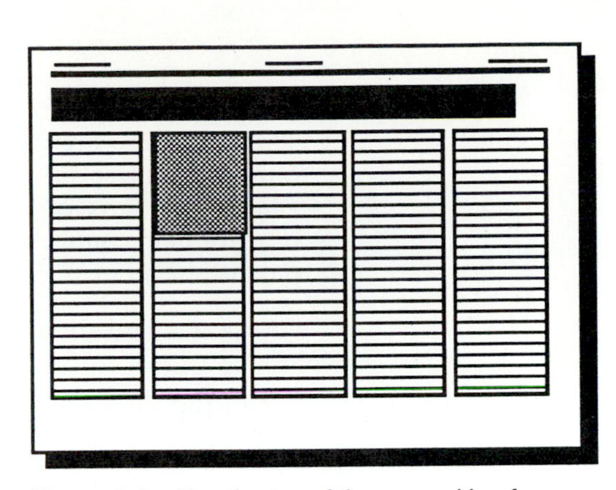

Figure 5-6 Use the top of the second leg for a story with more than three legs.

This would be a natural action of the eye when it runs into the border of the tape at the top of a pullout.

On the other hand, placing the pullout in the middle of a paragraph disrupts reading, and anything that does that is to be shunned. I lean toward the middle-of-the-graf placement, however, because the pressure to continue reading may well be greater than the pressure to stop when faced with a pullout. I would rather chance that than chance the reader stopping at the pullout, period.

Other good pullouts fall under the general rubric of the "At-a-glance" boxes. The placement rules for these are basically the same as for other pullouts. Some At-a-glance boxes are large enough to include art. These can be played as art elements, which will be discussed later.

Finally, you can use maps, charts, and graphs as additional elements of attraction to your page as a whole, and then to your individual stories on that page.

Surprise and Hold

Surprising and holding the reader after you have used strong visual elements to make that initial attraction is in large part a function of your content. But design plays a part as well.

The philosophy behind integrated editing is that content and design go hand-in-hand. If your design elements are interesting and surprising, and if you have selected and edited content that makes readers say "Gee Whiz!" then you have succeeded.

Your design can surprise by using the basic principles of visual attention and "adjusting" them in interesting ways. For instance you can run something bigger than usual, or smaller, or with lots of white space around it, or in bright and bold colors, or on a diagonal, etc.

Connect and Separate

These last two activities of laying out a page are the more mundane, but perhaps more important. Whenever you have more than one element on a page, your design must show quickly and clearly that they are either related or not.

To help connect related elements or separate unrelated ones, you should pay attention to:

- size and shape
- position
- line measure
- line justification
- typographical contrasts
- tape
- white space

If elements are the same size and shape, the eye makes a visual connection between the two. This, again, is gestalt at work. An obvious rule here is to make all legs of type in a story the same width and height—that is, use a modular layout. Readers prefer equal legs of type to an uneven, or **L**-shaped display (Fig. 5–6).

Another common positioning problem regarding shape is the play of a photograph with a story. A very natural position for a photo is above the story it goes with: Readers naturally look below artwork for explanatory words (Fig. 5–7).

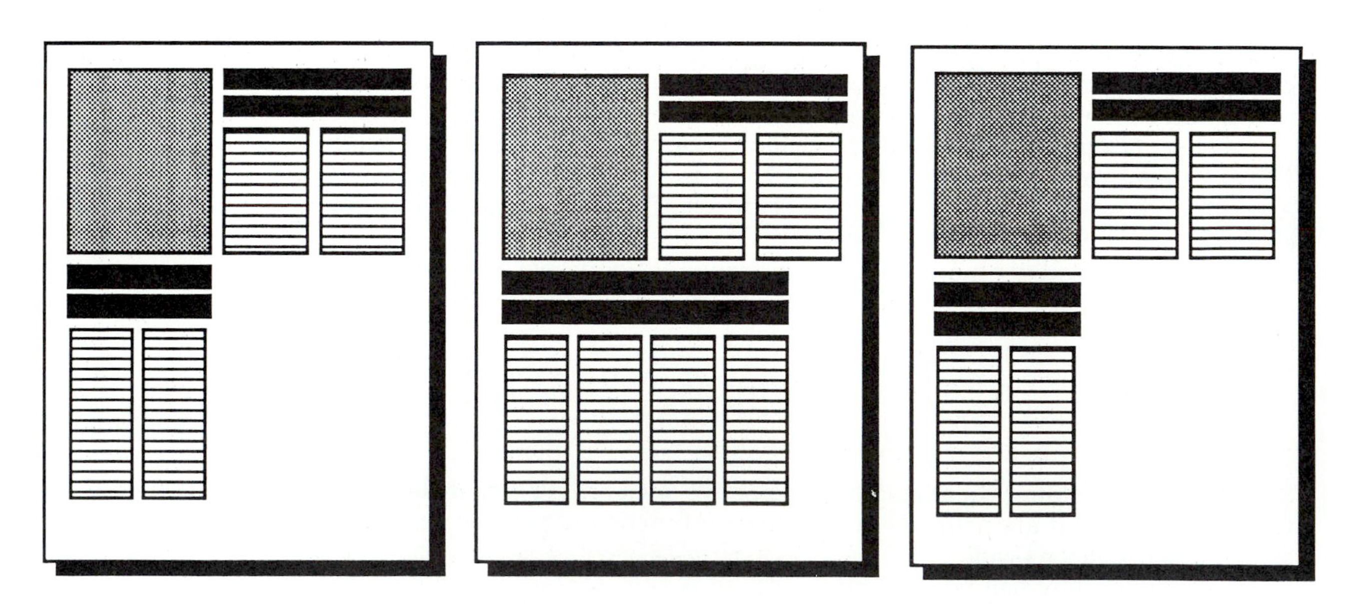

Figure 5-7 As a rule, place related type below art: People naturally look below photos for caption information. If you use a horizontal play, be sure to use a design tool (tape or white space) to connect or separate visually the proper elements. Here, the left-hand example shows ambiguous relationships: The photo could go with either story. In the center, the different width of the story below destroys the gestalt connection and helps stop the reader from following "reading gravity" to the type below a photo. On the right, a cutoff rule stops the vertical connection of art and story.

If playing art and type vertically, then, the photo should be exactly as wide as the story below. If either is a different width, the quick visual connection is not made, and the reader is confused.

With horizontal play, a photo can be on either the left or right of the type. The action in the photo should lead into the story, so let content be your guide in deciding which is better. Still, to allow gestalt to work for you, the photo should be the same width as your columns (if a one-column photo) and the depth should be approximately the same as the legs of type (see Fig. 5–7).

(If this seems to be pushing you toward modular design and layout, that's the point. Modular design is not just a personal taste: It is grounded solidly in the principles of visual gestalt.)

The line measure of contiguous stories can help separate those stories into discrete units because the reader will connect like line measures and not connect unlike line measure. The columns of type are seen as related elements because of the gestalt principles of size, shape, and proximity. To overcome this possible connection, use a different line measure. Then the stories will be quickly seen as separate units.

This is the reason behind, for instance, editorials in a newspaper being set in a wider line measure than anything else on the page. The "different" line measure is intended to signal to readers that the content in the columns is different from other content (Fig. 5–8).

And in a sense, isn't this really what layout is all about, namely the presentation of content in clearly defined packages? If the layout also is attractive, then so much the better. But functional layout must always come first.

A good basic principle for newspaper and other multistory pages is to have at least one story set in an odd measure. Because the difference will draw attention to itself, you might want to use the odd measure on a major story on the page. Be sure to keep the gutters between legs of type the same size, regardless of the line measure (and regardless of whether they are inside a box).

If you are using two different column widths on a page, use the narrower columns under the wider columns when possible. It looks better. For instance, on a four-column tabloid page, if you go to five columns, do it at the bottom of the page.

A full-size newspaper page would use the standard six-column format at the bottom, and use a four- or five-column format for a special story above. Or use seven columns at the bottom for a newsy, breezy column (see Fig. 5–13) and the standard grid above. A magazine-sized publication would probably shift between two and three columns, with the latter below.

Mixing justified type and ragged type is a good way to separate content. The eye can see very quickly the difference between several columns of justified type and several of ragged. You might, for instance, use ragged type for standing features or letters or news notes of some sort. Your regular content would be in justified type (Fig. 5–8).

Justified type, largely because of the many years of newspapers printing in justified columns, seems to say "news" much more than does ragged type. Because of this connotative meaning attached to ragged type, it just doesn't seem "right" to get serious news in ragged columns.

Typographical contrasts—bold vs. regular, caps, vs. U & lc, etc.—are the easiest ways to separate content on a page, but other than large type for headlines, they are infrequently used. As simplistic as it sounds, it is important to have headlines larger than body type: Headlines become graphic elements because of their relative size and boldness.

Here is where your "secondary" typeface comes into play (see Chapter 4). All your body type should be one face, naturally, but the type used in any other typographical element should be your secondary typeface. Mario Garcia calls

18 The Free Lance-Star
FREDERICKSBURG, VIRGINIA

OPINION

THURSDAY, JULY 21, 1988

EDITORIALS

Lt. Gov. Wilder stays neutral—to be safe

Despite circus atmosphere, job gets done

His convention proposal—rule out women speakers

JAMES KILPATRICK

New State Department watchdog makes headway

JACK ANDERSON

LETTERS TO THE EDITOR

Land use planning in city needs closer scrutiny

Train depot has one bright spot

Letters

Mayor best candidate to lead city

The Free Lance-Star

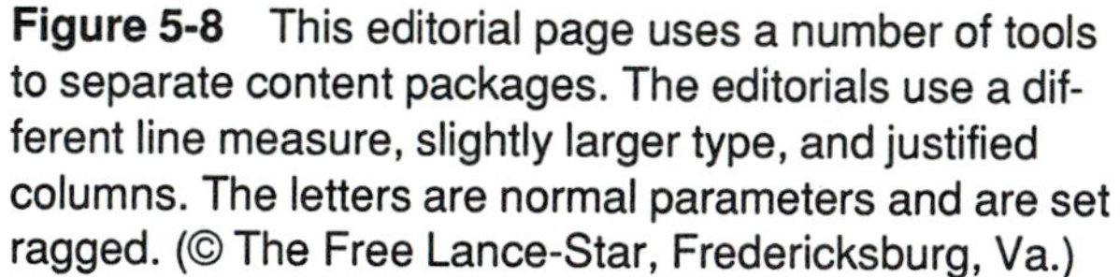

Figure 5-8 This editorial page uses a number of tools to separate content packages. The editorials use a different line measure, slightly larger type, and justified columns. The letters are normal parameters and are set ragged. (© The Free Lance-Star, Fredericksburg, Va.)

this an "accessory" face because, as with accessories in fashion, it is meant to accent the standard typography in a visually pleasing manner (Fig. 5–9).

The secondary face also contrasts visually with your standard face to differentiate the secondary content: bylines, jump lines (e.g., Please turn to page 5), from lines (e.g., Continued from page 1), cutlines, pullouts, maps, charts, and graphs. Some publications minimize the medley of typography on a page by using the headlines face as the secondary face as well.

In either your standard or secondary face, you can use all caps either to draw attention to content or to differentiate content. For instance, the main header over a graphic can be in all caps, and a secondary line in upper and lowercase. Or column logos can have the columnist's name in caps and the column title in U & lc (Fig. 5–10).

You also could use roman vs. italics and bold vs. medium or light here as well, or in a combination. For instance, a column logo could have the columnist's name in bold, sans serif caps, and the column title could be in roman light italic. Here several typographical contrasts are at work. Just be sure the two disparate faces look good together.

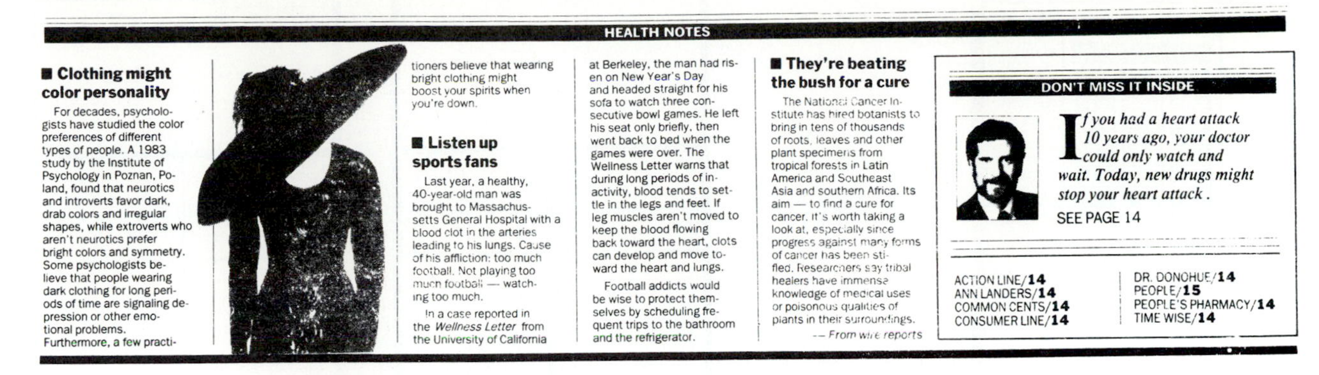

HEALTH NOTES

■ Clothing might color personality

For decades, psychologists have studied the color preferences of different types of people. A 1983 study by the Institute of Psychology in Poznan, Poland, found that neurotics and introverts favor dark, drab colors and irregular shapes, while extroverts who aren't neurotics prefer bright colors and symmetry. Some psychologists believe that people wearing dark clothing for long periods of time are signaling depression or other emotional problems. Furthermore, a few practitioners believe that wearing bright clothing might boost your spirits when you're down.

■ Listen up sports fans

Last year, a healthy, 40-year-old man was brought to Massachusetts General Hospital with a blood clot in the arteries leading to his lungs. Cause of his affliction: too much football. Not playing too much football — watching too much.

In a case reported in the *Wellness Letter* from the University of California at Berkeley, the man had risen on New Year's Day and headed straight for his sofa to watch three consecutive bowl games. He left his seat only briefly, then went back to bed when the games were over. The Wellness Letter warns that during long periods of inactivity, blood tends to settle in the legs and feet. If leg muscles aren't moved to keep the blood flowing back toward the heart, clots can develop and move toward the heart and lungs.

Football addicts would be wise to protect themselves by scheduling frequent trips to the bathroom and the refrigerator.

■ They're beating the bush for a cure

The National Cancer Institute has hired botanists to bring in tens of thousands of roots, leaves and other plant specimens from tropical forests in Latin America and Southeast Asia and southern Africa. Its aim — to find a cure for cancer. It's worth taking a look at, especially since progress against many forms of cancer has been stifled. Researchers say tribal healers have immense knowledge of medical uses or poisonous qualities of plants in their surroundings.

— *From wire reports*

DON'T MISS IT INSIDE

If you had a heart attack 10 years ago, your doctor could only watch and wait. Today, new drugs might stop your heart attack .

SEE PAGE 14

ACTION LINE/**14**
ANN LANDERS/**14**
COMMON CENTS/**14**
CONSUMER LINE/**14**
DR. DONOHUE/**14**
PEOPLE/**15**
PEOPLE'S PHARMACY/**14**
TIME WISE/**14**

Figure 5-9 This notes column from the *Dayton Daily News* is set in a sans serif type and not the normal roman body type. The same "accessory" typeface is used in bylines, cutlines, and pullouts. Note the excellent use of a narrow, seven-column format for "quick-read" items. (© Dayton Daily News)

Figure 5-10 Don't be timid about mixing typefaces. Get contrast in your column logos or standing typography by mixing serif and sans serif, bold and light, caps and upper/lower case, and so on.

Border tape is another handy way either to separate or connect elements on a page. Because it is so handy, and perhaps because it can be used both to separate and to connect, it is often slapped down on a page unthinkingly. For some people, tape has become a sort of Hamburger Helper of design. They think by merely throwing in various tapes hither and yon—even curvy line tapes!—one suddenly has a "designed" page.

Tape is most often used to separate, especially in today's modular design. When faced with bumping heads, you can use a thin tape to box one of the stories. Stand-alone photos are often boxed to separate them from the stories on the page.

Be sure to leave at least a pica of white space between the boxed element and the tape. The aim is to frame the element with the white. Thin tape will hold the boxed elements only if you allow white space to frame.

In situations when an unboxed story/photo package has another story beneath the photo, a *cutoff rule* is used to create a visual break (see Fig. 5–7). Tape is used to separate the nameplate, logo, or flag from the standard content.

The ability to separate content is one reason I'm no great fan of rules between the columns of type (at least on a regular basis). If you use too thick a tape, or if you allow the tape to run too high or low, it can serve to separate the legs of type visually. Column rules also create problems with column signs and other inserts.

Tape does not have to be very thick to perform its function. In fact, hairline tape can be used very well to box elements, assuming you've left ample white space. Column rules, if you really need to use them, must be no thicker than hairline!

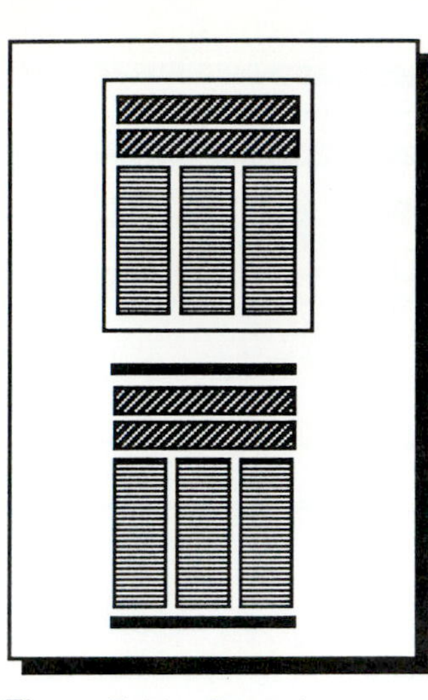

Figure 5-11 Sometimes an open box is a good way to create vertical "bookends" for the package. Heavier-than-normal rules and/or color are recommended here.

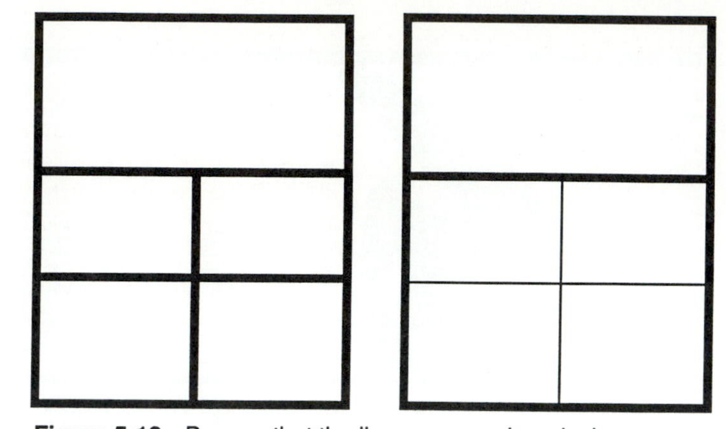

Figure 5-12 Be sure that the lines you use in a design communicate the divisions properly. Major divisions should be shown by heavier tape than that used between minor divisions. On the left, all the lines are the same width, making all the modules equal. On the right, it can be seen that there are two major modules, with four smaller modules within the one on the bottom.

Tape also can connect content or hold related content together. Looked at another way, boxes not only separate content from the rest of the page but they also can hold together many elements within their borders. A story/photo package can be held together by a box or by an open box: tape just top and bottom (Fig. 5–11).

An open box should have much heavier tape than a closed box to be functional. Use at least 4-point tape, and more if the size of the element and the size of your page allow you to do so.

For instance, on a magazine-sized page, using an 18- or a 24-point "tape" top and bottom would be graphic overkill. But the large size might work very well on a large spread on a broadsheet newspaper front. Don't use any graphic elements that are too strong for your page size.

Because tape is used in many places in your publication—under nameplates, logos, and flags; with column logos and standing headlines; with boxes; perhaps on the edges of your photos; and in other special places—you need to use tape hierarchically. In other words, tape used as major breaks or separations should be thicker than the tape used as minor separations.

For instance, in Fig. 5–12, we don't know whether we have four separate boxes or one big box divided into four in the left example. The tape is all the same thickness. But on the right, the internal—or minor—divisions are demarcated with thinner tape than the one around the entire group. Now we see it as five parts of one rectangle.

This idea has its largest application in the layout of advertising, but publication editor/designers can apply it as well.

If you use a 6-point tape under a section flag in a newspaper, for instance, you need to use thinner lines as your boxes and with column logos. I would suggest no thicker than 2-point for boxes (and one point may be better depending on the design of the rest of your publication) and 3- or 4-point for column logos.

This way the major separation has the thickest tape, the standing feature the next, and the separation at the content level the thinnest—that is, the tape is used hierarchically according to content level. This is the graphic equivalent of using large headlines for major stories and smaller ones for minor stories.

Tape used this way is *more* than a graphic element. It's a tool used by an editor to help readers understand content.

Finally, white space can be used to separate content, or even to connect. The white space used in your column gutters is small and meant to separate the columns of type and/or visual elements enough to be seen separately.

But even a multicolumn story must be seen as one element on the page. This is where the spacing formula for your publication (see Chapter 2) comes into play. The white space surrounding the story should be bigger than the column gutters. Thus, the legs of type are bonded together by the relative smaller gutter space and separated from other elements by the framing white space around it.

MODULAR LAYOUT

This approach to designing for information does imply modular layout, as mentioned earlier. Information in modules is easier for readers to access because they can see the separate elements—story, headlines, photo, other art—as a whole. They also prefer it this way. You will succeed if you give readers what they want.

MONDAY AUGUST 1, 1988 THE LEDGER-STAR SECTION D

■ COMMUNITY BRIEFS/D2
■ OBITUARIES/D3

Area News

CLASSIFIED/D4

Big brother: Boy longs for companionship

By Beverly Shepard
Staff writer

Robert Williams

■ SHIP TO SHORE ■

Still Strong

45 years after the fact, destroyer's ranks reunite

LARRY BONKO

MOTHER NATURE'S FURY

Firefighters work at the home of James and Patsy Boyd on McClure Road in Norfolk. A fire resulting from a lightning strike heavily damaged one side of the single-story house Sunday night.

Thunderstorms spark house fires, knock out power, cable TV service

Staff report

"(The car) completely lifted off the ground. You could feel the whole back end shaking. I was afraid we were going to be blown over."

Steve Patterson
Virginia Beach resident

Please see STORMS, Page D4

Suffolk school bus drivers sought

By Diane Tennant
Staff writer

Please see BUS, Page D4

Chesapeake Bay cleanup effort attracts international interest

By Diane Tennant
Staff writer

The Bay cleanup effort presents a unique perspective. . . because of its precedent-setting cooperation among three states, the federal government, private industry and environmental groups.

Figure 5-13 A good modular layout has an interplay of vertical and horizontal modules. (Courtesy of The Ledger-Star, Norfolk, Va.)

Readers like to see quickly the organization of a story and the full extent of coverage. Modular layout helps them to do this. A color-tint block added to type helps even more. This ability to assist the reader in organizing may overcome somewhat the loss of legibility of the type itself. Readers seem to prefer modular layout in newspapers.

Critics of modular layout claim that it is visually boring and that it creates difficult page layouts, In a sense, they are correct: Bad modular layout does indeed do those things.

Many people equate modular layout with horizontal layout. They are not the same. Horizontal layout of longer stories is good because the type mass seems shorter and less intimidating for the reader. But a good modular layout has both horizontal and vertical plays of stories (Fig. 5–13).

In fact, good rule for all modular layouts is

- be sure to include at least one strong vertical module.

All-horizontal modular layouts are boring visually because there is no contrast, no differentiation between elements. Good modular layouts have verticals and horizontals playing against each other, creating an interplay of visual shapes.

This pleasing interplay woks on a subliminal level, making the gathering of information more pleasing for the reader. Readers are not supposed to say, "Wow, what an effective layout!" They are supposed to spend some enjoyable and rewarding time on each page you present them with. You can do this by providing an interesting, even intriguing, display of your content.

A good way to check the condition of the underlying framework on your page is to trace the outline of each element on page-size tracing paper. Include border tapes. Then study the shapes alone on the "blueprint" of your page architecture. Are they pleasing to the eye? Is there a dominant element (by size anyway)? Are related stories shown to be so *by the layout alone*? Related stories should be evident on the blueprint alone, not by having the reader wrestle with content to see what goes where (Fig. 5–14).

Modular layouts can create some difficulties in page layout, but they are worth overcoming. One of the most common complaints of modular opponents is that it creates "bumping heads," especially on newspaper-sized pages, on which stories often have to lay side by side.

One of the reasons for all the **L**-shaped "armpit" stories on newspaper pages is that they are simply easier to handle. Instead of designing a good modular page, it is easier to "make up" a page filled with armpits.

On a modular page, you can easily avoid the few headline-bumping problems by

- writing the left-hand story's headline several counts short—at least half a column of type;
- making sure the two headlines are at least 12 points apart in size and that they have different numbers of lines in the head.

Another way to avoid problems is to use a "Dutch wrap." A Dutch wrap is a multicolumn story with a headline that does not cover the last leg of type. For instance, a Dutch-wrap headline for a three-column story would cover only the first two columns (Fig. 5–15).

The last leg of type's top line would line up with the top of the headline. Thus, the story on the right of the Dutch wrap would bump up against a type

THE LEDGER-STAR

SECTION C

Sports

■ COMMENTARY ■

Foul results

Title fights become theater of the absurd

Schrader takes high road for win

TALLADEGA 500

'WELL, THAT ONE'S OUT OF HERE'

"You can't hit a golf ball that far. In fact, Strawberry must lead the league in total yardage. Not too many of them just make it over the fence."

Pitcher Bob McClure

Met pitchers are throwing a challenge to NL - again

Straw keeps stirring up monsters

■ TOP OF THE SPORTS ■

BEST BETS

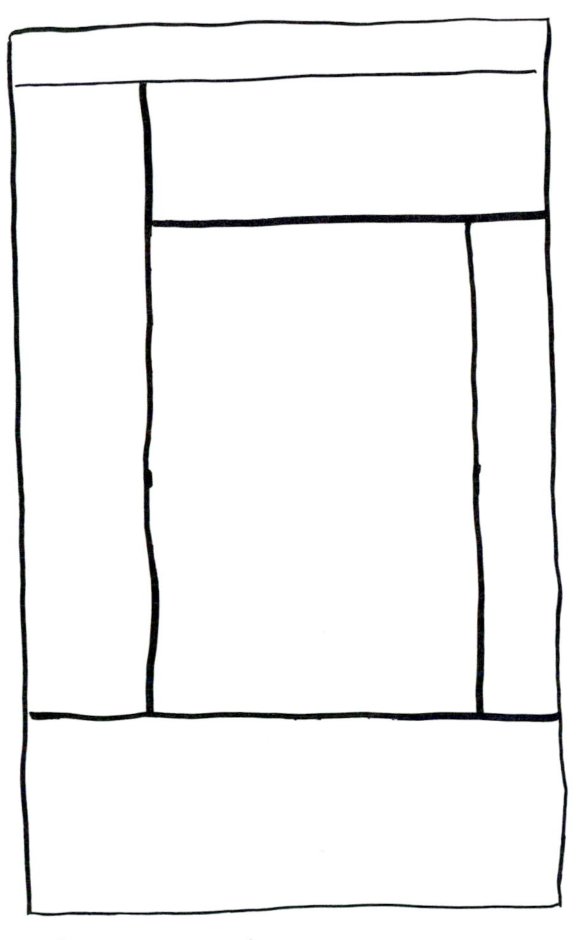

Figure 5-14 To see the underlying structure of your pages, create "blueprints" of them. The outline on the right represents the shapes of the major elements of the page on the left. (Courtesy of The Ledger-Star, Norfolk, Va.)

Figure 5-15 Modular layouts often lead to bumping headlines. One way to avoid this is to use a "Dutch wrap." The type in the last column wraps out from under the headline. To use this, the story above must have a clear break to avoid confusion. Or the Dutch-wrapped story can be boxed. In this example, a map is also used to separate the two headlines. (© The Free Lance-Star, Fredericksburg, Va.)

8 THE FREE LANCE-STAR, Fredericksburg, Virginia, Wednesday, May 31, 1989

Marine helicopter crashes off Okinawa; 14 missing

By ERIC TALMADGE
Associated Press Writer

TOKYO (AP)—A U.S. Marine helicopter crashed upside down into the sea during night training exercises off Okinawa, and 14 Marines were missing today and feared dead, U.S. military spokesmen said.

Authorities said eight other Marines on board the CH-46 Sea Knight helicopter, based in Kaneohe Bay, Hawaii, were rescued shortly after the 11:55 p.m. crash Tuesday about 30 miles south of Okinawa's Kadena Air Force base.

The names of the missing were withheld pending notification of next of kin, the Navy said. The cause of the accident was under investigation.

The Sea Knight helicopter had just taken off from the USS Denver, said Marine Master Sgt. Jake Rodrigues, spokesman for U.S. Forces, Japan.

Rodrigues said the helicopter, built in 1967, was carrying a crew of four and 18 Marines assigned to the 2nd Battalion, 3rd Marine Regiment, Okinawa, for six months' training as part of a unit-rotation program.

In Washington, Marine Corps spokesman Lt. Col. Fred Peck said the helicopter "pitched over to the right and went into the water inverted, upside down. I have nothing to indicate why it did that."

Peck said the four injured men were being treated aboard the Denver, an amphibious transport vessel designed for amphibious assaults and capable of carrying up to six CH-46 helicopters.

Capt. Lenny Ryan, a Kaneohe Marine Corps Air Station spokesman, said the four suffered minor injuries.

"An investigation will be initiated immediately," Ryan said. "As soon as they're able to talk, we'll start getting information immediately so we can start trying to piece together what happened in this tragedy."

He said the pilot was not wearing night-vision goggles at the time of the accident.

The helicopter went down 9½ miles southeast of Kiyan Cape, said Nagatoshi Naruse, spokesman for the Maritime Safety Agency, Japan's coast guard. He said three Japanese aircraft and six Maritime Safety Agency patrol boats joined two U.S. vessels, including the Denver, and four U.S. aircraft in the search.

Another coast guard spokesman, Kazuhiro Sameshima, said the weather in the area was fair at the time of the crash, with waves about three feet high.

Okinawa, Japan's southernmost prefecture, has the highest concentration of Marines outside of the United States, the 20,000 Marines stationed there comprise about 10 percent of the corps.

Okinawa was under American administration from 1945 until it was turned over to the Japanese in 1972. Under a mutual security pact, 64,000 U.S. troops are stationed throughout Japan.

CHINA
U.S.S.R.
Sea of Japan
N. KOREA
S. KOREA
JAPAN
Tokyo
Pacific Ocean
East China Sea
200 miles
Okinawa
Marine Helicopter Crashes
AP

Government increases tactics against students

By JIM ABRAMS
Associated Press Writer

BEIJING (AP)—In a new twist, thousands of farmers and workers today marched in support of Premier Li Peng's hardline policies at a government-sponsored rally opposing the pro-democratic student movement.

The first pro-government demonstration in China's six weeks of political upheaval occurred as Communist authorities pressed ahead with tactics aimed at intimidating and discrediting students occupying central Tiananmen Square.

Farmers and workers wearing straw hats marched to a stadium in Huangcun, a village southwest of of the capital, under banners saying "We support Li Peng" and "We oppose the small group causing turmoil."

Li is the main target of protesters, who demand he resign for imposing martial law in Beijing on May 20 and ordering a crackdown on tens of thousands of students and workers who have taken to the streets to demand a freer China.

The rallying farmers expressed support for the Communist Party's "four principles," which include allegiance to the dictatorship of the proletariat, socialism, party rule and to Marxist-Leninist-Maoist thought.

Sponsors said up to 10,000 people were taking part.

The Beijing Foreign Affairs Office informed foreign journalists of the march and several others in suburban sections of the capital. Under martial law regulations that have been widely ignored, foreign reporters are forbidden from covering student demonstrations.

On Tiananmen Square, China's symbolic center of political power, about 10,000 die-hard student protesters today entered the 18th day of a sit-in, resisting government demands that they disperse.

They planned a march to the Public Security Ministry tonight to protest the reported arrest Monday of three labor leaders sympathetic to the student cause. The three were involved in trying to establish an independent labor union, which is illegal in China's 40-year-old Communist system.

"We are now basically waiting for the government to take the initiative," student leader Mo Bin said. "Things are pretty calm with us. It's the government who's nervous."

More than a dozen military motorcycle convoys followed by jeeps sped down the main arteries of the capital, the latest warning that government tolerance for the student protests was nearing an end.

A military source said 200,000 troops surrounding Beijing under martial law orders have been told to "prepare for winter," meaning hardliners are digging in for a long battle with Communist Party moderates who sympathize with some of the goals of the students.

Reforms creating new dictator, Yeltsin says

By ANDREW KATELL
Associated Press Writer

MOSCOW (AP)—Boris N. Yeltsin charged today that reforms initiated by Mikhail S. Gorbachev have failed to improve people's lives and instead given the Soviet president so much power they could lead to a "new dictatorship."

The popular former Moscow party boss proposed radical changes that would wrest control of Soviet society from the 20-million-member Communist Party in favor of the nation's new competitively elected Congress in which he serves.

"The promises of four years have not been met," Yeltsin told fellow deputies. "People live worse ... the leadership knows that."

The former Gorbachev protege said the Soviet leader had been given "extraordinary powers" in the political overhaul that created the Congress and he suggested Gorbachev might be tempted, as past Kremlin chiefs have, to abuse his power.

Gorbachev, obviously sensitive to such charges, had promised the assembly when he stood for election last week that he would never take advantage of the increased power of the presidency.

But Yeltsin said his a 17-minute speech on the sixth day of the Congress' inaugural session that putting so much power in the hands of one man "could lead to the temptation to resolve our complex problems by means of force."

Yeltsin, 58, warned: "We can again be ... under a new totalitarian regime, under a new dictatorship."

On Thursday, the Congress elected Gorbachev to a 5-year term as president. Yeltsin proposed that Gorbachev instead submit to a nationwide vote of confidence each year to test popular support for his tenure.

Boris Yeltsin
Says reforms not working

Yeltsin, a member of the Communist Party's policy-making Central Committee, also called for renewal of the body, claiming current occupants have failed to fulfill their tasks.

He proposed drafting a law to regulate the powers of the ruling party, which has held a legal monopoly on power since 1917.

Initially denied a seat by fellow deputies in elections for the country's smaller, full-time legislature, Yeltsin was granted one on Monday in a deft parliamentary maneuver with Gorbachev's backing.

Tens of thousands of Muscovites, who overwhelmingly voted him into the Congress during the country's first contested elections in 70 years, had rallied on Sunday to protest Yeltsin's exclusion from the legislature.

Yeltsin, his bulky figure towering over the rostrum, addressed the Congress as one of many deputies recognized to respond to Gorbachev's state of the union address Tuesday.

leg, not a headline. Naturally, you would have to use border tape somehow—box; open box; tape below, story above, etc.—to keep the naked type leg from reading directly from the story placed above it.

A modular layout approach does not mean that every story simply must be in a module. If, for instance, within a box you had a major story and a related story, placing the secondary type in an "armpit" would be a good design move to help show the relationship between the two stories. And because the entire package would be a module, your overall page would still hold to the modular approach.

Modular layout is not just a design fad or something that has come about because of personal taste. It is a solid principle of design and organization of content for any printed communication. And readers *like* it. You could ignore modular layout, but you do so at risk to the efficacy of your message.

HEADLINE PLACEMENT

Quite simply, the best placement of a headline is over type: People naturally will look beneath a headline to get the story that goes with it. But a headline also can run to the left of the story, though not the right, and even beneath the story.

A headline placed to the left of a story does not have to be flush right, though sometimes that is acceptable. Even though more white space in-between the elements is introduced with a flush-left head, that style is probably still the best. Readers are simply used to flush-left heads, and if nothing else, readers are creatures of habit.

Regardless, a side head—sometimes called a rocket head among newspaper journalists—should have 3 to 6 more points of leading than your normal headline. Center the head in the space if the legs of type are short, or leave it flush with the top leg of type if that better fits your overall style. The bylines should run at the top of the first type leg.

If you choose to run a headline at the bottom of a story, it must be very dominant (large, color, etc.) and you must use a large initial letter or similar device to get readers back up to the story beginning from the head.

The initial letter should be in the same face as the headline, even if—or especially if—you use an art type, not your standard headline face. Remember, the brain searches for similarities; thus, use this device to help guide the readers where you want them to go.

SPECIAL EFFECTS

If you follow all the general principles of information presentation discussed so far, you will have a good, but not stunning, publication. It is extremely important to have all the basics—the typography, the page grid, the approach to element placement, etc.—in place first.

No publication can be well designed without a solid format, just as no building can win architectural awards for beauty without a solid foundation of raw cement and steel rods. Just because those elements are not seen doesn't make them unimportant.

Here are a few ideas that you can use every issue to build that element of surprise that keeps readers turning pages and reading the content of your publication. Be warned, however, that these tips can be used well or misused, used properly and sparingly or abused with overuse.

At Corporate Conference '84, top SBC managers heard that entrepreneurship is...

THE RIGHT STUFF

We cannot be afraid to take intelligent risks or to give people the freedom to do so.

"Not all risks will pan out quite the way we want them to," said Zane Barnes, chairman and chief executive officer of Southwestern Bell Corporation. "And that's okay, just so we win more often than not and learn from our experience.

"I'm looking to you, as this corporation's senior management team, to be the heroes of the entrepreneurial culture we need to establish. I want you to be heroes in questioning the status quo... living the vision... taking calculated risks... and exuding a confident, positive mindset."

Barnes was speaking to top managers of the corporation and its subsidiaries. The leaders came together in May for Corporate Conference '84. Every two years, senior managers use the four-day conference to immerse themselves in the most pressing issues facing the company.

The theme of the conference, "The Right Stuff," came from Tom Wolfe's book of the same name. The highly popular book portrays the courage and persistence of the seven original U.S. astronauts.

Good traits for managers

Those same qualities should characterize SBC managers and their approach to the company's new, partially deregulated working environment, according to a team of outside speakers especially assembled for the conference. The speakers included some of America's most highly regarded experts on management.

The experts focused on defining "the right stuff," putting it into action and using it to map strategic plans for meeting competition in the telecommunications industry.

They spoke with one voice in emphasizing this idea: The entrepreneurial spirit—one in which employees are encouraged to implement new ideas for new markets—is the right stuff for today's Southwestern Bell Corporation.

For example, Frank Lorenzo, chief executive officer of Continental Airlines who led his company through deregulation, bankruptcy and a recent reorganization, said:

"With deregulation, the consumer is king. As a result, you have to adapt and change the business to respond to the market. This change requires much more interaction among managers and a much sharper focus on goals to develop a different sense of spirit.

"Don't take deregulation lightly," he emphasized. "It produces truly profound changes in business. You must anticipate radical changes and be vigilant."

Another conference speaker countered the idea that large companies and corporate entrepreneurs cannot coexist.

"Many entrepreneurs in large organizations love their companies," said Gifford Pinchot, a consultant to several major corporations. "A company such as yours provides many internal resources and a tremendous support mechanism."

Pinchot's prescription

The bottom line, according to Pinchot, is that, for entrepreneurship to thrive, the right environment within the corporate structure must exist.

"Other companies are less bureaucratic (than yours), and many of those companies are your competition," Pinchot said. If Southwestern Bell Corporation loses a good number of "intrapreneurs" (corporate entrepreneurs) to other companies, a noticeable, negative impact will be felt, Pinchot said.

In his closing remarks, Barnes again emphasized the need for entrepreneurship.

"In the past, we spent much of our time playing from printed songsheets, melodies composed by someone else. Now we're the composers, writing our own scores," Barnes said.

"We have to take care not to overengineer those compositions. And we need to be ready to do some playing by ear, too. Our markets are moving fast, and so must we.

"In an industry moving as quickly as ours, the rules of the game are innovate or perish." ■

by Melinda H. Hart

10 *Enterprise / No. 2, 1984*

Figure 5-16 If you don't have good art to grab the reader, consider using large and/or bold type to attack the leader. Remember that type itself is pleasing to the eye and can be considered a graphic element if run large enough.

Attack the Reader

Readers are used to type on a page. Especially in this day of extreme communication overload and competition from electronic entertainment, print communicators must grab the reader with a strong design effort.

Ben Blank of ABC News talks of art attacks, type attacks, and color attacks for the graphics we see on the screen behind reporters' heads. An *art attack* uses compelling photos or illustrations to literally leap off the page (or the screen in his case), grab the readers by the lapels, and shout, "Hey you! Look at this!"

A *type attack* is a good strategy when you have no art (Fig. 5–16). I should say no art but type, because typefaces themselves are the work of artists. Type run three inches high or so can sometimes provide just the "attack" you need and act as art on your page as well.

A *color attack* is another strategy when your art selection itself is not worth large play and a type attack may not be appropriate. Using color as a backdrop for an entire page, or bright, sassy colors sprinkled throughout a spread, can create that moment of surprise (see Chapter 9).

As long as a shout for attention never becomes the strident scream of the sleazier supermarket tabloids, these attacks can be an effective tool.

3-D

A good strategy for bringing a special touch to feature and photo pages, according to Pegie Stark, former art director for the *Detroit Free Press*, is to add the third dimension (3-D) to the flat page.

"Making pages three dimensional makes them more interesting to the eye," Ms. Stark said. "Elements come to life because we see real life in 3-D."

Entrepreneur Mary Kay Ash found fame and fortune through her company, Mary Kay Cosmetics. She also has developed a reputation for being an expert in motivation.

run out of abilities–just possibilities, and the company will continue to lose its peak performers.

Enterprise: Fair enough. After you have a mission, what traits do you need to carry it out and be a peak performer?

Garfield: Based on all the peak performers we've studied, we can almost make a list:

- They all use foresight to help them plan strategically, whether it comes to their own career or a project they have to complete.
- They "stretch" to attain specific goals in the pursuit of excellence, even if that means taking risks.
- They have extremely high self-confidence and an equally high sense of self-worth.
- They have a significant need for responsibility and control and take ownership and credit for their good ideas.
- They know how to rehearse key situations mentally as a way of preparing for them.
- They learn from their mistakes and from the past.
- They utilize their time and capacities fully.
- They flourish even when other people don't understand their contributions, reasoning that hard, creative work and perseverence would eventually pay off.
- They are innovators. They know there is not just one way to do a job and are prepared to create a new way to get a job done.
- They know how to work with other people, and, in fact, know there is no way to complete most tasks without others' help on some level.
- They feel positive about their work environment, especially because they believe in their own ability to *make* it positive.
- They act decisively when opportunities develop for them.
- They anticipate difficulties and opportunities, adapt to change by growing along with it and regularly check themselves to see that they are on course with their mission.
- They never rest on their laurels–and never stop learning.

Enterprise: And how do the peak performers you studied manage people?

Garfield: First, they know how to draw the best out of the people they work with. They use a balance of autonomy and direction when it comes to "running" their staffs.

They hold their subordinates to goals but may also have them run independent, entrepreneurial units. Also, they are ready for mistakes to be made, looking at them as chances for their staff members' growth rather than as failures.

When a problem comes up, their first instinct is to solve it rather than assign blame. As a result of all this, their people give them their very best, and the peak performers are able to be that much more successful.

They realize that when you give power and opportunity to people working for you, it only comes back around to give *you* more power.

Enterprise: That makes sense. But tell me this: How can someone help people working for them become peak performers?

Garfield: Acquaint them with the characteristics of peak performers and challenge them to apply the principles at work and in their lives.

Let them know you'll value whatever effort they make in such a direction and that the way is clear for them to make a difference in your department.

Enterprise: You've given us a veritable checklist of traits that all the peak performers you've studied display. But for someone who reads your work and decides to use the information you present, won't there be a great risk for them to begin feeling guilty if they don't get to their peak quickly?

Garfield: You must understand that I'm not trying to engineer people's behavior or give them "Five Easy Steps to Nirvana."

This country is groaning under an avalanche of thin, little books that promise to make it easy for people to leap tall buildings at a single bound. I'm not offering my book of findings as that kind of self-help. ▶

Peak performer Nolan Bushnell, founder of Atari and Axlon, says: "Everybody who has ever taken a shower has an idea. It's the person who gets out of the shower, dries off and does something about it who makes a difference."

Jackie Robinson was determined to become the first black player in major league baseball. Only his talent and courage helped him overcome the flying spikes, beanballs and intolerant fans in one stadium after another.

5

Olympic tennis champion Stefan Edberg, Sweden's young superstar, captured the singles crown with a 6-4, 6-2 victory over Johan Kriek in the $277,000 Transamerica Open Tennis Championships, held September 23-29 in San Francisco. It was 19-year-old Edberg's first appearance in the Transamerica Open. Following his triumph in San Francisco, Edberg went on to score his first Grand Slam victory by winning the Australian Open.

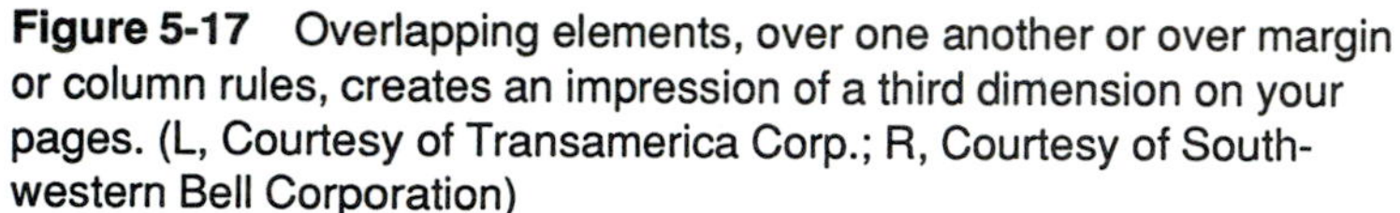

Figure 5-17 Overlapping elements, over one another or over margin or column rules, creates an impression of a third dimension on your pages. (L, Courtesy of Transamerica Corp.; R, Courtesy of Southwestern Bell Corporation)

She suggests starting with the various tones of gray available to those on even the tightest budgets. Use different sizes, tones, colors, proportions to create the look of sculpture on the page. Besides the obvious strategy of shadows behind elements and drawing in 3-D perspective, Stark says you can use color theory to create depths. She points out that cool colors recede and warm colors advance off the page toward the reader. This effect creates the feeling of a third dimension.

Another simple technique is to have elements, such as photographs, overlap, laying one on top of the other, in effect. Stark says it is okay to do this if the contents of the various photos are related.

Using border tape under elements (in a 3-D sense) to connect them, instead of simply on top or with a box, also creates another dimension (Fig. 5–17). This is the "continuation" principle of gestalt in action: The eye assumes the line is a continuing one, not simply bits between each element.

Finally, type contrast can add that third dimension as well.

Using all these approaches to a page can create a presentation of content that goes beyond simply being interesting to being intriguing to the reader. Moreover, such spreads obviously take a lot of time. The reader is led to believe the content is important, or why would you spend that much time on it?

It should go without saying—but I can't resist—that the best layout strategy is the one that gets your message to the most readers. Knowing what that particular strategy is for a particular story is the tough part. A large measure of that decision has to do with experience, and this book cannot help you with that.

At this point you should have a much fuller design toolbox than you had before. If you set up your design plan well ahead of time, then the creation of individual pages and spreads should come easier because you don't have to reinvent the wheel every issue.

The next step, after a brief run-through of production information, is to study the final three chapters of this book, which takes all the previous information and applies it to various kinds of publications.

CHECKLIST

1. A good layout is one that stops readers in their tracks, holds them still for a moment, and allows your sparkling content to draw them into the page. It is gratifying to have them read your content, but it is enriching to have them see the ads that are there as well.
2. Basically, a good layout connects elements that go together, separates those elements that do not, and helps the communication process in general.
3. Modular layouts are preferred by readers, in part because they can see the "edges" of each story so well. Readers don't want to commit to a story of unknown parameters.
4. A good layout follows all the general principles of design outlined in Chapter 3 (balance, proportion, etc.) as applied to real type and pages.
5. To see how clearly organized your packets of information are, use tracing paper to draw a blueprint of the underlying structure of your page. Trace just the outlines of elements and see how the shapes alone look.
6. Do you think you can plan modules, or even entire pages, ahead of time and fit your information to them? Is there something inherently wrong with this? (Yes.) But wouldn't there be some benefit to having a handful of suggested organizations (or blueprints) available for the time when inspiration isn't there or you are in a hurry?
7. Take a page you like and one you don't like from a couple of publications. Do blueprints of them. Tack them to the wall for a week or so. Learn what works well in the designs and what doesn't. Try to discover *why* some work and some don't.
8. Find some pages with simple bad placements of elements. Copy them, do blueprints, and then cut them up and put them back together again properly. Does your version present the information in more orderly fashion? If not, why not? Compare the before and after blueprints.
9. Define in your own words the relationship between design and content.
10. Write out as many design guidelines as you think you can use on a day-to-day basis and post them above your desk. Keep a file of well-designed pages and post some of those, on a rotating basis, as well.

CHAPTER

6

HEADLINES AND TITLES

Good typography is important to your message, and good typography in your display type—headlines and titles—is especially important. Readers look here first. If the headline or title is compelling, if it is typographically supportive of the message, and if it is attractive, then readers will be drawn first to the display type and then to the story.

Headlines and titles play two important roles. First, by virtue of their comparative size, or color, or just pure visual weight, they attract the readers' eyes. Thus, they first act as a graphic element, as much a piece of art as an illustration.

Second, they act as an agent of communication by giving the reader information. How well and how quickly and completely heads and titles impart their information are the criteria of good headlines and titles.

Because headlines and titles attract readers and tell them where to begin reading body copy to get more information, they should be close enough to the beginning of the story to make it easy on the reader. In general, headlines and titles are above the story they go with.

Sometimes, however, headlines can be elsewhere, even below the story. When this is the case, extra effort by the designer is needed to get the reader to the story beginning. One solution is an initial letter in the same typeface and/or color as the headline. The similarities will help the reader make the connection (Fig. 6–1).

The trend today is to have more display type than in the past. In part, this is a nod toward scanners and to a greater effort to grab their attention and detain them at that story. In a sense, magazines, using titles and blurbs, have been doing this for years. Only for newspaper communicators is this approach new.

The increased display type acts as a larger visual element, but mainly it gives readers more information on which to judge whether to read the story.

Showdown

Sales campaigns feature spirited regional battles

Like two gunfighters from the Old West, the Western and Southwestern regions face off at high noon under the blazing heat caused by the IRA and Charter/Charter Equity sales races. The dusty street is empty, but everyone is watching.

Western's gunbelt is filled with notches accumulated from previous successful sales efforts. It has earned respect from all corners of the state.

Southwestern represents a new breed, having quickly established its fast draw and unerring aim at every outpost along the Sales Trail. The time has arrived to challenge the reigning king.

Figure 6-1 An initial letter in the same typeface as the headline helps move the reader from the head to the beginning of the story, even if the headline is below the story.

Kicker headline

Main headline is larger

Reverse

Main headline is smaller and longer

Figure 6-2 Kickers are short, smaller headlines above the main headline, which is usually indented (top). Reverse kickers are just that.

NEWSPAPER HEADLINES

Because newspapers use so many stories, they must have a wide variety of different styles of heads to choose from.

When discussing headlines, you must take into consideration the number of columns a head covers, how many lines deep it is, the typeface, and the point size. A shorthand is used to communicate this: 3/48/2 Helvetica says that the head is to be three columns wide, two lines deep, and in 48-point Helvetica.

Besides the normal variations in columns, size, and the number of lines, there are some particular newspaper headline variations. Many, but not all, of these also are used in nonnewspaper publications.

Kickers. Small headlines above the main head, kickers have fallen into disfavor recently. This is because (1) no one is ever sure whether to read the *big* head or the *top* head first, and (2) they add awkward white space to the center of page designs. When they are used, they are usually half the size of the main headline (Fig. 6–2).

Reverse Kickers. Also called *hammer heads,* the larger type is used on the short top line, and the small type is used on the long second line (the opposite of the kicker).

Second Deck. These heads have gained favor as kickers have lost it. Also called *drop heads* or *readout heads,* this style is a return to a style of years ago. Under the main head, in much smaller type size, the second deck adds information about the story, much in the same way as the blurb does in magazines. Because they add information while not adding awkward white space, these heads have replaced the kicker in many publications.

Side Heads. Putting a headline on the left side of a story is one way to add a little variety to a page. Also called *rocket heads,* side headlines require a little additional leading to look good. They can be used successfully flush left, centered, or flush right. Usually the story is boxed. The byline should appear at the top of the first leg of type.

MAGAZINE TITLES

Headlines in magazine-style publications are more often called titles. But they differ in more than the name. Typographically, titles are allowed much more variation than are newspaper headlines. In general, headlines in newspapers are fairly standard typefaces, and 98 percent of all heads in the paper are the same face. The exception is on a newspaper's "magazine" pages: the features section front, the food section front, etc.

In magazines, however, the designer is freer to select a typeface that connotatively fits the tone of the story. Thus, an article about weddings might have a classy cursive whereas a story about bodybuilders may have a brassy slab serif or novelty face (Fig. 6–3).

Fore Play

Figure 6-3 Play with type to make it an art element, especially if you have no other art element to gain readers' attention.

When is a customer not a customer? When he or she is a "middleperson" —an insurance agent, an investment banker, a lending institution. An essential link in the transaction between Transamerica and the end-user of our services. Middlepersons are customers, too, and they require a large dose of personal service.

Figure 6-4 A small paragraph—called a blurb—often adds enough information to a story to tell a scanner whether to read the story. Newspapers are beginning to take this approach as well.

Magazine titles are generally shorter and more ambiguous than are newspaper headlines. Magazines rely on blurbs, or short paragraphs in display type that further explain a story; clear up the ambiguities from a "creative" but brief title; or, preceding the title, set up the meaning in the few words that follow (Fig. 6–4).

SIZE

Someone once asked Abe Lincoln, a tall man, especially for his day, how long his legs were. His answer was: "Long enough to reach the ground." Were we to apply this no doubt apocryphal story to display type size, we would answer the question "How big?" with "Big enough to function properly."

Unfortunately there is no ready answer to the size question.

Newspapers

The size of headlines in newspapers is one indication of a story's relative importance. If you use 72-point headlines to shout the normal news every day, what will you use when something really big happens? On the other hand, you can't use a 30-point headline for your main story just because it is the best of the bad selection on a slow news day.

In general, aim for the middle ground. Use a 60- or a 48-point head for the main news story on a broadsheet, and a 48- or 36-point head on a tabloid. For the size publication involved, these heads are neither too large nor too small: You can still go up for the big news; you are not so large as to be shouting about something relatively unimportant to your readers.

The remaining heads on the page should be either smaller or lighter or both to underline their relative importance. In general, inside pages should use somewhat smaller headlines. Broadsheets should generally start with 48 points, and tabloids with 36. Readout or second-deck headlines should be at least half the size of the main headline, and they can even go smaller.

Magazines

As is the usual case in this discussion of display type, more creativity in size selection is allowed in magazine titles. The guidelines for smallness still hold: 36-point would be about as small as you would want to go for most situations. Only for more intellectual-type digests would you want to have smaller display type (Fig. 6–5).

You could use type as large as you wanted to, even to the extent of covering an entire page or spread, if the story warranted that treatment. Remember that as type gets larger, it needs more kerning. Pay attention to the leading as well, which should increase with size.

As with all design decisions with type, make your final decision with the type *on the page.* Only experts should attempt to make design decisions in their heads. It is difficult to visualize how type will look, especially in large blocks and/or next to other type masses. The safest decision is always to do a proof before going to press.

By Gary Warren Melton and Gilbert L. Fowler Jr.

Female Roles in Radio Advertising

Males dominate radio ads to same extent other studies show they dominate television ads.

► Since 1971, more than 2,500 research studies have examined the effects of media on society.[1] Most of this research has dealt with television because it is the most pervasive medium. This concentrated research effort on the television medium would seem logical because the average individual spends more than three hours a day with this medium.[2] But all media have the potential to affect culture and socialization.

Research spanning the decades of the 60s and 70s also has focused frequently on female images. These research endeavors examined the visibility of women in professional and traditional roles through analysis of television programming and advertisements.[3]

Some studies have suggested that sex-role stereotypes perhaps socialize girls/-women to regard themselves as incapable of significant contributions to society, while others suggest that little evidence, if any, exists showing that television advertising was making efforts to reflect society where the sexes were equal.[4]

Research on television commercials suggest that males greatly outnumber women across many product categories. Indeed some evidence suggests limited support for the cause (media exposure) and effect (social reality perceptions) inferences which have been formulated through media cultivation research.[5]

Whatever the social, political, cultural or legal significance might be, the overwhelming evidence suggests that at least some dysfunctional activity has been brought about through interaction with television. But what about radio programs and their advertising?

With radio in 98% of American homes and 95% of U.S. automobiles it would seem logical to suggest that radio has some impact, either functional or dysfunctional, to some members of its audience.[6]

[1] Robert Liebert, Joyce Sprafkin, and Emily Davidson, *The Early Window: Effects of Television on Children and Youth* (New York: Pergamon, 1982).

[2] A.C. Nielson, *Nielson Report on Television* (Northbrook: A.C. Nielson Company, 1986).

[3] Linda Busby, "Sex-Role Media Research and Sources," in Dorothy McGuigam, ed., *New Research on Women and Sex Roles at the University of Michigan* (Ann Arbor: University of Michigan Center for Continuing Education of Women, 1976); Alice Courtney and Thomas Whipple, "Women in Television Commercials," *Journal of Communications*, Spring 1974, pp. 110-118; Alice Courtney and Thomas Whipple, "How to Portray Women in Television Commercials," *Journal of Advertising Research*, 20:53-60 (1980); Leslie Friedman, *Sex Role Stereotyping in the Mass Media: An Annotated Bibliography* (New York: Garland, 1977); Henry Bernstein, "Ads Ignore Real Women: Use Stereotypes," *Advertising Age*, June 16, 1975, p. 86.

[4] John Doolittle and Robert Pepper, "Children's TV Ad Content," *Journal of Broadcasting*, 19:131-141 (1975); Sunny Hansen, "We Are Furious (Female) But We Can Shape Our Own Development," *Personal and Guidance Journal*, 51:87-93 (1972); Eleanor Maccoby, "Effects of Mass Media," in Martin Hoffman and Lois Hoffman, eds., *Review of Child Development Research*, (New York: Russell Sage, 1964).

[5] Charles Atkin, *Effects of TV Advertising on Children. Report #2: Second Year Experimental Evidence. Final Report* (East Lansing: Michigan State University College of Communications, 1975); Muriel Cantor, "Comparisons of Tastes and Roles of Males and Females in Commercials Aired by WRC-TV During the Composite Week," in *Women in the Wasteland Fight Back: A Study of Treatment of Females and Males in WRC-TV Programming Aired During the Composite Week* (Washington: National Capital Center Press Chapter, 1972); Alexis Tan, "TV Beauty Ads and Role Expectations of Adolescent Female Viewers" *Journal Quarterly*, 56:283-288 (1979).

[6] Ray Hiebert, Donald Ungurait, and Thomas Bohn, *Mass Media IV: An Introduction to Modern Communications* (New York: Longman, 1985).

► The authors are faculty members at Arkansas State. Gary Warren Melton is in radio TV and Gilbert L. Fowler, Jr., is in journalism and printing. They wish to thank the Faculty Research Committee, Arkansas State Unversity for grant funding support of this research project.

Figure 6-5 A publication with a built-in readership—such as an academic journal—does not need to shout with display type to gain reader attention. *Journalism Quarterly* uses a blurb-type display to summarize the article. (© Journalism Quarterly, Association for Education in Journalism and Mass Communications)

OTHER DISPLAY TYPE

Display type also is used with accessory items on the page—for example, maps, At-a-glance boxes, etc., in subheadlines, and in initial letters. The use of these elements has been discussed previously.

Headlines for maps and At-a-glance boxes should generally be set in the headline typeface. They should be large enough to stand out, but not to overwhelm. In general, smaller elements, say 12 to 16 picas wide, should stick to 14- to 18-point type; larger elements may go as high as necessary to fit proportionally the size of the element.

Subheads allow creativity to come out. They may be little more than same-size, boldface versions of the body type (preferably with a line of white space above), or they may be as jazzy as you care to make them.

For instance, subheads can

- be in 12-point, in the headline face

"As the new tax laws are better understood, you will discover more people accepting and utilizing PMC's management concept and products," Koeniger says. "There is a strong demand and need for these sort of investments."

Fund generates publicity

Our Bank and the Financial Services Group received much favorable publicity for our recent involvement in a special trust fund. In early November, several innocent people were killed during a bizarre shooting

Figure 6-6 A subhead should be a sub-*headline*—that is, it should introduce the subsequent information. It should have a line of white space above it, and it can be in the headline typeface. Body type set in bold and a bit larger is also acceptable.

- use tape above or beneath
- be in color, or screened gray
- be centered or flush left or right
- any combination of the above.

Their size needs to be proportional to the package. Full-size newspaper spreads can take larger subheads than can an 8-1/2-by-11-inch corporate report.

Initial letters should be in the headline typeface. This visual connection between the headline and the beginning of the story is a valuable tool for delivering the reader to the story.

In general, the size of the first graf initial letter is up to you: It can be as large and dominant a visual element as you care to make it. If you have no other visual, using the type of the headline and the initial letters can make a dull gray presentation come alive. Ensuing initial letters should always be slightly smaller than the beginning initial letter.

Display type is a wonderful design tool because it plays the twin roles of communicating and attracting attention. In the hands of a good designer, type itself can become an exciting visual on your pages.

WRITING HEADS AND TITLES

Ah, and herein lies the rub. Good headlines and titles are crucial to quality publications. They should get a great deal of attention from the editor. The best answer to the question "How do I get good at writing headlines?" is: practice. Write headlines until it hurts. Then keep at it. One day, maybe, you'll be good at it.

Here is a brief list of some tips to help get you started:

- Leave out articles (a, an, the).
- Use comma for "and."
- Use semicolon between lines when each line has its own subject and verb.
- Headline and accompanying art must work together.
- Story must deliver what headline promises; that is, don't use a "cute" headline just because you like it.
- Use "key word" approach. Write down several words that would simply *have* to be in a headline and work with various sequences to find a head that works.

- Always use a verb in a headline.
- Use single, not double, quotation marks.
- Don't begin a headline with a verb.
- Be creative and clever with heads, but not on top of a serious story.
- Headlines should be neither too long nor too short.

MAKING HEADS FIT

With the advent of computers, the old skill of counting letters in heads to be sure they will fit in the allotted space has pretty much fallen by the wayside. Either the computer tells you whether the headline fits, or a page composition program, such as Aldus' PageMaker®, actually *shows* you on your computer screen.

Just in case you still need to count letters in heads, however, here is a suggested method.

The best way is to adopt a set unit spacing figure for every character you might use. The unit space compensates for variances in widths of letters. Compensating for different size type is done by allowing fewer of the larger sizes in a given column space. For instance, you might be able to get 8 letters of 36-point in one column, but you can only get 4 letters of 60-point.

Suggested unit values:
Capitals, except M,W = 1.5
M,W = 2
I = 1
Lowercase, except m,w,f,l,i,t,j = 1
m,w = 1.5
f,l,i,t,j = 0.5
Space = 0.5
Numbers except 1 = 1.5
1 = 1
Punctuation marks except ? — = 0.5
? — = 1.5
Symbols ($,%, etc.) = 1

With this system you would calculate ahead of time how many "units" of the various type styles would fit in a given column space. Then, when you are ready to write the head, you refer to the chart to see how far you can go.

A good way to keep track of heads in this method is to put a small hash mark below each full count and a hash mark above for each half count (Fig. 6–7). After

Writing the title = 13½

Figure 6-7

you have written the head, go back and simply count the full hash marks, and then pairs of half count hash marks to see if your head will fit properly.

CHECKLIST

1. Your typography is important because (1) it communicates your messages and (2) it is a graphic element.
2. If you have set up your typography style—including a style and spacing manual—and if you have mastered design basics, you are nearly ready to apply the principles to a specific page layout. It's one thing to lay out type and blocks in an attractive fashion; it's another when that type "says" something and when the blocks become stories with meanings.
3. If your assignments have been made with integrated editing in mind, it should be easier to write the head creatively to act as a "caption" for the accompanying art.
4. Remember that type can be used as a graphic element, as something to draw the reader's eye by its visual magnetism alone.
5. Should reporters/writers suggest headlines and titles, or is that strictly an editor's task? Why? If the *best* head or title doesn't fit the layout, which should be changed? Which communicates more, the head or the design? Which is usually changed? Why?
6. What is the main difference between newspaper headlines and magazine titles? Look at several examples of each and see if you can come up with a list of principles applied to each. What attributes make a headline a good one? A bad one?
7. Are headlines better communicators than titles? Take a story and write a head/second deck and a title/blurb for each one. Then run a small experiment and get some friends to tell you which one they think works better.
8. Have someone cover the headlines on a few newspaper pages and/or a few magazine openers. Then try to rewrite them. After peeking at what the other publications went with, evaluate your work against theirs.
9. Try to devise a "new" headline style (kicker, second deck, etc.), one that has never been used before. Remember that the point is to draw the eye, "sell" the story, and deliver the reader to the first word of the story. Does your new style do that better than, or at least as good as, present headline/title styles?

CHAPTER

7 PHOTOS AND ILLUSTRATIONS

One cannot communicate by words alone. Nearly any kind of written communication can benefit from the addition of visual images: photographs or illustrations. The old saw is that a picture is worth a thousand words. Extrapolating on that, a picture and a few words are worth *ten* thousand words.

Pictures themselves have communicative value. They must never be seen as something separate from the content of the publication. In other words, you don't have content, and then photos to "illustrate" that content, as if an illustrative visual was a second-class citizen.

Magazines always have used photographs, with *Life* magazine being the most obvious example. In recent years, newspapers have turned more and more to the photograph as a way to attract readers to the paper or to a particular page.

Research has shown that photos are usually the first, and often the second and third, stops a reader makes on a newspaper page. Photos are also strong visual attractors on smaller pages as well. They are important design elements as well as communicators (Fig. 7–1).

Other research has shown that newspaper readers, for instance, tend to see stories with photos more worth reading than stories without, and they tend to read deeper into stories with art than those without.

The photos and illustrations themselves, as well as the words that describe them, must be edited. The integrated editing approach considers this as part of the entire editing process, not something done after the word editing is done.

The work may in fact be done after the word editing, but the activities, from selecting the photo or illustration to editing to writing descriptive words, are not truly discrete events.

SATURDAY JULY 11, 1987

The Virginian-Pilot The Ledger-Star

SECTION D

■ THE NATION'S HOUSING/D3
■ THE HOUSING SCENE/D4
■ REAL ESTATE NOTEBOOK/D6

Real Estate

CLASSIFIED/D7

Breaking new ground

As rates rise, so does ARM use

New loan converts to fixed interest rate

THE OUTLOOK

More developers hiring MBAs

Peninsula condos have familiar look

Broad Bay Estates young, 'easy to sell'

THE SELLING PRICE

San Diego's slow-growth rule limits homes

Figure 7-1 A large photo is usually the entry point on a page. After traveling to the second photo, the reader is below the fold, so a strong main headline is necessary to bring the reader back to the top. (Courtesy of The Virginian-Pilot, Norfolk, Va.)

SELECTING PHOTOGRAPHS

An editor's job is a little different with a photographer than with a writer. Often an editor chooses a photograph from a proof sheet, which would be like looking over a reporter's notes and rough drafts. Selecting a good picture that will reproduce well from a proof sheet is chancy.

Generally, the best way to pick the best photo is to have the photographer select the best shots technically that seem to fit the photo assignment and submit those to the editor. The editor then picks the photo that best tells the story.

These choices should be submitted in full-frame 8-by-10s. Proof sheets, however, should also be submitted, more for information than for any selection purposes. If the content of the photographer's choices just won't work, then the editor can quickly refer to the proofs before conferring again with the photographer.

This approach means that photographers must shoot a wide variety of photos so that the editor has some choice. Frank Hoy, author of *Photojournalism: The Visual Approach* suggests a system he calls EDFAT: an acronym for *E*ntire, *D*etails, *F*rame, *A*ngles and *T*ime.

The photographer should

- shoot the *entire* scene in a general, overall shot,
- then shoot separate *details* of the overall scene,
- *frame* each shot into a strong composition,
- shoot from a variety of *angles,*
- *time* means to (1) vary shutter speeds and (2) continue to shoot the scene over as long a period of time as your deadline allows.

This method gives maximum selection possibilities to the editor. A good assignment that guides but does not dictate and a photojournalist who follows the EDFAT principles are the best ways to assure good selection during the photo-editing process.

With the photographer and editor working closely together, with each un-

THE TAMPA TRIBUNE
Saturday, July 30, 1988

Business

Section D

MARKET REPORT

Judge OKs loan for Sooner Defense

By CLAY ZEIGLER
Tribune Business Writer

TAMPA — Debt-ridden Sooner Defense of Florida Inc. got a new lease on life Friday when a federal bankruptcy judge allowed the ordnance maker to borrow money from one of its directors.

After a four-hour hearing, Judge Thomas Baynes endorsed Sooner's plan to borrow $400,000 from company director Lonnie Hawkins, but put restrictions on how the money can be spent. Baynes also denied a request from the company that it be allowed free use of its revenues, which are claimed by Sooner's banks.

Lakeland-based Sooner filed July 19 for protection from creditors under Chapter 11 of the federal bankruptcy code. It was unable to pay its employees on July 22, and about 500 of its 600 workers have been laid off. The company has $50,000 in operating capital, and is expecting between $1 million and $1.2 million in expenses during the next two months.

Sooner Chairman Edward Geoghegan testified Friday morning that if the company was not allowed to borrow the $400,000, "The company must cease operations. At the end of the day today."

Attorneys for Sooner's two lead banks argued vigorously against the loan, which takes precedence over their $13.75 million claim.

In making his ruling, Baynes summed up the hearing by saying Sooner's attorney "claims his client can struggle on. The banks have taken the position that we're all going to hell in a basket."

Baynes required that Sooner make its July 22 payroll of $218,391.51, that it pay off a $13,750 equipment loan, pay a Lakeland power company $60,000, and use the remainder for future salaries and wages.

The judge directed that most of the $50,000 the company already had be used to pay insurance premiums. Baynes prohibited any payments to company officers or directors.

Geoghegan testified that between 100 and 120 people are working at Sooner, and said that if Sooner continues to operate, it would be with a work force about that size.

After the hearing, however, he said he did not know if more layoffs would occur.

Geoghegan said efforts to line up investors or buyers for Sooner are continuing, and seven companies have expressed an interest.

At least four representatives of a major Sooner customer, Olin Corp. were in the courtroom Fri-

See SEVEN, Page 7D

Tribune graphics

Market throws surprise rally

A Tribune Wire Report

NEW YORK — Wall Street stocks posted their biggest gain in a month Friday as a rising dollar and higher U.S. bond prices kindled a lively and surprising rally.

Sale of Sheraton complete

Miami company pays $31 million for hotel

By STEPHANIE TRIPP
Tribune Business Writer

TAMPA — A Miami-based ho-

...transferred the deed to Continental.

The hotel opened in 1984 as part of Lincoln's $100 million Urban Centre office-hotel complex at West Shore and Kennedy boulevards. The developer completed a second 10-story office tower at the complex earlier this year. That building is owned by its anchor tenant, Aetna Life & Casualty Co.

The Sheraton Grand is one of several West Shore hotels suffering from a building boom that added hundreds of hotel rooms to the area during the mid-1980s. Since then, hoteliers have been forced to slash their rates to attract guests.

Continental's chairman, Sherwood Weiser, said that while overbuilding remains a concern, Tampa will be a good hotel market in the long term.

"It's been good," Weiser said. "It could be better. We certainly hope that it will improve."

The Sheraton name and its extensive reservations network are expected to bring in more guests, but the management company will not know the results of the changes it put into place last fall for several more months.

Also, Continental plans to renovate some of the hotel's public areas during the next six months.

Weiser said it was too soon to release specific plans, but added, "We are going to spend some substantial dollars."

Window painting

Bill Forish of St. Petersburg paints an advertisement on the windshield of a used car at Register Chevrolet in Brooksville. Forish paints car windshields for a living. He charges from $3 to $6 a windshield. He works for about 40 Tampa Bay area car dealerships and has done it for about six years. He said it's "a living".

Home builders predict bleak '89

By JERALD HYCHE
Tribune Staff Writer

ORLANDO — The outlook for the nation's housing industry through next year: Higher mortgage interest rates and the lowest rate of home construction since 1982.

Meanwhile, home ownership will remain only a dream for millions of the nation's working class unless government reduces construction fees and resurrects tax incentives to build rental housing for low-income families.

At least that's the perspective of Dale Stuard, president of the National Association of Home Builders.

Stuard, speaking at the Southeast Builders Conference on Friday, said the trade group's economists predict that mortgage interest rates will rise to 11.5 percent by the end of the year, a forecast shared by many economists.

Any rate increase knocks some would-be home buyers out of the market, but Stuard said government fees are as much to blame.

Florida builders complain that impact fees add as much as $7,000 to the cost of a new home, but California builder Stuard said his state's impact fees add $20,000 to every new home's price tag — which currently averages $211,000.

"About 30 percent of the people we see on the homeless list right now are 'working homeless' people," he said. "We have a country that has had a certain amount of low-income housing, so when some kind of catastrophe happens at the family level, a divorce, a death, what have you, there was at least some place for a person to move.

"Nowadays, they fall right down through that right down on the street."

He said a safety net could be created by reviving tax credits for building low-income rental properties that were killed by tax reform in 1986.

Tax reform's end to those tax credits and overbuilding are the main reasons multifamily construction has plummeted from 625,000 units in 1986 to 385,000 projected for this year.

He said the builders' group predicts 1.45 million housing starts this year, down from 1.6 million in 1986.

For 1989, the trade group expects 1.37 million starts — about a million single-family and 355,000 multifamily — the lowest level of production since 1982.

> "About 30 percent of the people we see on the homeless list right now are 'working homeless' people."
>
> — Dale Stuard
> President of the National Association of Home Builders

Peninsula, Georgia AAA groups merge

By ALINA MATAS
Tribune Business Writer

TAMPA — The Tampa-based Peninsula Motor Club and AAA Georgia will merge Aug. 1, forming the nation's fourth-largest American Automobile Association affiliate.

See NEW, Page 7D

Candy man

Associated Press photograph

A man bearing a striking resemblance to St. Nicholas tastes a candy cane at the National Candy Wholesalers convention in Boston on Friday. Americans will spend about $12 billion this year on about 5 billion pounds of candy. That is nearly 20 pounds a person.

Losing Medicare bidder claims contract was rigged

A Staff, Wire Report

JACKSONVILLE — The losing bidder for a $67 million Medicare data-processing contract claims Blue Cross and Blue Shield of Florida violated federal laws and regulations in awarding the contract to GTE Data Services Inc. of Tampa.

But Tom Albright, Blue Cross senior vice president for health industry services, termed the complaint "silly and nonsensical" bad-mouthing from a disgruntled loser.

Blue Cross and Blue Shield Inc. of Florida is the Jacksonville-based Medicare administrator for the state.

ADWEEK agrees to sponsor annual advertising seminar

TAMPA — Creative Seminar 14, an annual advertising seminar in Tampa, should get a boost in prestige following an agreement Friday that ADWEEK magazine will sponsor the event.

Enertin & Hall, the Tampa-based advertising agency that has sponsored the seminar for 14 years, agreed to the joint venture that calls for ADWEEK to sponsor the seminar beginning with the session planned for November.

Hall said he will manage the seminar for ADWEEK this year and next year.

Though the seminar has traditionally drawn participants from as many as 35 states, Hall said that because of its trade connections, ADWEEK would be able to draw more prominent speakers and more participants.

But just as importantly, Hall

See SPONSORSHIP, Page 7D

Figure 7-2 Instead of just a head shot, get the subject doing something. (Courtesy of The Tampa Tribune)

derstanding and respecting the other's craft, the best possible visuals can be shown to readers.

When looking over the photographic choices, editors must consider the same basic characteristics they look for in stories: impact, newsworthiness, clarity, brevity, etc. In addition, technical quality and design possibilities should be considered.

Naturally, the most important consideration in selecting a photograph is whether it is newsworthy and tells the story accurately. Clarity and brevity can be achieved through cropping. Design considerations do not often dictate photo selection: The function of design is to enhance content, not rule it. But with certain feature pages or spreads, the design may call for a special size photo or a photo with certain content or angle (Fig. 7–2).

An editor may, in good conscience, request or select a special photo in this instance as long as the content still accurately reflects the event or person.

Some people say that form should *never* dictate content, but never is a strong word. The best design is a marriage of content and functional form. Just as words can sometimes *suggest* a design, a page design can *suggest* effective ways the content—both word and visual—can best be presented.

EDITING PHOTOGRAPHS

Photographic information, as well as the word, must be edited. Just as stories need a strong focus, a good lead, and newsworthiness, so do photos. This can mean that the photo is *important* and contains essential information for the reader, or that it is *interesting* or entertaining.

Once this editing decision has been made, the photo content must still receive the same careful scrutiny that stories receive.

- Is the main action highlighted?
- Has extraneous material been deleted?

Also, editors must look for visual cues:

- Does the action in the photo lead *into* the photo?
- Is the focal point off-center?
- (Thinking of the page design) Does the action from the photo move the reader *into* the story lead (and not off the page)? This "gaze motion" has been shown to be a powerful force in moving readers' eyes.

Most of this editing is handled through *cropping,* or deleting portions of the photograph that do not meet the editor's requirements.

A good editor is ruthless in cutting away unneeded portions of both stories and photos. Readers today are too busy to have to wade through unnecessary information to get to what they want to know.

Photos are never actually cut during this process. Marks are placed on the edges of the photo that indicate the image area to be made into a halftone.

Because most people don't edit photos as tightly as they can go, a good rule of thumb is to crop the photo tightly. Then go back and crop a little tighter. Make sure that the central information area is played as large as you can handle it.

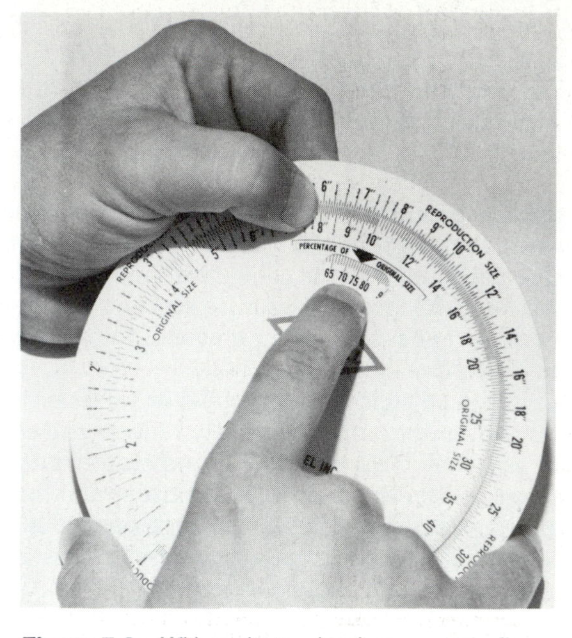

Figure 7-3 With a photo wheel you can easily calculate the proper dimensions for a photo. Here, the wheel shows that a 75 percent reduction is necessary.

On the other hand, beginners often overcrop, that is, they have taken the tight cropping sermon to heart so well that they crop away needed context in a photo.

The rule about cropping tightly to the heart of the photo—or as newspaper typographer and designer Edmund C. Arnold puts it, finding the picture in the photograph—does not mean to crop to the face in a sports action photo.

Nor does it mean to crop away "empty" background *if* that background is central to the *information* the photo contains. Considered this way, the editor is really editing *meaning,* not necessarily the physical manuscript or photograph. "Crop ruthlessly," then, is a relative phrase, allowing some photos to be published with little background and some with much background, depending on the meaning.

Because most photos are not published the same size as they are cropped, they must be *sized* after cropping. Considering the column grid of the publication, the editor either enlarges or reduces the size of the photo to fit.

Although sizing can be done using elementary math, most editors use some kind of scaling tool, usually a circular proportional scale.

A proportional scale consists of two wheels connected at the center. The larger or outside wheel represents the desired size in the publication; the smaller or inner wheel represents the size of the photo as cropped (Fig. 7–3). The inner wheel also has an opening that shows percentage figures. Sizing a photo is done by simply aligning the "original" dimension on the inner wheel with the "desired" dimension on the outer wheel and reading the percentage. A number larger than 100 percent means that the photo will be enlarged; a number smaller will mean it must be reduced.

Usually it is better to size the width first. Then, by keeping the wheel at the same position—to keep the percentage the same—find the original *depth* of the photo and read across to the figure now aligned with it on the desired wheel: That figure will be the new depth as published.

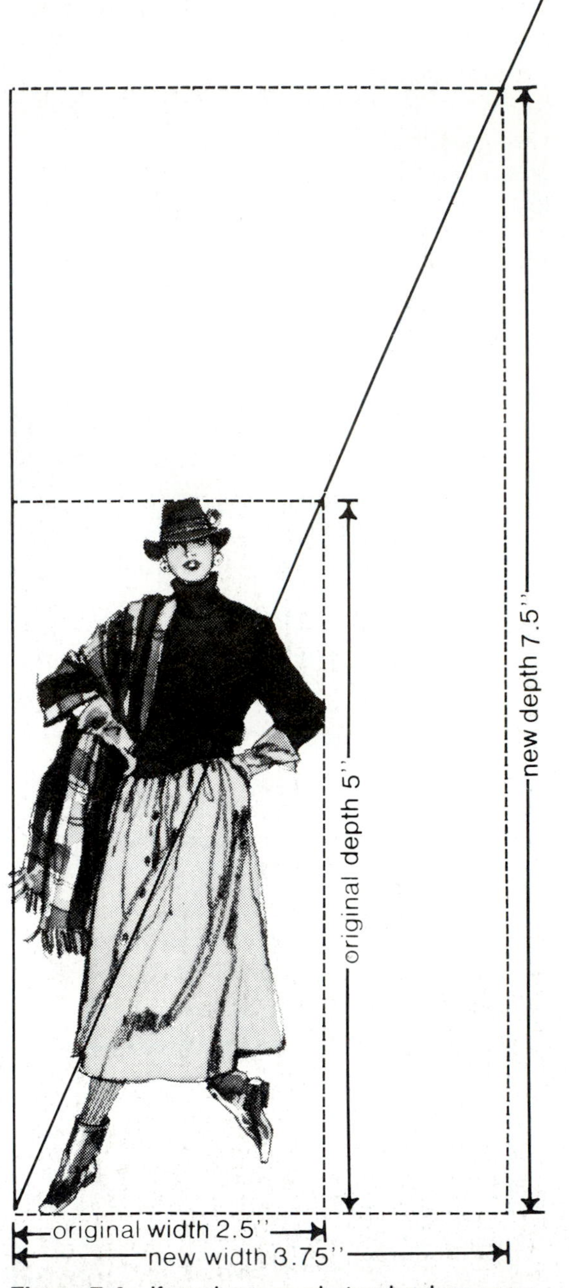

Figure 7-4 If you have no photo wheel, you can use a simple diagonal method to calculate the proper dimensions (see text). (Courtesy of The Virginian-Pilot, Norfolk, Va.)

If you have a high level of math anxiety, you could use the diagonal method to size the photo. On a sheet of tracing paper, mark the corners of the photo. Remove the photo and complete the sides. Draw the diagonal line. Then measure the width you desire along the base of this rectangle. By then drawing a perpendicular line from that point to the diagonal, you will have your new photo depth. This method works because both sides must be reduced or enlarged by the same ratio. The diagonal is the place to find the changed figure (Fig. 7–4).

Figure 7-5 Sometimes a special effects screen can add to a feature photo. Special screens, such as mezzotint, pictured here, should never be used for a news photo. (Courtesy of the St. Petersburg Times)

SPECIAL EFFECTS

Besides the standard halftone screen, many other screens are available for a special photo, such as mezzotint, steel etching, and circular, among others (Fig. 7–5). Like spices in cooking, these should be used sparingly and only when appropriate. Special screens should never be used, for instance, with a serious, news-oriented photograph because they remove the photo from reality, from what the readers would have seen had they been at the event.

Special screens also should never be used in an attempt to hide a weak photo. The effect becomes part of the meaning offered in the photograph. To use an inappropriate screen either confuses the reader or, worse, delivers a message you did not intend to send. Using a special effect on a photo turns it into a *photo illustration.* It demands different treatment from that accorded a standard photograph. Photo illustrations, in essence an artist's conception of reality, should be used with nonnews stories. The separation from "reality" makes them inappropriate for hard news.

CHANGING PHOTO CONTENT

Because the proper design calls for the action in a photo to point the reader into the story or at least into the page, editors often are faced with a dilemma: The

best photo doesn't fit the design. They will sometimes flop, or turn over the negative during printing, so that the action goes the proper way for the design.

Flopping should *never* be done. (And, yes, I remember saying earlier that never was a strong word. Here, I mean it.) First and most obvious, it puts wedding rings on the right hand, parts of the hair on opposite sides, and it makes people and places simply look different.

But the more important issue is the simple changing of reality for the convenience of the editor's design. Reality should not be changed; the design should be. This is an ethical issue. Mass communicators have an ethical responsibility to present the facts as they occurred. Much gets changed from reality during the communication process anyway. Changing reality purposefully simply should never be done. The pressure to change reality on deadline is even greater with the laser scanners used to separate color photographs into the four halftones needed to print a color photograph.

Scanners not only can adjust the color in any portion of the photo ("Gee, Suzanne, it would be great if that kid was a redhead") but they can also change the shape of any single element in the photo and even delete unwanted elements.

Not many people can mount a decent argument for the ethics of changing hair color. But is the electronic removal of distracting elements simply high-tech cropping? Or is it the changing of reality?

In essence, the scanner has given the editor a very powerful cropping tool, so powerful that it borders on a creative tool. These ethical questions have not been fully resolved by the communications industry, but some important questions about ethics should at least be asked before heavy changes on a scanner are made.

TWO-PICTURE PACKAGES

When selecting photos, an editor is often faced with a difficult decision: Which of several very good photos should be used? Is it the one that gives a good overview of the entire event, say of a county fair or an awards banquet? Or is it the one that shows only a small portion of the event?

Why not have your cake and eat it too: Use both!

With the increasing emphasis on the visual in today's mass communications, especially in newspapers, photos are being played larger and larger. In some ways, this is to be applauded: Readers like pictures and, as mentioned earlier, pictures have for too long been mistreated. But this does not address the problem of *which* photo to use: the overview or the anecdote. If you think in terms of a two-picture package, you can have both, and you can add some visual interest to your page design (Fig. 7–6).

The overview should be run smaller than the anecdotal or close-up photo. They should be run together as a package with one cutline. Frank Hoy's EDFAT approach for photojournalists plays right into this, as you can see.

This approach also forces some white space onto the page. Care should be taken with this white space, however, to ensure it is placed properly to the outside of a spread or page.

The total package of two photos, white space, and words would still be as big as one dominant photo, but more information is given to the reader, and little is lost in impact because it is the "crowd" shot that is run small. The anecdotal photo, the one most photographers would have picked anyway, is still run fairly large.

Figure 7-6 A two-picture package, with one photo a long-distance scene-setter and the other a close-up, is sometimes preferred to one picture. (Courtesy of Mike Vogl, Poudre Valley Hospital)

Figure 7-7 A "setup" photo or photo illustration is a useful approach for certain, difficult-to-capture subjects. At times a photo just can't set the right tone and you should use an illustration. (L, Courtesy Southwestern Bell Corporation; R, © Dayton Daily News)

ILLUSTRATIONS

Sometimes a photograph is simply inappropriate or unavailable. When that happens, the fortunate editor has access to an artist, either on staff or as a freelance artist (Fig. 7–7).

Illustrations are usually inappropriate for news stories because they don't say "real" and "now" to the reader. They are highly effective for stories such as child abuse or suicide or even obesity. Any topic that would be sensitive for either the reader or the subject of the photograph should be handled with an illustration or a photo illustration.

Because illustrations are not accepted as "real," as are normal photographs, you can feel freer to make a statement of your choice with the art instead of trying to reflect reality as seen by the artist or photographer.

Photo illustrations, therefore, must be identified as such either in the cutline or in the credit line under the illustration. Again, for ethical reasons, the reader must have no chance to believe the scene portrayed is real.

DESIGN

After the best photos and/or illustrations have been selected and edited, they must be placed on the page in an orderly and attractive fashion. Regardless of the size of publication, several principles should be followed:

- As stated earlier, the art should lead the reader to a related story, not away from it.
- Art elements should not be the same size, unless their content is related.
- In fact, *emphasize* size and shape difference when using more than one piece of art per page. This adds visual interest. This is the design principle of "contrast" in action.
- When using only one piece of art, use it very large so it dominates the page.
- White space should be used to frame art and separate it from other unrelated elements (see Chapter 3 for using white space in design).

Art and type must work together on a page. Sometimes type can be a dominant element on a page, but it should not fight art to do so. As you might expect, there are several principles for coordinating art with both body type and display type.

WITH BODY TYPE

- "Pictures over type." Readers habitually look below art for explanatory type. Cutlines, therefore, should be placed there for maximum ease of reading. You can place them at the side on occasion. If you do this, don't center the cutline in the vertical space. Place it at the top or bottom, aligning with the photo. Or place at a reasonable "off-center" point. Don't use caption blocks with photo essays. They are too hard on the reader.
- Pictures should also be placed *above* the stories they illustrate, if laid out in a vertical design. The best order (from top to bottom) is photo, cutline, headline or title, and story.

- Art inserted into legs of body type and below a headline or title should be inserted at the *top* of the type, not the bottom or in the middle. In a sense, this is still the "pictures over type" rule, if that helps you remember it.

DISPLAY TYPE

- Use the appropriate display type for the art: Art or photos with bold, heavy lines and tones call for bold type; delicately drawn art would be suffocated with a boldface. On the other hand, contrast might be attractive. Try each and let your eye decide.
- Remember pictures over type here, too.
- A "catchline," or a small display-type word or two above or directly below a stand-alone photo, helps catch the reader's eye.
- If you have no dominant art on the page, let your display type become an art element. But don't play a type attack against your art.

PHOTO GROUPS

Photos are often grouped to tell a story or even to make a point, as with a written essay. Technically, a two-picture package is a group, but here I'm mainly talking about large numbers of photos and especially photo pages (Fig. 7–8).

As mentioned earlier, readers tend to be attracted to photos first on any page. Giving them a plateful of photos will either dazzle them into confusion or, with a good designer, please them with an orderly stroll through the page.

RODEOGALLERY

RODEO

1986

The 1986 California Rodeo began on Thursday with the horse parade through Salinas to the Rodeo Grounds and ended on Sunday afternoon with the crowning of the all around cowboy. As the action wound down and the cowboys packed up for the next stop on the rodeo circuit, the winners collected their bounty and the competitors — two-legged and four-legged — headed for the next stop.

CLAY PETERSON/The Californian

RICHARD GREEN/The Californian

CLAY PETERSON/The Californian

Page 6 Salinas Californian Monday, July 21, 1986 Monday, July 21, 1986 Salinas Californian Page 7

Figure 7-8 A photo group should not fill every square inch of the page. (Courtesy of the Salinas Californian, Salinas, Ca.)

In order to design or plan a good photo page, observe the following:

- Have a center of visual impact or CVI. This is where the readers will start on the page. Then using the content of the photos, white space, and type, lead the readers in a logical sequence through the page.
- Use both horizontal and vertical shapes on the page.
- The white space between the photos should be small and consistent; the white space on the outside should be larger and it should vary. In other words, the elements should be clustered.
- Don't fill all four corners with photos or type. Leaving one corner white creates a visually interesting imbalance to the spread.
- Run individual captions under each photo. Block captions make the reader work too hard.

CAPTIONS AND CUTLINES

Photographs are always better with explanatory descriptions. Illustrations and photo illustrations can be published with no type, but true photographs need at least an identification of the person(s) or objects shown.

A caption is a small block of type that describes a photo, and a cutline is the "old-fashioned" term for the same thing. In the days of molten lead "hot" type, the metal engraved halftones were often called cuts. Thus, the lines of type used to describe cuts acquired the name cutlines.

Many editors today use "caption" to describe a line of display type, either above the photo (also called an *overline*), or more frequently, directly above the cutline.

This acts as a headline for the cutline information and can help attract the reader. It should be in 14- to 18-point type, and may be in the headline face (perhaps italics) to underline typographical consistency.

Cutlines should not simply describe what is in the photograph. It should add information to what the photo gives the reader. For instance, a cutline that said "Shown above is a fire hydrant spouting water..." would be redundant. We already can see *what* is happening in the photo. We want to know why.

Cutlines are written for two kinds of photographs: those that go with a story and those that stand alone. The style for each should be different. For obvious reasons, the stand-alone photo needs more space to add information. A photo with a story already has that additional information.

In general, keep cutlines for photos accompanying a story to one or two lines at most. The type should be in your "secondary" face and probably bold (not italic). I prefer boldface type for cutlines because this better matches the visual density of a halftone than does medium or lightface type.

Stand-alone photos should use a somewhat smaller size (if for no other reasons than differentiation and space) and they should have a catchline. This acts as the "headline" and helps draw attention to the type below the photo.

Photo credit lines can be played in several places:

- at the end of the cutline, often in parentheses
- in small type under the lower right-hand corner of the photo
- vertical at the lower right-hand corner.

Wherever you play them, don't just frivolously make them small and unobtrusive. Reporters get comparatively large bylines, often over small and relatively insignificant stories. Why should your photojournalists get short shrift when it comes to credit?

In fact, I would suggest being sure to give photo credits for photo pages in 14-point or larger type. Those pages call for a special effort, and the photographer deserves decent billing.

The photography and art in a publication can often make it or break it. It is all too easy to ignore the visual people who produce this part of your publication. Do so at great risk to the future of your publication.

CHECKLIST

1. Photographs are your best, most easily gotten, and probably most appreciated nontype visual. Do whatever it takes to get good photographs.
2. Every photo should have a cutline. Words-and-pictures together is your best communication strategy.
3. Color photographs are good, but not necessary for a quality publication.
4. Don't ruin the rectangle of the photograph by fiddling with inserts, or mortices, or circles, or anything else.
5. You can use art with spot color to add color easily and cheaply.
6. Be sure that photographers are part of the assigning and planning process.
7. What is the difference between a photographer and a photojournalist? Talk to several of each of them in your area to see if you can discover how they might differently approach the same basic assignment.
8. Check with other local publications to see how photographers and other visual people are used/abused in the editing process. Do they get to control content at all? Who makes final decisions on what pieces of art are used?
9. Some people like to have the art in hand before making a layout. Why might this be better for the design? How could you work around not having art on hand when you are designing pages?
10. Find some photos you have used in the past and select typefaces that "fit" the tones and meaning in them. In other words, would you use a bold Megaron or a light Palatino Italic? Do the same exercise with some illustrations as well. Do you like similarity or contrast better?

CHAPTER

8

INFORMATION GRAPHICS, CHARTS, AND MAPS

The previous chapter covered photographs, but they are not the only visuals that communicate information. In fact, the 1980s may be the decade of the information graphic, a combination of art and data.

Nigel Holmes of *Time* magazine was certainly not the first information-graphic artist, but he may well have created the modern interest in the form. In the 1970s, he was using clever combinations of an illustration and a bar chart or pie chart or "fever-line" chart to help numbers tell a story.

Then *USA Today* came along and made the information graphic into a "USA Snapshot" that told us something numerical about ourselves every day (Fig. 8–1). Coming along as well, however, was a host of imitators without the powerful vision and/or attention to detail necessary for this kind of data visual.

Edwin Tufte, in his excellent book on the subject (*The Visual Display of Quantitative Information*), describes excellence in an info graphic as "a well-designed presentation of interesting data—a matter of SUBSTANCE, of STATISTICS, and of DESIGN."

Too much of the work of imitators ends up as "chartoons" that are filled usually with too much ink, too much clutter and color: The data get hidden behind what Tufte called "chartjunk."

Maps, too, are wonderful visual ways to present information. For showing the scene of an accident, for instance, or a new plant site, nothing but a map will do.

A good editor should be able to see and understand information and then decide what form that information should be presented in for optimum accessibility by the reader: words or visuals or both. An information graphic, either as a stand-alone or accompanying a story, may be the proper decision more often than you would think because it combines so perfectly the word and the visual.

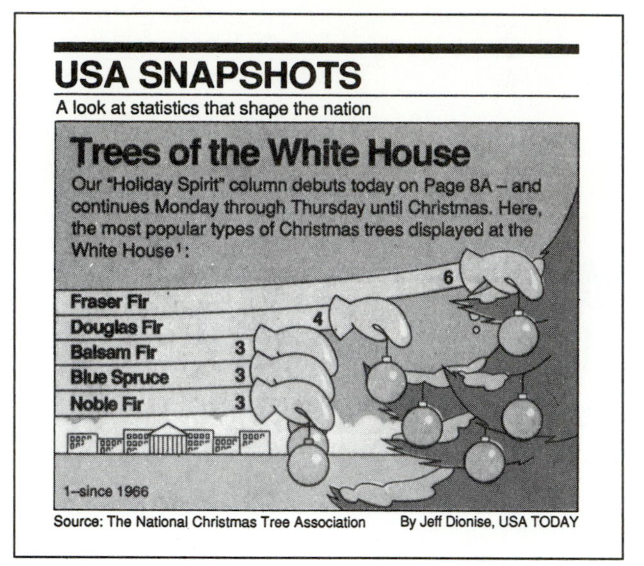

Figure 8-1 It is an easy, if not simple, task to turn interesting data into an interesting information graphic. (Copyright 1988, USA TODAY. USA TODAY and its associated graphics are federally registered trademarks of Gannett Co., Inc. Used by permission. All rights reserved.)

INFORMATION GRAPHICS

In the broadest sense, an information graphic is anything on a printed page that has both graphic and communicative value. Thus, even display type, in a sense, is an info graphic.

Here we will limit the discussion to nonheadline display type used graphically in a story and to tables, time series or fever-line charts, bar charts, pie charts, and maps.

We also should differentiate info graphics and art graphics. The former are primarily communicative with the added plus of being visually attractive and stimulating. The latter are primarily illustrative with the added plus of containing information of value. The function of a graphic element is to attract attention, to stop the reader. Information graphics are useful editing and design tools because they can fulfill two functions.

Pullouts

Another tool to help *stop* the scanner with a visual element and then *interest* him or her with content is the *pullout,* discussed previously in Chapter 1. They are worth a second look because, in a sense, they are also "information graphic" devices. Pullouts are generally direct quotes from a source in the story—often called *quoteouts*—but they can be anything at all of interest from the story.

Display type *will* stop the reader momentarily. You should select content that will intrigue the reader. One famous definition of news for a newspaper reader is, "Anything that will make a reader stop and say, 'Gee whiz!' " A good pullout will have a high "Gee Whiz Factor." If you can't find a good one in the story, then perhaps it isn't a good story in the first place. Or perhaps the writer needs to hit the streets or phones again.

Jobless rates

Unemployment rates in Virginia registered 4.2% in 1987, down eight-tenths of a percent from the previous year.

Locality	1986 rate	1987 rate
Fredericksburg	4.7	4.3
Stafford	2.7	2.5
Spotsylvania	4.1	3.9
Caroline	6.6	4.9
King George	4.1	3.8
Westmoreland	8.4	7.9
Culpeper	4.6	3.3
Fauquier	2.4	1.9
Louisa	5.3	5.3
Orange	5.0	4.5

JENNIFER LANE / *Staff graphic artist*

Figure 8-2 Alternating bars of gray and white make this table easier to read. (© The Free Lance-Star, Fredericksburg, Va.)

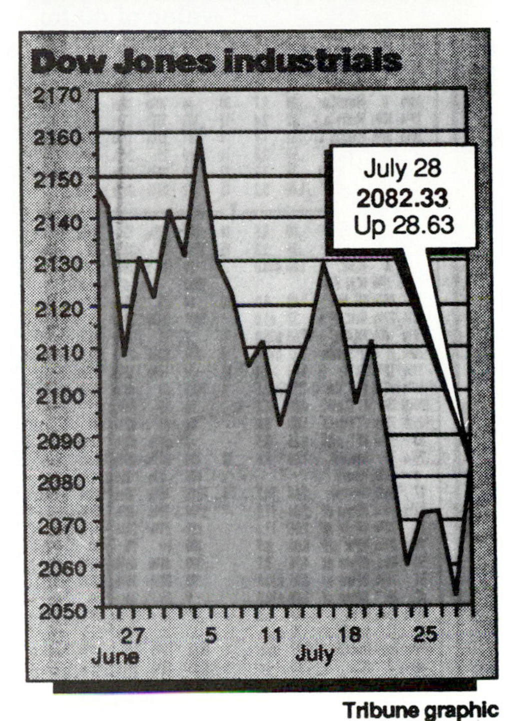

Figure 8-3 A time-series chart can show how something is changing over a certain time period. (Courtesy of The Tampa Tribune)

Tables

Tables are simple columns and rows of data. The juxtaposition of data allows comparison, but the data set must be small to allow comparison. A number of small tables can be put together into one large or "super" table, but don't be fooled: Super tables are not one large table.

Tables are often better than raw text for numerical data because they provide easy comparison, and usually that's why numbers are used in a story: to compare. If the differences between numbers are small, a table is preferred; if the differences are great, a fever-line is better.

To help the reader see the numbers quickly and clearly, tables need to be segmented somehow visually. One method is to separate every three rows in a table with a blank row. Another is to cover every other two rows with a gray screen. These methods allow readers to see the rows and columns clearly (Fig. 8–2).

Tables are better woven into the text of the article, or at the very least, immediately adjacent to it. Asking a reader to jump to a table on a facing page or overleaf and then return to the same point in the text is asking too much.

Charts and Graphs

Although a table is a better way to show numerical data than simple sentences and paragraphs, charts and graphs are an improvement on tables because they can show relationships among data. As with most information, it is the context, the relationship with other information, that often provides the most insight.

Time-series chart. One of the more interesting bits of information is how numbers change over time. A time-series graphic is usually set up with the time line on the horizontal axis of the chart and the measurement at that point in time on the vertical (Fig. 8–3).

Over time, as the line travels up and down—as does a fever-line on a hospital patient's chart—readers can see *relationships* clearly and quickly. Listing a value of 40 for 1975 and 80 for 1985 in a table may be mildly interesting, but showing that double-difference on a chart is superior, in terms of both quickness and clarity. The reader gets not only the raw data but also a visual representation of the relationship between the measurement on those two time points.

The time-series chart is appropriate for nearly any change in data over time. But if the data change so little over time that the visual change in the line is not clearly seen, then the numbers may be better in a table.

To be sure that the relationships are true, time-series charts should usually (I'd prefer to say always, but I can't bring myself to do it) include a zero point and equal time intervals on the horizontal axis.

Using unequal time intervals can either make the curve sharper or flatter, depending on the numbers. For instance, if you have been using months as your time interval and then suddenly switch to quarters in mid-graphic, the changes may seem suddenly more dramatic: The fever-line will take larger surges upward or downward.

In order to increase comparisons and/or context, you can put multiple fever-lines on a graphic. For instance, you might want to compare revenues and expenses, or salary increases and cost-of-living figures. Comparison is good, but don't add multiple lines if it will be too hard to separate the two (or more) lines on the chart visually—that is, if the numbers are very similar.

Also, you will have to be sure that the lines are clearly recognizable as different lines, either by using dashed or dotted vs. solid lines in black and white or different color lines.

In general, use no more than three comparison lines per chart, and two may even be better. If you have many comparisons, it would be better to create a series of charts—run small, close together, and with the same scale—that compare the various pairs of data points.

Bar Charts. Bar charts, like time-series charts, can be used to show differences in quantities over time. But unlike time-series charts, the bar chart can compare two or more quantities at a single point in time, not just how one element has changed over time (Fig. 8–4). A (fever) line is one element that may change; the bars represent different elements.

For instance, a time-series chart might show how advertising expenses for Company A have increased during the past 10 years. The data points would be plotted and connected by lines. This would show the ups and downs of the expenses.

A bar chart might be used to compare advertising expenses of Company A, Company B, Company C, and Company D this year. Or, if two bars per company were used (and remember, comparisons are *always* good), then it might be both this year's and last year's expenses for the four companies. Bar charts are usually best when used this way, to show comparative individual data points rather than change over time.

Because the visual volume (width × depth) of the bar conveys meaning as well as the end data point of the bar, it is especially important for a bar chart to start at the zero point of the data.

For instance, let's say you are comparing average salaries of reporters and editors for each of the past five years. In an effort to save space, you start the vertical axis at $20,000. This may mean that after a few years, depending on the scale interval you use, the bar size or volume on the chart for either group may be *twice* as tall, even though the salary increase during the period may have been only 18 percent (Fig. 8–5). This is misleading visual information. Your

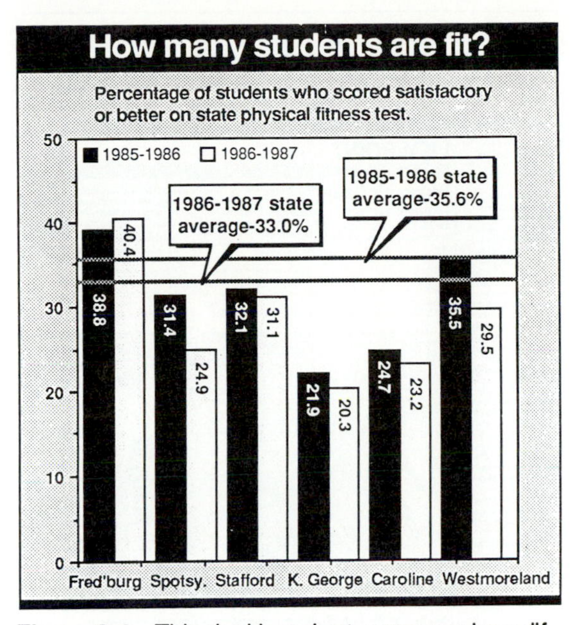

Figure 8-4 This dual bar chart compares how different counties fare on student physical fitness. The two bars at each column represent two school years. This is a good way to give readers a lot of data in a small place. (© The Free Lance-Star, Fredericksburg, Va.)

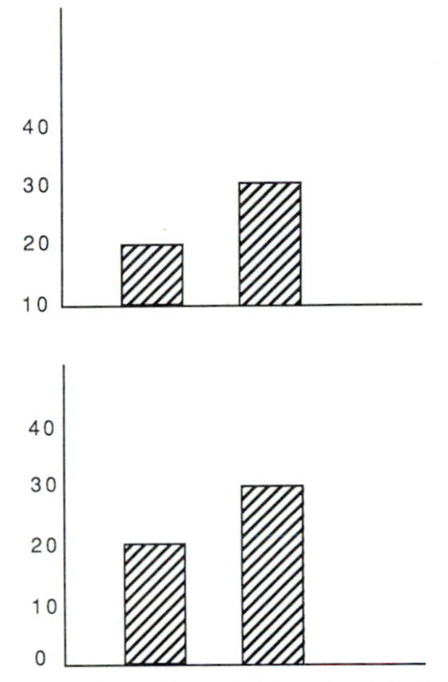

Figure 8-5 Bar charts should always have a zero point. The visual interpretation can change if you don't. The chart on top uses 10 as a zero point, making the second bar appear twice as large. Using zero, however, shows the bars in their true visual proportion (bottom chart).

visual information and your data must match, or confusion could set in. And especially with numbers, even momentary confusion is the enemy.

Tufte says that getting too creative with bar charts adds information that is unnecessary, and perhaps even confusing. Even using a 3-D effect can lead not only to confusion but also to erroneous conclusions thought by the reader to be correct. For instance, a reader may be comparing volume of the bars when it is the height that shows the relationship. On the other hand, putting the data in a visual context (Fig. 8–6) helps to draw in the reader and provide further information.

Worse yet is to try to show pictures of people or things increasing or decreasing: barrels of oil, doctors, dollar bills, and such. It is too easy to confuse the reader by mis-manipulating the sizes of these multidimensional objects (Fig. 8–7). Again, it is often the volume that confuses. A representational graphic *can* be effective, but caution is advised.

Tufte's rule is: "The number of information-carrying (variable) dimensions depicted should not exceed the number of dimensions in the data." In other words, if you are trying to show a simple set of numbers, use simple two dimensions: a flat bar chart. Use three dimensions only with three related variables.

Pie Charts. These charts are used to show the various parts of a whole. The most common use of these is to show the components of a budget. The slices of the "pie" depict the relationship between the components (Fig. 8–8).

Tufte says that pie charts should never be used because they do not order numbers along a single visual dimension. He also says that accurately comparing slices of the pie is difficult.

Nigel Holmes argues that pie charts are fine as long as they do the job—that is, as long as the visual comparisons are easy to see and are accurate. If

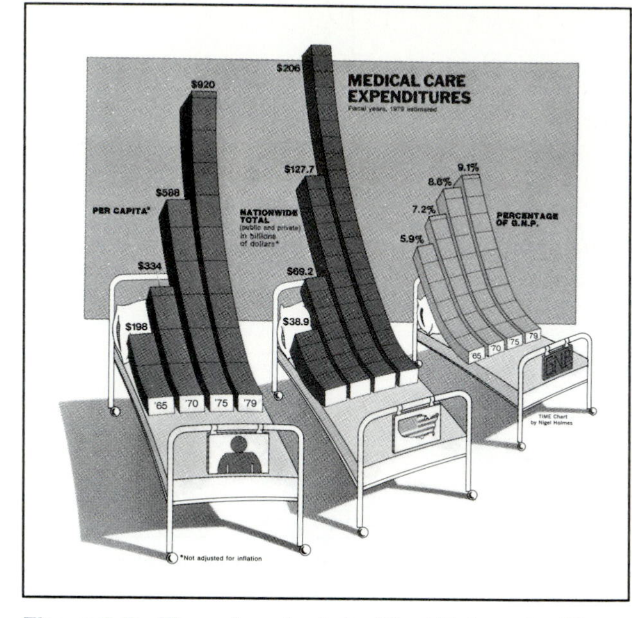

Figure 8-6 These bar charts by Nigel Holmes for *Time* magazine show that accuracy with data can be achieved with an artistic approach. The numbers by the top of the bar help one's total understanding. The creative idea of the hospital beds to show medical expenditures supports the idea while drawing reader attention in the first place. (*Time* chart by Nigel Holmes, ©*Time* magazine)

3

"We also metallize sites for future attachments, so the customer can affix a chip and the wires," says Robert L. Reber, Metaramics chairman.

Motorola buys Metaramics packages to protect power transistors on chips in two-way radios of police cars and taxis. These transistors amplify the signal coming into the radio speaker. Other power transistors, protected by beryllia, drive the solid-state transmitter connected to an antenna in each cell of the cellular mobile radio telephone network, now going national. This honeycomb system permits more drivers to use car phones at the same time.

With 80 products and 100 employees, Metaramics predicts sales to grow by a factor of four between 1983 and 1988. Power transistors will pack more wallop. Circuitry will get denser and react faster. "Even today," Mr. Reber declares, "you can put the whole *Encyclopedia Brittanica* on one four-inch chip." An IBM personal computer whizzes through 78,000 additions of seven-digit numbers in one second! All this tots up to more heat and sales.

Reviewing Grace's plunge into new materials, Robert W. Samuels, a Grace executive vice president and ICG's new group executive, forecasts: "Ceramics and composites will take us increasingly toward fabrication. The profits will probably be in the value we add, not in chemical raw materials. Fabrication is within our culture. Cryovac, Polyfibron and Servicised are examples. But we must keep our ceramic and composite ventures in perspective. The real engine is still our existing businesses. We're going to build the new acquisitions into major profit contributors, starting in the 1990s." ■

VIEWPOINT

Economic Gain Favors Grace

The U.S. economy is headed for strong expansion again this year.

Business Economics expects real gross national product (GNP) to grow 5.5% in 1984, following a robust 3.4% rebound in 1983 from the 1981-1982 recession. Inflation, which fell from 9.4% in 1981 to 4.2% last year, is forecast to increase only 5% in 1984. Business Economics reports a favorable outlook for Grace businesses.

Consumer Spending—Bolstered by Reagan tax cuts, consumers hiked outlays 4.2% in constant dollars last year after a lackluster 1.4% gain in 1982. Real consumer spending is likely to jump 4.4% this year. While the rebound will center on durable goods—1984 car sales are projected to surge more than 25% ahead of 1982—all consumer areas from restaurants to apparel will share in the recovery.

Construction—From a 35-year low of 1.1 million units in 1982, housing starts increased 60% to 1.7 million units last year as mortgage rates declined about three percentage points, 1982 to 1983. Although 1984 interest rates may rise slightly, housing starts are expected to continue increasing this year, reflecting higher income and growing acceptance of variable-rate mortgages.

Real nonresidential construction, which lags the business cycle, fell 6.1% last year. However, with the economy expanding, businesses are starting to invest in new plants. Business Economics projects real nonresidential construction to advance 3% this year.

Industrial Production—Since Grace's specialty chemical business relates to industrial production, the company's prospects are positive. The past 14 months since the end of the recession have seen one of the strongest recoveries in industrial output on record. After falling 8.2% in 1982, industrial production advanced 6.5% last year. Despite this growth, inventory-sales ratios fell to new lows at the end of 1983, suggesting stronger production gains, 9-10%, in 1984.

—By Leonard Kamsky

Mr. Kamsky, a Grace senior vice president, heads the Business Economics Group.

Figure 8-7 Be careful with art: It can sometimes get in the way of the data. The comparisons here are a little hard to make because the top points vs. mass of objects confuse the data. (Courtesy of the Bernhardt Fudyma Design Group)

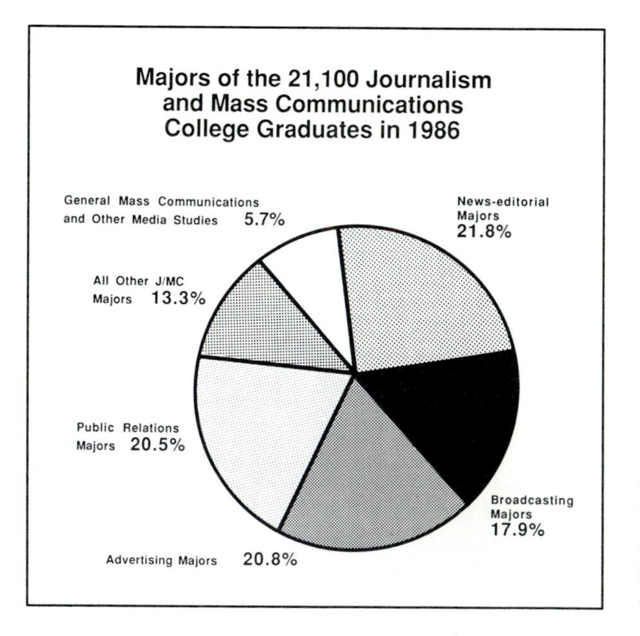

Figure 8-8 Pie charts are shown when you want to show parts that make up a whole. But pie chart pieces are difficult shapes to compare and should be used sparingly. A bar chart will do just as well, and maybe better. (Courtesy of The Dow Jones Newspaper

the chart is a simple circle divided up into eight or fewer components (any more than eight and you can't truly do much comparing of slices), and if the circle is not made into 3-D and/or slanted and/or modified into another shape, it can serve a useful purpose.

The slices of the pie can be shaded to help separate them visually. But do not do this if you have more than four components. After that, the differences are too tough to see. Just allow them to be the same color or shade, the lines being the only separators. Avoid the temptation to use color on the components too. Color, which is more quickly perceived than is shape, will almost certainly interfere with quick and clear understanding of the data.

Maps

Information with a geographic base simply must have a map. Maps need no justification or explanation. Here is a list of points to remember when using maps:

- Always use a locator or inset map that puts the area under scrutiny into geographic context.
- Always provide a distance scale and an arrow pointing north.
- Provide only enough detail for the reader to understand the information, and not a drop of ink more.
- Create a style guide for all your maps so that water, the country, state, etc., will always be a certain screen, tone, or color.
- Create a typographical style guide as well.
- Type always should be horizontal for ease of reading.

Maps easily can be created in 3-D. This is not necessarily adding clutter, as Tufte might say, because topography *is* three-dimensional. Showing a "picture" of reality as close as possible to reality will help the reader understand.

One technique is to take photographs of a globe from every conceivable angle and file those away to use as base maps for world events. A map can be traced easily from the photo.

Adding a 3-D perspective to maps of an office complex downtown, or a university campus can bring a routine map to life. This approach is well worth the effort. And remember that maps can always be filed away and used again. Time spent initially is time saved later.

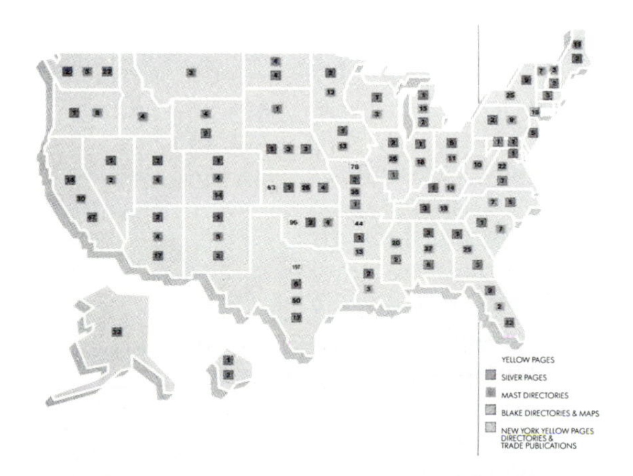

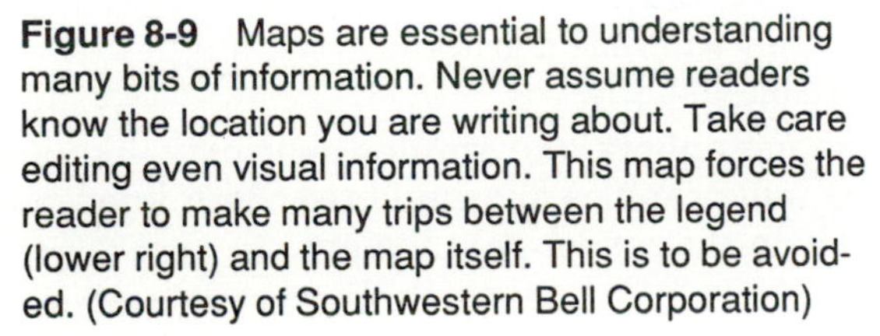

Figure 8-9 Maps are essential to understanding many bits of information. Never assume readers know the location you are writing about. Take care editing even visual information. This map forces the reader to make many trips between the legend (lower right) and the map itself. This is to be avoided. (Courtesy of Southwestern Bell Corporation)

Maps are interesting to most folks because many know so little about geography, even the geography of their own area. Never assume that all your readers know where "X" is: Your new readers never knew and many of your older readers may have forgotten. Maps can add the necessary context for an event.

In fact, I think context is the most important contribution an information graphic can add to a story (besides the visual color it adds to a page). Context is crucial to understanding certain kinds of information. Without context, some information is virtually meaningless to the reader.

As you assign, write, and edit stories, think of ways context can be added with some kind of information graphic.

Many homilies and maxims are contradictory ("Look before you leap" vs. "He who hesitates is lost"), and here come two more. Tufte says that more information is better than less information in a graphic and that they should often be based on large data matrices.

Nigel Holmes suggests keeping graphic simple. How can you keep graphics simple while shoe-horning in information?

The answer, as I hope you would expect to hear by now, is in *editing.*

Edit graphics and maps so that every bit of visual information is essential. A graphic can pack a lot of information. If all is essential, the graphic may have a lot of ink. "Crop" the graphic to its leanest form.

Tufte lists five principles of graphical excellence:

1. Above all else show the data.
2. Maximize the data/ink ratio.
3. Erase nondata ink.
4. Erase redundant data ink.
5. Revise and edit.

Don't hesitate to use numbers in some sort of graphic form, but be sure to use the appropriate format for the data. In today's visual world, information graphics, charts, and maps can also add pleasing visuals to nearly anything that can be set in type.

CHECKLIST

1. Be sure you understand how different data can best be displayed. For instance, data best shown in a pie chart cannot be shown well in a bar chart. This is in the finest tradition of integrated editing: You need to select the *best presentation* of the information, not just the most convenient, the one you like best, or the one you happen to know best.
2. Some information is simply better communicated graphically. This is especially true with comparisons.
3. In a sense, information graphics are visual metaphors, aren't they? A metaphor or simile compares two seemingly unlike things to illustrate one (though both are often illuminated). For instance, a writer might say "high as an elephant's eye," whereas a graphic artist might draw an elephant and show the comparison visually.
4. Good writers use metaphors and similes sparingly, like spices in cooking. Good editors use info graphics sparingly too. Both know the importance of the metaphor to help the reader gain insight.

5. Sometimes an information graphic can be combined with a photograph to good effect.
6. Avoid chartjunk and cuteness.
7. Information graphics, in a sense, are just visual ways to segment information into interesting and easily digested chunks. Writers and editors need to segment stories by using "true" subheads (as discussed in Chapter 6). Good reporters and editors need to go a step further by including info graphics in their segmentation strategy. Here's the information. How shall we slice it up? One long story with subheads and a map? A main story, a sidebar, a map, and an info graphic? As always, discovering the best way to present the information is the most important job of the editor. More important than simply editing copy.
8. Always use a locator map with a map. With any communication, give the reader some context. Using only a local map is rather like telling a joke's punchline without first sharing the narrative (Gads, another simile...).
9. Take some data and create both a horizontal and a vertical bar chart. Do the data appear different? Why?
10. Try some statistical manipulation. Who knows? If you are good at it, you may have a future in politics. Create a grid and a fever-line for some time-series data of your choice. Now keep the horizontal units the same and double the value of the vertical. How has the data changed? Try it the other way: Keep the vertical the same and double the horizontal. Compare all three. Can numbers be made to lie?
11. Read through some magazines and newspapers, looking for information in a story that would have been better presented in an information graphic. Create that information graphic. Then try a new layout for the page or spread using the graphic and the shorter story length.
12. Create a list of "key words" to help you recognize information that would be better in an information graphic. To get you started, consider the following: key "players," budget increases (decreases), victims (think photos here as well), chronology, list, agreement, larger, smaller, etc. Post the list above your desk and give a copy to each of your writers/reporters/photographers.

CHAPTER

9 COLOR

Human beings see in color. Therefore, as many studies have shown, readers believe color photos are more realistic than black-and-white photos, and they prefer them.

Color also is a very strong attractor of the eye. A good page layout uses color to help the reader with the content; a poor layout often allows color to get in the way of communication. Color can move a reader through a page in a coherent way or it can be used haphazardly to create confusion.

Color can add meaning to the content. Color is quickly and easily processed by the brain. It is a simple, though not an easy, tool to use, but a difficult one to use well. As with any design element, it should not be applied cosmetically or as a visually exciting bandage on an otherwise weak layout. Good color is a planned part of a good design.

COLOR DEFINED

Defining color involves both physics and psychology. Basically, color involves reflected light waves and absorbed light waves: An object we see as red absorbs all other wavelengths except those in the "red" portion of the spectrum, which are reflected and reach our eyes.

But the mind plays a part in the process as well. We expect to see certain things in certain colors: grass is green, the sky blue. Even if you showed us red grass, we might "see" it as green because of our expectation. Pure color from a physics standpoint—let's say the color red as light of a frequency of 650 millimicrons—is changed by many other factors, including the viewer's expectations and intentions in viewing.

Note: All figures in this chapter are on the color insert.

For the purposes of this discussion, however, we will accept a working definition of color as simply the property of reflected light of a particular wavelength.

The eye is capable of seeing several million colors, but we have names for very few of these colors. In fact, the basic color vocabulary is only about a dozen words. Other words for colors are (1) qualifiers [light or dark], or (2) the name of something else [gold or lemon or puce, which comes from the Latin word for flea, *pulex*—yes, a flea's belly is colored puce], or (3) the putting together of two colors [blue-green, red-orange], or (4) just pulling a name out of a hat [magenta, a dye created in 1859, was named after the Battle of Magenta in northern Italy].

Color itself conveys meaning. Red, in almost any culture, in almost any period of human development, has meant danger. It was found to be the third color word added to a culture's vocabulary (after black and white) in nearly all of 2,000 cultures studied. In the West, black is the color of mourning and funerals; in China, white is used for mourning.

So, to a certain extent, color is cultural. Eskimos, for instance, have no word for brown in their vocabulary, but they have many words for different shades of white. A number of studies have shown that reactions to certain colors—red, for instance—are similar. Red, an active color, actually excites brain waves. Thus, regardless of cultural background, someone seeing the color red has certain physiological reactions.

Red has been found in several studies to raise the respiration rate, blood pressure, the number of eye blinks per minute, and the amount of hand tremors. Blue, on the other hand, lowers all three.

Time spent before a red screen was estimated as shorter than the same amount of time spent before a blue screen in one interesting test. Thus, red, the "active" color, perhaps made the subject feel "busier," so time went faster. Blue, the "passive" color, calmed the subjects so much that time seemed to lag.

Another study found that the warm colors have a strong excitation effect and may cause people problems in concentrating on a task. Yet another test found reaction times to be 12 percent higher than normal under a red light. A green light actually slowed responses.

Red has been found to be more arousing than green, but violet has also been found to be more arousing than green. Thus, it may be that the ends of the color spectrum (red and violet) are more arousing than the center. In other words, in terms of arousal red > orange > yellow > green < blue < indigo < violet.

Several researchers have tried to attach personality attributes to color preferences, or vice versa. Faber Birren, a leading authority on color and the author of many books on the subject, said that red is preferred by active people, orange by friendly, yellow by the high-minded, and blue-green by fastidious.

Birren also noted that blue is the most-cited favorite color, with red second. In fact, the ends of the color spectrum, where apparently more arousal strength exists, seemed to be preferred in general over the middle (green).

He found that Latins tended to prefer reds and oranges, Scandinavian people liked blues and greens, and that red is better for emotionally determined actions; green is better when the goal is exact fulfillment of a task.

Many color psychologists believe that people are either warm-color dominant or cool-color dominant and that these general color preferences are tied to many other personality traits.

E.R. Jaensch says that with warm colors goes the primitive response of children, excitation, extroversion. Warm colors tend to be preferred by brunettes, he says. On the other hand, cool colors, preferred by blonds, go with more mature responses and introversion.

Other psychological associations commonly attached to certain colors:

red:	passionate, exciting, rage, fierceness, intensity.
orange:	jovial, energetic, hilarity, exuberance, forceful.
yellow:	cheerful, inspiring, celestial, high spirit, health.
green:	peaceful, refreshing, quieting, ghastliness, terror, guilt.
blue:	subduing, melancholy, sober, gloom, furtiveness, fearfulness.
purple:	mournful, dignified, mystic, loneliness, desperation.
white:	pure, clean, frank, youthful, normality.
black:	depression, funereal, negation of spirit, death.

Only younger children have been found to prefer bright, intense colors. Once a child reaches the teen years, and then throughout adulthood, the preference is for pastels. There appears to be little differences between the sexes on color preferences.

Some people even claim that certain colors of light will actually heal medical problems. In other words, depending on the illness, a specific color shone on the affected part of the body can cure the problem. Blue, for instance, is supposed to be good for a sore throat.

Faber Birren says that it may be generalized that color affects muscular tension, brain wave activity, heart rate, respiration and other functions of the autonomic nervous system, and that color certainly arouses emotional and esthetic reactions.

Many of the studies referred to, however, have been severely criticized. In fact, it appears that little is known for sure about how people react to color. Dr. Robert Chestnut, while research director of the Ted Bates Agency in New York, pointed out that color preferences change throughout a day for no other apparent reason than the passage of time.

COLOR BASICS

The primary colors we generally think of are only the primaries in pigment: red, yellow, and blue (Fig. 9–3). From these can be made the secondary colors: green, orange, purple, etc. When the primary colors in pigment are combined, a brown/black is created.

The primary colors of the physical spectrum are red, blue, and green. Light beams of these colors can produce any of the other colors of the visible spectrum. When these three colors are combined in light, white light is created. They are called "additive" primary colors because of this property.

If any one of the three primary colors is taken away from white light, a different color is produced. Red and blue only (with green removed) produce magenta; blue and green create cyan; red and green make yellow (remember, these are colors in *light,* not pigment). Because these colors are created by the removal of a primary color, they are called "subtractive" primary colors.

It is these subtractive primaries—magenta, cyan, and yellow—that are used in color printing to make color photographs. Any color can be made by a combination of these three colors (see Fig. 9–4). These "process colors" and

The Free Lance-Star
Fredericksburg, Virginia

Area news

Monday, July 6, 1987 21

Lots of hot chili and a cool river whet appetites for a fun-filled . . .

4th of July

Working on a quilt at the Heritage Festival craft fair are (from left) B. B. Merrels, Vera Cooper and Joan Hellmann. Kathy Dellinger of Woodbridge (at left) reacts to one of the spicier entries in the Chili Cookoff.

As they finish the July 4th Raft Race, the Spirit of Penola from Caroline County (on the left) takes on the Anrapo Antiques raft in a drenching water battle.

Variety of activities marks weekend event

By MICHAEL ZITZ
Staff Reporter

Galen Haynes of Fredericksburg does a little flag-waving at the City Dock.

Terry Labar of Stafford cheers on the rafters.

Figure 9-1 Color photos are becoming part of even smaller newspapers' day-to-day operations. It's hard to imagine that the Fourth of July was ever covered in only black and white. (© The Free Lance-Star, Fredericksburg, Va.)

Figure 9-2 With magazines, color has long been a necessity. It was what separated them from newspapers. Here, a color illustration fills the cover of *Enterprise* magazine. (Courtesy of Southwestern Bell Corporation)

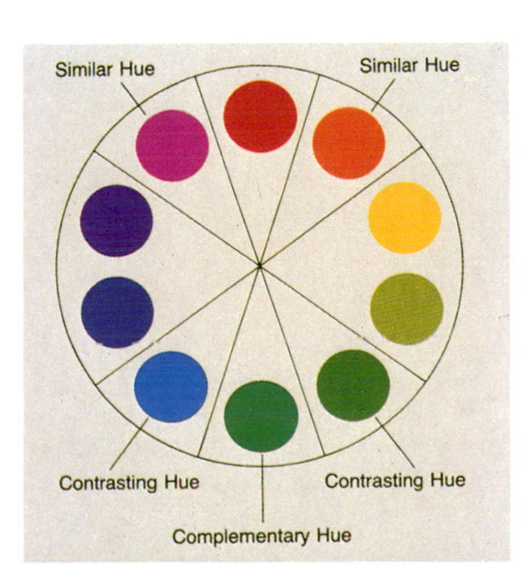

Figure 9-3 This color wheel shows the primary and secondary colors. (From *Color Harmony: A Guide to Creative Color Combinations.* Courtesy of Rockport Publishers)

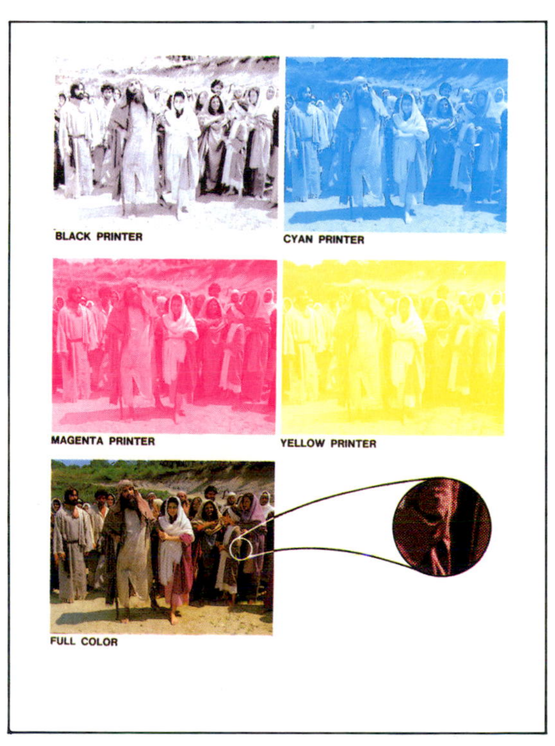

Figure 9-4 The colors are separated into four (or sometimes more) versions of the photograph to be printed in the four-color inks. The circle in the lower right shows the four-color dots that merge into one when viewed at actual size. (Courtesy of The Virginian-Pilot, Norfolk, Va.)

USA TODAY

Sports

SPORTSLINE

Heat will win next game — someday

Bears won't have to leave den

Blind-sided in Buffalo

Chicago tops in NFC; Buffalo has AFC edge

WEEKEND ON CAMPUS

TUESDAY

Oilers' rival could turn into friend

Crenshaw gives USA golf victory

COVER STORY

Fans in funk: It's Monday mourning

Florida team can win it all by winning one

Inside SPORTS

USA SNAPSHOTS

How Professional Bowlers Association prize money has grown in the '80s

Figure 9-5 *USA Today* moved newspapers into the color era of the 1980s. (Copyright 1988, USA TODAY. Reprinted with permission. USA TODAY and its associated graphics are federally registered trademarks of Gannett Co., Inc. Used by permission. All rights reserved.)

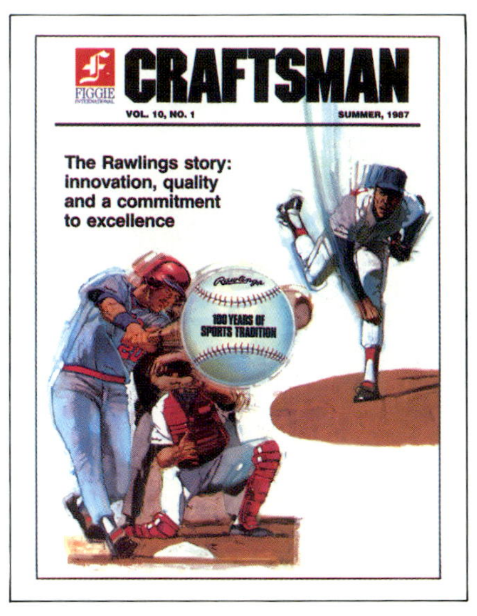

FIGGIE INTERNATIONAL

CRAFTSMAN

VOL. 10, NO. 1 SUMMER, 1987

The Rawlings story: innovation, quality and a commitment to excellence

Figure 9-6 FIGGIE International uses red as its corporate color. It appears on all its printed communication. (Courtesy of FIGGIE International, Inc.)

FOOD

Smart shopping

EVERYTHING IS JUST

PEACHY

WITH THIS FRUIT

Turkey great in microwave, but store leftovers properly

NUTRITION BRIEFS

Figure 9-7 The peach color from the photo was picked up to be used in the color bars on this spread. The similar colors help define the block in which the story appears. (Courtesy of the Salinas Californian, Salinas, Calif.)

Weekend Californian

Experts: Sewer crisis threatens economy

AIDS: A killer aimed at us all

Syria sends troops into West Beirut

THE AIDS CRISIS

AIDS victim faces 'death sentence'

Priest finds affinity with city landmark in 25-year tenure

INSIDE TODAY'S CALIFORNIAN

Figure 9-8 The gray screen surrounding the color photo helps the light colors and white pop out of the photo. Using gray or a complementary color around a color photo can enhance it if used carefully. (Courtesy of the Salinas Californian, Salinas, Calif.)

Business perspectives for managers of GRACE — *May/June 1983*

SUNBELT KEEPS SMILING ON CHEMICALS, CONSUMER LINES

The Sunbelt* siren, still serenading business, is expected to radiate its allure through the year 2000, at least.

The Census Bureau predicts Sunbelt population will bump up 1.1% a year, 1980-2000, because of natural increase and in-migration. This figure is ahead of the projected U.S. population increase, .8%, but tails the Sunbelt's brisker pace of 1.9% a year, 1970-1980. That decade saw the nation grow 1.1% a year. About 48% of Americans live in the Sunbelt, earning 46% of the total U.S. personal income. But the income gap is narrowing.

Stealing some of the Sunbelt's steam, though, are tumbling birth rates, recession, slower migration from the Snowbelt, declining energy sales—and taxes—and infrastructure headaches such as water shortages and traffic jams. Not all subregions will prosper either. The Kosciusko, Mississippis, and the Baxley, Georgias, haven't grown in years. And not all businesses will fit.

Nevertheless, the bloom is still on the yellow rose of Texas and other Sunbelt states.

As J. Peter Grace has said, "Texas is one of the most important states in terms of our business." In 1982 Texas accounted for almost half a billion dollars in sales from Grace's natural resources, chemicals, agricultural chemicals and consumer lines.

Industrial Chemicals Group chose Texas for the glycine, Daxad* dispersants and nitroparaffins plants of Organic Chemicals. (Forty-three percent of ICG's 90 U.S. plants are in the Sunbelt.) Texas has environmental laws "based on science," asserts Vance M. Bakeman, ICG's vice president, environmental affairs and engineering.

Within Texas, ICG picked Deer Park near Houston for the plants. The area offers labor experienced in petrochemicals, and a climate favoring the work-style ICG

(Cont. on p. 2)

*Sunbelt, as defined here, covers 22 states and Washington, D.C., stretching from Delaware to Florida and west to California.

Figure 9-9 Spot color can be used effectively, if full-color photos cannot be. In the examples above, one color is used in the heavy rule at the top of the front and two inside pages to connect the pages in the readers' minds. (Courtesy of Bernhardt Fudyma Design Group.)

...Sunbelt
(Cont. from p. 1)

wanted: flexibility, automation and high technology. Deer Park also has abundant energy and feedstocks. ICG prefers Deer Park's workers "to nonskilled people who would need training from ground zero," Mr. Bakeman says.

About 40 employees run the glycine and Daxad facilities, now on-stream. They are all salaried. And instead of laboring at fixed tasks, they rotate from shipping to laboratory to operations.

"Our people identify with the whole concept," Mr. Bakeman says. "They are participants in the business and pinch-hit for one another. We will gain in productivity and the ability to change as technology changes."

Others subscribe to the ICG approach. Shervin Freed, vice president, A. T. Kearney, Inc., a management consultant, reports a leading manufacturer stresses flexibility at its southern plant. Mr. Freed says, "One of their managers told me: 'We make the best products, but in six months we may want to make them differently. We need the freedom to switch.'"

Many apparently agree. According to the U.S. Bureau of Labor Statistics, Texas is fifth in U.S. manufacturing jobs. Margaret R. Scripsema, senior consultant, Alexander Grant & Company, reports Texas is also runner-up for "ideal manufacturing climate" in a study by her public accounting firm. (Florida is first.) Adds Frank J. Magrino, vice president, Texas Commerce Bank: "Our state puts strict limits on welfare and unemployment benefits. We don't support idleness; people who stay have a positive work attitude."

Retail Follows the Sun

Two-thirds of Grace's 370 home centers are buckled into the Sunbelt with 68 Handy Dans and Cashways in Texas alone. Robinson Jewelers, Bermans and Sheplers are also there. The company's sun-kissed stores tap the third most populous state with the third largest personal income.

For the 21 Handy Dans in metro Houston, getting in early helped. "Since many people were as new in town as our stores," reports Harry E. Pierson, Retail Group's senior vice president, real estate, "they had no established store loyalties."

Retail searches for growing metro areas, "not small, mañana towns," Mr. Pierson explains. "In Houston and other Sunbelt markets, our home centers are in a beautiful position to capitalize on new housing. The Sunbelt had 72.4% of U.S. single-family building permits in 1982, with Florida, Texas and California in the forefront. And it has builders who can put up smaller homes that are still attractive."

The Restaurant Group also likes the region. Out of 608 Grace units nationwide, 78% call Sunbelt home. Why? "The first companies we acquired—Far West and El Torito, plus jojos later—were already there," explains Anwar Soliman, a Grace executive vice president and head of the Restaurant Group. "Development has emphasized the Sunbelt for these companies and Del Taco. People there are out all year; northerners hole up in their homes in cold weather."

Further west, 32 Angels and Orchard Supply home centers prosper in California, "one of the best do-it-yourself markets," Mr. Pierson avers. "California spends more on home modernization than any other state."

California has the most people, 25 million or 11% of the U.S. total. About 95% live just where Mr. Pierson likes them to live: in metro areas. "With its emphasis on health and the outdoors, California will also be a natural one day for Herman's," Mr. Pierson believes. "And I would urge Robinson Jewelers to consider it because of the young population and good income."

The Restaurant Group has a table-thumping 195 units in California "where eating out is part of the life-style," according to W. Robert Schmidt, the group's vice president, strategic planning and market research.

However, California's soaring home prices could discourage future out-of-staters from moving to the "golden land," and high wages could drive California businesses to add plants in other states, warns Gregory A. Jackson, associate professor at Harvard and coauthor, *Regional Diversity: Growth in the United States, 1980-1990*.

"In Silicon Valley," Kearney's Mr. Freed adds, "an employee can walk across the street and get $10,000 more."

Across the border, metropolitan Phoenix with 11 Angels stores "has grown with the momentum of fire," Mr. Pierson says. The population, now at 1.6 million, is expected to ratchet up 26%, 1980-1990. Phoenix is also among the top 25 metro areas in personal income growth.

"Outside Phoenix's core, corners at intersections of wide streets offer generous sites for stores," Mr. Pierson adds. "Lots of vacant land. You don't get that in Philadelphia or Hackensack."

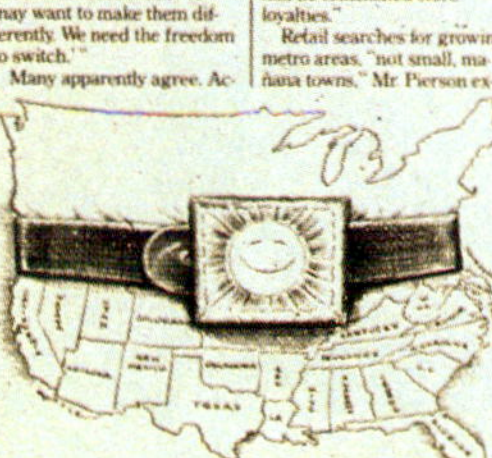

Restaurants in Arizona

The Restaurant Group enjoys the Arizona advantage, too. It operates a total 23 units of Far West Services, Gilbert/Robinson and El Torito-La Fiesta in metro Phoenix and Tucson.

Over in Louisiana, Retail is blitzing the New Orleans market with five House Works units, Grace's latest home center venture. House Works has also broken into Florida with a Sarasota unit, and more are on the way.

Thomas J. Thornton, vice president, finance, Home Centers Division, says Florida basks in the Sunbelt's "good weather—which lets people fix up their homes year-round—and has the third fastest-growing population and excellent store sites." Mr. Pierson is also surveying Florida for Robinson Jewelers.

The Restaurant Group has 14 units in Miami, West Palm Beach, Tampa, Orlando and Jacksonville. All are rooted in that state's fastest-growing counties.

"Florida is in the path of trade with Latin America—good for local banks, export/import companies and satellite stores and restaurants," according to Reynolds Farley, research scientist at the Population Studies Center, University of Michigan.

However, John Pitkin, research associate at the Harvard-Massachusetts Institute of Technology Joint Center for Urban Studies, believes "that state's population growth rate may have peaked."

Stephen R. Adams, manager of facilities location studies for The Austin Company, an engineering construction firm, points out that "Florida has many opportunities for regional consumer activities, but faces limitations for certain national consumer businesses. This is because the state is remote from the U.S. population centroid and because of the heavy concentration of economic infrastructure in the North."

Professor Jackson speculates that other businesses, including "footloose" types, may opt instead for the South Central—Alabama, Georgia and Mississippi—with its available labor, lower wages and high birth rates. "South Central has been a Singapore for assembly plants needing low skills," he says. "Now Georgians ask, 'How can we get into high-tech research and be more like Boston?'"

Gene D. Sullivan, research officer, Federal Reserve Bank of Atlanta, says certain information industries are "growing fast" in South Central, particularly in Atlanta and Huntsville. He contends, though, that South Central's birth rates will decline as incomes rise.

Atlanta is headquarters for Del Taco. Among past problems, Mr. Soliman recounts, was that Mexican cooking—popular in California where Del Taco originated—was alien to Atlantans five years ago. "Since then," he says, "these customers have developed a taste for Del Taco's food. We now hold a position in Georgia, and because we were here first, we have the edge."

T. J. Applebee's, Grace's new pub concept, is based in Atlanta, too. "We look to expand in the Southeast by opening units and by franchising," Mr. Soliman reports.

From Retail's vantage, "you don't get the store sales in lower income South Central, or even in the Carolinas, that you get in Houston, Dallas and San Antonio," Mr. Pierson says. Even the research triangle—that university/high tech complex linking Raleigh, Durham and Chapel Hill—doesn't do it for retailers, he declares. The area has economic promise, but a few dozen miles away are old tobacco warehouses and high unemployment.

Growth to Peak

Mr. Farley puts a cap on Sunbelt growth sometime in the early 21st century; U.S. population is expected to stabilize at 308.9 million by the year 2050.

But no matter what, five percent of Americans will keep moving long distances every year, says Dr. Peter A. Morrison, director, Population Research Center, The Rand Corporation. The United States, Canada and Australia have the highest moving rates of any Western industrial nation.

In explanation, Dr. Morrison points out that the three were populated mainly by immigrants. Continuing in that mode, U.S. easterners rolled West in the 1800s. In the 1940s southern blacks migrated North. Americans left small towns in the 1950s to change it in big cities. In the 1960s, city people departed for the suburbs. And starting in the 1970s, northerners—mainly young and well educated—headed South and West for "salary plus scenery," Dr. Morrison says. As Gene D. Steiker, coordinator for regional economics, Grace's Business Economics, puts it, "A palm tree in your front yard isn't the worst thing."

The next hot spot? Dr. Morrison is watching high-tech spill across Massachusetts' borders into northern New England. "New Hampshire is going from the past directly into the future," he says. "It never had a present." ■

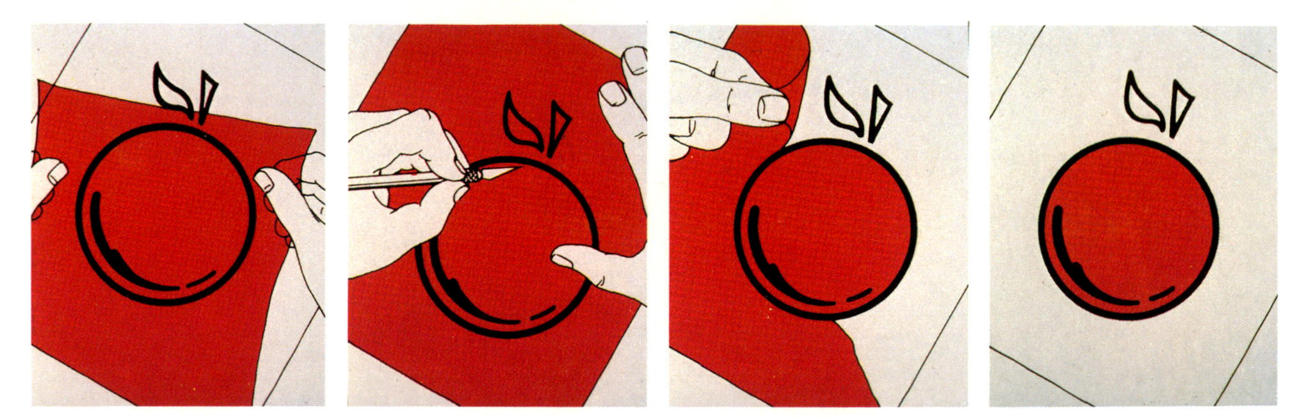

Figure 9-10 Spot color is usually added by cutting out film in the shape of the object to be colored. By carefully lining up the colored part from one part of the printing press with the black inked elements from another part, the finished product looks correct. In the above sequence, the film is laid over the object, the outline is cut with a razor blade knife, the noncolored area is carefully pulled away, and only that area to be colored is still covered with the film. (Courtesy of The Associated Press)

More hugs than medals There are no losers at the International Special Olympics Page 1F

THE TAMPA TRIBUNE

3 area men on doomed gulf copter

Weinberger says Reagan was misled

Pristine beauty

Elderly may consolidate growing political clout

Older Americans' voting strength

Tornadoes in Canada claim 32

THE STATE OF RETIREMENT

Men on shrimp boat deny mutiny charge

Inside

Cancer removed 4A

Suicide rate highest in Tampa Bay area

RETURN TO VIETNAM

Coming Sunday

Figure 9-11 The information graphic in the middle of the page was created by having a different film overlay for each color. On the right, the four components are (from upper left) the black type and outlines, the red bars, the gray screen background, and the blue behind the stars. (Courtesy of The Tampa Tribune)

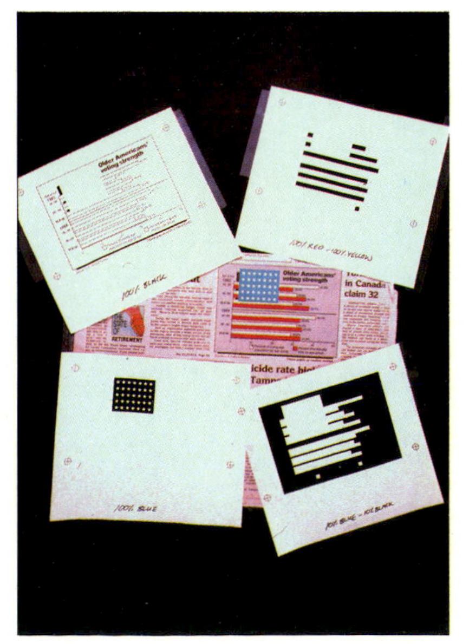

usually black are used to create color photographs in newspapers and magazines. In some of the more expensive magazines, more colors are used.

The terms we use to describe color are hue, value, and intensity.

Hue refers to the property of color we commonly call an object: red, blue, and so on.

Value or *brightness* refers to the relative lightness or darkness of a color, or how the color would be seen on a gray scale. *Shades* (in printing, usually black dots over a pure color) and *tints* (in printing, usually screened color so the white paper shows through and mixes visually with the color ink) are more common terms.

Intensity refers to the purity of a color. A hue with high intensity has little or none of its complement mixed in; for example, an intense red would have little or no green.

COLOR PRINTING

Putting color ink on paper, especially if that color is part of a color photograph, is an exacting process. Basically, color is used two different ways in print: as *flat* or *spot* color and as *process* or *full* color.

Flat color refers to a single color ink, usually used at 100 percent. When colors are combined, either at 100 percent or screened, they are often referred to as *mechanical color.*

Many different flat colors are available through ink manufacturers, often with a specified formula. The Pantone Matching System®[1] uses a book with removable color swatches. If you want a brick red, for instance, you might select Pantone No. 194. You could rip out a small "chip" of the color and attach it to the job with your request. That way you are assured that you will get the exact color you requested.

The process colors of cyan, magenta, and yellow, because they are transparent, can create any color of the rainbow. These colors are used in color printing of photographs, but they also can be used to create spot colors. Flat colors from specific companies, however, cannot be exactly reproduced with process colors.

COLOR IN DESIGN

As mentioned earlier, color is one of many tools that can be used to enhance communication or confuse it. The main purpose of color in design is to draw attention to a design element. Tests have shown that readers will generally look at all the color elements on a page before moving on to reading a story. In this way color is a "people mover," and is an important editing and design tool.

Too much color can create a hyperactive page. Learning how to use color well is one of the more difficult tasks facing the visually literate editor.

Unfortunately, little research has been done outside of advertising studies. So although we know a little about how people react to advertising in color vs. black and white, we don't really know how people approach editorial copy with color on it or around it.

One study that dealt with newspaper spot color was done on the background color on a tabloid insert aimed at architects. Red had a much higher attraction rating than any other color. The other colors tested—yellow, brown, red, and green—were rated nearly the same. Bright yellow scored better than muted

[1]PANTONE is a registered trademark of Pantone, Inc.

yellow, but muted green was better than bright green. No difference was found in the reds and blues.

In Ruth Clark's study about newspapers, *Relating to Readers in the '80s,* readers were asked to respond to the following statement: "I wish newspapers would use more color and color pictures." Somewhat surprisingly, only 46 percent agreed, although the figures were higher for the 18-to-24 age group (52 percent), minorities (52 percent), and nonreaders (61 percent). It is surprising because most newspapers spent the early part of the 1980s splashing themselves with both process and spot color.

A 1985 International Newspaper Advertising and Marketing Executive Association (INAME) survey found that newspaper readers see run of the press (ROP) color as "progressive." The study also learned that readers found color photos more realistic than black-and-white photos, that readers dislike poor color reproduction, and that the use of color may boost readership.

In ads, color *generally* pulls more reader attention. Also, the more color surrounding an element, the less attractive power that element has. Among other results:

- On 9 of 11 color vs. black-and-white ad pairs, the color version was remembered better. Color ads with lots of color surrounding them were weaker against black-and-white ads.
- Color is more important in gaining attention than is illustration.
- In a study of color and store design, red tended to attract the most attention, but its active nature made people more tense than did the other colors.
- In a Newspaper Advertising Bureau study, body type in a color ad was read by 80 percent of subjects; in a black-and-white ad, only 50 percent.
- In another test—this one testing *recall,* not attention—color was recalled more frequently, but black-and-white beat color in depth of recall.
- Color scored well in a recognition test for ads, but black-and-white ads did better in an aided recall test.
- In a study of a long-term ad campaign, the content of black-and-white ads were remembered better than was color ad content.
- Two-color ads increase readership by 20 percent, but they have no advantage over black-and-white ads in attention-getting power.

It appears, then, that color is better for the fast grab, for the quick appeal, but that black and white is better for a response needing more in-depth thinking. The good page designer will keep these ideas in mind when planning color.

USING COLOR

The first color to master is color in black and white: An informed use of typography can create contrast on the page, as covered in the previous chapters. Contrast creates visual interest, much as color does, and that is why we can talk of "color" on a page when none is available.

The important considerations are the size and boldness of the type, the amount of white space, the use of border tape, and the use of gray screens.

Body type is the basic mode of communication, but it is the least interesting visually to the reader. No matter how intriguing a story may be, presenting it only in body type will cost you readership.

To create visual interest, at least a few visual stopping-off points must stand out against the sea of gray. For instance, subheads a few points larger than the body type, and perhaps even in the headline face, are good visual magnets, as well as information organizers. Subheads may also use border tape above and/or below for additional contrast. Depending on the personality of the publication, gray screens can add a special touch.

In a sea of gray, often all you need for visual excitement is a little contrast in black and white.

Contrast in color is useful as well. Some colors have different hues, but the same value. Thus, their appearance on the page is flat, lacking visual contrast (despite the difference in hue). Johannes Itten lists seven kinds of contrast in his book *The Art of Color:*

1 Contrast of hue, of pure color contrast. A vivid contrast, which can be heightened further by black and white.
2. Light-dark. Tonal or value. An important and often misused contrast.
3. Cold-warm. This is greatest when red-oranges and blue-greens are juxtaposed. However, any color can appear "warm" or "cool" compared to a cooler or warmer color next to it.
4. Complementary color, or colors opposite on the color wheel.
5. Simultaneous contrast. The eye simultaneously produces a color's complementary if it is not actually present. For instance, a red next to a gray block will induce a greenish contrast (the complementary) to the block of gray.
6. A contrast of saturation opposes brilliant and dull (achieved by adding black or white or both or the color's complementary).
7. Opposition of color areas of different size.

Using process color is nearly always a good idea—if you can afford it. Color separations alone are expensive, and then you have to add in more printing negatives and plates, ink, labor, and paper waste.

Color photographs are not only more realistic but they say "class." If your publication needs or wants to say that, or if you merely want to separate yourself from your competitors, then process color may be the way to do that.

Using spot color is trickier. The general approach by beginners is to splash the one spot color available everywhere possible. Even halftones are sometimes published in blues or, worse, pinks.

Care should be taken with spot color because it can literally ruin an otherwise good layout. One of the purposes of a layout is to connect elements that belong together or to separate those that do not.

The eye tends to connect elements of the same color. In fact, *New Woman* magazine used this principle by taking a dominant color from a four-color ad on one page and using it as an editorial spot color on a facing page. The harmonized colors drew the reader from the ad to the content and back again. *Enterprise* magazine uses this principle on editorial content alone.

So using the one spot color available on several disparate elements would disrupt the effect of a good layout: The layout might be saying "different," while the color would be saying "similar."

The other extreme is to create a Hawaiian shirt effect on the page with an entire rainbow of spot colors. To a certain extent, *USA Today,* and many of its less capable imitators, uses color this way. Blues, pinks, purples, greens, reds and yellows fill the page (Fig. 9–5). *USA Today* does this as a marketing concept to separate it from other newspapers. The editors know what they are doing with all that color. You may not, so be careful.

Using *too much* color may even be worse than overusing just one. Although no reader would make incorrect connections between a purple and a blue, the page simply becomes too busy. Also, one advertising study found that the use of more than one spot color often caused subjects to rate the ad as "cheap."

How should spot color be used properly?

First, when the urge to use spot color hits, lie down for 15 minutes. Try to solve the layout without color. If the urge remains, then refer to the following suggestions:

1. Remember to use the color wheel to help you pick colors. "Analogous" color pairs are next to each other on the color wheel, or nearly so. "Triad" color combinations, using an equilateral triangle to point to the three colors, gives you three you can use together. "Complementary" colors are opposite on the wheel, and "split-complementary" colors are on either side of the color opposite. Several books that show you color combinations that work are available.

2. *Complementary colors and value.* Remember that opposite colors are often at the same value level and therefore lack the necessary contrast for effective color use. This lack of attention to the *values* of color is the most frequent cause of bad color. If nothing else, be sure you understand the concept of a color's value.

3. *Use as a corporate identifier.* IBM is big blue; Coke is red. By creating a logo or nameplate in color, you have added information that will help the reader identify your publication from a host of others (Fig. 9–6).

4. *Use as a content connector, or as a "people mover."* This can be done two ways: (a) as a background for an entire spread, thus helping your layout tie everything in a neat package; and (b) by coloring similar items; for example, news nugget boxes in an information graphic or top and bottom tapes on a spread, to help the reader see the layout as a whole, not a bunch of parts (Fig. 9–7).

5. *Color "things," not background.* Use the color on elements on the page: certain type, tape, illustrations and graphics, or maps. Screening the background of a type box is a weak use of color.

6. *Tint blocks.* Although it is a weak use, coloring the background of type is one way to use color. Care should be taken to assure the type can still be read through the tint. Use no more than a 10 percent screen, and possibly a 5 percent screen to assure readability. This is best used when there is no other art for a particular page.

7. *Use as a background for color photographs.* Sometimes a complementary color can be used to help a photograph pop out from a page. Again, the working principle is *contrast.* Selecting the dominant color from the photograph is a weak choice because of the lack of contrast. A light gray is a good choice: The colors look brighter compared to the gray. White is rarely a wrong choice as well.

8. *If you must use color display type, don't screen it.* If you wish to use cyan or magenta, use 10 percent black over the top of 100 percent color to tone down the color. *USA Today* uses a 10 percent black over the 100 percent cyan on its nameplate.

Color is an important design tool. It should not be used just because "it's available," or just because the boss wants color. Its use has to be informed, or it is counterproductive. If it does not help communication, then it must hurt it. Don't use it.

CHECKLIST

1. Remember that color must be used functionally, that it must assist in the understanding of content.
2. Color has communicative value.
3. In a design, color is more easily processed than shape. Thus, people tend to look at similar colors before they look at similar shapes (driven by visual gestalt as they are). Don't use the same color on unrelated elements.
4. Find a color page or spread from a magazine or newspaper ad and "edit" the color from it. In other words, make a photocopy to get it in black and white. Trace/redraw dark photos or illustrations. How does it look without the color? What is lost? What (if anything) is gained? Can you make the design workable by using type contrast and white space, those tools of "color in B&W"?
5. Don't make color choices based on a generic color sampler. You need to know how *your* press handles color on *your* paper stock. The best bet is always to do a test sheet with a wide variety of color choices so you know that what you ordered will be what you wanted to get.
6. Create a color stylebook for a (or your) publication. How should color be used? How much is too much on a page? What colors should be used and what avoided? With the help of a color expert, pick several colors or even color combinations that you should use on a regular basis.
7. Find examples of uses of color (not content, not type, not anything else but color use) that look classy and some that look "cheap." What is the difference? Create a list of publications that use color well and those that use color poorly. Post examples of *both* where you can see them. Let the differences between the two soak subliminally into your brain.
8. Take *USA Today*'s color scheme and, using colored pencils or pens, hand-color a *New York Times* front page to look like the Gannett paper. How important is color to a publication's personality? Color two disparate elements on the page the same color. Does your eye want them to be related?

CHAPTER

10 TYPESETTING AND PRINTING

Print communicators need to understand, at least in basic terms, how their work is processed after the creating of it is complete. The final goal is always to get the best possible message in the best possible form. The methods used to get the ink on paper may affect how the message will be created.

TYPESETTING

Most typesetting today is phototypesetting, or the setting of type on photosensitive paper. The other major methods of setting type are mostly of historical importance. They do not need to be covered here.

Most modern typesetters are digital or laser. This means that the characters are created dot-by-dot or line-by-line inside the computer and then projected onto a screen for viewing and/or to the photosensitive paper.

Earlier generation typesetters, often called "photo-optic" systems, used film strips—much like negatives in photography—and a series of lenses, often mounted on a circular plate that would rotate the selected lens into the proper position, to expose the letters onto the paper.

With digital typesetting, you have much more flexibility in choosing point sizes, line spacing figures, and so on, than you could have with a photo-optic system. With the latter, you were limited in point sizes, for instance, to only those lenses that could be fit onto a wheel inside the typesetter.

This could mean that you had only 6 to 72 points in 6-point increments. But with digital typesetting, you can get from 4 to 127 points of type in half-point increments. Not only that, but the type can be manipulated by the computer in any number of ways: obliqued, condensed, expanded, etc.

With this much flexibility (literally!) with type, designers can be much freer to select and then adjust appropriate type for a given job. Another benefit is that digital typesetters can also set type very quickly. Some systems are capable of up to 10,000 lines per minute.

WHAT TO TELL A PRINTER

When you have type set at a commercial printer, make sure you specify the following:

- point size of the type
- line measure, or width, you want the type to be
- line spacing
- family name, including variation (oblique, bold, condensed, etc.)
- additional kerning, if desired
- any special effects, such as wraps or initial letters

FRONT-END SYSTEMS

With the increase in power and decrease in cost of personal computers (PC), they are being used more and more as word processing/typesetting terminals by newspapers as well as corporate publications. Most large newspapers, however, still use front-end systems created specifically for that use.

A typical newspaper front-end system and a smaller, PC-based system perform many of the same functions. The differences are largely in speed and in the number of programmed functions addressable by special keys on the keyboard.

Any system consists basically of a keyboard, for direct input of stories; some software, for the manipulating of the stories; a memory unit, for storing the stories prior to editing or for later issues; and a phototypesetter, which takes the specially coded stories and sets them into galleys of type.

Very advanced systems have the ability to compose a page entirely inside the computer. Instead of pasting down galley after galley of type in columns, an entire page is sent through the phototypesetter, with headlines, cutlines, and body type properly placed on the page. This is called *pagination.*

Generally, only larger front-end systems have the capability to do pagination. However, the Apple Macintosh® and the IBM® PC have several software packages available that allow them to be used as pagination terminals.

PRINTING

Modern communicators have a variety of printing methods to choose from: from relief or letterpress, the oldest form of printing, to xerography and laser printing. The trick is not necessarily to understand the methods as well as your printer, but to know enough about the processes to work with your printer to choose the best method.

The major methods are relief, intaglio (or gravure), lithography, xerography, thermography, flexography, and laser printing.

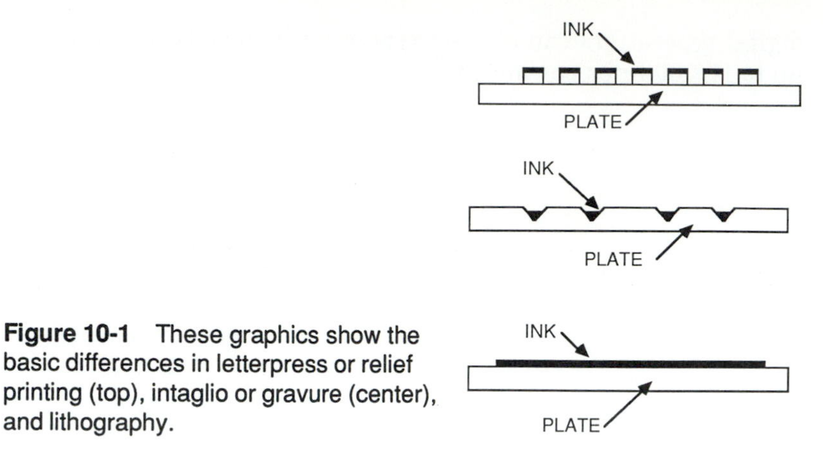

Figure 10-1 These graphics show the basic differences in letterpress or relief printing (top), intaglio or gravure (center), and lithography.

Relief. With relief printing, the image to be printed lies above the rest of the printing plate. The raised surface is inked and pressed directly against the paper. Thus, it is often called *letterpress* printing (Fig. 10–1).

Because pressure must be exerted to transfer the image, the image is often not as sharp: Some ink is blotted out around the edges. But still, letterpress printing can be of very high and consistent quality. Getting proofs from a letterpress job is relatively easy and cheap. Preparing the press and plates—called "makeready"—is long and involved.

Intaglio. Intaglio printing, called gravure or rotogravure today, uses the exact opposite technique from letterpress: The image to be printed lies *below* the level of the rest of the plate. Pressing paper against the plate causes the ink to be lifted from the depressions.

With gravure, *everything* on your page is screened, even type. Small type and type with thin serifs should be avoided when printing with gravure. But for halftones it is unsurpassed by any other printing method. Good gravure halftones look nearly like continuous-tone photos. Proofing is expensive, and gravure is economical only if the press run is very large.

Lithography. The newest of the three major printing methods, lithography, was invented about 1796 by Aloys Senefelder, a German. Lithography is a planographic printing method in that the image is neither raised nor lowered from the rest of the plate.

Lithography uses the theory that oil and water do not mix. The image area is treated to hold a grease-based ink while the nonimage area is washed free of ink during the printing process. Thus, only the image area has ink on it when the paper is pressed against the plate. This is called *direct lithography.*

The most popular form of lithography is called "offset" because the inked image is first transferred to another (blanket) roller and then to the paper. The plate is "set off" from the paper in this method. Most newspapers today use offset, as do most of the instant printers around the country (Fig. 10–2).

With lithography, the plates are inexpensive and the makeready is fairly short and simple. But the press run needs a lot of attention throughout to keep quality consistent.

Xerography. This printing method, which uses electrically charged particles, was named after the first company to develop a marketable copying machine. The printing quality of xerography has improved greatly in recent

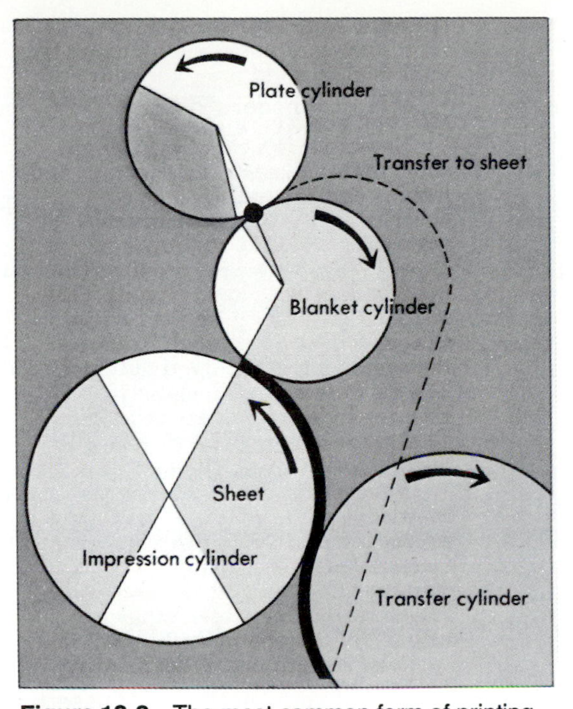

Figure 10-2 The most common form of printing for publications today is offset, a form of lithography in which the printing plate is "off set" from the paper. The image is transferred from printing plate to paper via a blanket cylinder. (Courtesy of The St. Petersburg Times)

years. For certain jobs with a short shelf-life and perhaps a deadline yesterday, xerography can provide a quick and relatively inexpensive answer.

Thermography. Really an after-printing process, thermography creates raised letters and images. This is achieved by using a slow-drying ink. Immediately after printing, the job is dusted with a powder and then vacuumed. The powder sticks to the inked areas. Then the job is passed under a heater, which causes the ink and the powder to fuse into a raised image, much like an engraving. It is used most often for business cards and letterheads.

Flexography. This process, basically relief printing with a soft, rubber-like plate, is being studied carefully by newspapers. In fact, some newspapers have even gone to "flexo" instead of offset. Flexography uses a light ink that dries quickly and smudges less, especially on newsprint, the bane of newspaper readers. Right now it is used mainly for product packaging.

Laser Printing. Laser printing is similar to xerography. Using a laser, an image is created on a photosensitive drum. That image is transferred to paper using a dry toner and heat. There is little difference between a laser copier and a laser printer. In fact, many laser printers can also be used as a copier. Also, for short runs, a laser printer can create multiple copies of a page.

The main goal of the professional communicator is to get information into print in a pleasurable and accessible package. However, this must be done under deadline pressure, and more importantly, under budget constraints.

Knowing which printing method gives you the best combination of quality for your particular job, speed, and cost control is information worth having.

CHECKLIST

1. Type has become very flexible with modern digital phototypesetters. This does not mean, however, that some of the "old" principles of effective typography should be discarded.
2. Work with your printer to learn how to communicate more effectively using the type that you now use.
3. Personal computers are becoming very important in the typesetting industry. In fact, in 1986, Apple Computers surpassed Compugraphic as the major producer of type-producing equipment in the country. You would do well to learn how to use a microcomputer immediately, if you have not already done so.
4. The three major forms of printing are letterpress, gravure, and lithography.
5. Gather samples of all the major printing methods. Then, using the information in this chapter, but gathering some more, create a list of the advantages and disadvantages of each printing method. You might want to interview local printers for this. Make a display of all the samples and of the lists for your easy reference.
6. How does your specific printing method fit into your publication design plan? How should it?
7. Have you checked recently to see if your method of typesetting and printing is the cheapest/fastest/whatever for what you want? I have known people who have cut their publishing bill in half by switching to PC typesetting and laser printing instead of standard typesetting and printing. Make a comparison of what it costs to get a story typeset by a local typesetter and by a local microcomputer/laser printing shop. Often you can rent time on a PC and laser printer at a local quick-copy shop.

CHAPTER

11

PASTEUP AND PRODUCTION

No matter how good your design, if it is not pasted up properly you haven't gotten the most from your effort. Pagination systems, either mainframe or microcomputer, have returned publications to the precision of the hot type days. But if you don't use a pagination system, the pressure is on you or your production staff to carry out the design plan, to deliver it to the reader.

Pasteup takes place after all the pieces of the page—stories, photos, art and headlines, and such—have been gathered. The pasteup process is one of following the design plan and layout approach to the half pica: There is no room for lack of precision.

Newspaper communicators almost never do their own pasteup. The same is true for magazine communicators. But many small publications are pasted up by the same people who write the stories and take the pictures. Understanding how pasteup is done—even if you are never going to do it yourself—is helpful information for the designer.

The secrets to good pasteup are:

- neatness
- precision
- planning and *following* the plan

Because most publications today are printed by offset lithography, neatness is extremely important. In a sense, a "picture" of the pasteup is taken. Thus, smudges, dirt, thumbprints, folded-back type galleys and such show up just as clearly as does your type.

Precision is important as well. If, in your design, you have worked out set-spacing guidelines that call for exact placement of elements, then those guidelines must be followed exactly. The best way to gain precision in pasteup is to have a plan.

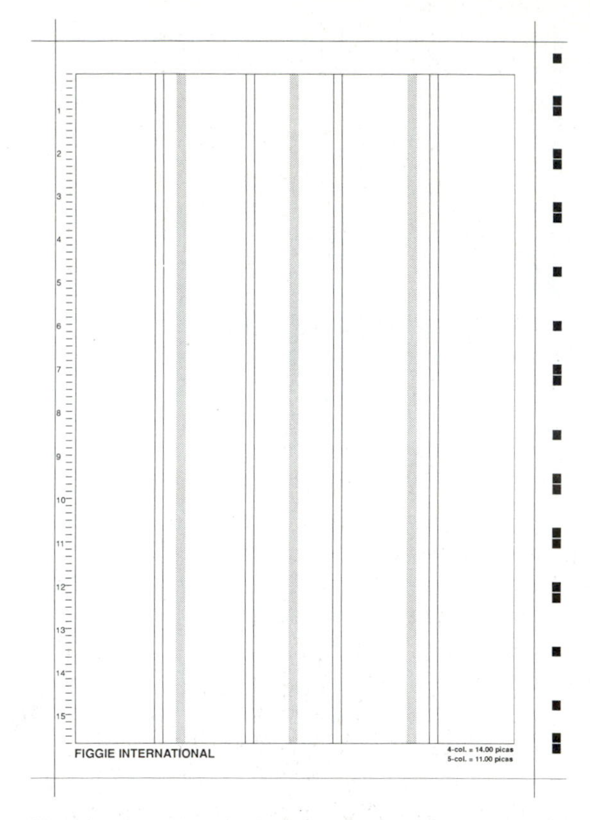

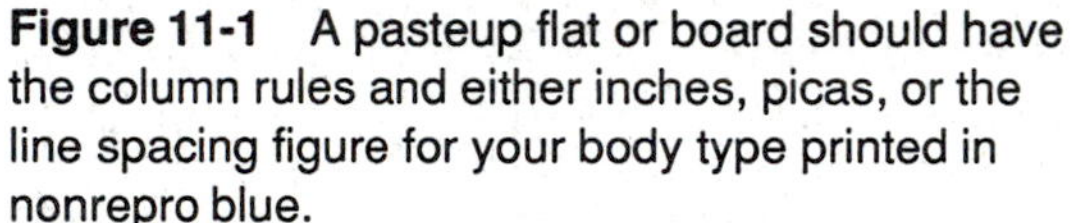

Figure 11-1 A pasteup flat or board should have the column rules and either inches, picas, or the line spacing figure for your body type printed in nonrepro blue.

Part of your overall design plan should include the setting up of a page format/grid plan (discussed in Chapter 2). Part of the page grid plan should include spacing guidelines. A page grid for pasteup, often called a *flat,* is a grid of blue lines (that won't photograph when the page negative is made for printing) representing the proper spacing for margins, columns, and gutters.

The best way to get a good pasteup grid is to design your own. Set up your margins, your columns and gutters, and then horizontal lines to help those who do the pasteup get type straight. The usual spacing for horizontal lines is 12 points, or one pica. Inches are marked as well (Fig. 11–1). Then make an exact replica of the flat, in reduced form, for your page dummy.

Another benefit of designing your own flats is that you not only can customize the blue lines for your needs but you can also have some of your "constants" printed on the flats in black.

For instance, on a classified ad page for a newspaper, the column rules can be printed in black on the flat itself. Thus, these don't have to be pasted down week after week, saving time and increasing precision in pasteup on the other elements.

Publications that use a Swiss grid approach to layout would have the horizontal lines spaced the same distance as their leading. A publication with body type of 9 point on 10.5 points of leading would have lines marked off every 10.5 points.

This approach would make it very easy to do pasteup because all edges of art elements and all baselines of type would line up on a blue line on the grid.

Some newspapers have gone to this system. Many magazines have special grids as well.

Even if you don't use a Swiss grid, your pasteup flat is the key to success in pasteup. It should have the standard columns—as well as the main one or two alternate column widths—lined out. This way, the pasteup staff can easily line up type on the grid no matter what column width the page layout calls for.

Another part of your pasteup plan is to have all the necessary tools easily at hand in a space set aside for pasteup. I often liken this to a NASA "clean room": Do whatever it takes to have a separate, well-lighted, and clean space for pasteup.

In general, the following tools are needed to do your own pasteup:

- a pasteup flat of card stock. This is usually better than one made of paper. Because the page is, in a sense, a mechanical assemblage of the page components, the pasteup is often called a *mechanical.*
- a cutting tool, such as an X-acto knife. Scissors are helpful too. Also, a cutting surface. You won't want to gouge your work surface.
- pica poles. These are absolutely necessary for measuring the distance between elements on the page and for drawing and cutting straight lines. Clear plastic ones make the job even easier.
- wax or glue to stick down the type, photos, and art.
- a nonrepro or photo-blue pen or pencil to use for marking on the pasteup. The light blue will not reproduce.
- a series of border tapes. You should at least have hairline, 1-point, 2-point, 3-point, 4-point, 6-point, 12-point, and an assortment of miscellaneous tapes, such as rounded corners, Oxford or Scotch rule (a thick and a thin tape together), benday (a "screened" tape), and so on.
- cellophane tape and white tape. Some printers dislike cellophane tape on pasteups (so check with yours), but it is often helpful in holding down smaller elements. White tape is handy to mask out errors and such.
- a table with square edges (for your T-square should you choose to use one) for card stock flats, or a light table for paper flats. A light table allows you to see through your type galleys to the grid for alignment.

If you have a plan, and if you have all the tools at the ready in a clean area, pasteup isn't a chore; it's an opportunity to give the final touch of professionalism to the design with the care of a dedicated artisan.

PASTING UP

After checking the dummy to be sure it is complete and you understand it, begin by placing constants, art, and display type first. If the design plan is to be effective, these stronger visual elements must be placed right where they are indicated on the dummy. Body type is a little more flexible because lines can be cut or the story can be continued on a following page.

Using your razor-blade knife, slip the blade under an element and place it properly on the grid according to the dummy. If possible, all elements should be waxed ahead of time and placed near the flat. If you are using rubber cement, you would put the cement on each element individually.

Don't rub the elements down too firmly now: You may have to move them later. Paste up is always a compromise. The dummy may have called for one layout, but the reality of the page may call for another, or at least an adjustment.

Place the flag and or folios first, then the art elements, then the headlines. At this point, you will know exactly how much space you have remaining for body type. If the copy fitting was done properly, you should have just about the right amount.

Now is a good time to stop and remeasure your galleys of type and compare the length to the space left for them. Major adjustments should be made now, before you have started to cut the galleys.

After putting down flags, folios, and such, the art should be placed. Photographs are handled on a mechanical in two ways: as veloxes (halftones of the photograph) or as "windows" for the stripping in of halftone negatives by the printer. The window is opaque black or red film or paper the same size as the desired halftone pasted down in the desired position.

When the negative of the final page is shot, the photo area becomes clear, thus the "window" term. The printer then takes a halftone negative and attaches it into the proper position in the window.

With veloxes you get more control of the cropped photo, and you can see for sure what photo will go where before printing. With stripped-in negatives, you get higher-quality printing (because of one less generation of print), but you have to trust your printer to get the right negative in the right window.

Thus, you have to include an extra checking step in the process. Also, you are leaving a pasteup skill—getting the halftone in straight and cropped correctly—to someone who is skilled at camera work, not pasteup. You should work with your printer and pick the best method for your publication and scheduling needs.

Now begin to place the body type. If you have three legs of type, lay down the first column *exactly* where it should go. Mark the cutoff point with a blue pen. Then pick up the galley and gently fold (without creasing the galley) into thirds as indicated by the first type leg.

In a perfect world you would end up with exactly the same number of lines in each type leg. Many slick publications insist on this because they want lines of type in each column to line up perfectly.

In an imperfect world—especially in the imperfect world of newspaper pasteup—you don't always end up with the proper number of lines in each leg. Here the key is to make sure that all three legs have as close to the same number of lines as possible and that the top line and bottom line of type align.

Make up space in the "short" leg by cutting between each paragraph—never between lines of type—and adding air. Cut between every paragraph in the leg so that spacing can be spread out over as much cuts as possible. It is less noticeable this way.

This is another reason for writing in short paragraphs. If you need to air out a leg that has only one graf in it, you are stuck with only one place to make up all the room. It ends up looking like a dropped line.

Be sure to line up body type on the exact left-hand edge of the column, right on the blue line. Beginners often err by placing the trimmed edge of the paper against the blue line. This leaves the type starting several points indented from where it should be. Lines of type must be precisely horizontal; edges of type must be precisely vertical.

After everything has been placed on the page, recheck the spacing of all elements and recheck the proper alignment of the elements to the pasteup grid. Only after you are confident that everything is ready should the page be burnished and set aside. You should have a solid box—often you can use page negative boxes—for keeping and transporting your flats.

When the page is complete and ready to go, you will lay a tissue or tracing paper over the page and rub all the elements with a burnisher or brayer. This will ensure that the elements properly adhere to the flat. After you do this, elements are difficult to move, so be sure that the page is truly ready to go without further adjustments.

After all the pages have been completed, go back over all the flats, in sequence, and look for errors for the last time. Solid editing and proofreading should have caught all the typographical errors. This is the time to look for what I call the "mega-errors," the ones so big you overlook them.

If you do this final check on the actual mechanicals, *be careful!* It would be better to make this check on a proof of the page.

- Check to see that cutlines/captions and photos match. Especially don't mix up the Kiwanis award-winner's photo with that of the rapist.
- Check folios, both the dates and the page numbers.
- Check and follow all jump lines: Are they accurate? Be sure no lines are missing from one page to the next.
- Check the "from" lines: Are they accurate?

Are headlines or titles placed over the proper stories? Read heads and blurbs (anything in display type, actually) backwards—force yourself!—to look for those "invisible" errors.

- Are all special effects marked properly?

Sometimes small errors slip through even the most careful publication staff, especially publications that exist on deadline—such as daily newspapers. But don't ever let the big error get by: One major error on one page can ruin reader perceptions of an entire issue, if not the publication itself.

SPECIAL TECHNIQUES

Border tapes are used in nearly every publication today, from neighborhood newsletters to the *New York Times* to *Time* magazine. They are relatively easy to use—at least compared to technical pens—for the rookie, and they are cheap.

Always tape on a grid line. If one doesn't fall exactly where you want a line, then you may be better off to carefully draw a blue line with a nonrepro pen. It is not as easy as you may think to get a straight line with the tape, especially the thinner sizes.

The secret is to pull the tape just tight enough that it is straight, but not so tight that you are stretching it (Fig. 11–2). How tight is that? Have fun figuring that one out for yourself! You'll know you've pulled too tightly if, after you've cut the tape, it pulls back from the corner or springs up in your face in a circle.

Then try it again.

Border tape should never overlap. At the corners of boxes, then, you must make mitre cuts. Let the tape overlap at first. Then go back and carefully make a 45-degree angle cut (Fig. 11–3). The top tape can easily be lifted off. With care, the bottom tape from the overlap can be coaxed out. Rub the corner hard to keep the cut from separating.

Some designers, and many photographers, like a thin black rule surrounding their black-and-white halftones. To a certain extent these create design problems because they just increase the amount of tape automatically on a page.

Figure 11-2 Stretch border type *slightly* as you put it down to keep it straight.

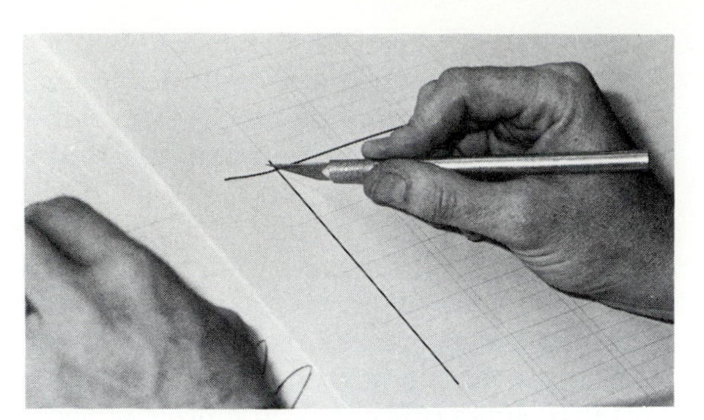

Figure 11-3 Corners of a box should be overlapped and then mitered, or cut at a 45-degree angle to keep all tape on the same plane. Overlaps could appear fuzzy in print.

Figure 11-4 A screen can be created inside a computer typesetter, but if you are doing hand pasteup, all it takes is an acetate overlay.

But they do help some photos by giving them a good, clean edge. Use only hairline or 1-point tape.

Your printer may be able to create boxes for your halftones on the typesetting computer. A velox can be carefully trimmed inside the box so that the line falls on the edge.

If you use tape, don't use thin tape on a clear acetate backing that will cover the halftone dots: The tape ends up distorting the dots at the edge of the photo, and anything you've gained from a sharp edge is lost.

You can get 1-point tape on the side of a one-quarter-inch clear backing. The clear acetate backing would go down on the mechanical, not the halftone, and the line would appear on the edge of the photo. An experienced printer can deal with the very thin 1-point tape, but it is not easy to do. If you must tape photos, let your printer handle it.

Overlays are used to indicate where screens and/or color are to be placed on the page. These are done two ways: Either you use a tissue overlay to make a rough outline of what you want and where, or you use a clear film overlay and other materials to make a precise version of what you want (Fig. 11–4). With this latter version, the printer will actually shoot what you do, so it must be extremely accurate.

If you have enough money in your budget to have the printer do all overlays, I'd suggest you do that. Doing the work yourself requires a certain amount of expertise that your printer will surely have, and you may not.

For instance, if you want a color tint block surrounding elements on a page, you could tape a tissue overlay on the top of your mechanical and indicate on it exactly where you want the spot color to go. The printer, following these instructions, will do the work on a clear acetate overlay that will be used to make a second printing plate for that page.

The material must be placed exactly because the ink will be laid on the paper from two separate units of the press. Do you want that responsibility?

If you do, then you would use a material called Rubylith or Amberlith. This is either red- or amber-colored translucent material on an acetate base. Laying the Rubylith over the area of interest, you can cut away unwanted Rubylith by tracing the shape on the flat (see Chapter 9 examples).

You would cut the *exact* shape of what you want to be screened or in color and lay that *precisely* where you want it to be. To help the printer line up the position, you should use register marks—rather like little bull's eyes—on both the mechanical and the overlay.

This method of getting spot color is called "cut color." By cutting overlays for anything you wanted in color, you could create very complex color illustrations. Even if you had access to only the process colors—cyan, magenta, and yellow—you could create nearly any color in the rainbow by merely combining overlays in varying combinations.

For instance, some of the wonderful color illustrations in *USA Today* were created by artist George Rorick with up to *15* overlays calling for various combinations of the process colors. Only the usual careful registration and color work of *USA Today* pre-press and printing staff kept such work from being jumbles of unregistered screened mush.

The beauty of cut color is that *anyone* can do it, if he or she is careful. By combining only black and one color in various combinations, it would be possible to design a page that looked much more colorful than simple one color to readers.

Overlays also are used for surprints and dropout headlines. Anything printed in ink on top of a photograph is a surprint or overprint. It is done by burning the page's printing plate a second time with the headline you want surprinted (Fig. 11–5). Be sure that the background is plain, and don't overprint over several images on the photo.

A dropout is when the letters are pulled out of the photo so the color of the paper shows through. Dropout headlines are usually white. This must be done when the halftone negative is made at the printers, but the pasteup technique for both is the same (Fig. 11–6).

Simply tape an overlay over the photograph and carefully place the headline where you want it to appear. Use at least two register marks if placement is crucial.

PAGE DUMMIES

If you are working on an 8-1/2-by-11-inch publication, you would sketch out your layout on dummies that are full-size replicas of your full-size grids. If you have a tabloid or full-size newspaper-type publication, however, you should probably use page dummies, or proportionately reduced replicas of the page.

Figure 11–7 shows some of the usual ways to indicate various elements on a newspaper page dummy. Magazine and other publication dummies should be similar.

Regardless of which size you use, you will still probably need to dummy a page several times to get the best layout. Sketch quickly, trying this arrangement, then another one, remembering always the rules/principles of effective design and layout.

The final version you produce must be an accurate "road map" of your page, especially if someone else will be following that map!

Notice the instructions to "fit," "cut," or "jump" on the dummy. It is important to tell your pasteup staff as much as you can on the dummy. The more they know, the less likely work will stop while they track you down to ask a question.

FREDERICKSBURG, VA. The Free Lance-Star MAY 2, 1987

Town & County

Coaching Da
at Stratford
Pages 10–11

Pony cart owned by Mr. and Mrs.
William H. Rewis of Beverly,
Mass., arrives for triennial event.

Figure 11-5 A surprint is the printing of type "on top" of a photo. Here, the type should have been kept off the horse's leg because it is too dark and the letter is lost. (© The Free Lance-Star, Fredericksburg, Va.)

FREDERICKSBURG, VA. The Free Lance-Star JULY 11, 1987

Town & County

The kayaker
takes his cue
Pages 11–12

Figure 11-6 Here, the headline is "dropped out" of the photo, allowing the white of the paper to show through. (© The Free Lance-Star, Fredericksburg, Va.)

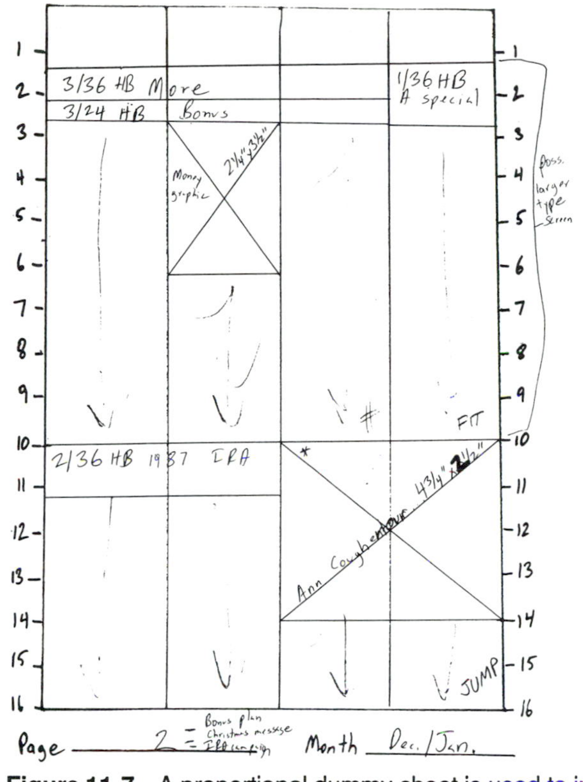

Figure 11-7 A proportional dummy sheet is used to indicate where elements should be placed during pasteup. Headlines are noted on the dummy as well. Notice that the final layout had to be changed from what was planned on the dummy. (Courtesy Central Fidelity Bank)

Page 2

More money for you!

Bonus plan rewards outstanding performances

Our new non-exempt bonus plan was designed to reward outstanding performance *and* encourage similar types of future commitment.

Because our company achieved record levels of profitability during 1986, bonus pools to reward those responsible for the outstanding work are substantially higher for non-exempt and exempt staff members. But we need continued high levels of performance if we are to maintain our excellent record.

We initiated our discretionary, performance-based non-exempt bonus plan this year to better reward *every* employee responsible for our superb accomplishments. You responded as expected by working harder and more efficiently than ever before. Such quality efforts are being rewarded with quality compensation.

"The amount accrued for the non-exempt bonus pool is substantially higher than the amount distributed in last year's Christmas gift program," explains Les Rutledge, director of our Personnel Division. "On the average, amounts could be two-to-three times higher than the non-exempt awards made under our former program."

Bonus pools have been distributed to executive managers who have passed allocations through the ranks. First-line supervisors and managers submitted input so non-exempt staff members could receive their awards on Friday, December 19. The non-exempt bonus plan reflects the same philosophy as well as administrative procedures that have characterized the exempt bonus plan for several years. This year's exempt plan is again designed to reward outstanding performance. Exempt bonuses should be paid in late January or early February.

Our unique system has generated inquiries from other major state banks that have been intrigued by the idea of rewarding those directly responsible for success.

"The extra money we've accumulated is a direct result of the efforts, commitments and sacrifices of many employees in the field," Rutledge says. "Paying larger bonuses is one of the ways we can allow them to share directly in the company's success.

"If money accrued because of outstanding performance isn't used to reward those responsible, we have missed the purpose. This system provides us with an excellent opportunity to communicate throughout the company what we believe is important and what will be rewarded. It also enables us to recognize people who perform at exceedingly high levels and reward them accordingly. We hope they will feel appreciated and continue to demonstrate the same level of commitment in their work."

Such an effort is essential in the coming year. Tax reform will have a significant negative impact on our Bank's earnings as will increased expenses for expansion and automation.

"If we are to maintain profitability at record levels and continue as one of the top earning banks in the country," concludes Rutledge, "we must absolutely have the top level of performance and commitment from *everyone* in the company."

A special message

To My Associates:

At this very special time of the year I want to extend to you my sincere thanks for a job well done in 1986. It was through your efforts that this period will be recorded as the most outstanding year in our history and further enhanced our reputation as one of the finest quality financial institutions in the country.

Our company has succeeded in the past and will continue to be successful in the future because of the strengths demonstrated by the uniqueness of the commitment, dedication and teamwork of the members of the Central Fidelity family. It is my honor and privilege to be associated with each and every one of you.

To you and your loved ones the very happiest of holiday seasons, and may your new year be filled with joy and satisfaction.

IRA campaign incorporates many themes

Our branches indicated the desire and need for a sales campaign featuring numerous winners as well as inner-regional competition. The 1987 IRA campaign fully incorporates both of those suggestions.

During this campaign, we want to educate our customers and prospects on the IRA's continuing benefits for both the 1986 tax year and after tax reform changes. To accomplish that goal, we trained our branch staff members to sell this product more effectively.

Attractive product line offered

We offer a most attractive, full line of IRA products, with maturities from 12 to 60 months. Our most popular product is the Best Rate IRA, a variable rate product that has an 18-month maturity. We guarantee the rate will go no lower than seven percent during the 18-month term of the IRA—the *only* Virginia bank offering such a guarantee. The Best Rate IRA is very popular with customers since its rate adjusts every two weeks, enabling them to take advantage of market trends.

Our other IRAs are fixed-rate accounts with maturities ranging from one to five years. Our Self-Directed IRA lets customers choose how and where their funds are invested.

So our customers can continue simply and conveniently opening IRAs, we've made minor revisions to our popular 3-Step IRA booklet. We have developed a similar booklet for Self-Directed IRA sales.

"We want to provide our branches with the proper tools to make opening any type of IRA as easy as possible," states Cindy Ellis, IRA product manager.

We also developed a document on tax reform changes exclusively affecting IRAs so branch staff members can easily answer customer questions. In addition, we are inserting a statement stuffer into fourth quarter IRA statements as well as attaching a special supplement in the Winter Edition of *The Central Fidelity Bank Book* informing customers how their IRAs will be affected by tax reform.

An exciting incentive campaign will kick off at the start of the year to stimulate IRA sales further. Our statewide goal through April 15 is $32 million in total IRA growth.

For the campaign, our regions have been divided into 13 tiers—four in the Western and Southwestern regions, three in the Eastern Region, three in Northern Virginia, Charlottesville and Culpeper and three in Richmond, Southern and Fredericksburg—based on IRA branch goals. Staff members of the branches achieving the highest percentage of their goal in new accounts *and* additional deposits to existing IRAs in each of the 13 groups will earn $130 each. Staff members of branches with the second highest percentage of goal will win $100 each.

"We're providing branches with the type of competition and incentives they want," Ms. Ellis explains. "Our goal is to encourage existing and new customers to fund their IRAs at Central Fidelity, and we believe our campaign will be successful."

IRA Product Manager Cindy Ellis (far left) explains the 1987 IRA campaign and how tax reform will affect IRAs to a group of Central Region managers.

Ann Coughenour, Cindy Ellis, Linda Fisher and Kim Dugan helped plan the IRA sales campaign and conduct training around the state.

CENTRAL FIDELITY NEWS
Published monthly by
Central Fidelity® Banks, Inc.
Third and Broad Streets
P.O. Box 27602
Richmond, Virginia 23261
Telephone: (804) 782-4792

Jim Belcher, Editor

Contributors in this issue: Pat Burton, Chris Dodge, Jim Fish, Debby Franz, Betty James, Ginny Lewis, Betty McKinney, Jane Rhodes, Debbie Shaffer, Jane Shields, and Peggy Varney.

An equal opportunity employer.
© Central Fidelity Banks, Inc.
January, 1987

"Fit" means to get the story on the page, no matter what you have to do to other elements on the page. "Cut" tells the pasteup artist to end the story at that point on the dummy. The "cut" material—often called *overset*—should not be discarded until after the issue has gone to press. You never know when your plans might change. "Jump" means to end the story at that point and continue it on a following page.

A dummy has to be as neat and precise as you want your final page to be. Again, it is like a map: If the map is fuzzy, your trip will no doubt be "fuzzy" as well.

Draw the line precisely where you want your body type to begin. If you leave enough space, in general, for the headline, the pasteup person will be sure that the final spacing will follow the guidelines.

Indicate odd measures. In fact, the pasteup person should be aware of all special treatments, including color.

Draw all boxes and border tapes just where you want them, and label the kind of tape you want. Write down a few words of identifying information for every element on the page: photos, art, headlines, and body type. This way your "map" is intelligible, even if you aren't available to interpret it.

PAGINATION

Of course, much of this discussion becomes moot in the face of recent advances in electronic page composition, or pagination. With pagination, pages are put together completely within the computer. Instead of galleys being run out of the typesetter, complete pages come out, ready for alignment on a grid and for shipment to the platemaker.

Highly sophisticated pagination systems can even store halftones in memory (dot by dot and, yes, it takes many K's of memory) to be called up on a screen, cropped, sized, and placed on the electronic page. Most systems, however, are not that sophisticated.

Even microcomputers, such as the Apple Macintosh® and the IBM® PC[1], have programs written for them that allow the user to place text and illustrations on a page. Hooked to a laser printer, these programs are especially useful for creating newsletters, fliers, and brochures.

But even with electronic composition, dummies of some kind need to be made. Planning is not abrogated; dummies not abolished. Spacing guidelines must still be strictly adhered to. All that is changed is that the page is under more control of the creator and pasteup time can be minimized.

Remember, however, that although pasteup time *can be* minimized, in the hands of a tyro pagination actually can take longer than old-fashioned pasteup. Another point to remember is that pasteup then becomes an additional chore for a desk person, not a job done by someone "out back." This can change the work flow dramatically.

Before switching to PC-based "desktop publishing," consider staff needs and skills. You may be better off using the PC system as a cheaper typesetting alternative alone and continue with standard pasteup. The savings may still be substantial, you may keep *all* your staff members happier, and the product may even be better and easier to produce. *Don't be seduced by technology.*

Quality time on the pasteup—by hand or by microchip—is always worth it when the final product comes out. You wouldn't meet your important readers and advertisers dressed in mussed up and/or dirty clothes. Don't send out your valuable words in a mussy format either.

CHECKLIST

1. The secrets to good pasteup are: (a) be neat, (b) be precise, and (c) have a good dummy to follow.
2. The secrets to a good dummy are: (a) be neat, (b) be precise, (c) be complete, and (d) have a good design plan to follow in your page-by-page layouts.
3. Be sure to indicate the proper spacing on the dummy. Leave appropriate spaces for headlines, pullouts, etc.
4. During pasteup, place constants first. You *know* the nameplate has got to go in this issue. Then place the major graphic elements: your photos and headlines. The design is based on their position. Then fit the body type as best you can, making the appropriate decision to fit, cut, or jump.
5. You simply have to try pasteup before you can appreciate the skill it takes to do it well. After you have fumbled with it for a while, visit a professional print shop or newspaper composing room and watch and learn from a pro. Write down and save all the tips and shortcuts you will learn.
6. It's always seemed to me that production personnel are about the most important members of the publication team, yet they are rarely made to feel that way. How can you expect your publication to look good if the craftsmen (and, of course, I mean women too) involved in the hands-on part can't or

[1]Apple Macintosh is a registered trademark of Apple Computer, Inc. IBM is a registered trademark of International Business Machines Corporation.

don't do their job well? Work closely with production people and (a) you will learn what you need to know to be a better designer and (b) your work will be handled a little more lovingly because you have paid some attention to them. Everyone gains. Especially the reader, our No. 1.

CHAPTER

12 PAPER AND IMPOSITION

Selecting the proper paper is an important aspect of editing and design. If the goal is to communicate as quickly, completely, and pleasurably as possible, then even the paper on which your message is to be seen is important.

Paper, like design, can add meaning to the message. Some paper says "rich" and "classy," whereas other paper says "cheap" and "quickly done." If your message is "classy" and you use "cheap" paper, you can confuse the reader.

Another factor is cost. Classy papers, naturally, cost more money. But you may not need to increase the budget by using expensive quality paper. Newspapers, for instance, use lots of paper and they need to print quickly. It would not be sensible for a newspaper to use anything other than newsprint.

On the other hand, if your publication—let's say an annual report or a brochure—needs to look expensive or elegant, then the proper paper could do that for you, and do it possibly cheaper than adding other effects, such as color.

Selecting paper is not an important part of being newspaper communicators, who are stuck with low-quality newsprint. But other communicators often must select the proper paper for a job.

Imposition has to do with the positioning of individual pages on large sheets of paper on the press. For the editor/designer, knowing imposition can help design, even though it is really the concern of the printer.

HISTORY

Humans have not always had paper. Early written communication took place on cave walls, stone and clay tablets, and animal skins. Necessity being the mother of invention, however, humans searched for ways to make the storage of written information more convenient.

The Chinese are credited with inventing a papermaking process around 100 A.D. Making paper was a laborious process, much of it done by hand, until the early 1800s. It was then that the Fourdrinier papermaking machine was invented. The process involved—as it still does today with the modern machines that bear the same name—a "wet end" where pulp was created and processed, and a "dry end" where the pressed pulp was processed and dried before being rolled or cut into sheets.

The Fourdrinier machine was a godsend for printers, especially American printers during the colonial period. Although the first paper mill in America was built in 1690, paper was still very scarce in the years prior to the American Revolution. The printers who produced the broadsides and newspapers that helped fire the patriotic fever often had to take their carts through the cities and towns and beg for old rags to be made into paper.

PAPER TERMS

Before discussing how to select the proper paper for the job, you need to understand the terminology of paper. Paper is described in terms of:

- Weight
- Finish
- Coating
- Color
- Grain
- Special touches:
  - Calendering and supercalendering
  - Embossing
  - Die cuts

Paper weight numbers really better describe its thickness than its actual weight. Different types of paper come in different pretrim sizes. Using the ream (or 500 sheets) as the standard, the *basis weight* of the paper is then figured. If the ream weighs 80 pounds, it is considered 80-pound paper. Forty-pound paper would logically have to have thinner individual sheets because the number of sheets in the ream would always be the same.

To add to the slight confusion, there are various basis sizes of papers. Thus, it would be possible for certain 40-pound papers to be *thicker* than certain 50-pound papers.

For instance, a ream of 12-by-22-inch paper that weighed 50 pounds would have to be thicker stock than a ream of 25-by-38-inch paper that also weighed 50 pounds. The larger size would dictate that each sheet would have to weigh less.

The best way to choose the proper paper weight is to feel a sample. You can't beat touch when it comes to selecting paper.

The following list should clarify matters:

Bond: Basic typing paper. Basis size = 12 × 22

Book: Used, oddly enough, in books. Basis size = 25 × 38

Text: Used for high-quality books. Basis size = 25 × 38.

Offset: Similar to book, but resists moisture of offset printing better. Basis size = 25 × 38.

Cover: Heavier versions of text papers. Basis size = 20 × 26.

Bristol Board: Like index cards or folders. Basis size = 22.5 × 28.5.

There are other basic grades of paper, but these are the most common.

Papers also have different finishes, ranging from very smooth to rough texture. Smoothness makes a difference in the ink you lay on the paper. The smoother the paper, the higher-quality reproduction you get, especially with halftones.

The roughest paper, besides most handmade papers, is newsprint. Some have likened newspaper printing to printing on toilet paper: It's no wonder the quality of printing for newspapers is generally so low. The main reason for the low quality is the roughness. The image ink ends up being laid on hills and valleys instead of a flat and smooth surface. The edges then begin to look fuzzy to the eye. This effect is especially important with halftones because of the very small dots. Some typefaces—notably those with very thin strokes—also don't show up well on rough paper.

In general, if you want to use halftones, especially color halftones, you should avoid textured papers. Other common finishes are antique (textures such as eggshell and vellum), English, machine, calendered, and supercalendered.

Calendering is a process that uses pressure to create a smooth paper, almost as smooth as coated papers. *Supercalendered* papers are made even smoother—and thinner—by putting the paper through more rollers. This process is used where thin (and light) paper—for instance, in magazines that are mailed—is desired. *English* is a special form of calendering that produces a thick, opaque paper.

Coated papers have pigments, such as zinc oxide or clay, laid on the paper with adhesives, such as glue or casein. Generally the coating is put on the paper during the papermaking process. However, more expensive coatings are often added at a different plant after the paper has been made. Coated papers are good for covers, quality printing of halftones, and for very special printing jobs.

Papers come in nearly any color you could want, including a variety of whites. Colored paper, however, affects what is printed on it. Type looks better on a muted, matte white, for instance, but halftones look better with a brighter white.

Printing halftones on colored paper sometimes creates odd and unpleasant effects. For instance, on blue paper a photograph comes out with black shadows and blue highlights. It can look very odd.

The grain of paper mostly affects how it folds. Folding with the grain is easily done. Trying to fold the paper against the grain is difficult and involves more waste—and that means more cost to you. A good printer will help you make sure a paper's grain is right for the job you want.

Other special effects with paper are also available to the editor/designer. *Embossing* is a process that raises a portion of the paper, such as a corporate logo on a letterhead. Foil can be added to the embossed part for an additional effect. When the embossed part is not inked, it is called "blind embossing."

Die cuts are nothing more than holes in the paper. On a folded piece, these are often used to allow the reader to "peek" at something on the inside. Both embossing and die cuts can be done with any shape, and in combination on the same page.

CHOOSING PAPER

A number of factors should be kept in mind when choosing paper. First, perhaps, is cost. Fine papers cost money. Typically, the cost of the paper alone represents 20 to 25 percent of the cost of the entire job. In general, select the highest-quality paper that is right for the job and allows you to stay within your budget.

Type

Your paper selection may affect how your typography will look. For instance, you may desire a rough textured paper. This means that you stay away from modern roman type with its very thin strokes. Thin lines will be lost on the texture.

Certain dark colors will reduce the contrast so much between your type and the background that legibility will be affected. Don't let design choices impede communication. Make decisions always as an editor, not just as a designer.

Thin papers may have too much show-through, especially with bold or heavy typefaces. Be careful with type selection on supercalendered papers especially.

Halftones

Photos are affected in nearly the same ways. Halftones lack clarity on a rough textured paper. The dots themselves lose sharpness, and highlight dots (the small dots in the whiter areas of the halftone) will be hard to hold. This may also affect the accuracy of colors.

As mentioned above, colored stock is never advisable for photos, unless light brown paper is used to gain a sepia effect.

Thick papers, because of their opacity, are good for photographs. Coated papers are even better because the very smooth finish allows the halftone dots to be very crisp around the edges.

Perhaps the best way to learn about paper is to go to your local printer and spend some time with the many sample books the printer no doubt has. The samples will allow you to feel the different papers and to check their opacity for yourself. Many samples also have type and/or halftone examples.

Better yet, talk to the printer about your job and get some expert advice on paper selection. Printers know paper the way a carpenter knows wood. The printer's experience with certain papers from certain companies or mills in your area will also be invaluable. This will be time well spent.

IMPOSITION

Imposition is a term that refers to how pages need to be put together so they come out in the proper sequence after being printed. As mentioned earlier, paper comes in sizes larger than the final printed form. The pages are printed in such a way that after some folding and cutting, the pages end up in the proper order.

Here's an example. Take an 8-1/2-by-11-inch piece of paper. Fold it in half and then in half again. Now it's a small quarter-page booklet. Number the eight pages and open it up again.

As you can see, on one side of the paper you've got pages 1, 4, 5, and 8. On the other side, you've got 2, 3, 6, and 7. Note two important positioning facts: First, the pages properly line up back-to-back and, second, the page pairs on

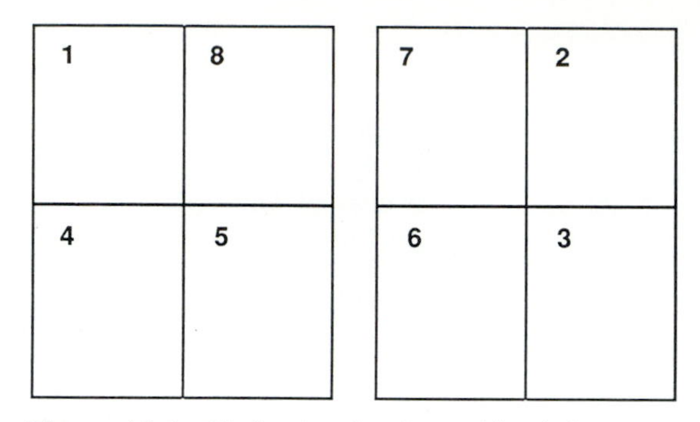

Figure 12-1 Understanding imposition is important because it can help you save money. For instance, printing color on only one side of the sheet (pages 2,3,6,7 or 1,4,5,8) is cheaper than trying to color both.

each half of a side add up to 9, or one more than the number of total pages (Fig. 12–1).

Imposition is not a decision made by an editor, although the size of the publication and the number of pages affect the imposition. The printer and the binder, if you have a magazine, are the main persons concerned with imposition.

Still, a visually literate editor needs to be aware of how imposition works. Imposition especially affects color decisions.

Let's take the simple eight-page example. If you can afford full-color only on one side during a press run, that means you can have color only on pages 2 and 3, 6 and 7, or on the front and back covers (1 and 8) and pages 4 and 5.

Because pages 4 and 5 represent the centerspread of the publication, and because you might like color on your "cover," you may want to opt for color on that side of the paper.

Or, let's say you have a 16-page publication. Your budget is limited, so you can run process color only on one side, but you can run two spot colors on the other side. Full color will appear throughout the pages (for example, pages 1,4,5,8,9,12,13,16), with two-color interspersing them.

Readers will think that color is available for all 16 pages. The more important issue, however, is that you need to be aware ahead of time which pages have full color and which do not. Then you can design in functional color properly and get the most for your money.

CHECKLIST

1. The kind of paper you choose for your publication communicates something about that publication: Thick textured paper can mean rich and classy; newsprint can mean quick and dirty.
2. Be careful when choosing paper based on its "weight." You are always better off selecting paper by looking at and holding a sample.
3. Coated papers are good for halftones; textured papers are bad for halftones.
4. Paying attention to imposition can maximize your use of color *and* save you money.

CHAPTER

13

NEWSLETTERS AND BROCHURES

In this and the final two chapters we will discuss briefly the application of "integrated editing" to various types of publications. Then we will look at real publications and how they have followed (or ignored) the dictums covered in this book. It is sort of an "integrated editing in action" approach, one I feel can better illuminate the process than can many additional words from me. Each chapter will begin with a few words about designing the publication(s) in general.

Even though many communicators prepare for the world of big-time newspapers and magazines, most spend a lot of time on newsletters and brochures. When communicators are "found out" in whatever community or church group they are members of, they are often asked to be the newsletter editor.

So no matter how you've prepared, or what your career goals may be, get ready for at least a few newsletters or brochures.

A newsletter is nearly always 8-1/2-by-11-inch paper. Sometimes it is stapled in the upper left corner. Sometimes it is printed on 11-by-17-inch paper and folded.

Typographer Edmund Arnold defines a brochure as a publication with the pages fastened by thread or staples. Stretching the definition a bit, you also can include the ubiquitous single sheet, letter-folded. For convenience sake, I also will call that a brochure.

NEWSLETTERS

The easiest and perhaps best approach to newsletters is to follow another KISS formula: Keep It Short and Simple. The nature of a newsletter is to get information to people quickly, cheaply, and if you can at all manage it, attractively.

Thus, little time is available for snappy special effects. The job of the newsletter designer is largely in the effective setting up of the basic design plan: the format, the column grid, the typographical constants, and such.

This is the maxim mentioned earlier: First freeze the pond, then let the skaters dance. The pond is more important than the dancers: Without a solid base of ice, there will be no dance. Period.

With a solidly conceived plan, the individual pages can be consistent variations on a typographical theme—well-choreographed steps of a dance.

FORMATS

Typeset Newsletters

If you can afford to have your stories set in type, and not done on a typewriter, you are fortunate. Not only will your publication look more professional but you may even save paper. Stories set in type take up to 50 percent less space than does typewritten copy.

In fact, the production of newsletters has changed significantly in recent years with the advent of page composition programs on personal computers and with laser printers. This type of system can provide the user with typeset quality and maximum control over the product at a much lower cost than standard typesetting. In rough terms, a newsletter produced on a laser printer can look nearly as good as one using professional typesetting, and it will cost about half as much, sometimes less.

The first step in designing a newsletter is to select a paper size. Because nearly all are 8-1/2-by-11-inch, we will discuss that size. In a sense, two different 8-1/2-by-11-inch formats are available: one that is stapled in the upper left-hand corner, and one printed on 11-by-17-inch paper and folded.

Each has its own design strategy. With a stapled newsletter, the reader sees only one page at a time. The act of reading is done by flipping one page over the others. Because the reader sees the bottom of the page first, you should have a strong design element at the top of each page to get the eye to travel up there (Fig. 13–1).

On the larger-sized sheet, it is possible to see two pages at one time. Therefore you must consider the spread as seen together, as well as individual pages. This is even more important for slick magazines, and it is covered more fully in the next chapter.

Next, decide upon the size of the type page. In other words, how big will your margins be? This is an important decision. Margins that are too small will make the type appear crammed into the space. Margins that are too big will waste valuable space on unnecessary white space (Fig. 13–2).

The largest margin should be the bottom, or foot margin. This follows the principle of the optical center being higher than the actual center of a space. The other margins can be the same, or the top or head margin can be slightly larger than the side (but smaller than the foot). I would suggest five picas for the foot margin, and three picas for the others.

The next decision is the number of columns. For a publication this size, the choices are one, two, or three columns. Each has its benefits and drawbacks. A one-column newsletter looks too much like a letter. It shouldn't. If you want your newsletter to be read, it should look different from other printed communication.

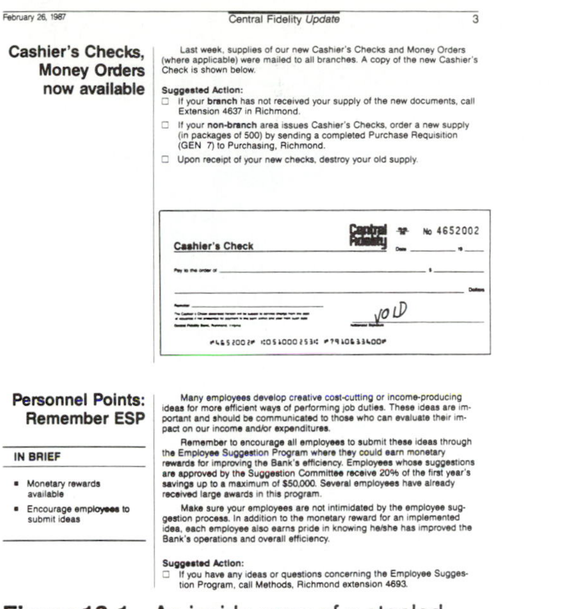

February 26, 1987 | Central Fidelity *Update* | 3

Cashier's Checks, Money Orders now available

Last week, supplies of our new Cashier's Checks and Money Orders (where applicable) were mailed to all branches. A copy of the new Cashier's Check is shown below.

Suggested Action:

☐ If your **branch** has not received your supply of the new documents, call Extension 4637 in Richmond.

☐ If your **non-branch** area issues Cashier's Checks, order a new supply (in packages of 500) by sending a completed Purchase Requisition (GEN 7) to Purchasing, Richmond.

☐ Upon receipt of your new checks, destroy your old supply.

Cashier's Check — Central Fidelity — No 4652002

VOID

Personnel Points: Remember ESP

IN BRIEF

- Monetary rewards available
- Encourage employees to submit ideas

Many employees develop creative cost-cutting or income-producing ideas for more efficient ways of performing job duties. These ideas are important and should be communicated to those who can evaluate their impact on our income and/or expenditures.

Remember to encourage all employees to submit these ideas through the Employee Suggestion Program where they could earn monetary rewards for improving the Bank's efficiency. Employees whose suggestions are approved by the Suggestion Committee receive 20% of the first year's savings up to a maximum of $50,000. Several employees have already received large awards in this program.

Make sure your employees are not intimidated by the employee suggestion process. In addition to the monetary reward for an implemented idea, each employee also earns pride in knowing he/she has improved the Bank's operations and overall efficiency.

Suggested Action:

☐ If you have any ideas or questions concerning the Employee Suggestion Program, call Methods, Richmond extension 4693.

Figure 13-1 An inside page of a stapled newsletter needs strong type—or better yet, strong art—at the top of a page to get the reader up there. Here, the relatively small type is made stronger because it is surrounded by white space. (Courtesy of Central Fidelity Bank)

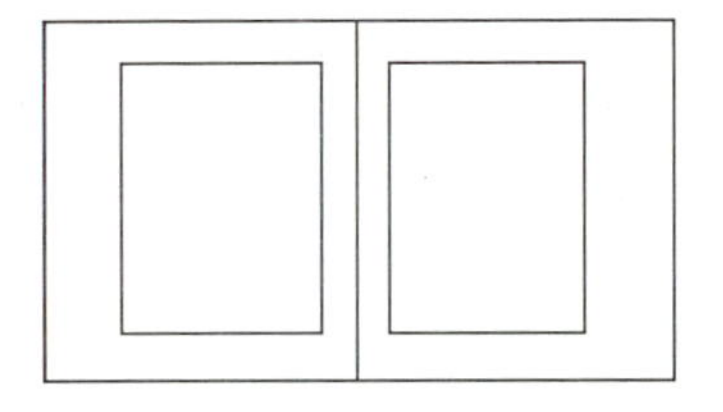

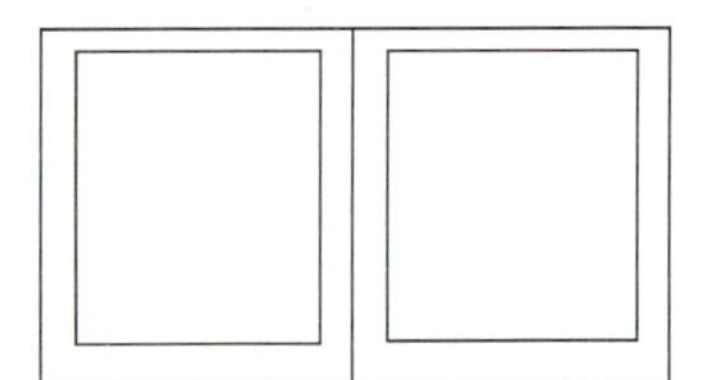

Figure 13-2 Margins are an important part of the overall look of the page. The top page has margins that are too small, the middle too large. The page on the bottom uses progressive or book margins. Here the proportion of type page to margins is more appropriate.

Two columns work well, though the line measure can be a bit on the long side. If you used three-pica side margins and a 1.5 pica gutter between the columns, your type would be 21.09 picas wide (Fig. 13–3).

Two columns give you little opportunity for design variations. Worse yet, any art is forced to be wide. This is difficult if you will be using a lot of small face-only photos, or mug shots. One solution is to run small art, such as mug shots, half column, or as mentioned in the discussion on formats, a six-column Swiss grid with type running two "columns" wide. This, however, means that you either have to wrap type around the photo, run two photos to fill the space, or have a block of white space that may be unattractive.

That is why I prefer the three-column format for newsletters, especially newsletters that will use occasional photos. The columns are sized about right for type, three columns give you a number of design opportunities, and the column width is more conducive to mug shots, usually your smallest graphic element. And, in general, you should select your column size based in part on the optimum play for your smallest graphic element.

Another interesting option, especially for newsletters with no art at all, is the odd-sized two-column format. In this format, the left-hand column is narrower than the right-hand column. Headlines and other graphic elements appear in the narrow column; body type goes in the wide column (see Fig. 13–1).

Figure 13-3 A two-column grid for a newsletter can appear wordy and gray if you are not careful. On the left, slightly larger margins would have helped make the page more readable. On the right, tight margins on a four-column grid appear more appropriate. (L, Courtesy of Pantone Color Institute; R, Courtesy of the Bernhardt Fudyma Design Group)

This approach can also be used with a standard three-column format, but setting up optimum columns is usually more effective. Either way, this approach is good for typewritten newsletters, either with rub-on headlines or with typewritten ones.

Although setting type flush left is preferred, this is one situation in which flush-right type is acceptable. The right-hand edge of the headlines of a number of short items creates a virtual line on the page. If you use flush-left headlines in this format, a thin column rule might be helpful. Do not use a thick line, as that will serve more to separate the content than connect it.

Many simple newsletters must be created on typewriters, either in full or in part. If you must use a typewriter, use the best you can find, one with a good film ribbon and proportional spacing, if possible.

After the basic format has been settled, attention should be given to the typographical "constants," elements such as nameplate, folios, content organizers, and so on. If you can, use rub-on type, available from nearly any art supply store for as much display type as you can.

Because this type is often fairly expensive, especially if you get a number of sizes, you may wish to use rub-on type for only the nameplate and certain regular features, not for headlines.

These standard typographical features can then be photocopied for use in each issue. Photocopying is much less expensive and quicker than rubbing on new type each issue.

If you use rub-on type for headlines, follow all the rules on headline typography covered in Chapter 6. Be especially careful with the leading.

If you use rub-on type for only the constants, use all caps and/or boldface type for headlines. The principle here is to differentiate the heads from the body type somehow.

If you are using a word processor with a dot matrix printer set at "letter quality," you may be able to use a feature that prints the letters at double width as well. This option gives you a larger size as well as the boldness or caps to gain the necessary typographical contrast.

The last and least favorable choice is to use no headlines at all. Because each item needs a graphic element to draw the eye to the beginning of the content, you should at least use all-caps (and bold, if you can) lead-ins. This means that the first word or two (and no more than four) should stand out visually on the page.

The content of these can be either the first few words of the item itself or, like headlines, it can be a few words of summary.

Even halftones can be produced for a newsletter fairly cheaply. Obviously the best choice is to have halftones created by a professional on a good copy camera. But many print shops have the capability to screen even an instant-print color photo into a usable halftone. The exposure of the photo is crucial, and you should check with the print shop before taking the picture.

Another option for visuals for newsletters are books of clip art, or drawings without copyright that can be used for anything at anytime. These range from modern drawings created specifically for this purpose to old engravings that have endured past their copyright period and are now in the public domain.

Either gives you the opportunity to add visual interest to the copy on your page. Do not use modern material, such as cartoons in magazines or newspapers, because they are almost certainly protected under copyright law.

Attention to detail on the format—and this includes spacing between elements—and on the typographical constants will give your newsletter a professional look, even if it is done on a typewriter.

Sending out your professionally produced and important copy in a less-than-professional format and design only serves to undermine the effectiveness of your communication. Package your message well and it will be heard. Throw information together on a sheet of paper and you may as well have remained silent.

BROCHURES

Brochures come in many shapes and sizes. But because the most common is the 8-1/2-by-11-inch sheet folded twice into a three-panel brochure, that is the format that will be covered here. Most of the principles carry over into the other sizes and shapes anyway.

Although some brochures this size are designed to open horizontally, most open vertically (Fig. 13–4). This method makes the brochures easier to display on a holder, and the unfolding of the pages creates interesting opportunities—and challenges—for the editor.

The cover of a brochure must sell the content inside. It must tease the reader, intrigue the reader, question the reader, and demand a response—in short, it must do anything to get the reader to see the brochure, pick it up, and open it.

The cover can be just type ("type attack") or art or a combination. Here's where you can pull out the tricks mentioned earlier: type contrast, add a third dimension through type and/or design, use screens, spot color, etc. All the rules of margins apply here as well. Set your margins large enough to give a sizable frame to your type. Remember that type never bleeds—or runs off the edge of the paper—unless you are using it as an "art element" and not just type.

The real trouble spot in designing a trifold brochure is after the cover panel has been opened to reveal the next step (Fig. 13–5). At this point the reader is looking at one panel that is truly on the back side of the paper (right panel) and the far left panel of the inside, where most of your important message is printed.

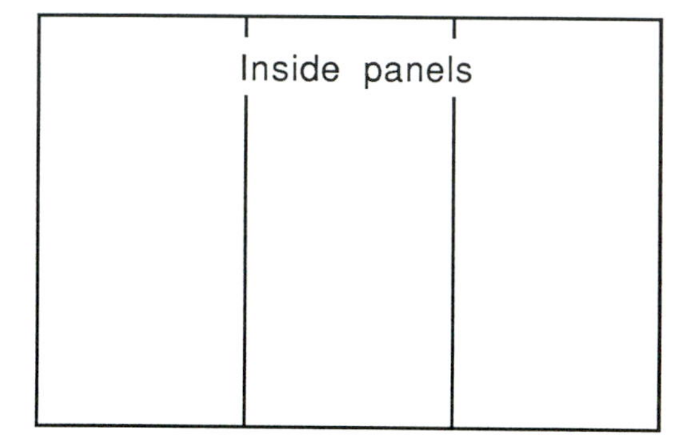

Figure 13-4 The classic letter-fold brochure is used frequently by many businesses and corporations. Filling each panel appropriately is difficult.

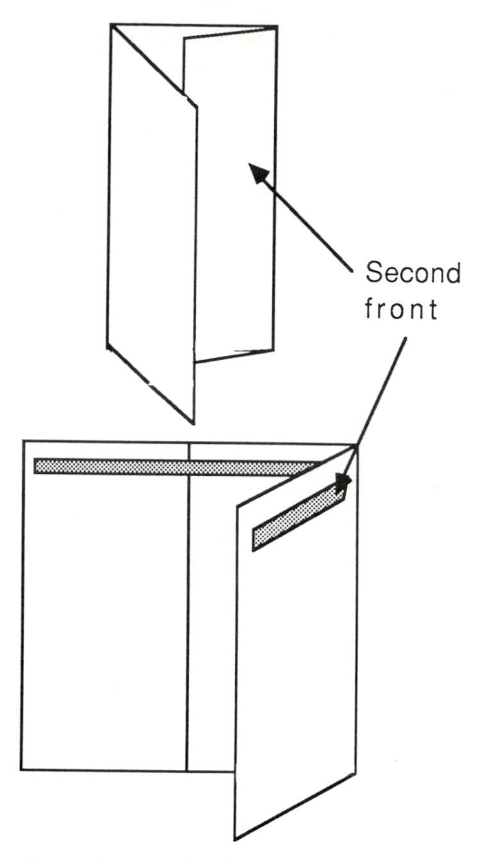

Figure 13-5 After the cover panel is opened on a letter-fold brochure, the problem comes in guiding the reader: Which panel does the reader look at next—the left or the middle? Use graphic elements, such as a color bar or tape, to create visual continuity between "second front panel" and inside content.

The key here is use a graphic element—type, border tape, color, white space, or perhaps an illustration printed half on one panel and half on the other—to connect those two panels and to carry over into the inside three-panel presentation. Make it easy for the reader to understand where to enter your message and where to go next.

On the inside three panels, you are free to design the space—inside your well-chosen margins—in nearly any way you please. You do not have to stick to three columns of information. Most brochure designers seem to feel stuck in the three-column mode, but it is absolutely not mandated.

The middle panel of the back side can be used for a message, but generally your message should be short enough that you do not need this area. Either leave it blank except for your corporate identification and address or set it up as a self-mailer by leaving space for an address. Be sure to follow U.S. Postal Service regulations if you are going to mail your brochure.

A brochure that is opened horizontally still faces the same problem of how to deal with what the reader sees after the first panel is opened. The solutions are found in the same area of graphic devices that tie panels together and show the reader where to go.

All the rules we have been discussing so far apply: Set up ample margins, set up some kind of column grid, follow your spacing guidelines, follow the principles of design and layout, and use special effects judiciously.

All printed communications are meant to be read and understood. Brochures are special, however, because they are meant to have a short shelf life. They are designed to be read quickly, to provide information on the run, if you will. Therefore, on brochures most of all, you must follow the KISS principle corollary of Keep It Short and Simple.

INTEGRATED EDITING AND NEWSLETTERS

Integrated editing means attention to presentation of content from beginning to end of the process. With newsletters, the audience is generally preselected and stable. Editors don't have to "sell" the newsletter itself so much as sell the content. The goal of the editor is to make the generally standard and "expected content" somehow more interesting and appealing. Design is probably the best way to do that.

Because newsletters usually have little opportunity for art at all, much less compelling art, the best way to approach integrated editing techniques with a newsletter is through type.

Remember that the two questions to ask are:

1. What is the best way to communicate this information? Is it visual?
2. Is there a visual element that can enhance this information?

With newsletters, these questions tend to refer not to photos or illustrations, but to tables, charts, graphs, maps, and pullouts (quoteouts, At-a-glance boxes, etc.).

A well-constructed numerical table with perhaps a few lines of explanation is often better than trying to talk about numerical information within a story. Most often, however, newsletter editors must deal with the second question: What visual can be added to break up the gray?

Because newsletter readers, especially those in a corporate setting, are often in a hurry, the At-a-glance box or "in brief" is a good strategy (see Fig. 13–6B). By working in a quick summary of the important details of a story, you have done your most important job: to provide information to those who need it. Some need only a little information, and some quite a bit. With an At-a-glance box, you have served both groups of readers.

If you have an interview or a feature-oriented story, the quoteout is good *IF* (and that's a big if) you have a compelling quote. There is little worse than a sleep-inducing quote played large in display type.

Maps, charts, and graphs also can be done quite well in the newsletter format. These do not have to be complicated or use art to jazz them up.

You can easily set up a grid for a fever-line graphic, for instance, by using the blue-lined graph paper available in any paper store or college book store. Using the lines as a guide, ink your background grid lines in black. Or use border tape. (The light blue lines will not reproduce when printed.)

Do the graphic twice as large as you would like to use it. Then, before you add type, reduce it 50 percent on a good copy machine. Make sure the lines you draw are thick enough to stand this kind of reduction.

Then add the numbers on the X and Y axes (typed or typeset). Carefully draw the straight or dotted lines—or better yet use border tape again.

If you have followed the typographical rules and the rules for making a fever-line chart, then you have a terrific visual information-giver instead of just gray type.

Bar charts can be made quickly the same way. Draw a standard rectangle that you will use for your bar chart. Again, draw it twice the size, with thicker lines than you would like them to be in the final form. Draw it longer than your longest possible data point. Then copy a bunch of them.

To make the graphic, lay the rectangles down on your predrawn grid. Use 18- or 24-point border tape to make it easy and precise. Line them up just the way you need them to be and carefully razor-blade them at the baseline. Then tape or glue them into their final position.

After the initial setup, these information graphics take little time and little "artistic" talent. Actually, you need to understand numbers and their relationships more than you need to understand art.

One final thought on this: If you have access to a personal computer with graphics capability, then these can be done in the computer. And no art talent is needed to work a computer! In fact, many quick-print shops have Apple Macintosh computers available on a rental basis. Some editors are putting entire newsletters together on a Mac in a quick-print shop and still saving money over having them typeset.

Naturally, all of this discussion holds for brochures as well. The main difference is that a brochure, by its nature, has to "sell" its content a little more. For that reason, integrated editing is an important marketing tool.

Brochure readers also want the information quick and easy. Attention to the nature of your information and whether it may be presented better visually then becomes crucial to the success of your communication plan.

Remember that the most important time for integrated editing is at the planning stage. The first question, above, includes the second question, in a sense. If you have thought out the best way to *gather* the information, then the second question—are there visuals?—may well be redundant.

The second question needs to be asked if the first question was not, or if the answer turned out to be wholly or partly wrong. Whether you decide to present the information visually or whether you just add visuals and follow design basics as you present the information doesn't matter much. What matters is that you are aiming for the best presentation. Period.

CASE STUDY

Company: Central Fidelity Bank, Richmond, VA

Publication: *Update.* A weekly 8-1/2-by-11-inch stapled newsletter sent to all bank branches. Content includes rate changes, important news and information, etc.

Redesign Goals: Flag needs to be changed to follow corporate design changes. Format needs to be more interesting. Looks like standard letter-type memo now. Design needs to fit capability of computer-page composition system in word processing department. Design needs to be simple because newsletter is put together quickly.

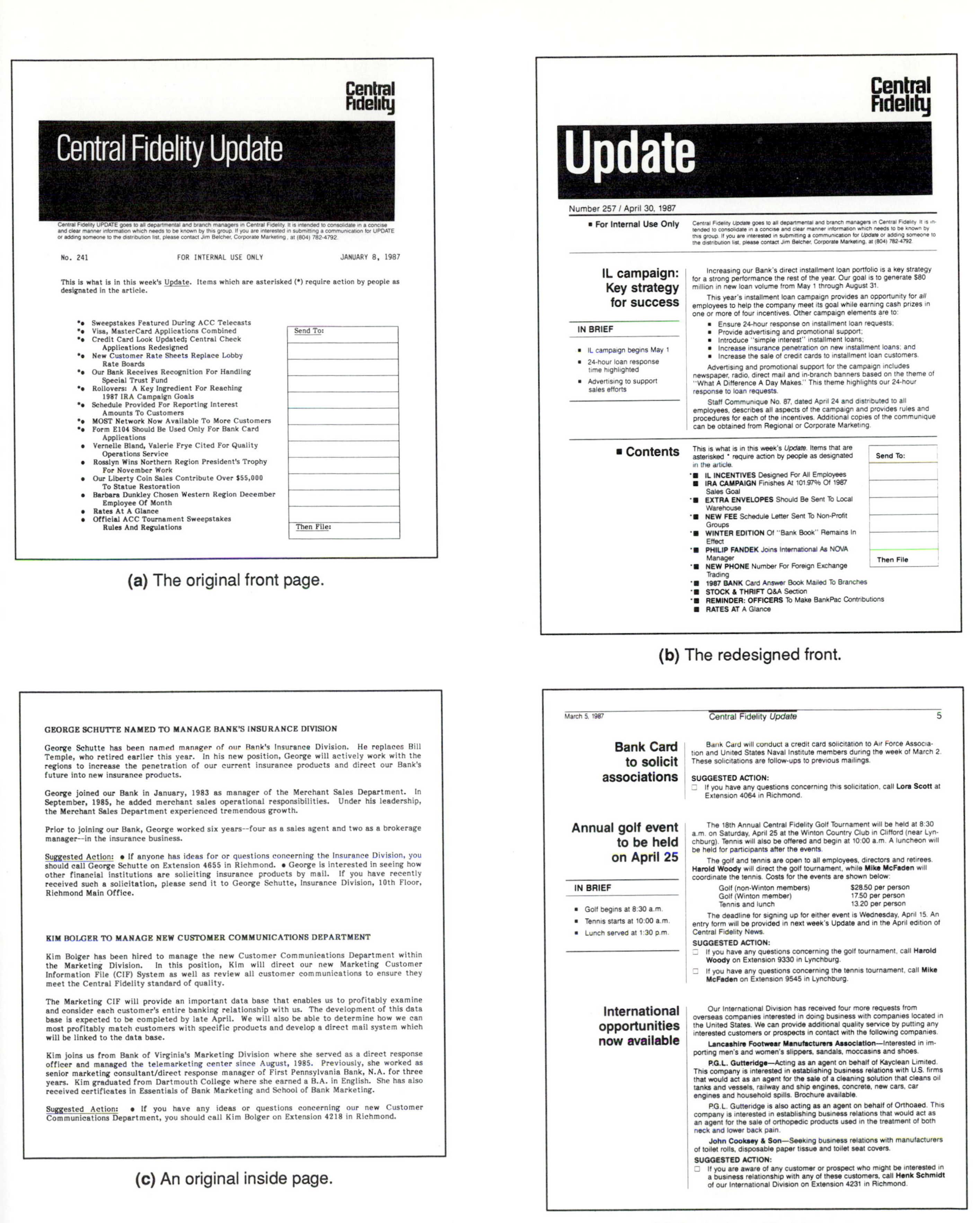

Central Fidelity

Central Fidelity Update

Central Fidelity UPDATE goes to all departmental and branch managers in Central Fidelity. It is intended to consolidate in a concise and clear manner information which needs to be known by this group. If you are interested in submitting a communication for UPDATE or adding someone to the distribution list, please contact Jim Belcher, Corporate Marketing, at (804) 782-4792.

No. 241 FOR INTERNAL USE ONLY JANUARY 8, 1987

This is what is in this week's Update. Items which are asterisked (*) require action by people as designated in the article.

- *• Sweepstakes Featured During ACC Telecasts
- *• Visa, MasterCard Applications Combined
- *• Credit Card Look Updated; Central Check Applications Redesigned
- *• New Customer Rate Sheets Replace Lobby Rate Boards
- *• Our Bank Receives Recognition For Handling Special Trust Fund
- *• Rollovers: A Key Ingredient For Reaching 1987 IRA Campaign Goals
- *• Schedule Provided For Reporting Interest Amounts To Customers
- *• MOST Network Now Available To More Customers
- *• Form E104 Should Be Used Only For Bank Card Applications
- • Vernelle Bland, Valerie Frye Cited For Quality Operations Service
- • Rosslyn Wins Northern Region President's Trophy For November Work
- • Our Liberty Coin Sales Contribute Over $55,000 To Statue Restoration
- • Barbara Dunkley Chosen Western Region December Employee Of Month
- • Rates At A Glance
- • Official ACC Tournament Sweepstakes Rules And Regulations

Send To:

Then File:

(a) The original front page.

Central Fidelity

Update

Number 257 / April 30, 1987

■ For Internal Use Only

Central Fidelity *Update* goes to all departmental and branch managers in Central Fidelity. It is intended to consolidate in a concise and clear manner information which needs to be known by this group. If you are interested in submitting a communication for *Update* or adding someone to the distribution list, please contact Jim Belcher, Corporate Marketing, at (804) 782-4792.

IL campaign: Key strategy for success

IN BRIEF

- IL campaign begins May 1
- 24-hour loan response time highlighted
- Advertising to support sales efforts

Increasing our Bank's direct installment loan portfolio is a key strategy for a strong performance the rest of the year. Our goal is to generate $80 million in new loan volume from May 1 through August 31.

This year's installment loan campaign provides an opportunity for *all* employees to help the company meet its goal while earning cash prizes in one or more of four incentives. Other campaign elements are to:

- Ensure 24-hour response on installment loan requests;
- Provide advertising and promotional support;
- Introduce "simple interest" installment loans;
- Increase insurance penetration on new installment loans; and
- Increase the sale of credit cards to installment loan customers.

Advertising and promotional support for the campaign includes newspaper, radio, direct mail and in-branch banners based on the theme of "What A Difference A Day Makes." This theme highlights our 24-hour response to loan requests.

Staff Communique No. 87, dated April 24 and distributed to all employees, describes all aspects of the campaign and provides rules and procedures for each of the incentives. Additional copies of the communique can be obtained from Regional or Corporate Marketing.

■ Contents

This is what is in this week's *Update*. Items that are asterisked * require action by people as designated in the article.

- *■ **IL INCENTIVES** Designed For All Employees
- ■ **IRA CAMPAIGN** Finishes At 101.97% Of 1987 Sales Goal
- *■ **EXTRA ENVELOPES** Should Be Sent To Local Warehouse
- *■ **NEW FEE** Schedule Letter Sent To Non-Profit Groups
- *■ **WINTER EDITION** Of "Bank Book" Remains In Effect
- *■ **PHILIP FANDEK** Joins International As NOVA Manager
- *■ **NEW PHONE** Number For Foreign Exchange Trading
- *■ **1987 BANK** Card Answer Book Mailed To Branches
- *■ **STOCK & THRIFT** Q&A Section
- *■ **REMINDER: OFFICERS** To Make BankPac Contributions
- ■ **RATES AT** A Glance

Send To:

Then File

(b) The redesigned front.

GEORGE SCHUTTE NAMED TO MANAGE BANK'S INSURANCE DIVISION

George Schutte has been named manager of our Bank's Insurance Division. He replaces Bill Temple, who retired earlier this year. In his new position, George will actively work with the regions to increase the penetration of our current insurance products and direct our Bank's future into new insurance products.

George joined our Bank in January, 1983 as manager of the Merchant Sales Department. In September, 1985, he added merchant sales operational responsibilities. Under his leadership, the Merchant Sales Department experienced tremendous growth.

Prior to joining our Bank, George worked six years--four as a sales agent and two as a brokerage manager--in the insurance business.

Suggested Action: • If anyone has ideas for or questions concerning the Insurance Division, you should call George Schutte on Extension 4655 in Richmond. • George is interested in seeing how other financial institutions are soliciting insurance products by mail. If you have recently received such a solicitation, please send it to George Schutte, Insurance Division, 10th Floor, Richmond Main Office.

KIM BOLGER TO MANAGE NEW CUSTOMER COMMUNICATIONS DEPARTMENT

Kim Bolger has been hired to manage the new Customer Communications Department within the Marketing Division. In this position, Kim will direct our new Marketing Customer Information File (CIF) System as well as review all customer communications to ensure they meet the Central Fidelity standard of quality.

The Marketing CIF will provide an important data base that enables us to profitably examine and consider each customer's entire banking relationship with us. The development of this data base is expected to be completed by late April. We will also be able to determine how we can most profitably match customers with specific products and develop a direct mail system which will be linked to the data base.

Kim joins us from Bank of Virginia's Marketing Division where she served as a direct response officer and managed the telemarketing center since August, 1985. Previously, she worked as senior marketing consultant/direct response manager of First Pennsylvania Bank, N.A. for three years. Kim graduated from Dartmouth College where she earned a B.A. in English. She has also received certificates in Essentials of Bank Marketing and School of Bank Marketing.

Suggested Action: • If you have any ideas or questions concerning our new Customer Communications Department, you should call Kim Bolger on Extension 4218 in Richmond.

(c) An original inside page.

March 5, 1987 Central Fidelity *Update* 5

Bank Card to solicit associations

Bank Card will conduct a credit card solicitation to Air Force Association and United States Naval Institute members during the week of March 2. These solicitations are follow-ups to previous mailings.

SUGGESTED ACTION:

☐ If you have any questions concerning this solicitation, call **Lora Scott** at Extension 4064 in Richmond.

Annual golf event to be held on April 25

IN BRIEF

- Golf begins at 8:30 a.m.
- Tennis starts at 10:00 a.m.
- Lunch served at 1:30 p.m.

The 18th Annual Central Fidelity Golf Tournament will be held at 8:30 a.m. on Saturday, April 25 at the Winton Country Club in Clifford (near Lynchburg). Tennis will also be offered and begin at 10:00 a.m. A luncheon will be held for participants after the events.

The golf and tennis are open to all employees, directors and retirees. **Harold Woody** will direct the golf tournament, while **Mike McFaden** will coordinate the tennis. Costs for the events are shown below:

Golf (non-Winton members)	$28.50 per person
Golf (Winton member)	17.50 per person
Tennis and lunch	13.20 per person

The deadline for signing up for either event is Wednesday, April 15. An entry form will be provided in next week's Update and in the April edition of Central Fidelity News.

SUGGESTED ACTION:

☐ If you have any questions concerning the golf tournament, call **Harold Woody** on Extension 9330 in Lynchburg.

☐ If you have any questions concerning the tennis tournament, call **Mike McFaden** on Extension 9545 in Lynchburg.

International opportunities now available

Our International Division has received four more requests from overseas companies interested in doing business with companies located in the United States. We can provide additional quality service by putting any interested customers or prospects in contact with the following companies.

Lancashire Footwear Manufacturers Association—Interested in importing men's and women's slippers, sandals, moccasins and shoes.

P.G.L. Gutteridge—Acting as an agent on behalf of Kayclean Limited. This company is interested in establishing business relations with U.S. firms that would act as an agent for the sale of a cleaning solution that cleans oil tanks and vessels, railway and ship engines, concrete, new cars, car engines and household spills. Brochure available.

P.G.L. Gutteridge is also acting as an agent on behalf of Orthoaed. This company is interested in establishing business relations that would act as an agent for the sale of orthopedic products used in the treatment of both neck and lower back pain.

John Cooksey & Son—Seeking business relations with manufacturers of toilet rolls, disposable paper tissue and toilet seat covers.

SUGGESTED ACTION:

☐ If you are aware of any customer or prospect who might be interested in a business relationship with any of these customers, call **Henk Schmidt** of our International Division on Extension 4231 in Richmond.

(d) Redesigned inside page.

Figure 13-6

Rates at a Glance

DEPOSIT PRODUCTS

Product	Effective Through	Rate	Yield
3-Month Certificate	December 16	5.50%	--
6-Month Certificate	December 16	5.80%	--
12-Month Certificate	December 16	6.00%	6.13%
18-Month Certificate	December 16	6.10%	6.24%
24-Month Certificate	December 16	6.50%	6.66%
30-Month Certificate	December 16	6.50%	6.66%
36-Month Certificate	December 16	7.00%	7.18%
60-Month Certificate	December 16	7.15%	7.34%
Alert Investor Account	December 16	5.40%	5.53%
SuperNOW	December 16	5.25%	--
Check 6000	December 16	5.25%	--
12-Month IRA	December 16	6.00%	6.13%
Best Rate IRA	December 16	8.50%	8.77%
24-Month IRA	December 16	6.50%	6.66%
36-Month IRA	December 16	7.00%	7.18%
60-Month IRA	December 16	7.15%	7.34%

LOAN PRODUCTS

Product	Effective Through	Rate	APR
1-Year Adjustable Rate Mortgage	December 25	7.875%*	--
3-Year Adjustable Rate Mortgage	December 25	9.750%**	--
Charter Account	December 25	--	9.504%
Employee Charter Account	December 25	--	8.508%
Charter Equity Account	December 25	--	9.120%
Employee Charter Equity Account	December 25	--	8.120%

*The index for the 1-Year Adjustable Rate Mortgage is 5.875%.
**The index for the 3-Year Adjustable Rate Mortgage is 6.500%.

(e) Old Rates at a Glance page.

March 5, 1987 Central Fidelity *Update* 7

Rates at a Glance

■ Deposit Products

Product	Rate	Change	Yield	Change
Certificates (Effective through March 10, 1987)				
3 Month	5.50%		—	
6 Month	5.75%		—	
12 Month	6.00%		6.13%	
18 Month	6.00%		6.13%	
24 Month	6.50%		6.66%	
30 Month	6.50%		6.66%	
36 Month	7.00%		7.18%	
60 Month	7.25%		7.44%	
Money Market Accounts (Effective through March 10, 1987)				
Alert Investor Account	5.30%		5.43%	
Check 6000	5.25%		—	
Individual Retirement Accounts (Effective through March 10, 1987)				
12 Month	6.00%		6.13%	
Best Rate - 18 Month *	8.50%		8.77%	
Best Rate - 18 Month **	7.00%		7.18%	
24 Month	6.50%		6.66%	
36 Month	7.00%		7.18%	
60 Month	7.25%		7.44%	

* Opened or renewed on or before December 31, 1986
** Opened or renewed after December 31, 1986

Product	Rate	Change	Yield	Change
Checking / Savings Accounts				
Interest Checking	5.25%			
Statement Savings	5.50%			

■ Loan Products

Product	Rate	APR
Mortgages (Effective through March 30, 1987)		
1-Year Adjustable Rate	7.500%*	—
3-Year Adjustable Rate	9.000%**	—
Charter / Charter Equity (Effective through March 25, 1987)		
Charter Account	—	9.504%
Employee Charter Account	—	8.508%
Charter Equity Account	—	9.132%
Employee Charter Equity Account	—	8.136%

* The index for the 1-Year Adjustable Rate Mortgage is 5.875%
** The index for the 3-Year Adjustable Rate Mortgage is 6.500%

(f) New Rates at a Glance Page.

Figure 13-6 (Continued)

Editor Jim Belcher also wanted a way to hit the highlights quickly for the person who did not have the time to read through the entire publication. "We found that *Update* was not being read quickly enough by those people who most needed the information," Belcher said.

First, the nameplate was changed to reflect changes in other corporate publications. One decision that had to be made was whether to keep the redundancy of the corporate logotype—Central Fidelity—near the nameplate, which also had "Central Fidelity" in it. It was cut, or rather edited out.

"We had just received some new equipment at our internal typesetting department," Belcher said. "I had been interested in the narrow/wide column format, but our previous equipment could not do that. Finally, we had just gone through a corporate identification program. We needed something to bring this along through a changed look.

"A benefit of the change was the new, easier-to-read Rates At A Glance box. We decided to take the 'At A Glance' concept to the rest of the publication. If people don't have time to read every word, they can get an idea of what's going on by just reading the left-hand column.

"The reaction has been positive. *Update* has always been considered the most indispensable of our publications because it's the most timely."

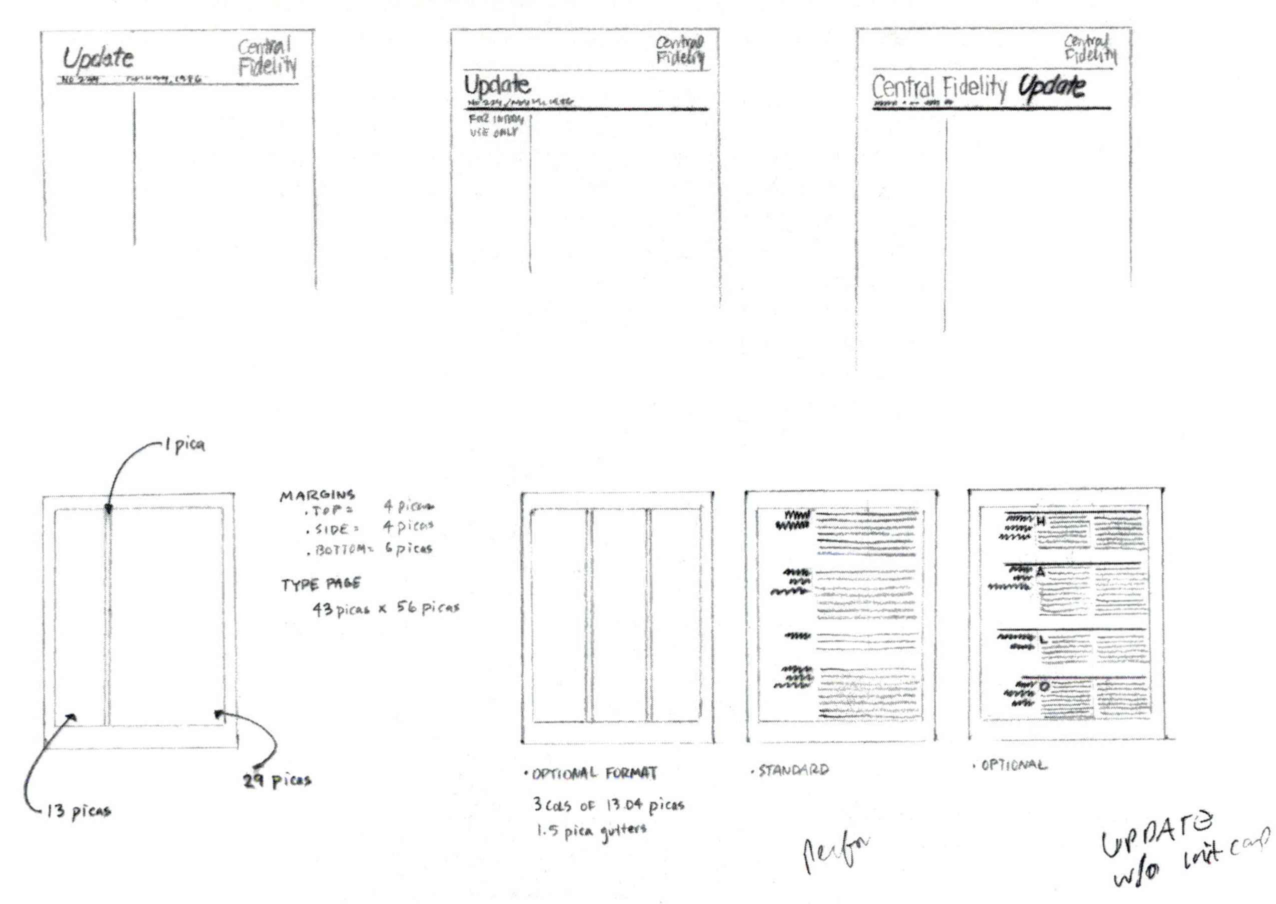

Figure 13-7 Sketches of possible formats for "Update." (All examples courtesy of Central Fidelity Bank)

My Analysis

The original front page consisted of only the contents list. Without any typographical contrast, the page appears flat and uninteresting. The flag was changed to just say "Update." With the logotype in the upper right (where it is located on all letterhead, business cards, and signage, etc.), the bank's name again in the flag is simply redundant. The change was minimal, but effective.

Inside pages. Even though display type was used for headlines in the original, the look of the newsletter was still typewritten. The move to the narrow/wide format is a good one. With the addition of the "In Brief" boxes in the left-hand column, the scanner can truly get the most important information quickly.

The new pages also have more type contrast, using both boldface and caps better. The "Rates At A Glance" box was also improved by putting the information in a more sensible order. Indentations, just like the standard outline format, are used to indicate the different levels of information. Redundancies were removed.

The information is better organized and it is packaged more clearly and more attractively. That's a good example of "integrated editing": Readers get clearer information and the package looks better.

CHECKLIST

1. Even though a newsletter is a "simple" publication, attention to all the previously covered design information—type, design basics, white space, color, etc.—needs to be given. The same goes for a brochure. In fact, right now would be a terrific time to go back and reread Chapters 2, 3, and 5 before experimenting with your own newsletter or brochure design. You don't learn the good stuff with just one quick read. It's like sweeping dust in a dustpan: It takes several sweeps of the broom to get it all in.
2. First, always "freeze your pond": Set up your type page and margins, columns and gutters (and alleys, if you are using a Swiss grid). Then, if you have set up good spacing guidelines, and if you have selected good typography with guidelines for use, you are ready to produce organized and—with luck—attractive pages. Following accepted principles will nearly always lead at least to a not *un*attractive publication.
3. With attention to detail, even a typewritten newsletter can look professional. If it is *done* professionally, if the editor has followed all the guidelines, then it will look good.
4. Remember that information graphics are useful ways to communicate certain kinds of information. These do not have to be complicated at all. Just use them to show the relationships among data.
5. Get a newsletter from a local corporation or community group. Design three different nameplates, all the same size as the original. Make sure each has a distinctly different "personality." Lay the new nameplates on top of the old and photocopy each front page. Compare them. Which one works best? Worst? Why? Does the "feel" of the publication change with each one?
6. Do the same for the cover of a three-panel brochure. Do up a type attack, a color attack, and an art attack cover that fits, in general, the content needs of the particular brochure. Which one works best? Why? Ask disinterested others to look at all three and choose the one that has the most "pick-me-up" appeal.
7. Pick something of interest to you—a sport, hobby, or other similar outside activity—and create a prospectus and mock-up of a newsletter for that group. For instance, you might decide to come up with Central State Runners Club. The prospectus should include the prospective audience, its size and nature, the number of pages, how created, how printed and distributed, etc. Design a column grid and a brief typographical style manual, and create a mock-up of the front page and an inside page.
8. Design a brochure for an organization you are involved in. Don't bother with writing copy (unless you want to, of course!). Just set up the format and grid, columns, margins, gutters, etc. Cut out rectangles of tone paper (or gray construction paper) to represent the art and use greeked (faked) typeset copy—available from art stores—to represent copy. You can use rub-on type for display type, or trace what you need from a type book and transfer it to your mock-up (called a "comp" or comprehensive layout) with carbon paper.

CHAPTER 14

MAGAZINES

Magazines have many of the same design challenges of newsletters, and a few more as well. Magazines are often thicker, have more elements, have a more diverse audience, and generally have to compete for readers' attention, whether they are corporate magazines or general-circulation magazines. Newsletters often have built-in audiences with interest in the subject at hand. In general, magazines have to compete for their share of the audience. Design then becomes very important.

It becomes important in two ways. First, as we have seen throughout this book, design helps make content easier to consume. Design makes publications user-friendly. This is important in the hectic pace of today's society. Second, design is one way to set your publication apart from others, to give it a unique personality in the crowd of competitors.

So, besides the basics of format (Chapter 2), design (Chapter 3), and layout (Chapter 5) covered earlier, a few other specific comments about magazine design need to be covered. Then we'll look at a magazine spread being designed and watch problems being solved.

FORMAT

Choosing the format and personality for a publication is an important first step. The first step in designing, or redesigning for that matter, is to ask a number of questions:

- What is the nature of your intended audience?
- What are other publications in this field like?

- What is your "personality" going to be—that is, urbane and sophisticated or wild and raucous?
- How much color do you want or, better yet, can you afford?

You need to answer all these questions with an eye on your audience and another on your budget. And if you had a third eye, you had better look over your competition as well.

Much of this process of selecting a format and personality involves marketing concepts. You must decide exactly who your readers are, what their needs are, what their interests are, what advertisers have products they would like to sell to them.

Once you have identified your particular segment of the audience, you need to decide how to "position" yourself within the market. Assuming there are a number of other publications trying to reach the same readership, how are you going to separate yourself from them?

Design is only one way, but it can be a very important way. If you decide to take an intellectual approach to your subject matter, then the design must be very different from the magazine that has taken the gossipy approach to the same subject matter.

An intellectual approach to the content calls for wide columns, small headlines that quietly announce the title, not shout it out. It is a gray, pin-striped suit, not a flashy, plaid sports jacket.

On the other hand, if you want to take that wild and crazy approach, then by all means, add wild color, let your titles shout, run type on diagonals (mild, please!), and just let your design go a little wild too.

Another way to separate yourself from your competition is the format. Naturally both the kind and the amount of content say something about what kind of page size you select. But one certain way to separate yourself from possible competitors is use a different format.

The main formats are:

- Small or miniature: 4-1/2 × 6
- Book size: 6 × 9
- Standard: 8-1/2 × 11
- Picture: 10-1/2 × 13

First, let your content decide the format. Are you going to run a lot of high-quality photos? Then the small sizes are out. Is your content to be read on the move, or seated near a coffee table? If the former, than a small size would be suitable. If the latter, the large size would probably be better. If you have a small amount of content, you may be better off with a smaller size. The larger pages would give you a thin publication. Readers would think they were not getting much for their money.

The most common size is the 8-1/2-by-11-inch. This is because the size is convenient: typing paper, file drawers, and folders all are this size. Also, with 11-by-17-inch paper, there is virtually no paper waste and accompanying costs.

The miniature size is not used much. *Reader's Digest* and *TV Guide* are the best-known publications this size. The small page size limits what can be done with design anyway, so it needn't concern us here. A designer often will set up the grid, select readable and attractive type, use white space well, and let it go at that.

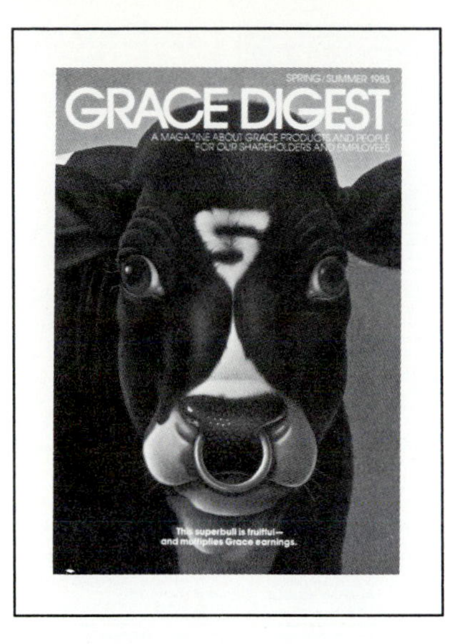

Figure 14-1 Even a small-format magazine, such as *Grace Digest,* can be well edited and designed. Small pages do not design themselves. (Courtesy of Bernhardt Fudyma Design Group)

Grace Digest (Fig. 14–1) is a well-designed small publication, an exception to the rule of miniature publications. This magazine shows that a format is not the limit; the designer's imagination and skill are.

The largest size is close to that of a tabloid-sized newspaper. Many of the principles are the same, and they are covered in the following chapter. For that reason, only the ubiquitous 8-1/2-by-11-inch format will be looked at in any detail here.

COLUMN GRID

There is no end to the ways you can set up a column grid. The standard formats are three-column and, to a lesser extent, two columns. The two columns provide more of a bookish look, and it is used with more intellectual, more bookish publications (Fig. 14–2).

But if you have an adventurous design spirit, you can work with unusual column configurations. One unusual, but highly effective, grid was adopted by *Enterprise* magazine, designed by Hawthorne/Wolfe, Inc., for Southwestern Bell (Fig. 14–3). It has a three equal-column format with a fourth narrower column that floats. The narrow column can be used anywhere.

This approach gives the designer the best of both worlds: a solid and familiar grid and freedom to make the grid flexible.

Along with the grid, you have to decide upon your margins and gutters and such. To a certain extent, even the size of these nonelements should be dictated by your design personality. Wide, bookish columns call for wider gutters and more margin than do narrower, active columns.

COVER

This is the most important single page in your magazine, especially if your publication has to shout from newsstands to sell itself. It should be a window to the content inside, and it should reflect the design personality you have selected for your publication.

Lorem ipsum dolor sit amet, consectetuer adipiscing elit, sed diam nonummy nibh euismod tincidunt ut laoreet dolore magna aliquam erat volutpat. Ut wisi enim ad minim veniam, quis nostrud exerci tation ullamcorper suscipit lobortis nisl ut aliquip ex ea commodo consequat. Duis autem vel eum iriure dolor in hendrerit in vulputate velit esse molestie consequat, vel illum dolore eu feugiat nulla facilisis at vero eros et accumsan et iusto odio dignissim qui blandit praesent luptatum zzril delenit augue duis dolore te feugait nulla facilisi. Lorem ipsum dolor sit amet, consectetuer adipiscing elit, sed diam nonummy nibh euismod tincidunt ut laoreet dolore magna aliquam erat volutpat. Ut wisi enim ad minim veniam, quis nostrud exerci tation ullamcorper suscipit lobortis nisl ut aliquip ex ea commodo consequat.
Duis autem vel eum iriure dolor in hendrerit in vulputate velit esse molestie consequat, vel illum dolore eu feugiat nulla facilisis at vero eros et accumsan et iusto odio dignissim qui blandit praesent luptatum zzril delenit augue duis dolore te feugait nulla facilisi. Nam liber tempor cum soluta nobis eleifend option congue nihil imperdiet doming id quod mazim placerat facer possim assum. Lorem ipsum dolor sit amet, consectetuer adipiscing elit, sed diam nonummy nibh euismod tincidunt ut laoreet dolore magna aliquam erat volutpat. Ut wisi enim ad minim veniam, quis nostrud exerci tation ullamcorper suscipit lobortis nisl ut aliquip ex ea commodo consequat. Duis autem vel eum iriure dolor in hendrerit in vulputate velit esse molestie consequat, vel illum dolore eu feugiat nulla facilisis at vero eros et accumsan et iusto odio dignissim qui blandit praesent luptatum zzril delenit augue duis dolore te feugait nulla facilisi. Lorem ipsum dolor sit amet, consectetuer adipiscing elit, sed diam nonummy nibh euismod tincidunt ut laoreet dolore magna aliquam erat volutpat.
Ut wisi enim ad minim veniam, quis nostrud exerci tation ullamcorper suscipit lobortis nisl ut aliquip ex ea commodo consequat. Duis autem vel eum iriure dolor in hendrerit in vulputate velit esse molestie consequat, vel illum dolore eu feugiat nulla facilisis at vero eros et accumsan et iusto odio dignissim qui blandit praesent luptatum zzril delenit augue duis dolore te feugait nulla facilisi. Lorem ipsum dolor sit amet, consectetuer adipiscing elit, sed diam nonummy nibh euismod tincidunt ut laoreet dolore magna aliquam erat volutpat. Ut wisi enim ad minim veniam, quis nostrud exerci tation ullamcorper suscipit lobortis nisl ut aliquip ex ea commodo consequat. Duis autem vel eum iriure dolor in hendrerit in vulputate velit esse molestie consequat, vel illum dolore eu feugiat nulla facilisis at vero eros et accumsan et iusto odio dignissim qui blandit praesent luptatum zzril delenit augue duis dolore te feugait nulla facilisi.
Lorem ipsum dolor sit amet, consectetuer adipiscing elit, sed diam nonummy nibh euismod tincidunt ut laoreet dolore magna aliquam erat volutpat. Ut wisi enim ad minim veniam, quis nostrud exerci tation ullamcorper suscipit lobortis nisl ut aliquip ex ea commodo consequat. Duis autem vel eum iriure dolor in hendrerit in vulputate velit esse molestie consequat, vel illum dolore eu feugiat nulla facilisis at vero eros et

Lorem ipsum dolor sit amet, consectetuer adipiscing elit, sed diam nonummy nibh euismod tincidunt ut laoreet dolore magna aliquam erat volutpat. Ut wisi enim ad minim veniam, quis nostrud exerci tation ullamcorper suscipit lobortis nisl ut aliquip ex ea commodo consequat. Duis autem vel eum iriure dolor in hendrerit in vulputate velit esse molestie consequat, vel illum dolore eu feugiat nulla facilisis at vero eros et accumsan et iusto odio dignissim qui blandit praesent luptatum zzril delenit augue duis dolore te feugait nulla facilisi. Lorem ipsum dolor sit amet, consectetuer adipiscing elit, sed diam nonummy nibh euismod tincidunt ut laoreet dolore magna aliquam erat volutpat. Ut wisi enim ad minim veniam, quis nostrud exerci tation ullamcorper suscipit lobortis nisl ut aliquip ex ea commodo consequat.
Duis autem vel eum iriure dolor in hendrerit in vulputate velit esse molestie consequat, vel illum dolore eu feugiat nulla facilisis at vero eros et accumsan et iusto odio dignissim qui blandit praesent luptatum zzril delenit augue duis dolore te feugait nulla facilisi. Nam liber tempor cum soluta nobis eleifend option congue nihil imperdiet doming id quod mazim placerat facer possim assum. Lorem ipsum dolor sit amet, consectetuer adipiscing elit, sed diam nonummy nibh euismod tincidunt ut laoreet dolore magna aliquam erat volutpat. Ut wisi enim ad minim veniam, quis nostrud exerci tation ullamcorper suscipit lobortis nisl ut aliquip ex ea commodo consequat. Duis autem vel eum iriure dolor in hendrerit in vulputate velit esse molestie consequat, vel illum dolore eu feugiat nulla facilisis at vero eros et accumsan et iusto odio dignissim qui blandit praesent luptatum zzril delenit augue duis dolore te feugait nulla facilisi. Lorem ipsum dolor sit amet, consectetuer adipiscing elit, sed diam nonummy nibh euismod tincidunt ut laoreet dolore magna aliquam erat volutpat.
Ut wisi enim ad minim veniam, quis nostrud exerci tation ullamcorper suscipit lobortis nisl ut aliquip ex ea commodo consequat. Duis autem vel eum iriure dolor in hendrerit in vulputate velit esse molestie consequat, vel illum dolore eu feugiat nulla facilisis at vero eros et accumsan et iusto odio

(a)

Lorem ipsum dolor sit amet, consectetuer adipiscing elit, sed diam nonummy nibh euismod tincidunt ut laoreet dolore magna aliquam erat volutpat. Ut wisi enim ad minim veniam, quis nostrud exerci tation ullamcorper suscipit lobortis nisl ut aliquip ex ea commodo consequat. Duis autem vel eum iriure dolor in hendrerit in vulputate velit esse molestie consequat, vel illum dolore eu feugiat nulla facilisis at vero eros et accumsan et iusto odio dignissim qui blandit praesent luptatum zzril delenit augue duis dolore te feugait nulla facilisi. Lorem ipsum dolor sit amet, consectetuer adipiscing elit, sed diam nonummy nibh euismod tincidunt ut laoreet dolore magna aliquam erat volutpat. Ut wisi enim ad minim veniam, quis nostrud exerci tation ullamcorper suscipit lobortis nisl ut aliquip ex ea commodo consequat.
Duis autem vel eum iriure dolor in hendrerit in vulputate velit esse molestie consequat, vel illum dolore eu feugiat nulla facilisis at vero eros et accumsan et iusto odio dignissim qui blandit praesent luptatum zzril delenit augue duis dolore te feugait nulla facilisi. Nam liber tempor cum soluta nobis eleifend option congue nihil imperdiet doming id quod mazim placerat facer possim assum. Lorem ipsum dolor sit amet, consectetuer adipiscing elit, sed diam nonummy nibh euismod tincidunt ut laoreet dolore magna aliquam erat volutpat. Ut wisi enim ad minim veniam, quis nostrud exerci tation ullamcorper suscipit lobortis nisl ut aliquip ex ea commodo consequat. Duis autem vel eum iriure dolor in hendrerit in vulputate velit esse molestie consequat, vel illum dolore eu feugiat nulla facilisis at vero eros et accumsan et iusto odio dignissim qui blandit praesent luptatum zzril delenit augue duis dolore te feugait nulla facilisi. Lorem ipsum dolor sit amet, consectetuer adipiscing elit, sed diam nonummy nibh euismod tincidunt ut laoreet dolore magna aliquam erat volutpat.
Ut wisi enim ad minim veniam, quis nostrud exerci tation ullamcorper suscipit lobortis nisl ut aliquip ex ea commodo consequat. Duis autem vel eum iriure dolor in hendrerit in vulputate velit esse molestie consequat, vel illum

dolore eu feugiat nulla facilisis at vero eros et accumsan et iusto odio dignissim qui blandit praesent luptatum zzril delenit augue duis dolore te feugait nulla facilisi. Lorem ipsum dolor sit amet, consectetuer adipiscing elit, sed diam nonummy nibh euismod tincidunt ut laoreet dolore magna aliquam erat volutpat. Ut wisi enim ad minim veniam, quis nostrud exerci tation ullamcorper suscipit lobortis nisl ut aliquip ex ea commodo consequat. Duis autem vel eum iriure dolor in hendrerit in vulputate velit esse molestie consequat, vel illum dolore eu feugiat nulla facilisis at vero eros et accumsan et iusto odio dignissim qui blandit praesent luptatum zzril delenit augue duis dolore te feugait nulla facilisi. Lorem ipsum dolor sit amet, consectetuer adipiscing elit, sed diam nonummy nibh euismod tincidunt ut laoreet dolore magna aliquam erat volutpat. Ut wisi enim ad minim veniam, quis nostrud exerci tation ullamcorper suscipit lobortis nisl ut aliquip ex ea commodo consequat. Duis autem vel eum iriure dolor in hendrerit in vulputate velit esse molestie consequat, vel illum dolore eu feugiat nulla
Lorem ipsum dolor sit amet, consectetuer adipiscing elit, sed diam nonummy nibh euismod tincidunt ut laoreet dolore magna aliquam erat volutpat. Ut wisi enim ad minim veniam, quis nostrud exerci tation ullamcorper suscipit lobortis nisl ut aliquip ex ea commodo consequat. Duis

autem vel eum iriure dolor in hendrerit in vulputate velit esse molestie consequat, vel illum dolore eu feugiat nulla facilisis at vero eros et accumsan et iusto odio dignissim qui blandit praesent luptatum zzril delenit augue duis dolore te feugait nulla facilisi. Lorem ipsum dolor sit amet, consectetuer adipiscing elit, sed diam nonummy nibh euismod tincidunt ut laoreet dolore magna aliquam erat volutpat. Ut wisi enim ad minim veniam, quis nostrud exerci tation ullamcorper suscipit lobortis nisl ut aliquip ex ea commodo consequat. Duis autem vel eum iriure dolor in hendrerit in vulputate velit esse molestie consequat, vel illum dolore eu feugiat nulla facilisis at vero eros et accumsan et iusto odio dignissim qui blandit praesent luptatum zzril delenit augue duis dolore te feugait nulla facilisi. Nam liber tempor cum soluta nobis eleifend option congue nihil imperdiet doming id quod mazim placerat facer possim assum. Lorem ipsum dolor sit amet, consectetuer adipiscing elit, sed diam nonummy nibh euismod tincidunt ut laoreet dolore magna aliquam erat volutpat. Ut wisi enim ad minim veniam, quis nostrud exerci tation ullamcorper suscipit lobortis nisl ut aliquip ex ea commodo consequat. Duis autem vel eum iriure dolor in hendrerit in vulputate velit esse molestie consequat, vel illum dolore eu feugiat nulla facilisis at vero eros et accumsan et iusto odio dignissim qui blandit praesent luptatum zzril delenit augue duis dolore te feugait nulla facilisi. Lorem ipsum dolor sit amet, consectetuer adipiscing elit, sed diam nonummy nibh euismod tincidunt ut laoreet dolore magna aliquam erat volutpat.
Ut wisi enim ad minim veniam, quis nostrud exerci tation ullamcorper suscipit lobortis nisl ut aliquip ex ea commodo consequat. Duis autem vel eum iriure dolor in hendrerit in vulputate velit esse molestie consequat, vel illum dolore eu feugiat nulla facilisis at vero eros et accumsan et iusto odio dignissim qui blandit praesent luptatum zzril delenit augue duis dolore te feugait nulla facilisi. Lorem ipsum dolor sit amet, consectetuer adipiscing elit, sed diam nonummy nibh euismod tincidunt ut

(b)

laoreet dolore magna aliquam erat volutpat. Ut wisi enim ad minim veniam, quis nostrud exerci tation ullamcorper suscipit lobortis nisl ut aliquip ex ea commodo consequat. Duis autem vel eum iriure dolor in hendrerit in vulputate velit esse molestie consequat, vel illum dolore eu feugiat nulla facilisis at vero eros et accumsan et iusto odio dignissim qui blandit praesent luptatum zzril delenit augue duis dolore te feugait nulla facilisi.
Lorem ipsum dolor sit amet, consectetuer adipiscing elit, sed diam nonummy nibh euismod tincidunt ut laoreet dolore magna aliquam erat volutpat. Ut wisi enim ad minim veniam, quis nostrud exerci tation ullamcorper suscipit lobortis nisl ut aliquip ex ea commodo consequat. Duis autem vel eum iriure dolor in hendrerit in vulputate velit esse molestie consequat, vel illum dolore eu feugiat nulla facilisis at vero eros et accumsan et iusto odio dignissim qui blandit praesent luptatum zzril delenit augue duis dolore te feugait nulla facilisi. Lorem ipsum dolor sit amet, consectetuer adipiscing elit, sed diam nonummy nibh euismod tincidunt ut laoreet dolore magna aliquam erat volutpat. Ut wisi enim ad minim veniam, quis nostrud exerci tation ullamcorper suscipit lobortis nisl ut aliquip ex ea commodo consequat.
Autem vel eum iriure dolor in hendrerit in vulputate velit esse molestie consequat, vel illum dolore eu feugiat nulla facilisis at vero eros et accumsan et iusto odio dignissim qui blandit praesent luptatum zzril

euismod tincidunt ut laoreet dolore magna aliquam erat volutpat. Ut wisi enim ad minim veniam, quis nostrud exerci tation ullamcorper suscipit lobortis nisl ut aliquip ex ea commodo consequat. Duis autem vel eum iriure dolor in hendrerit in vulputate velit esse molestie consequat, vel illum dolore eu feugiat nulla facilisis at vero eros et accumsan et iusto odio dignissim qui blandit praesent luptatum zzril delenit augue duis dolore te feugait nulla facilisi. Lorem ipsum dolor sit amet, consectetuer adipiscing elit, sed diam nonummy nibh euismod tincidunt ut laoreet dolore magna aliquam erat volutpat. Ut wisi enim ad minim veniam, quis nostrud exerci tation ullamcorper suscipit lobortis nisl ut aliquip ex ea commodo consequat.
Duis autem vel eum iriure dolor in hendrerit in vulputate velit esse molestie consequat, vel illum dolore eu feugiat nulla facilisis at vero eros et accumsan et iusto odio dignissim qui blandit

praesent luptatum zzril delenit augue duis dolore te feugait nulla facilisi. Nam liber tempor cum soluta nobis eleifend option congue nihil imperdiet doming id quod mazim placerat facer possim assum. Lorem ipsum dolor sit amet, consectetuer adipiscing elit, sed diam nonummy nibh euismod tincidunt ut laoreet dolore magna aliquam erat volutpat. Ut wisi enim ad minim veniam, quis nostrud exerci tation ullamcorper suscipit lobortis nisl ut aliquip ex ea commodo consequat. Duis autem vel eum iriure dolor in hendrerit in vulputate velit esse molestie consequat, vel illum dolore eu feugiat nulla facilisis at vero eros et accumsan et iusto odio dignissim qui blandit praesent luptatum zzril delenit augue duis dolore te feugait nulla facilisi. Lorem ipsum dolor sit amet, consectetuer adipiscing elit, sed diam nonummy nibh euismod tincidunt ut laoreet dolore magna aliquam erat volutpat.
Ut wisi enim ad minim veniam, quis nostrud exerci

tation ullamcorper suscipit lobortis nisl ut aliquip ex ea commodo consequat. Duis autem vel eum iriure dolor in hendrerit in vulputate velit esse molestie consequat, vel illum dolore eu feugiat nulla facilisis at vero eros et accumsan et iusto odio dignissim qui blandit praesent luptatum zzril delenit augue duis dolore te feugait nulla facilisi. Lorem ipsum dolor sit amet, consectetuer adipiscing elit, sed diam nonummy nibh euismod tincidunt ut laoreet dolore magna aliquam erat volutpat. Ut wisi enim ad minim veniam, quis nostrud exerci tation ullamcorper suscipit lobortis nisl ut aliquip ex ea commodo consequat. Duis autem vel eum iriure dolor in hendrerit in vulputate velit esse molestie consequat, vel illum dolore eu feugiat nulla facilisis at vero eros et accumsan et iusto odio dignissim qui blandit
Lorem ipsum dolor sit amet, consectetuer adipiscing elit, sed diam nonummy nibh euismod tincidunt ut laoreet dolore magna aliquam erat volutpat. Ut wisi enim ad minim veniam, quis nostrud exerci tation ullamcorper suscipit lobortis nisl ut aliquip ex ea commodo consequat. Duis autem vel eum iriure dolor in hendrerit in vulputate velit esse molestie consequat, vel illum dolore eu feugiat nulla facilisis at vero eros et accumsan et iusto odio dignissim qui blandit praesent luptatum zzril delenit augue duis dolore te feugait nulla facilisi. Lorem ipsum dolor sit amet, consectetuer adipiscing elit, sed diam nonummy nibh euismod tincidunt ut laoreet dolore magna aliquam erat

(c)

Lorem ipsum dolor sit amet, consectetuer adipiscing elit, sed diam nonummy nibh euismod tincidunt ut laoreet dolore magna aliquam erat volutpat. Ut wisi enim ad minim veniam, quis nostrud exerci tation ullamcorper suscipit lobortis nisl ut aliquip ex ea commodo consequat. Duis autem vel eum iriure dolor in hendrerit in vulputate velit esse molestie consequat, vel illum dolore eu feugiat nulla facilisis at vero eros et accumsan et iusto odio dignissim qui blandit praesent luptatum zzril delenit augue duis dolore te feugait nulla facilisi. Lorem ipsum dolor sit amet, consectetuer adipiscing elit, sed diam nonummy nibh euismod tincidunt ut laoreet dolore magna aliquam erat volutpat. Ut wisi enim ad minim veniam, quis nostrud exerci tation ullamcorper suscipit lobortis nisl ut aliquip ex ea commodo consequat.
Duis autem vel eum iriure dolor in hendrerit in vulputate velit esse molestie consequat, vel illum dolore eu feugiat nulla facilisis at vero eros et accumsan et iusto odio dignissim qui blandit praesent luptatum zzril delenit augue duis dolore te feugait nulla facilisi. Nam liber tempor cum soluta nobis eleifend option congue nihil imperdiet doming id quod mazim placerat facer possim assum. Lorem ipsum dolor sit amet, consectetuer adipiscing elit, sed diam nonummy nibh euismod tincidunt ut laoreet dolore magna aliquam erat volutpat. Ut wisi enim ad minim veniam, quis nostrud exerci tation ullamcorper suscipit lobortis nisl ut aliquip ex ea commodo consequat. Duis autem vel eum iriure dolor in hendrerit in vulputate velit esse molestie consequat, vel illum dolore eu feugiat nulla facilisis at vero eros et accumsan et iusto odio dignissim qui blandit praesent luptatum zzril delenit augue duis dolore te feugait nulla facilisi. Lorem ipsum dolor sit amet, consectetuer adipiscing elit, sed diam nonummy nibh euismod tincidunt ut laoreet dolore magna aliquam erat volutpat.
Ut wisi enim ad minim veniam, quis nostrud exerci tation ullamcorper suscipit lobortis nisl ut aliquip ex ea commodo consequat. Duis autem vel eum iriure dolor in hendrerit in vulputate velit esse molestie consequat, vel illum dolore eu feugiat nulla facilisis at vero

eros et accumsan et iusto odio dignissim qui blandit praesent luptatum zzril delenit augue duis dolore te feugait nulla facilisi.
Lorem ipsum dolor sit amet, consectetuer adipiscing elit, sed diam nonummy nibh euismod tincidunt ut laoreet dolore magna aliquam erat volutpat. Ut wisi enim ad minim veniam, quis nostrud exerci tation ullamcorper suscipit lobortis nisl ut aliquip ex ea commodo consequat. Duis autem vel eum iriure dolor in hendrerit in vulputate velit esse molestie consequat, vel illum dolore eu feugiat nulla facilisis at vero eros et accumsan et iusto odio dignissim qui blandit praesent luptatum zzril delenit augue duis dolore te feugait nulla facilisi.
Lorem ipsum dolor sit amet, consectetuer adipiscing elit, sed diam nonummy nibh euismod tincidunt ut laoreet dolore magna aliquam erat volutpat. Ut wisi enim ad minim veniam, quis nostrud exerci tation ullamcorper suscipit lobortis nisl ut aliquip ex ea commodo consequat. Duis autem vel eum iriure dolor in hendrerit in vulputate velit esse molestie consequat, vel illum dolore eu feugiat nulla facilisis at vero eros et accumsan et iusto odio dignissim qui blandit praesent luptatum zzril delenit augue duis dolore te feugait nulla facilisi. Lorem ipsum dolor sit amet, consectetuer adipiscing elit, sed diam nonummy nibh euismod tincidunt ut laoreet dolore magna aliquam erat volutpat. Ut wisi enim ad minim veniam, quis nostrud exerci tation ullamcorper suscipit lobortis nisl ut

Lorem ipsum dolor sit amet, consectetuer adipiscing elit, sed diam nonummy nibh euismod tincidunt ut laoreet dolore magna aliquam erat volutpat. Ut wisi enim ad minim veniam, quis nostrud exerci tation ullamcorper suscipit lobortis nisl ut aliquip ex ea commodo consequat. Duis autem vel eum iriure dolor in hendrerit in vulputate velit esse molestie consequat, vel illum dolore eu feugiat nulla facilisis at vero eros et accumsan et iusto odio dignissim qui blandit praesent luptatum zzril delenit augue duis dolore te feugait nulla facilisi. Lorem ipsum dolor sit amet, consectetuer adipiscing elit, sed diam nonummy nibh euismod tincidunt ut laoreet dolore magna aliquam erat volutpat. Ut wisi enim ad minim veniam, quis nostrud exerci tation ullamcorper suscipit lobortis nisl ut aliquip ex ea commodo consequat.

(d)

Figure 14-2 The number of columns in the basic grid should be decided before any other design decisions are made. Two-, three-, or four-column grids can be used, depending on the content and personality of the publication. If you use a "half-column grid,"—that is, if you use smaller basic columns and then run type two "columns" wide—even more creative possibilities are opened up. The art in (d) is a half or two-and-a-half columns wide. Any layout still shows that it is tied to that underlying grid skeleton.

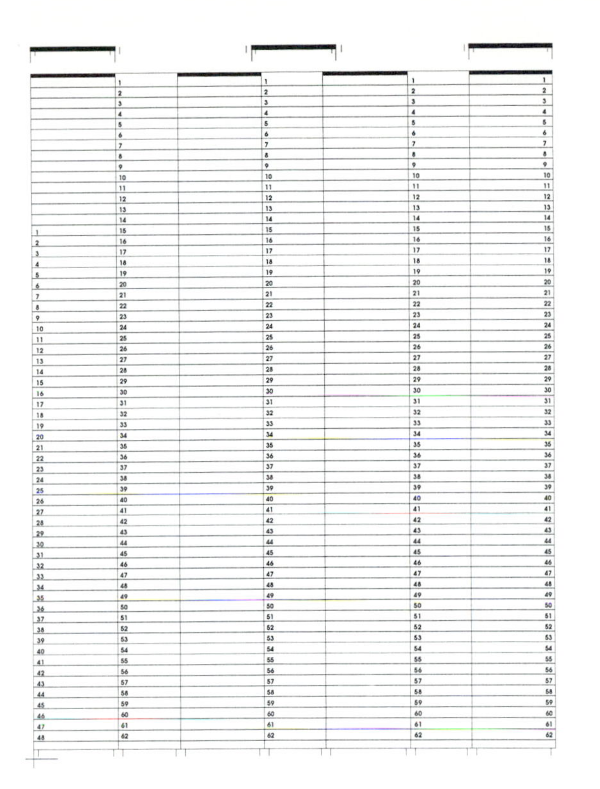

(a)

line of high-quality, competitively priced telephones for residence and small business customers."

(For a look at how the Electra employees reacted to the acquisition, see the box at right.)

Telecom's other major new venture is a consulting division named Southwestern Bell/ISI–Information Systems Integrators.

"The biggest problem facing today's information systems managers is how to plan for both business growth and technological change," says Scott Pool, president of ISI. "Our services have been developed especially to address this problem.

"ISI services cover two main categories. First, we offer general telecommunications consulting to help customers define their telecommunications requirements.

"Second, we can handle the analysis and design, equipment evaluation, and job management and coordination for private local information transport systems. Our capabilities extend from the smallest telephone system up through today's most advanced local area network."

ISI's chief advantage is its unique combination of technical and economic judgment, Pool says.

Mobile Systems keeps rolling toward success

AT Southwestern Bell Mobile Systems, innovation is keeping the company at the forefront of the evolving cellular industry.

Here are just a few of the new avenues SBMS is pursuing in the cellular field:

- The company has filed a waiver request with the U.S. district court in Washington seeking permission to offer consulting and monitoring services for other cellular companies.
- SBMS also is seeking permission to offer cellular system management services for firms throughout the United States, Canada and the Caribbean.
- In many of its markets, Mobile Systems has introduced a phone rental plan with only a one-month minimum term. The plan makes it much easier for customers to experience the benefits of cellular service before they buy the cellular phone outright.
- In St. Louis and Dallas, cab companies have equipped some of their vehicles with SBMS cellular phones. The cab driver collects payment from passengers using the phones.
- In various cities, Mobile Systems has an agreement with Budget Rent-A-Car to make cellular phones available in rental cars. Budget pays SBMS for the calling time and then charges its customers for the time.

In addition to all these developments, SBMS is operating cellular systems in six cities, more than any other cellular company in the country.

"We've been able to do all this because people in all areas of our company — from engineering to billing to marketing — are finding methods to put our systems in operation quickly," says John Atterbury, president and chief executive officer of Mobile Systems.

Intelligent risk-taking makes for a bright future

THE various new ventures within Southwestern Bell Corporation point to a bright future for the company. We're building on our strengths by taking intelligent risks.

How do we judge whether a risk is worth taking? It boils down to one thing: A risk makes sense when there's a reasonably good chance that customers will respond enthusiastically to a new offering at a reasonable price.

Our risk on new ventures is reduced by one important strategy: We stick close to the businesses we know best. Few would challenge our expertise in telecommunications and directory services. As we keep finding new revenue streams within those areas, we'll ensure a stable present and an exciting future. ■

Indianians open their hearts to Telecom

THE announcement came as a pleasant surprise to the affected employees of Electra Company. The 50 or so workers were relieved to learn a half year ago that they were about to become the Freedom Phone® Division of Southwestern Bell Telecom.

"Our employees knew the company was for sale, and they were very concerned that the purchaser would move the work out of Indianapolis," explains Sam Martin, president of the Freedom Phone Division. "You can't imagine how happy they were to stay here.

Sam Martin

"The other thing they appreciate is being associated with a company as substantial as Southwestern Bell Corporation and the Telecom subsidiary. There's a feeling of security that comes with being employed by a well-established company."

Martin says some changes were easy to digest for the Freedom Phone Division's 50 employees and others weren't.

"The pension plan we've come into is better, and so is the holiday schedule," he explains. "And we had neither a dental plan nor a vision care plan before.

"The hard part to accept, however, was that like all new Southwestern Bell Corporation employees, our employees couldn't be eligible for some benefits for six months. Also, they're having to pay their own health plan premiums for the same amount of time.

"In the end, however, the employees will have a better benefit plan." ■

Enterprise / No. 1, 1985 13

(b)

then it can't make accurate forecasts, and it can't depend on its cable and switches being used. If the plant is not used, it goes to waste, and ratepayers end up shouldering needless expense.

Also, if the company must wait to install facilities until it's certain its services will be used, the obligation to provide service on a *timely* basis is compromised.

Obligations are welcomed

"We welcome the obligations outlined in the certificates as long as we continue to have the right to be the sole provider of local service," Waetzig says.

"In fairness to all interests involved, our request to the commissions is this: Quickly clarify our status as exclusive providers of exchange service and declare that those who are not certificated have no right—as they have no obligation—to provide alternative service, in any form, within our franchised service territory."

Would-be resellers often could operate less expensively than Southwestern Bell Telephone precisely because they don't have the obligation to serve everyone. The situation is similar to what has happened in the long-distance business.

Competitors succeeded in that business, in part, by skimming the cream away from the old Bell System, serving only the profitable, high-volume routes such as St. Louis to Chicago and New York to Washington. They were more than happy to leave to the Bell System the less used, less profitable routes—such as Cash, Ark., to Odessa, Tex.

By taking revenues away from the Bell System, competitors jeopardized and eventually eroded the practice of using long-distance revenue to subsidize local service.

In the local exchange, would-be competitors—if allowed by the state commissions—again would have the advantage of serving only in profitable situations.

They'd also have another advantage: If a real estate developer were to use a large switch to serve various tenants in his complex, he could use fewer trunks than would be necessary if each customer were served directly by Southwestern Bell Telephone. This would result in a savings the reseller could pass on to customers.

Some companies seeking to enter the resale business have advanced the argument that it's already allowed. Hotels, motels and hospitals have been doing it for several years.

"That situation is so special that there's a compelling reason to allow it," Waetzig explains. "You can't expect a hotel guest or a hospital patient to call the Telephone Company, have a line put in and order it disconnected when he leaves. It's just not practical, so the best workable alternative is to allow a special type of resale in that unique instance."

What's causing the push toward resale?

What conditions have come together to make resale an issue that must be faced by the company?

Thomas Garvey, staff manager-market management-intermediaries, explains: "First of all, it really hasn't been possible—technologically and economically—to think about reselling local service until recently. Now those obstacles have been removed, and both new and old office complexes can be equipped so a real estate developer can be a little telephone company for people on his premises.

"Also, divestiture has presented an opportunity. Developers are seeing a chance to become a single point of contact for their tenants in the telecommunications area.

"They can buy the wiring, switches and equipment, negotiate for long-distance services, and sell a whole telecommunications package to their customers. It potentially makes it much easier for a tenant to arrange and modify phone service."

In states inside and outside Southwestern Bell Telephone's territory, developers already have tried or have begun to offer multitenant services. That puts pressure on other developers throughout the United States to do the same, Garvey notes.

In the battle to win tenants, every service that can be promised by a real estate developer becomes important. As much as anything, this explains why developers seek to offer such services within Southwestern Bell Telephone's five-state territory, Garvey says.

Besides the concern about losing revenue and watching plant go to waste, Garvey says, there's another potential hazard for the Telephone Company if resale starts happening on a large scale.

"Every time our service is resold, it moves us one step away from the customer. If that happens often enough, we start to lose our market presence. Also, we're that much further removed from being able to determine our customers' needs. If we lose that contact, it becomes much harder to understand the people we serve.

"This puts us at a distinct disadvantage when we try to bring new products and services to the marketplace."

Garvey points out several risks for the customer using a developer's telecommunications services, especially if the developer isn't a regulated provider of such services.

"For one thing, the developer would have no regulations or obligations in regard to the quality of service. And if the developer

"The issue at hand is more complicated than whether or not competition should be allowed in the local exchange. The issue is this: Who should pay for the competition if it is allowed?"

4 *Enterprise / No. 3, 1984*

(b)

(c)

Figure 14-3 *Enterprise* magazine uses a three-column grid with a floating half-size extra column. It can appear anywhere on the page (a). The two pages show that the extra half-column can be used to separate a main story from a sidebar (b) or as an outside column with a quoteout (c). (Courtesy of Southwestern Bell Corporation)

Figure 14-4 Even a cover that is largely an ad can make for an attractive approach. (Editor & Publisher. Reprinted with permission)

Figure 14-5 A cover limited to black and white can still be powerful. If you can't afford to hire artists, then the photo is probably the strongest cover art. (Courtesy of Mike Vogl, Poudre Valley Hospital)

With more expensive magazines, the cover is printed on heavier stock than are the inside pages. This "separate" cover adds the extra touch of class that these magazines desire. Another option is the "self-cover," or a cover that is printed on the same stock as the inside pages. This is cheaper, and it gives you the option of carrying color from the cover inside the book fairly cheaply. A self-cover is part of the same signature (see "Imposition" in Chapter 12) as many inside pages. If you do this, however, you may have to use a higher-quality inside stock than you may have wished to.

Financial considerations may dictate that you have advertising on your cover sheet (Fig. 14–4). If you have a solid subscription list that doesn't need the "sell" of a snappy cover, then by all means take the money and run!

Covers usually cry out for a large photo or illustration. These will draw the most readers. Use a little type to indicate what the photo is about and where inside the magazine readers can turn for more. Add perhaps a teaser or two about a few other top stories and you have a good formula for a cover. Naturally you have to work in the flag and folio information as well.

Once you come up with a good working format for your cover, keep it much the same each issue. Readers will become familiar with the format, even as the content of the cover changes from issue to issue. *National Geographic,* for instance, uses that yellow frame and *Time* the red. We immediately recognize each magazine, regardless of what content is being highlighted on the cover.

Figure 14-6 Many company magazines have covers that rival the best consumer magazines. Usually a tease to the inside should have a page number. (Courtesy of Transamerica Corp.)

Figure 14-7 A cover can tell readers a lot about the contents. *Enterprise* magazine will obviously provide readers with provocative and professional content inside. (Courtesy of Southwestern Bell Corporation)

INSIDE

Inside, all content should fit the basic column grid you have set up. Even the important table of contents should fit that basic grid. Other elements of concern inside are the masthead, letters column, briefs columns, other columns, and story layouts.

The table of contents page is important (the basic format was discussed in Chapter 2), especially if you do not have much "tease copy" on your cover. Readers will want a brief rundown of what's in the issue whether it's on the cover or on an easily read contents page.

The contents page does not have to be merely a boring list. Take the opportunity to have fun while letting your readers know what's inside. At the same time, don't let the fun interfere with communication.

Organize the content through design. Think of it in terms of an outline. An outline indicates by its design both the major and the minor points. Likewise, you can showcase your major stories through emphasis or the use of art, while listing the continuing columns.

The masthead usually appears on the contents page. The masthead rarely needs more than simple attention to the typography. Make the information accessible, but keep the type small and unobtrusive.

Letters columns and your other columns should stand out from your other editorial matter. Use any of the tools available to you to differentiate that content: typographical contrast, different line measures, standing heads, color, etc.

These regular features also should be anchored in the same general positions every issue. The usual positions are at the front of the book, the back, or both.

After the contents page, you could position your letters, and/or a regular column or two. This allows you an opportunity to give your scanner some short items to read before hitting the main story. More important, you can fit some more ads in those early pages.

After saving the middle spreads for the main editorial content of the issue. you can ease your reader out of the magazine with some more standing matter, such as jumps from the letters or front columns, items in brief, and another columnist or two.

Putting popular standing features at the back as well is important for another reason. Many magazine readers begin from the back and leaf toward the front. Having something there for them besides just the jumps from stories and a few ads is a good strategy to keep them interested in your pages.

Page Spreads

One of the major decisions you need to make as you plan your magazine is whether to open stories only on two-page spreads, or whether some (or all) spreads will open on a right-hand, single page.

The latter decision is fine, but it means you must coordinate your story opener with the unrelated, left-hand page next to it. This is no problem because by now you know a lot of ways you can connect related content and separate un-

GUMSHOE

MICKEY SPILLANE AND RAYMOND CHANDLER WROTE ABOUT DIZZY DAMES AND DEAD-EYE DICKS WITH GUNS, GUTS, AND GLAMOR. REAL-LIFE DETECTIVE WORK IS AN EXTREMELY DIFFERENT CASE.

The Nick Harris Detective Academy is no gumshoe fantasy from the paperback racks. Located in Van Nuys, Calif., it was founded in 1907. For several years, Nick Harris detectives provided law enforcement for the unincorporated areas outside Los Angeles. When the suburbs became more established, the Harris detectives got out of formal police work and stuck with the private eye beat. By the 1920s, Harris himself had become so popular with the publication of his personal case history book, *Out of the Shadows*, that he started broadcasting his cases on national radio. His stories were the forerunner of the popular detective shows of the 1920s and '30s.

The Agency has been responsible for solving some of L.A.'s more bizarre and baffling cases involving missing heiresses, kidnappings, thefts and, even, murder. So why continue an academy if you already have a reputation as one of the top detective agencies? "Simple," says Milo Speriglio, director of the agency since 1959. "We get our pick of the best people." Despite the TV mythology, the agency is not in a sleazy downtown walk-up. It is in a simple stucco building on a pleasant suburban sidestreet. The academy is committed, in fact, to dispelling certain fantasies about the life of a private peeper.

I could see that my trenchcoat, fedora and heater were going to fit in with this Harris bunch like a fur coat in Hawaii. My classmates were young suits from the financial district, silver haired grannies, middle-aged housewives and a cross-section of virtually every walk of American life.

When Speriglio addressed the class in his welcoming speech, every bit of hardbitten fantasy I'd heard about this racket vanished. Speriglio's a small, wiry guy with curly hair, Caesar Romero moustache, and a "Welcome to L.A." tan. He wears enough gold to start dispensing stock.

His introduction was a tough pill to swallow: no guns, no glamor, no glory. He shot straight from the hip: We were in for hard

BY KENNETH CLARK

ILLUSTRATION BY DOUGLAS TAYLOR/PHOTOS BY ERIC MYER

Figure 14-8 A photo or piece of art is a good way to tie together two pages into one visual entity. (Philip Morris USA. Reprinted with permission.)

related content. The decision involves a little extra care in planning, but you gain by having another option for spread openers.

With two-page spread openers, the main goal—besides the standard strategy of stopping and detaining the reader through design—is to connect the two pages visually.

The design must conquer the power of the page gutter to split the pages into two separate parts of the spread. The reader sees both pages at once (though paying attention to only one at a time), so your design must emphasize that tendency.

One strategy is to have the art carry across the gutter (Fig. 14–8). This is good only if (1) your printer can handle the delicate task of making sure the photo halves line up properly during printing and binding, and (2) if you have art that can be used that large.

If your art is not able to go beyond one page, at least bleed that art to the gutter. That will help the eye make the desired visual connection.

Another strategy is to use a line (one of your basic design tools from Chapter 3) to carry the eye across. This can be a real line or an imaginary one (Fig. 14–9). Gestalt principles tell us that the eye/brain is drawn to lines, so it is an obvious tool to use.

You could try to line up a headline that carries across two spreads, but getting a headline to line up exactly is difficult. If you must do that, be sure that the space between two words falls on the gutter. Never try to carry a word across a gutter.

Besides these powerful visual connectors, you can use color (or in B & W, tone), either as a backdrop or on elements on each page of the spread; shape, perhaps as a continuing series logo throughout; or type, such as initial letters.

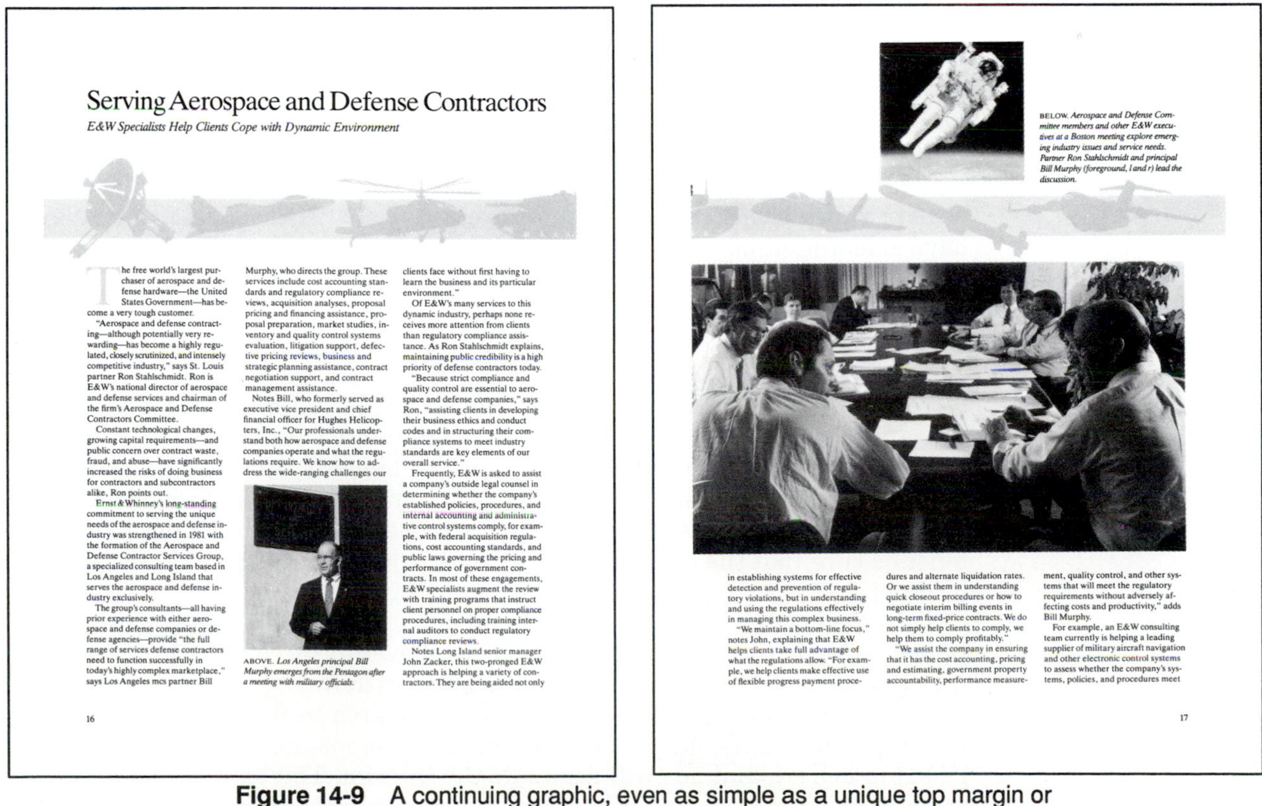

Serving Aerospace and Defense Contractors

E&W Specialists Help Clients Cope with Dynamic Environment

The free world's largest purchaser of aerospace and defense hardware—the United States Government—has become a very tough customer.

"Aerospace and defense contracting—although potentially very rewarding—has become a highly regulated, closely scrutinized, and intensely competitive industry," says St. Louis partner Ron Stahlschmidt. Ron is E&W's national director of aerospace and defense services and chairman of the firm's Aerospace and Defense Contractors Committee.

Constant technological changes, growing capital requirements—and public concern over contract waste, fraud, and abuse—have significantly increased the risks of doing business for contractors and subcontractors alike, Ron points out.

Ernst & Whinney's long-standing commitment to serving the unique needs of the aerospace and defense industry was strengthened in 1981 with the formation of the Aerospace and Defense Contractor Services Group, a specialized consulting team based in Los Angeles and Long Island that serves the aerospace and defense industry exclusively.

The group's consultants—all having prior experience with either aerospace and defense companies or defense agencies—provide "the full range of services defense contractors need to function successfully in today's highly complex marketplace," says Los Angeles mcs partner Bill Murphy, who directs the group. These services include cost accounting standards and regulatory compliance reviews, acquisition analyses, proposal pricing and financing assistance, proposal preparation, market studies, inventory and quality control systems evaluation, litigation support, defective pricing reviews, business and strategic planning assistance, contract negotiation support, and contract management assistance.

Notes Bill, who formerly served as executive vice president and chief financial officer for Hughes Helicopters, Inc., "Our professionals understand both how aerospace and defense companies operate and what the regulations require. We know how to address the wide-ranging challenges our clients face without first having to learn the business and its particular environment."

ABOVE. *Los Angeles principal Bill Murphy emerges from the Pentagon after a meeting with military officials.*

Of E&W's many services to this dynamic industry, perhaps none receives more attention from clients than regulatory compliance assistance. As Ron Stahlschmidt explains, maintaining public credibility is a high priority of defense contractors today.

"Because strict compliance and quality control are essential to aerospace and defense companies," says Ron, "assisting clients in developing their business ethics and conduct codes and in structuring their compliance systems to meet industry standards are key elements of our overall service."

Frequently, E&W is asked to assist a company's outside legal counsel in determining whether the company's established policies, procedures, and internal accounting and administrative control systems comply, for example, with federal acquisition regulations, cost accounting standards, and public laws governing the pricing and performance of government contracts. In most of these engagements, E&W specialists augment the review with training programs that instruct client personnel on proper compliance procedures, including training internal auditors to conduct regulatory compliance reviews.

Notes Long Island senior manager John Zacker, this two-pronged E&W approach is helping a variety of contractors. They are being aided not only

16

BELOW. *Aerospace and Defense Committee members and other E&W executives at a Boston meeting explore emerging industry issues and service needs. Partner Ron Stahlschmidt and principal Bill Murphy (foreground, l and r) lead the discussion.*

in establishing systems for effective detection and prevention of regulatory violations, but in understanding and using the regulations effectively in managing this complex business.

"We maintain a bottom-line focus," notes John, explaining that E&W helps clients take full advantage of what the regulations allow. "For example, we help clients make effective use of flexible progress payment procedures and alternate liquidation rates. Or we assist them in understanding quick closeout procedures or how to negotiate interim billing events in long-term fixed-price contracts. We do not simply help clients to comply, we help them to comply profitably."

"We assist the company in ensuring that it has the cost accounting, pricing and estimating, government property accountability, performance measurement, quality control, and other systems that will meet the regulatory requirements without adversely affecting costs and productivity," adds Bill Murphy.

For example, an E&W consulting team currently is helping a leading supplier of military aircraft navigation and other electronic control systems to assess whether the company's systems, policies, and procedures meet

17

Figure 14-9 A continuing graphic, even as simple as a unique top margin or border tape, can tie together continuing pages. Here, the screened aviation graphics tell the reader that the content on the second two-page spread is a continuation. (Courtesy of Ernst & Whinney)

LEFT. *The gleaming fuselage of a new McDonnell-Douglas MD-80 airliner mirrors Ron Stahlschmidt (l) and Douglas Aircraft Company vice president-controller Ray Kleinberg.*

government contract requirements, while maintaining desired cash flow, profitability, and allowable cost recovery. The engagement also includes management and auditor regulatory compliance training.

A similar project assisted Eaton Corporation in reviewing its compliance with regulations governing contracts for such projects as microwave landing systems and electronic countermeasure devices for the Air Force's B-1B bomber. The engagement, directed by Bill Murphy with the assistance of Long Island partner Alex Cover, encompassed reviews of Eaton's major defense contracting divisions across the country and often drew on the skills of local E&W audit specialists.

"Specific rules govern how and where costs are to be charged under government contracts," says Alex. "Our analyses determine whether these rules are being followed and whether they are being followed effectively."

Sometimes these analyses pinpoint specific opportunities to improve a company's competitiveness. For example, an E&W review conducted for an eastern defense contractor resulted in a complete restructuring of the company's product pricing.

Says Bill Murphy, "We found that their pricing structure, which allocated costs over too large a base, resulted in lost business in some products and lost profits in others. We helped the company restructure their costing to improve the assignment of engineering costs. E&W also assisted the company in moving away from a pure direct labor base allocation of overhead to the type of machine algorithm method factories of the future will require. The result, reports Bill, was a pricing structure that helped make the client more competitive and profitable across the board.

Training programs of the kind Dallas partner Billie Parker recently helped design and conduct for E-Systems educate client personnel to their continuing responsibilties in maintaining effective regulatory compliance systems. Billie points out the emphasis on this type of service is growing as regulations continue to change and evolve.

"To gain membership in the Aerospace Industries Association, companies must now have a specific, written code of ethics," Billie says. "We are helping clients develop systems that support compliance with such codes."

Monitoring emerging aerospace and defense issues is Ernst & Whinney's Aerospace and Defense Contractors Committee. Made up of more than a dozen E&W partners with varied responsibilities and expertise in aerospace and defense, the committee initiates and integrates the full range of E&W's aerospace and defense accounting and auditing, tax, and consulting services.

One area receiving close committee scrutiny is tax reform, which, according to National tax partner Jim Godbout, could have significant impact on the capital-intensive aerospace and defense industry.

"The loss of investment credit, for example, will be an important issue for aerospace and defense companies," says Jim, who also notes that tax reform-induced changes to the completed contract method of accounting will cause acceleration of defense industry tax payments to where some companies will pay taxes on profits they have yet to realize. "Under the new tax law, companies will need more cash sooner," Jim concludes. "Our clients can look to us for assistance in successfully addressing these changes."

Another area of extreme importance to the industry—and one drawing strong E&W response—is data security. Says Long Island senior manager Larry Gader, "Safeguarding information is critical to all organizations, but particularly so to defense contractors. Much of their work is classified, which places increased emphasis on system integrity. When helping a client design and implement an information system, we place special emphasis on protecting that system from unauthorized access."

Companies such as Schweizer Aircraft call on Ernst & Whinney for assistance in preparing contract proposals, negotiating contracts, and in addressing other customer-regulatory issues.

Similarly, Los Angeles senior manager Charles Wilkens and manager Stephen Kiraly are aiding Motorola in

18

BELOW. *At the McDonnell-Douglas Long Beach facility, Ron Stahlschmidt (r) and Ray Kleinberg observe technicians readying a KC-10—one of the world's largest cargo/tanker transports—for delivery to the U.S. Air Force.*

documenting and preparing company proposals and billings under government contracts, in defining systems requirements, and in organizational structuring.

Subcontractors such as Gemcor, developer of a unique aircraft wing riveting process, rely on Ernst & Whinney professionals for help in formulating pricing strategies.

E&W audit teams serving defense clients turn to the Aerospace and Defense Contractor Services Group for assistance in estimating contract cost at completion, or in evaluating contract provisions and performance contingencies that could affect financial results. Market studies, strategic planning, operational capability analyses, merger and acquisition analyses, and litigation support are other services drawing increased client interest.

The Ernst & Whinney commitment to the aerospace and defense industry also includes "Defense Contracting Briefs," a monthly newsletter that keeps industry participants abreast of emerging developments. Moreover, E&W-conducted seminars apprise lending institutions of the unique risks and opportunities inherent in defense contracting.

"Aerospace and defense is far different today from what it has ever been before," summarizes Ron Stahlschmidt. "Our commitment is to help our clients prepare for the rewards—and challenges—certain to come in the future."

19

Figure 14–9 (Continued)

Using visual connectors such as these is important because the reader is guided through the content by familiar signposts. Let's face it—readers are inherently lazy and demanding. They want their information easy, and they want to be visually entertained at the same time. They are also fickle. Make it tough on them and they spurn you for another.

Openers on right-hand pages follow the same basic rules, but you don't have to worry about tying two pages together. You still use ample white space, have a dominant image to attract attention, and use typographical contrasts to add visual interest to the message.

Pages with Ads

Here's where reality rears its greenbacked face. If you must have ads to continue publishing, then it's a reality the designer must deal with.

The ads themselves will be strong visual elements, and readers *like* to look at ads. (Personally, I think the ads in the *New Yorker* are about the most entertaining things in there, except for the cartoons of course.) The designer then must be sure that the editorial content, even a jump with no art, is visually appealing.

In magazines, ads have been placed along the outside edges of the pages. In one sense, this is good planning. It keeps the editorial content grouped to the inside where the designer can do a little more with it.

On the other hand, and there is some research to support this, if readers see only ads peeking out as they flip through the magazine's pages, they may be led to believe that ads will dominate the interior. This impression may lead them to another magazine that seems less driven by Mammon.

One solution may be to run the ads in an **L**-shape around the copy, leaving the upper corners clear. The space given to advertising would be about the same, and the magazine flippers would see, at least occasionally, editorial content instead of all ads.

Regardless of your approach to ads on pages, try to work with your ad department to find out what the ads on a page look like, if you can. Readers see a page in its entirety; thus, editorial content and ads must work together visually.

In some ways, it makes no sense that ads are designed individually, with no thought as to what they will be placed next to in the publication, and then the ads are placed and the editorial content is designed with no thought given to what the ads look like.

Is this any way to design a publication? I think that the best-looking pages are *totally* designed, ads and all. Find a way to work that out on your publication.

INTEGRATED EDITING AND MAGAZINES

As mentioned several times previously, a good editor will ask two questions prior to or during editing:

1. What is the best way to communicate this information? Is it visual?
2. Is there a visual element that can enhance this information?

Editors of monthly magazines have more time than nearly any other publication editor to ask these questions. Even though magazine editors have the same busy and hectic day-to-day pace that a newspaper editor has, magazine content is often planned as far as six months in advance. This leaves plenty of time to decide the optimum presentation of information.

It especially leaves time for high-quality photos and illustrations. These have been shown to be the most compelling visuals to present to readers.

Beyond these, good information graphics, maps, charts, and such take time to produce. The best use of these elements is in the creating of *context* for the story at hand. Again, because of the time frame monthly magazines—and even newsweeklies, for that matter—operate in, one of the best information/entertainment services they can provide is the giving of context.

For instance, I once saw a magazine article about a safari in Africa. Incredibly, there was no map to show what part of Africa I was reading about. What was needed was a map of the area of the safari, and then a locator map showing what part of Africa the story took place in. The article had less *meaning* and was less pleasing to the eye because of *bad editing*. Not badly edited, in that mistakes were made in spelling or grammar, but bad editing. You know the difference.

The article also talked about declining numbers of wildlife due to poaching and the natural creep of civilization into formerly untouched areas. I would have liked to see a fever-line chart or two showing me the decreasing numbers over time of lions or elephants or whatever. *Put news in context.* Do this with good information graphics and you have taken two positive steps toward successful editing: The words will make more sense, and the page will be more attractive.

These would not have been mere decorations on the page. They would have helped me understand what the safari story was really about. Instead, I read a page and a half or so of gray type (I'm a glutton for punishment), and then I gave up.

Other stories need context as well. In one story about building a dam on a "wild" river, we might want to see on a map the exact boundaries of the new lake the dam would create, especially in relation to the present bed of the river and rapids.

Or we might want to know, perhaps in list form, what other "wild" rivers in the country have fallen to those who want dams built, what ones have not, where they are, how long they are, etc.

Or maybe we might want to know how a dam is built. Do engineers divert the water, and if so where and how? How big? How much? How many? These are all questions that readers will ask. How you answer them—with words or with visuals—may influence whether readers pick you up again or put you down. This is also true with company magazines.

There is no set answer to any of these questions or problems—only the set process. Thus, there is little more, really, that I can tell you about integrated editing. That is the folly, in a sense, of this book.

Good editing *is* integrated editing. If you have selected the proper presentation of the information in the first place, and if you have edited the words to their best and briefest and clearest, and if you have edited the visuals to their most informative, then you have done it. You have succeeded. Readers will appreciate it. And your advertisers will appreciate them.

CASE STUDY

Publication: *Enterprise,* Southwestern Bell Corporation, St. Louis, Mo. Monthly magazine published for employees of the company. News, features, briefs.

Editor: Susan Darr; writer, Carol Crosthwaite; designer, John Howze, Hawthorne/Wolfe, Design Consultants, Inc.

Susan Darr: The idea came from an awareness of problems with ethics in other industries and from the stories in the media about Ivan Boesky, the Bakkers, Oliver North, etc. Plus our own industry has experienced heightened competition, and some employees could get the idea that we were ready to do anything for a buck. To avoid this from developing, I wanted to discuss workplace ethics in a series of articles. I wanted to bring the issue into a spotlight so that managers would be sure to think about ethics in everything they did.

My personal interest in ethics runs deep. As a public relations manager I see ethical questions raised often. Some people still turn to the "PR guy" to fast-talk the company out of a tight spot. I feel good about working for a department of peers who realize the value of a strong ethical stance. Carol—the writer and my boss—suggested the survey of employee attitudes. She said that she'd like to know what employees think about ethics. It is the individual's ethical practices that ultimately make up the ethics of a business.

Carol Crosthwaite: Right off the bat I knew that I didn't want to write a finger-wagging, accusative article that laid the whole problem on the employees' doorsteps. I read and read for weeks. I read so much that when I finished I wasn't

ENTERPRISE

VOL. 4/NO. 2, 1987

WORKPLACE ETHICS
HANGING IN THE BALANCE?
PAGE 16

Southwestern Bell Corporation

Your copy of *Enterprise* to take home and share with your family

Figure 14–10

16 Enterprise / No. 2, 1987

Figure 14–11

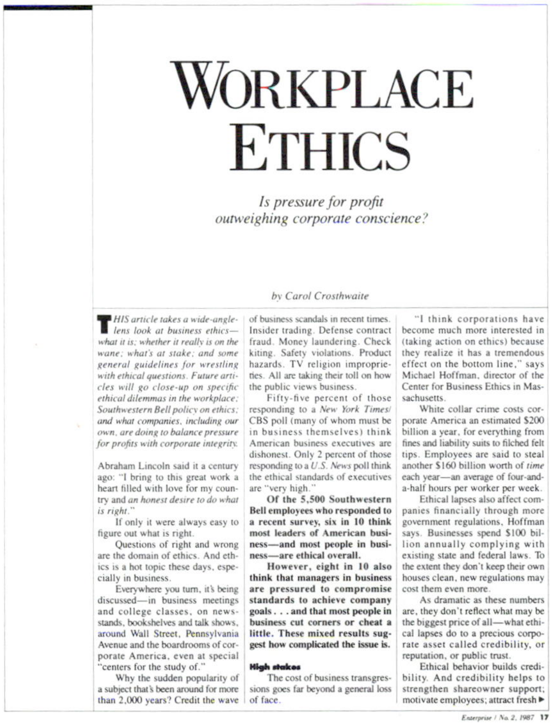

WORKPLACE ETHICS

Is pressure for profit outweighing corporate conscience?

by Carol Crosthwaite

THIS article takes a wide-angle-lens look at business ethics—what it is; whether it really is on the wane; what's at stake; and some general guidelines for wrestling with ethical questions. Future articles will go close-up on specific ethical dilemmas in the workplace; Southwestern Bell policy on ethics; and what companies, including our own, are doing to balance pressure for profits with corporate integrity.

Abraham Lincoln said it a century ago: "I bring to this great work a heart filled with love for my country and *an honest desire to do what is right.*"

If only it were always easy to figure out what is right.

Questions of right and wrong are the domain of ethics. And ethics is a hot topic these days, especially in business.

Everywhere you turn, it's being discussed—in business meetings and college classes, on newsstands, bookshelves and talk shows, around Wall Street, Pennsylvania Avenue and the boardrooms of corporate America, even at special "centers for the study of."

Why the sudden popularity of a subject that's been around for more than 2,000 years? Credit the wave of business scandals in recent times. Insider trading. Defense contract fraud. Money laundering. Check kiting. Safety violations. Product hazards. TV religion improprieties. All are taking their toll on how the public views business.

Fifty-five percent of those responding to a *New York Times*/CBS poll (many of whom must be in business themselves) think American business executives are dishonest. Only 2 percent of those responding to a *U.S. News* poll think the ethical standards of executives are "very high."

Of the 5,500 Southwestern Bell employees who responded to a recent survey, six in 10 think most leaders of American business—and most people in business—are ethical overall.

However, eight in 10 also think that managers in business are pressured to compromise standards to achieve company goals . . . and that most people in business cut corners or cheat a little. These mixed results suggest how complicated the issue is.

High stakes

The cost of business transgressions goes far beyond a general loss of face.

"I think corporations have become much more interested in (taking action on ethics) because they realize it has a tremendous effect on the bottom line," says Michael Hoffman, director of the Center for Business Ethics in Massachusetts.

White collar crime costs corporate America an estimated $200 billion a year, for everything from fines and liability suits to filched felt tips. Employees are said to steal another $160 billion worth of *time* each year—an average of four-and-a-half hours per worker per week.

Ethical lapses also affect companies financially through more government regulations, Hoffman says. Businesses spend $100 billion annually complying with existing state and federal laws. To the extent they don't keep their own houses clean, new regulations may cost them even more.

As dramatic as these numbers are, they don't reflect what may be the biggest price of all—what ethical lapses do to a precious corporate asset called credibility, or reputation, or public trust.

Ethical behavior builds credibility. And credibility helps to strengthen shareowner support; motivate employees; attract fresh ▶

Enterprise / No. 2, 1987 17

Figure 14–12

talent; improve supplier, media and government relationships; and earn community respect.

Even more, it influences relationships with customers and whom they vote for with their consumer dollars. "The public is becoming much more sensitive and educated as to what kind of company they want to deliver their goods and services," Hoffman says. Loss of public trust can translate to loss of sales.

As one business leader said, "You may not find credibility directly in the operating income of rates of return, but I can assure you it's there, somewhere."

The usual suspects

So what's the cause of the current rash of corporate wrongdoing? Like Louie in the movie *Casablanca*, experts have rounded up the usual set of suspects. And the list includes almost every major institution.

Families. The family has been the traditional way of mediating values through the generations, but trends such as divorce and working couples cause children to spend less time with their parents. To the extent family life is disintegrating, some experts say children aren't being taught the most basic values about lying, cheating or stealing.

Schools. "It's hard to know where young business people would get what used to be thought of as mainstream values," said a writer in *Fortune*, "given schools that strive to be inoffensively value-neutral and teach that everything is relative (nothing is ultimately right or wrong).

"It's hard to know where new workers would acquire a strong sense of responsibility for their actions when they've been taught that the cause of wrongdoing is the economic and psychological environment of the wrongdoer (rather than the wrongdoer himself)."

Religion. Some say a factor in the demise-of-ethics equation is the declining role religion has played in people's lives. However, concern over ethics may lead to a reversal of that trend as people turn back to their religious roots in search of answers and real meaning.

Government. All branches have had scandals of their own, under each administration . . . and starting long before Watergate. Many observers blame business wrongdoing on the bad example set by politicos who support basic American values in rhetoric but play fast and loose with them in deed.

The media. Those who point the finger at the media say we're constantly bombarded by information that's really disinformation. Some see TV advertising as the main villain. Ad executive Jerry Della Femina doesn't disagree. "We're conceived, born and deceived," he said. "By the time someone reaches age 10, he's pretty cynical."

Then there is TV's portrayal of business people as devoid of morality. "How can you live with yourself?" a fellow Dallas character asks J.R. Ewing. "Oh, it's not hard," J.R. responds. "You'll see. Once you give up integrity, it's a piece of cake."

A Media Institute study found that TV portrays business people 70 percent of the time as foolish, greedy or evil, and more than half of all prime-time CEOs commit illegal acts. "In TV's vision of business," said a United Technologies ad, "ethics are about as rare as rowboats in the Sahara."

Such portrayals may not directly cause unethical behavior, but they also don't give future business leaders anything to live up to.

"The good life." Ironically, the country's prosperity since World War II may share the blame. Sociologists claim that baby boomers, those born between 1946 and 1964, are the group most lacking an ethical orientation. Some call boomers "Corrupies" and charge that they expect wealth and instant gratification to be givens, overemphasize material values and don't take responsibility because they've never experienced anything but the good life.

Others dismiss the "Corrupies" theory, saying there are more ethical lapses among bopmers simply because they are a larger group.

Business itself. Some people point to mounting competition and the intense pressures it places on employees, especially middle managers. Competition in consumer markets, competition for jobs and promotions, and pay-for-performance programs all may tempt employees— or cause managers to pressure their staffs—to cut corners and bend the rules. This often is done in the name of short-term results, at the expense of the long-term health of the organization or the people it affects.

Linked to this are the increasingly pervasive notions of standard practice and pragmatism. The first says something is OK if everyone does it; the second says it's OK to do "whatever is necessary to succeed." One place these notions come into play is in doing business overseas, where financial "lubricants" are often the rule.

Others blame ethical lapses on the restructuring of corporate America. Mergers, acquisitions and divestitures can weaken established cultures and cause confusion about values and about what behavior is "acceptable" in the new environment.

The increased bigness of business, some say, creates an environment where traditional moral values can get diluted or pushed aside. What comes to matter, according to Robert Jackall, associate professor at Williams College, "is not a person's willingness to stand by his actions but his agility in avoiding blame; not what he believes but how well he has mastered the (beliefs) that serve his corporation; not what he stands *for* but whom he stands *with* in the labyrinths of the organization."

Certainly, the bigger the business, the more people its decisions affect . . . and the more important ethical behavior becomes.

A moral meltdown?

Clearly there's not consensus on who or what is to blame. In fact, there's not even consensus that the business world really has gone through a moral meltdown. Maybe wrongdoing just gets more media exposure these days. Or maybe people just expect more.

In a sense, it doesn't matter. Either way, if people *perceive* busi-

18 Enterprise / No. 2, 1987

Figure 14–13

Figures 14–10 through 14-16 *Enterprise* magazine, the company publication of Southwestern Bell Corporation and designed by Hawthorne/Wolfe Design Consultants, does an excellent job of integrating words and art. The cover art is repeated inside to help continuation from cover to story. The unique grid is used on the inside pages to keep the columns of type together in a unit. Sidebars not only have screens to separate them from the main story, but also have extra column space.

ness as less ethical, that's danger enough.

As *U.S. News* said, "The danger is the same as if the erosion (of honesty) were real: A widespread fall-off of confidence in national institutions and the resulting development of an every-man-for-himself ethic that would threaten the social contract itself."

A free and open society is based on people having trust in their institutions—which, in turn, is based on ethical conduct.

What there *does* seem to be consensus on today, then, is the need to correct the image of business as indifferent to the public good. Business has come to realize it must manage the factors that influence reputation (ethics being basic among them) just as carefully as it manages operations, finance and other business functions.

The prize, as a growing body of evidence attests, is that businesses which do good, do well.

Ethics defined

As often as the term is used these days, people may mean different things by it. So what is ethics, really?

The study of moral values and duties, says Webster. Each author of three current books on ethics has his own definition.

The most basic ground rules by which a person or a firm acts, says Mark Pastin, author of *The Hard Problems of Management: Gaining the Ethics Edge.*

The art of mutually agreeable compromise, given that our interests and those of others are forever intertwined, say Robert Solomon and Kristine Hanson, authors of *It's Good Business.*

Any decision that has an effect on other people, or where interests collide, has an ethical dimension to it, according to James O'Toole, author of *Vanguard Management.* Which means that business people carry the burden of ethics daily in almost every transaction.

In recognition of this fact, more than half of Southwestern Bell survey respondents said they're constantly or frequently faced with ethical decisions in their daily work environment. ▸

Our own house

HOW ethical is Southwestern Bell?

Eighty-five percent of the 5,500 Southwestern Bell employees responding to a recent survey think the company is committed to ethical practices.

Despite the massive changes brought by and since divestiture, 60 percent of employees say the company's ethical commitment matches or exceeds what it used to be; 35 percent say it has declined. Close to 90 percent of employees think it equals or exceeds that of other companies in our own and other industries.

Most employees see Southwestern Bell as a company that produces products and services and has a reputation they can be proud of, trusts employees and treats them fairly. Slightly more than half say the company does *not* condone cutthroat competition or pressure employees to compromise their principles. However, four in 10 say it *does* . . . and 70 percent say the company values results more than integrity.

Yet, eight in 10 employees say their own job makes them feel proud of themselves and their company and that they are doing something worthwhile. More than eight in 10 also say their job does *not* make them feel unethical.

The questions on "what percent of Southwestern Bell employees you think have ever considered doing or done something ethically wrong" were inconclusive. Three in 10 employees answered 0 percent, three in 10 answered 100 percent and the rest were scattered quite evenly in between. This may reflect the wide differences in how people define right and wrong.

The final question was asked not about business specifically but about ethics in general. Almost four in 10 employees said they've never had to make a decision or take an action contrary to their ethical principles; almost six in 10 say they have had to, but infrequently.

Other results are highlighted in the main article.

More specific mention of some of the write-in comments will be made in future articles. In general, though, what came through most clearly was employees' dedication to customers and to the ethical health of Southwestern Bell . . . and the extent to which their opinions on ethics are formed by what they see daily in the actions of employees around and above them in the workplace. ■

Enterprise / No. 2, 1987 19

Figure 14–14

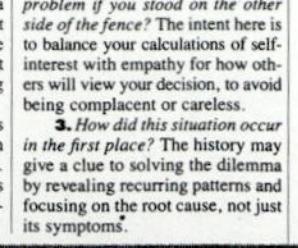

The word ethics comes from the Greek "ethos," which means good character. "Ethics is not just obedience to rules," say Solomon and Hanson, "so much as it is concern for your personal and company character—your reputation and good name—and more important, how you feel about yourself."

Southwestern Bell employees defined ethics most often as "doing what is right," "good moral conduct," "values," "standards to base decisions and actions upon."

A number of company employees also see ethics as a relative concept based on personal beliefs. As one said, "Ethics is not a fixed commodity. Each person has his own measurements of what is ethical."

Legal? Moral? Nonfattening?

Lacking a universal definition (philosophers have debated this for centuries), and if what's ethical can change with the situation at hand, how do we know if we're behaving ethically?

Not all ethical questions are relative; there are some absolutes. Some situations are easy to call, as they involve sharply delineated rights and wrongs. The instances of corporate wrongdoing listed at the start of this article—defense fraud, safety violations and the like—are examples. The "right" course of action clearly is dictated by laws or regulations.

These situations get most of the media play, and they often have far-reaching effects. They are the ones covered most often in business codes of conduct, as well. But they account for only a small portion of the ethics-related decisions made each day.

The vast majority fall into areas where right and wrong are much harder to gauge—where the choice often may be between right and right. Most ethical dilemmas consist of contradictions between equally valid claims.

What you owe the longtime employee who can't be retrained. What you owe the community that's no longer producing business. What you owe the longtime supplier who wasn't the low bidder but needs your business to survive. What to do about a friend who is breaking a company rule. How you act affirmatively to hire and promote women and minorities and yet don't discriminate in hiring and making promotions.

These much subtler decisions require independent and often complex thinking and judgment. These are the types of decisions employees could most use guidance on.

The 12 questions

One tool toward this end is a list of 12 questions devised by Harvard professor Laura Nash. She suggests asking yourself these as a way to clarify thinking on ethical dilemmas.

1. *Have you defined the problem accurately?* How you assemble the facts weights an issue before the moral examination ever begins, and a definition rarely is accurate if it articulates your loyalties rather than the facts.

2. *How would you define the problem if you stood on the other side of the fence?* The intent here is to balance your calculations of self-interest with empathy for how others will view your decision, to avoid being complacent or careless.

3. *How did this situation occur in the first place?* The history may give a clue to solving the dilemma by revealing recurring patterns and focusing on the root cause, not just its symptoms.

4. *To whom and what do you give your loyalties as a person and as a member of the corporation?* As a way of probing conflicts of loyalty, Nash suggests playing various roles: What will I say when (my boss) (my peer) (my child) asks me why I did that?

5. *What is your intention in making this decision?* Intentions matter because they set the standard on which an entire series of actions will be based.

6. *How does this intention*

20 *Enterprise / No. 2, 1987*

Figure 14–15

compare with the likely results? Goodness of intent pales before results that cause injury or simply do little good. Nash cautions that overconfidence about results often precedes a disastrous mistake.

7. *Whom could your decision or action injure?* This is borrowed from the ancient Greeks. Greek physicians 2,500 years ago adopted the Hippocratic oath as a simple gauge for ethical behavior. *Primum non nocere*, the oath says: "Above all, not knowingly to do harm."

8. *Can you engage the affected parties in discussing the problem before you make your decision?* This principle can be highly effective but often is forgotten because of time pressures, inconvenience or fear of facing hostile questions.

9. *Are you confident your position will be as valid over a long period of time as it seems now?* A difference in time frame can change the meaning of a problem. Decisions should do their best to anticipate changes of fortune.

10. *Could you disclose without qualm your decision or action to your boss, CEO, board, family or society as a whole?* Disclosure is a way of sounding out conscience and loyalties.

11. *What is the symbolic potential of your action if understood? If misunderstood?* Business decisions have symbolic value in signaling employees and outside constituents about the rules of the game. How the symbol actually is perceived is as important as how you intended it to be perceived.

12. *Under what conditions would you allow exceptions to your stand?* Despite the need for consistency, what conflicting principles or situations would provide a morally acceptable basis for making an exception?

Nash's complete article gives specific examples of the 12 questions in practice. If you would like a copy, please write in your request and your return address on the *Enterprise* feedback card.

More to come

This article has presented the panoramic view of business ethics. Clearly it's a complex subject that defies easy definitions or easy answers.

Building ethical awareness and skill is not an add-water-and-stir process. As one Southwestern Bell survey respondent said, "If you think ethical behavior can be stimulated by a slick magazine article, you're wrong."

We don't. All articles can do is raise the issue (as this one has) and clarify Southwestern Bell's commitment to it (as future articles will do).

Book definitions aside, the real issue of ethics is nothing less than how we treat each other as human beings. On this the success of our economic, political and social systems depends . . . as does the self-respect which is at the heart of our personal happiness.

The stakes for business and for the individuals who comprise it are high. And the rewards of conscientious adherence to highest ethical standards are great. ■

Toward internal drivers

PSYCHOLOGISTS have identified several stages we go through in developing our moral fiber. In each stage, our behavior is driven by different factors.

In the early stages, moral behavior is based on *consequences* and the physical power of those who dole them out. Whatever brings rewards is right; whatever brings punishment is wrong.

In the middle stages, behavior is based on the *desire to belong*, to be accepted by the group (family, friends, community). We conform to the social order and support and justify it.

Finally, we may progress to the point where we're driven by *our own principles and beliefs* about concepts such as fairness, community good and human dignity. We question the rules and get involved in making or changing them.

Most Southwestern Bell survey respondents are operating out of the last stage. Two internal drivers, "high personal standards" and "living up to your responsibilities," are placed by 75 to 80 percent of employees in the top five factors guiding ethical behavior at work.

Company drivers come next for 30 to 40 percent of employees: "knowing the company expects it of you," "you are being paid to uphold company standards," "concern for the company's reputation," "the company's high standards" and "explicit company policies."

"Religious dictates" was ranked in the top five by 30 percent of employees.

Only a handful are motivated by consequences—hope of reward or fear of punishment. ■

Enterprise / No. 2, 1987 21

Figure 14-16 Sketches by artist Cary Henrie for the cover and main art for the story inside. Henrie was working with the concept of the story, not just freely creating art work that may or may not fit the story well.

sure where to start. I made outlines of important points and of points brought up by respondents to the survey.

I wanted to be sure that I left employees with something they could hold onto. And in everything I read, the most usable information on how to address ethical concerns came from Laura Nash's list of 12 questions. It helped me end the article on an upbeat note.

John Howze: One of the fun things about working on this magazine is that Carol and Susan really get excited about the articles they are coming up with. Their articles on downsizing the workforce, the profile of the chairman of the board, and the ethics piece are not just pablum. Nor are they mandates from top management.

During the preparation process I had several discussions with the writer and editor concerning the article content. I obtained a synopsis and read through a random sampling of the survey results. I prefer to have finished copy, but I just didn't have it this time. After gathering the background information, I discussed several cover illustration ideas with the editor and writer. I recommended the concept we went with, which was my favorite.

Figure 14-17 The cover art is beginning to take shape (L) as is the lead art for the article (R), even to the "classical" border. This back-and-forth between editor and artist is integrated editing at its best. The final result is excellence and, better yet, communication.

②

Figure 14-18 The cover art is approaching its final form. A version without the hand lifting the blindfold was tried and discarded (L), then one with the hand emphasizing the point of peeking from under the blindfold. Putting the figure in more of a business suit attire (R) was discarded. (All examples courtesy of Southwestern Bell Corporation)

Everyone agreed almost instantly. The traditional, but nonthreatening—in fact, almost innocent-looking—figure of Justice, the raised eyebrow, the dramatic lighting—they all make you think: "Are we as individuals and as a company managing our ethics? Or are we letting the circumstances determine our ethics?" In a nonthreatening way, it raises your awareness of the ethical implications of what we do every day.

Why is the photo on page 20 (Fig. 14–15) centered, forcing the reader to jump over it in three columns? I wanted overall page balance. It didn't work at the top. In concept it was nice to have the points around it. We use this type of layout a lot in the book, so reader habit should overcome any problems with reading flow. I think we can take some liberties with the layout given our audience.

Why use boldface paragraphs throughout the article? Both Susan and Carol wanted the type for the Southwestern Bell survey results to stand out from the rest of the story. They wanted the type in color as well as bold. Italic was ruled out because then the grafs would look like editor's notes. We tried Futura (the same face as the subheads), but they didn't like it. So we just used boldface body type (Times Roman). [From Carol Crosthwaite: Normally we yield to John on design and layout, but not this time. He didn't like the boldface at all.]

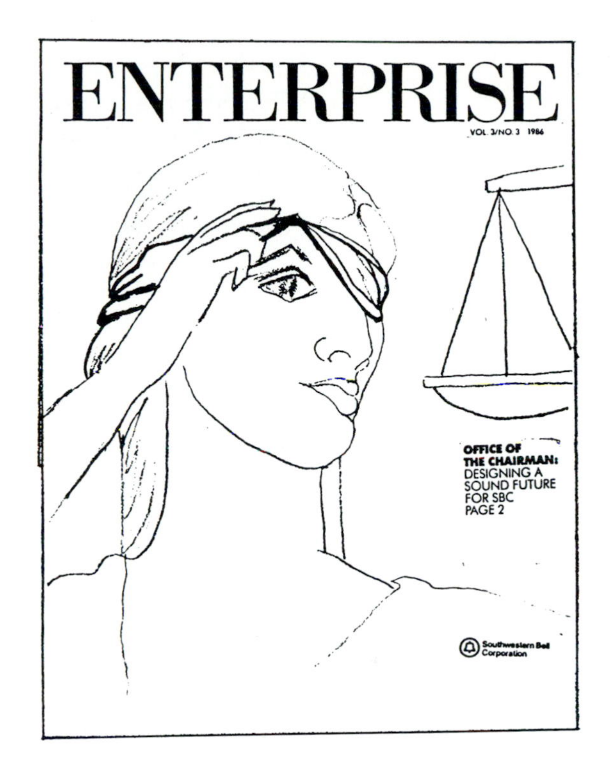

Figure 14–19 These sketches represent the final shape of the cover art. Compare to Figure 14–10.

My Analysis

This story is an excellent example of good corporate *journalism,* not just corporate PR and hype. The story is important, well-researched, and well written. It does indeed bring an important issue to the attention of the employees.

The illustrations also are excellent. I was glad to see that the words and the visuals were discussed and planned at the same time early in the process.

I like a lot of aspects of the design and layout of the article, and I dislike very little. The layout of the two "inside" spreads are similar, in both layout and use of color. This helps readers see immediately which is article and which is sidebar. Again, *the layout supports the content.* This is what good functional page layout should do, no matter what kind of publication you are working on.

The subheads are just about perfect, to my thinking. First and foremost, they are *functional* in that they key the reader to parts of the story that take off in a new direction. Although they are good at washing out the gray, the fact that they are functional subheadlines as well makes the difference. Skimmers might find something in the middle or at the end of the story that draws them into the story.

Another neat touch is the use of small triangles at the end of the last line on a page to indicate story continuation (and then a square to indicate the end). In a very short space you have done what an additional line of type (jump line or continued line) often must do. I like the graphic approach, but I would like to see another triangle at the start of the copy jump on the following page to help the reader understand the jump. If the break is at a paragraph (as it is here from pages 19–20), a back-to-front reader might not be aware that the top of page 20 is a continuation.

Summary

Just an excellent job. Persons interested in corporate magazines would do well to get on the *Enterprise* mailing list. My initial thought was to disagree with the use of bold Times Roman in the midst of the story, but the other options typographically are not any better. In the end, I agree that it's the best solution.

My other initial reaction to those boldface grafs would have been to group them in a sidebar. But because two other very good sidebars exist in the package, a third would have been difficult to manage well. I also toyed with the idea of suggesting a small graphic, perhaps even the Southwestern Bell corporate logo, and/or a subhead-sized (but probably in caps) tag line, such as "Your Response" or something. But I rejected that as busying up the page too much.

Ultimately I had to agree again with John. What we are looking at here is perhaps a new animal: a segmented information graphic, disguised as paragraphs and placed throughout a story at pertinent stopping points!

CHECKLIST

1. Integrated editing, as you have learned by now, is a (catchy, I hope!) smoke screen. What we are talking about here is really good, thoughtful editing of the words, and attention to the visual as a method of communication.
2. If you say "design" to some word people, they immediately recoil with a high and uncalled-for fear and loathing. But design can be done by word people with a little attention to easily followed principles of *typography, format,* and *design,* or really, *how people see.* Maybe that's what we should say instead of design so we don't scare word people away from good design.

3. Good design is nothing something only artists care about. Crusty word editors should care about it too.
4. Magazines have more opportunity than do most publications to use the integrated editing concepts to their fullest. Even "bookish" magazines would benefit from the occasional display-type pullout. It would be the equivalent of the doctor-prescribed looking away from your reading once in awhile to give your eyes a break.
5. One of the easiest design concepts to use in magazines is white space. Set ample and pleasingly proportional margins, and allow white space to appear on each spread. White space can be used to tie spreads together, and when used on the *outside* of a package it helps to tie the elements together. Be sure to use white space on *all* your spread openers.
6. For an 8 1/2-by-11-inch general-interest magazine, design two column grids. First, design a standard three-column grid. How big will your margins be? Your columns? Your gutters? Indicate where the folio/page number will be. Then design an "odd" grid, or one with uneven column widths.
7. Take the page grids you designed above and create a mock two-page spread opener for each. You can choose any subject matter you want. Try to use the integrated editing and design concepts on both spreads. If you want, you could find two weakly designed two-page spreads and fix them. Use gray paper for halftones and greek your body type.
8. Write a prospectus, including a mock grid and a basic design plan (use thumbnails, or very small and rough layouts of pages) for a new magazine in your area. Be realistic. Find an audience that would benefit from such a magazine. The prospectus should include a description of this audience, printing specs and bids from a print shop or two, distribution plans, etc. Make the prospectus complete enough to present to a prospective venture capitalist who might want to support such a project.

CHAPTER

15 NEWSPAPERS

Newspapers represent the biggest challenge for the integrated editing idea, but they need the concept most of all. Newspapers are created literally on the spot. Therefore, planning is crucial. Also, broadsheet newspapers are simply difficult visual fields for the editor to design. They are too large to be seen in one glance by readers. But somehow the editor must impose order on the natural chaos.

Newspapers also are suffering from a declining readership, or at least one that is not growing as fast as the population. So they need to pay attention to what readers want. We have seen that, in general, readers want easy-to-find and easy-to-read information.

Newspapers come in two sizes, broadsheet or full-size, and tabloid (Fig. 15–1). Nearly all daily newspapers and many weeklies are broadsheet. Some weeklies have gone to the tabloid format in an attempt to position themselves differently in the newspaper marketplace. Also, many entertainment or soft-news weekly and monthly publications use the tabloid format.

The ideas behind integrated editing are the same for all, but we will look briefly at a few design challenges for each separately.

BROADSHEET

Most newspapers follow a standard six-column format based on Standard Advertising Unit (SAU) column widths (Fig. 15–2). The SAU plan was instituted to create a set of standard sizes for national advertisers to make it easier to create one ad that would fit all newspapers.

The basic grid for a newspaper will almost certainly use the six-column format and add standards for five and seven columns as well. The wider columns might be used for the opinion page, and the narrower for calendars or briefs.

BACK OFF: Ease after-work tension/25

FINALLY, FAME: Baseball hall picks/28

Dayton Daily News
THE JOURNAL HERALD

Dayton, Ohio, Thursday Evening, Jan. 15, 1987

Air museum not aiding contras, director says

Arms talks on menu: one-on-one
1st session a warm one between Soviets, U.S.

Digging out in Sweden

County richer by $1.8 million
GGFC pays outstanding claims

Principal screened for jail-diversion

Son got AIDS at hospital, parents say in suit

W. Germans nab suspect in 1985 TWA hijacking

Sam Hall reported to be OK
U.S. officials get brief visit with hostage

INSIDE

On the Town

Tow, tow, tow your boat

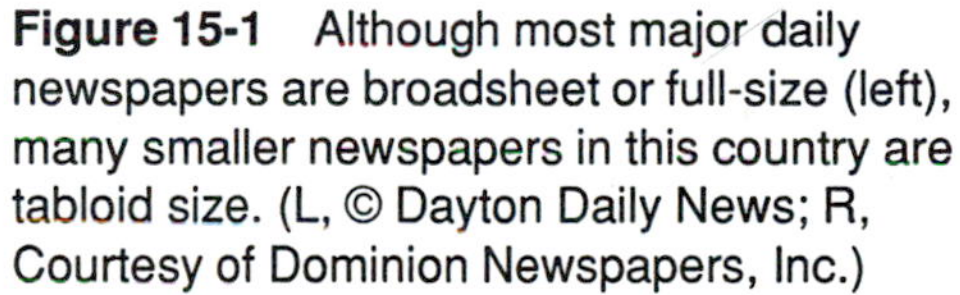

Figure 15-1 Although most major daily newspapers are broadsheet or full-size (left), many smaller newspapers in this country are tabloid size. (L, © Dayton Daily News; R, Courtesy of Dominion Newspapers, Inc.)

After the grid is set up, attention must be given to the typography (body type, headlines, accessory type for standing features).

Then, to save time on deadline, many newspapers have worked out a number of flexible formats for certain pages. This allows for the news of the day to shape the content, while at the same time reducing the number of decisions an editor has to make under deadline pressure.

On page one, for instance, constants might include the nameplate, tease boxes above the nameplate, an index and a column either of briefs or of more teases to inside content (see Fig. 15–1). These can be in any number of configurations. When the design and typography plan for the newspaper is set up, a number of these suggested "templates" for the page can be created for reference. These can be used as guides by the editor. You might also include some layouts to avoid as well.

Section fronts can benefit from much the same approach. One way, suggested by Mario Garcia, is to create an **L** shape for standing elements, leaving the remaining rectangle—almost the same size as a magazine front—for the page editor to worry about each week (Fig. 15–3). This plan has enough flexibility in it to create a number of different shapes that, with differing art, typography, and graphics, will look different every day.

Critics of this approach may worry about form taking precedence over content, but that is not meant to be the case here. Form, however, is important. If

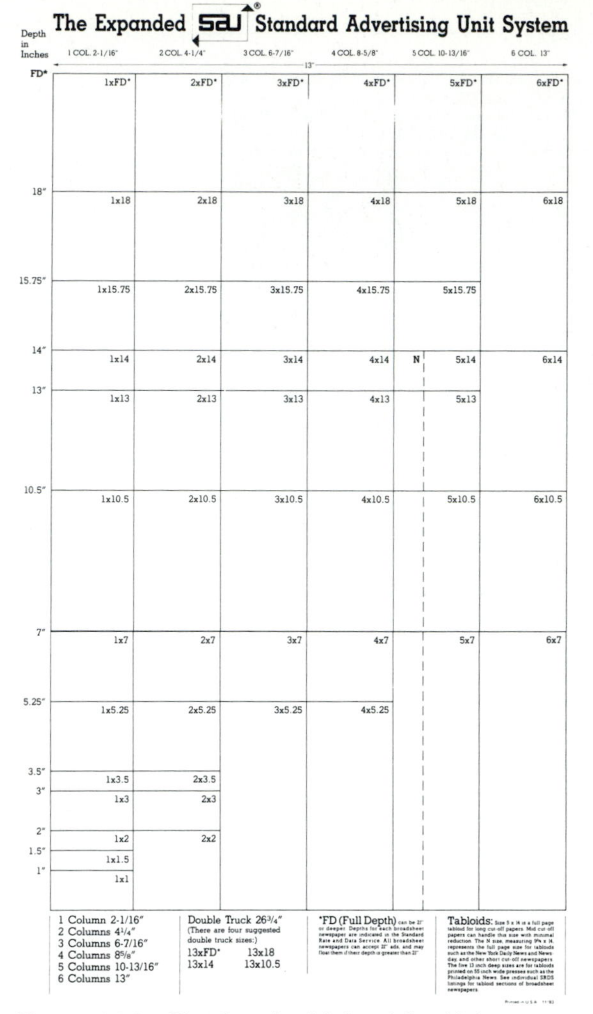

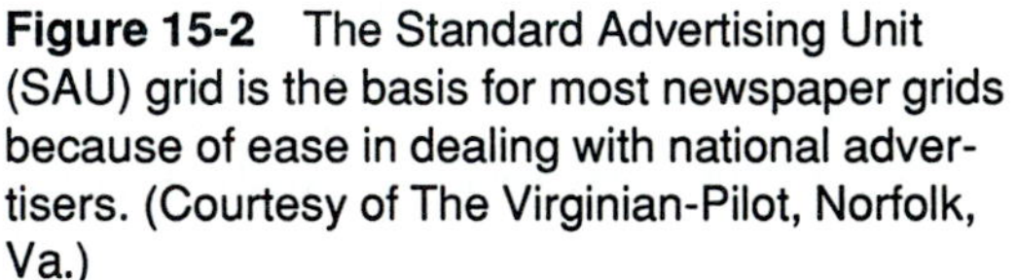

Figure 15-2 The Standard Advertising Unit (SAU) grid is the basis for most newspaper grids because of ease in dealing with national advertisers. (Courtesy of The Virginian-Pilot, Norfolk, Va.)

the underlying shapes of the elements are pleasing, the layout has a better chance to work.

Naturally, if the news of the day calls for adjustments to the basic format, fine, as long as the changes follow the general premises of the format and grid designed for use by the paper.

On any page, it is important to mix both vertical and horizontal modules. Having only one or the other would be boring visually. Longer stories look better horizontally. A good plan then would be to run one or two shorter stories vertically to counterpoint your longer, horizontal stories.

Section front design in the early 1980s moved toward the domain of the artist. The pages that won the most design awards looked as much like posters as newspaper pages, and critics of the trend began to use "poster page" as a derisive term.

Research has indeed shown that readers can only "look at" about two-thirds of a broadsheet page at a time, even though they can "see" the entire page. It makes more sense then to give over no more than two-thirds of a page to a special spread.

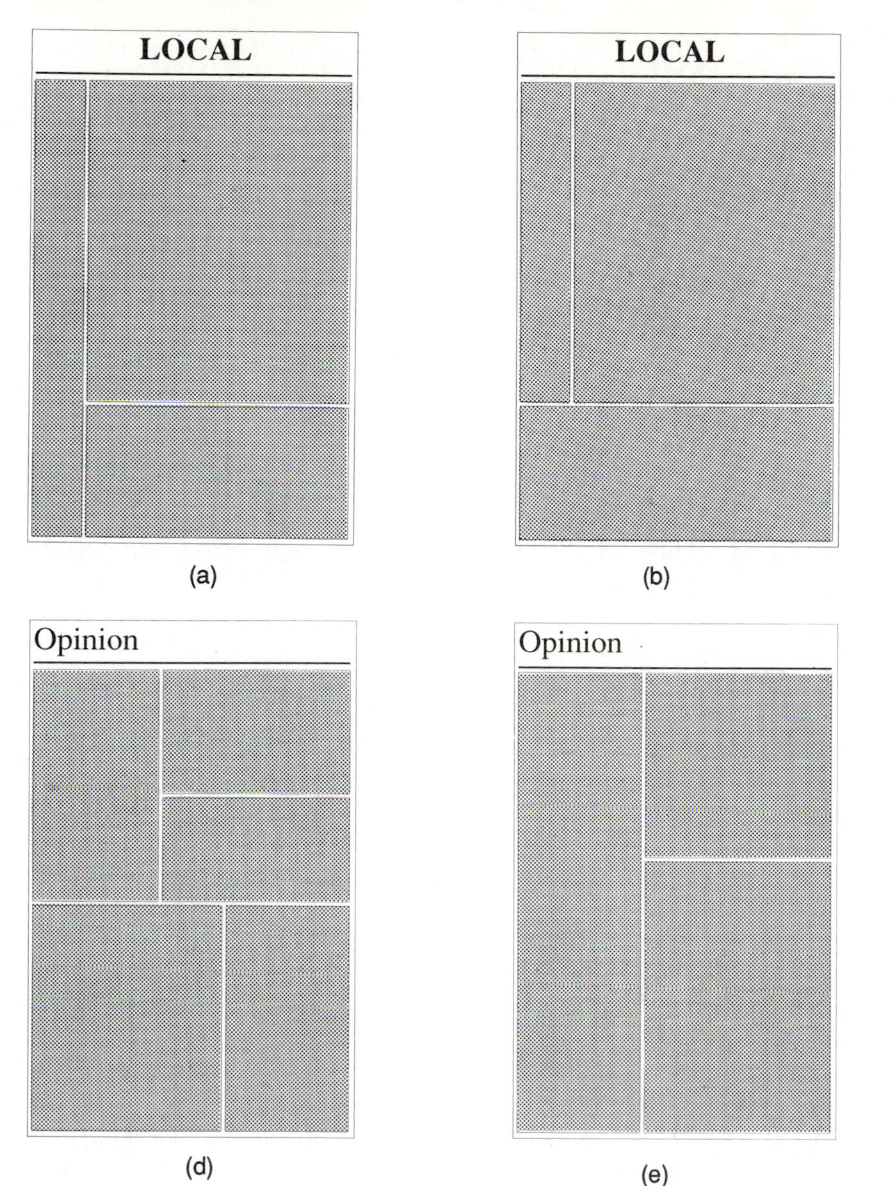

Figure 15-3 By setting up a number of different basic shapes for a section front, leaving only a magazine-sized "cover" for a special treatment, editors can concentrate on creativity each issue and not on reinventing the wheel. Besides, readers *like* features anchored in the same place each issue. These basic formats for content can be used as templates or simply as a starting point for ideas.

Sometimes the award winners also tend to be pages with two pieces of headline type, one jazzy initial letter, two grafs of body type to a jump, a larger-than-life-size photo of an artichoke on a silver platter, and a pullout box on "Ten Ways the Rich and Famous Eat Artichokes."

These pages can be enormously attractive, and I applaud the artistic talent it takes to conceive them and carry them out. But what if your readers don't care about artichokes? What else have you given them on their own silver platter of the information of the day? And would the spread lose all that much impact if it were reduced a bit so that a few other elements could appear on the page as well?

The Register-Guard

EDITORIALS

LETTERS OPINIONS

An Independent Newspaper

18A Eugene, Oregon, Sunday, April 12, 1987

Assessors need state help

Eugene's piece of 'pork'

LETTERS IN THE EDITOR'S MAILBAG

Pay for mistakes

Fresh still better

Respect all teachers

Park site questioned

Rates unfair now

James J. Kilpatrick

The 'staggit eve' and a cultural legacy lost

Figure 15-4 Editorial pages tend to use somewhat wider columns and differing typography to separate comment from the news. (©, The Register-Guard, 1987, Eugene, Ore., 1987)

Figure 15-5 Try for modular ad holes on a page. But when you must have a stairstep effect, use the edges of the stairs to create modules on the page. Then, within those modules, you can modify column measures and use other creative techniques.

Editorial pages call for yet a different approach, largely because of the different nature of the content. The important opinion function of American newspapers cries out for a different treatment, both typographically and with the grid itself.

Historically, most editorial pages have used a different column grid, usually four or five, for this reason. Also, the headline race or group on the page is often different from the rest of the paper (Fig. 15–4). Although the change in headline group is not necessary, changing at least to an italic version of your normal headletter is a good idea. Changing the grid to a five-column format is easiest to work with.

With a five-column format you can create a number of standard layouts you can rely on each day. Again, the content of the page may well call for a layout not suggested. As long as it follows the basic guidelines, fine.

Pages with ads fill most of a newspaper. But these pages are often given mere afterthought in a design plan. The sheer numbers of pages with ads should tell you that this is the wrong approach. If that won't, your advertisers might: They don't want your readers glossing over pages with ads because they have received scant attention.

Your highest goal on an inside page is probably to organize the content so that it is easily accessible. This means getting it into modular shapes, even if the ads themselves stairstep down the page (Fig. 15–5).

Better yet, persuade your advertising manager to go along with modern research that has shown that a well-designed ad *does not* have to touch editorial content to be seen. Thus, a modular ad hole, one that is in rectangular shape instead of stairstep, will help you lay out better-looking inside pages.

Whenever you can't do this, just try to get as close as you can. For instance, no leg of type should have fewer than six or seven lines of type in it. If an ad hole is shaped so that you have an awkward typographical situation such as this, just go ahead and allow a little dogleg anyway. An occasional dogleg is better than a forced module.

The rest of a newspaper—the miscellany of the classified ad section, the stocks, the weather, etc.—should follow the basic typography and design of the major portion of the paper. The main goal is to make these standing items easy to find and easy to read. The design doesn't have to wow people.

Remember that one of the important points of good design is *unity*. By designing in typographical unity for each section, subsection, and minor piece of your newspaper, you create that feeling of unity. Readers appreciate this. The typographical signposts guide them through the story.

TABLOIDS

Tabloid *news*papers can follow the same basic concepts mentioned above in the broadsheet section. Tabloid-sized entertainment, or other nonnews, publications can follow somewhat different rules.

Tabloid newspapers also have an SAU format that they can follow. A standard grid, with different column measure options, should be set up as part of an overall design plan. The editorial page also should have a different grid from the rest of the paper.

Certain pages, including the front, can and probably should have a series of suggested layout shapes planned. The basic **L** shape can be used, although a tabloid page is not big enough for more than three elements, and one or two is probably better for a section front (Fig. 15–6).

Large tabloid newspapers may have sections that run on for many pages. Broadsheet sections are actual sections within the paper. Tabloid sections are usually all inside one fold, although some newspapers do run several separate sections. With tabs, I like to see the use of "pagetopper" section logos that tie into the folio on each page. Run no larger than about 18-point, the pagetoppers can provide continuing identification of the section within the tabloid.

The tab has a centerspread in which the two pages are actually one sheet of paper. This part of the tab is an opportunity to overcome the limitations on your design that the smaller pages give. On this two-page spread alone you can run art, heads, even body type across the gutter without worry. The *Free Lance-Star* (Fredericksburg, Va.) gives the centerspread of its weekly tab "magazine" a special touch each week (Fig. 15–7).

Tabloid entertainment publications are a cross between a magazine and a newspaper. Because they are aimed at a different segment of the audience, they generally can depart from the more standard newspaper approach and lean toward magazines.

For instance, many have full photo covers, tables of contents, a section with the main stories of the week, and smaller front- and back-of-the-book columns and briefs—all common to magazines as well.

Business

Business Briefs

Old Colony names new management

Expanding to the government market

Businesses can increase revenue through public sector

Alexandria woman in Job Corps

Baker lands contract

A few purchasing agents in Alexandria

Preview

BEST BETS

'The Mission' solemn, noble failure

'Buckeye Barndance' mixes stage, live radio

Dance concert

Michael Cooney

Fruited plains

The latest business news begins on Page 19

Figure 15-6 An **L**-shaped structure (on the left, a reverse **L**) is a good way to approach a page. The main story appears in the largest module, with two thin modules, one horizontal and one vertical, filling out the page. The right-hand page shows excellent use of accessory type in the Best Bets column on the left, and of white space, by leaving that one corner blank. The page clearly is not a news page with this kind of treatment. (L, Courtesy of Dominion Newspapers, Inc.; R, © Dayton Daily News)

For that reason, a designer of this type of "newspaper" would do well to study magazine design as well as newspaper design (Fig. 15–8).

One final tabloid-sized publication should be mentioned: the corporation newspaper. Many corporations use a tabloid-sized publication for a more "newsy" approach (Fig. 15–9). These then are similar to a tabloid *news*paper, even though the writing may be more public-relations oriented than news writing.

Again, however, the same rules apply: Attention to the grid, to typography, and to basic shapes of modules on pages should be done ahead of time. Also, thought should be given as well to covering certain information visually.

Although the audience for this kind of publication is a little more captive than for a standard publication, the tactics of drawing readers to content are still important. Many corporate publications go unread because they have been put together with little thought given to how they look.

10 Saturday, June 11, 1988 — TOWN & COUNTY — THE FREE LANCE-STAR | THE FREE LANCE-STAR — TOWN & COUNTY — Saturday, June 11, 1988 11

WAR GAME

STORY AND PHOTOS BY JIM MANN

FORT CHAFFEE, Ark.—The sound of gunfire burst into the early morning hours.

Sgts. Lloyd Perkins of Stafford, Duane Bryant of Spotsylvania and Warren Hinman of Newport News were ready.

The tree-lined perimeter around Echo Company was under attack by the forces of Atlantica—a fictional Soviet-style country in Central America.

For a week, when they weren't on duty as helicopter crew chiefs for Echo Company of the Virginia Army National Guard, Perkins, Bryant and Hinman were reinforcing their bunker. The latest addition was flooring placed in the trenches where the three stood to fire their two M-60 machine guns.

"Our goal here is to stay alive—nothing more, nothing less," Bryant said. "That's why we have surrounded ourselves with what we need to stay alive."

Hinman was on watch when the firefight started at 2:25 a.m. Forty-five minutes later, half of the 26 aggressors had been "killed" in the Army's version of harmless laser tag to three casualties for the friendly forces.

This would be a rare victory for the National Guard units from Virginia and Maryland taking part in a 10-day mock conflict at the nation's new Joint Readiness Training Center at Fort Chaffee. The Guard troops made up a task force from the 29th Light Infantry Division, including four different elements—infantry, artillery, engineers and aviation. The infantry came from Maryland and the other elements from Virginia.

Company C of the 229th Engineer Battalion at Fredericksburg was among the support units for the 3rd Brigade ground troops from Maryland.

Perkins, 27, and Bryant, 25, who do auto repair work in civilian life, and Hinman, 30, a quality control supervisor at Newport News Shipbuilding, agreed the training offered a good look at what war might be like.

"It's been a positive experience, a learning experience for everyone" Perkins said. "Something we can all take away from here and know more about is our own personal capabilities and our unit's capabilities."

The Virginia and Maryland soldiers were the fifth group and the first National Guard troops to train

Please see War Game, page 13

Above: An Echo Company helicopter is loaded on a C5 Galaxy. The giant airplane can pack in five UH-1 helicopters as well as 78 soldiers on its upper passenger deck.
At right: Sgts. Warren Hinman, Duane Bryant and Lloyd Perkins outside their camouflaged machine gun bunker on the perimeter at Fort Chaffee, Ark.

Spec.4 Susan McDonald

Housewife, mother, crew chief

Susan McDonald is an attractive, blue-eyed, blonde. She is a housewife, mother and secretary at Fort Eustis.

She is also a part-time helicopter crew chief and door gunner with the Virginia Army National Guard.

"This is totally different — it's an escape from the everyday things that I do," McDonald said sitting next to her pup tent in the woods at Fort Chaffee, Ark. She was taking part in two weeks of annual training with Echo Company, one of the Virginia Guard's assault helicopter companies based in Richmond.

"I've got a 15-year-old daughter and it just amazes her that I do the things that I do, because her friends' mothers are settled down."

As a crew chief—she's Echo Company's only woman crew chief—McDonald is responsible for the daily maintenance of the UH-1 helicopter assigned to her. On combat training missions she serves as a door gunner firing one of two M-60 machine guns on the aircraft.

She said she thinks women can handle combat duty.

"For some women, it would work and for some women I know, it wouldn't work. The same way I know for a lot of men it wouldn't work."

The mock war at Fort Chaffee was "a good challenge," she said. "People pay money to go through this kind of adventure training."

Figure 15-7 The center spread of a tabloid should be used for a special feature because it is the only position in the publication where you have the ability to go across the fold on the same sheet of paper. (© The Free Lance-Star, Fredericksburg, Va.)

Calendar

WEEK OF JULY 22 - 28

This Week

COMIC BOOK AND SCIENCE FICTION CONVENTION, Holiday Inn: July 23, 10 a.m.-5 p.m. 1489 Jefferson Davis Highway, Rt. 1. $3 at door. For more information call 292-4587.

COLONIZATION LECTURERS, The Lyceum: Two noted authorities on colonization in the New World and in Africa will speak July 22 at 7:30 p.m. 201 S. Washington St. Free.

PAN AMERICAN FESTIVAL, Market Square: Bolivian theme. July 23, noon-6 p.m. 301 King St.

LIFEGUARD COMPETITION, Chinquapin Park Recreation Center: July 23, 6-10 p.m. 3210 King St. $35 per team of six, $2 for each additional. 931-1127

ART EXPO, The Village at Shirlington: 20 artist members of The Arlington Arts Center will display their works. July 23, 11 a.m.-4 p.m. South Quincy and South 28th Streets, Shirlington Exit off of I-395.

FAD FESTIVAL, Arlington: July 23. Ballston Mall, Level 1, Corner of Wilson Blvd. and Glebe Road. 243-8088.

STEP DANCING, Smithsonian: Demonstration on July 23, 7 p.m. Baird Auditorium, National Museum of Natural History (10th Street and Constitution Ave. N.W.) Tickets $10 members, $15 nonmembers.

BARBERSHOP QUARTETS, Fort Ward Park: Concert. July 28, 7:30 p.m. 4301 West Braddock Road. Free.

PAKISTAN FESTIVAL, Washington Monument Grounds: Cultural shows, music, foods and exhibits. July 24, 10:30 a.m.-9 p.m.

WASHINGTONIAN'S 10TH ANNIVERSARY "BEST AND WORST" PARTY, Capital Hilton Hotel July 27, 6:30-9 p.m. Presidential Ballroom, 16th and K Streets, N.W. $25 to benefit Juvenile Diabetes Foundation.

CARIBBEAN SUMMER IN THE PARK, President's Park: July 24, noon-8 p.m. 1500 Constitution Ave., N.W. 659-9100.

G.W.U. SWINGS, G.W.U. Marvin Center: Swing dance party night featuring hot jazz. July 27, 7:30-8:30 Dance Instruction, 8:30-? Swing Party. 3rd floor Continental Ballroom, 21st and H Streets, N.W. $7. 547-6419.

Performance

"ANNIE," West End Dinner Theatre: Through July 31 at 4615 Duke St. 370-2500.

MUSIC AT TWILIGHT CONCERTS, Fort Ward Park: Thursday evenings, 7:30 p.m. 4301 W. Braddock Road. Through July.

WATERFRONT PARK CONCERTS, Waterfront Park: Monday evenings, 7:30 p.m. Strand St. (between Prince and King). Through July.

U.S. MARINE BAND PERFORMANCE, U.S. Capitol Building: Summer Concert Series. Performance is free and no tickets are required. 8 p.m. For information call 433-4011.

COMMUNITIES IN CONCERT, Smithsonian: Sundays at 3 p.m. July 17-Aug. 28. Jacksonville Bandstand, West Lawn of the National Museum of American History. 357-2700.

"KISMET," The Little Theatre of Alexandria: A musical adapted from the works of Alexander Borodin. July 22-Aug. 13, Wed.-Sat., 8:30 p.m.; Sun. at 3 p.m. 600 Wolfe St. $8-$10. 683-0496.

"WENCESLAS SQUARE," Kennedy Center: A comic drama about a professor of theater. Terrace Theater. Through Aug. 6, 7:30 p.m. Tickets from $19 to $35. For information call 857-0900.

"THE KING OF THE INSTRUMENTS AND THE INSTRUMENT OF KINGS," Washington Cathedral: July 26, 8 p.m. Free 537-6200.

"LA CAGE AUX FOLLIES," The New Hayloft: Opened June 14, 8:30 p.m., Sun. 7 p.m. 10501 Balls Ford Rd., Manassas. Tickets $20-$31.

NAVY BAND, Navy Memorial: Country Current. July 23, 8 p.m. 8th & Pennsylvania Ave., N.W. Free.

See CALENDAR Page 24▸

SOUSA

The United States Marine Band, whose 17th director was the renowned John Philip Sousa, celebrates its 190th birthday this year. To enjoy free concerts by "The President's Own" band, see listings under Performance.

Friday, July 22, 1988 — Alexandria Gazette Packet • 23

Figure 15-8 This calendar section from a weekly newspaper looks more like a magazine. Bold type, narrower than usual columns, ragged right type, column rules, and an art/photo combination make this page stand out. (Courtesy of Dominion Newspapers, Inc.)

■ Special Edition on new Central Fidelity Bank Building

Central Fidelity News

SEPTEMBER 1987

Commitment

New headquarters makes major impact

The new Central Fidelity Bank Building shines brilliantly as the brightest evidence to our increased commitment to the Virginia market.

During the last few weeks, we have moved 350 employees into our new corporate headquarters located in the heart of Richmond's business and financial district.

Quality emphasized above all

Every feature of our building emphasizes quality—from the mahogany paneling, brass chandeliers and marble floors in our retail branch and commercial loan office on the first floor to the comfortable working spaces on each of the other nine floors; from the luxurious environment in the Retail Atrium that connects our building with the Omni Hotel and Three James Center to our art collection that beautifully depicts the state's many different landscapes.

The Central Fidelity Bank Building makes quite a statement.

"It makes *more* than a statement," says Carroll L. Saine, our Bank's Chairman of the Board and Chief Executive Officer. "This building represents a major financial commitment on our part to the state of Virginia. A new headquarters further indicates that we are committed to being a major, independent financial institution for Virginians."

Extensive coverage, publicity

Because of that commitment and our move into the new headquarters, many publications have prominently featured Central Fidelity. One major newspaper, on the cover of its weekly business magazine, reported that all Virginia banks were moving—but while others were busily moving across state lines, we were moving across town to increase our level of service here at home.

Another major newspaper also featured us on its business magazine's cover. In an interstate banking feature, it highlighted our concept of serving only Virginians.

"The Central Fidelity Bank Building is the most visible evidence of our philosophy to remain independent and stay solely in Virginia," Mr. Saine explains, "but it's certainly not the only evidence. Our aggressive branch expansion program and the Farm Fresh Project also represent sizeable commitments to those ends.

"We would not go to this expense and magnitude if we were not committed long-term to our Bank, to our shareholders, to our employees and to our customers. We still do not plan to participate in interstate banking and are not interested in attracting takeover offers.

"We're committed to being a Virginia-only bank; we ignore what others are doing and pursue our own course."

Future planning pays off

That course is now anchored by a new flagship that will be the hub of Richmond's business and financial district—both in terms of location and activity.

The Central Fidelity Bank Building contains a total of 340,000 square feet on its 22 floors. We will initially occupy approximately 165,000 square feet on the first 10 floors. All of our floors have been designed to meet each department's unique needs as well as possible future expansion. Our extensive use of mahogany, brass and marble has enabled us to combine the best of both the modern and traditional worlds.

Two years ago when we decided to build this new headquarters, we believed that the James Center would become "the place to be." Today, we're even more convinced of it and understand fully *why* it's the place to be.

All of the state's other major bank holding companies have corporate or

☐ See **Commitment**, page 4

AT A GLANCE

Some of the major advantages provided by our new corporate headquarters are:

- Locating in the heart of Richmond's business and financial district
- Making a positive statement concerning our commitment to Virginia
- Strengthening our stance as an independent financial institution
- Being close to major companies, financial analysts and key customers/prospects
- Having each floor designed to meet specific needs of individual departments

Central Fidelity presidents Lewis N. Miller, Jr. and William F. Shumadine, Jr. have led our Bank to the threshold of a new era at the Central Fidelity Bank Building, our new corporate headquarters.

Grand Opening Week schedule

The following is a tentative schedule of all the exciting events that will be held September 8–13 during Grand Opening Week at the Central Fidelity Bank Building, our new corporate headquarters:

Day	Time	Event
Tuesday, September 8 through Friday, September 11	11:30 a.m. – 1:30 p.m.	Entertainment in our plaza provided by local musicians, refreshments in lobby, scheduled tours
Monday, Sept. 8	11:30 a.m. – 1:30 p.m.	Walt Howell's Swing Sextet
Tuesday, Sept. 9	11:30 a.m. – 1:30 p.m.	Jazz Ladies
Wednesday, Sept. 10	11:30 a.m. – 1:30 p.m.	Secrets
Thursday, Sept. 11	11:30 a.m. – 1:30 p.m.	Continentals (Accompanied by Mariana's Ballroom Dancing Synchronized Exhibition)
Friday, September 11	6:00 p.m. – 8:00 p.m.	Prospective customer entertainment Music: Richmond Pops
Saturday, September 12	8:00 p.m. – midnight	Customer entertainment Music: Natalie Cole
Sunday, September 13	1:00 p.m. – 5:00 p.m.	Employee Day

Employee Day highlights week of exciting events

Since the Central Fidelity Bank Building is one of a kind, it's fitting that we do something unique to highlight the Grand Opening Week.

For the very first time, *every* employee is invited to attend one of our Bank's events. Employee Day will be held at our new corporate headquarters on Sunday, September 13, and everyone who works for our Bank can attend the festive celebration.

Culminates exciting week

Employee Day is the culmination of a highly exciting week of activities. Following the Labor Day holiday on Monday, September 7, we will provide many entertainment opportunities for a wide variety of guests.

Every day during the week, we will have local Richmond musicians performing in the beautiful plaza adjacent to our building. (See related schedule for more information.)

We will also serve refreshments in our first-floor lobby. Commercial loan officers and retail staff members of our James Center Branch will be provided with special business development packages to solicit new business.

Scheduled tours of our new headquarters, which is located in the center of Richmond's business and financial district, are available during the week. Ginny Lewis, Regional Marketing Coordinator for the Central Region, will head up this effort.

Beginning at 6:00 p.m. on Friday,

☐ See **Opening**, page 2

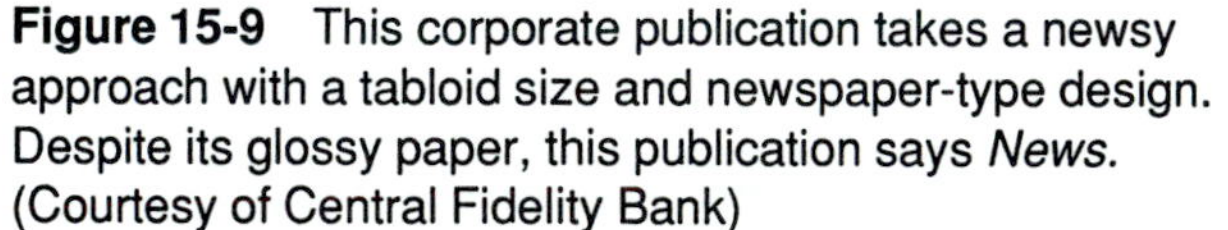

Figure 15-9 This corporate publication takes a newsy approach with a tabloid size and newspaper-type design. Despite its glossy paper, this publication says *News*. (Courtesy of Central Fidelity Bank)

INTEGRATED EDITING FOR NEWSPAPERS

Let's go ahead and list the two integrated editor's questions one last time and get it over with:

1. What is the best way to communicate this information? Is it visual?
2. Is there a visual element that can enhance this information?

These questions are the toughest for newspaper editors because they historically have not been concerned with the visual. For years, newspapers have been gray and the reader be damned.

Now that newspapers have to fight a little harder for those damnable readers, design has become something of concern.

First, newspaper reporters have to become visually literate. As they gather their stories on their beats, they need to bring in maps, charts, graphs, and anything else they can get their hands on. When they turn in their stories, the visuals should be turned in as well.

Another approach they could use would be to turn in with the story a suggested pullout or quoteout. The editor could do it, but because the reporter is closer to the story, it would be easier and quicker if the reporter would at least suggest the pullout. The editor could then decide to use it or not, and then edit if necessary.

Editors need to make assignments with visuals in mind as well.

Just as photographers at newspapers have become photojournalists, artists need to become art-journalists. Art alone will not fit in newspapers, but news presented in an artistic form will. The artist has to be able to recognize and present news before this trend toward more art will work.

Nearly any newspaper story can use an At-a-glance box. These can take many forms:

- checklist
- highlights
- background
- key players
- organization
- chronology
- briefly
- how to...
- looking ahead (or back)
- how this affects you, etc. (See also the list you may have created as an exercise earlier in this book.)

Naturally, all this is in the story as well, but integrated editing provides attractive presentations of facts-on-the-run for the reader in a hurry as well as the more in-depth coverage for those readers who want that.

These news summaries are useful tidbits of information and pleasing visual points on an otherwise gray page. If the goal of the newspaper editor is to communicate as many facts as possible to as many people in a short time, then integrated editing is the way to go.

CASE STUDY

Publication: *Salinas Californian,* Salinas, Calif. A Gannett newspaper. Circulation of 23,000 six days a week (p.m.). The paper won the "Best in Gannett" award for papers its size in 1988.

Editor: Dave Doucette. Responsible for total news product, including photography. A "Founding Editor" of *USA Today.*

Dave Doucette: One of the attractive aspects of the story idea was that it would make a good "Saturday" story. Because we have no Sunday paper, we like the Saturday paper to be salable all weekend. Soledad Street has been a part of Salinas for 50 to 60 years. Though many readers must have been aware of the history of the street, Salinas had grown so much we knew that many of the newer readers would not know about it. The reporter who suggested the story also had

Saturday morning

115 years serving Monterey County

Salinas Californian

Home edition

A Gannett Newspaper

SATURDAY MORNING, Dec. 13, 1986

Burglars take advantage of holiday opportunities

By Fred Alvarez

Soviet jet crash kills scores

TV-Time dates

Summary

A WALK ON THE WILD SIDE OF SALINAS

By night, Chinatown takes on an eerie glow. It's a primary hangout for addicts, alcoholics, prostitutes and pimps. As long as anyone in Salinas can remember, the city has wanted to clean up the area. But this time, the city is looking for a more permanent remedy.

Soledad Street: Diamond in the rough

By Mike Wennergren

In the daylight, the area seems less forbidding and supports City Manager William Carlson's notion that Chinatown could become colorful and prosperous.

Schools get caution flag on lottery fund spending

By Jeannine Guttman

PLASTIC JUNKIES

Credit cards can be a curse

Documents reveal arms dealer's high life

Saturday, Dec. 13, 1986 Salinas Californian 3A

Diamond

Continued from page 1A

Police decoys 'complicate' street action

By Mike Wennergren

A young woman in hot pants stands on a Soledad Street corner. Police decoys also patrol the street from time to time as an attempt to discourage "johns."

A shadowy figure walks along a dimly-lighted section of Soledad Street. City officials have wrestled for generations with the problem of trying to cleanup the area. Some see a potential for development and prosperity.

Figure 15-10 The weekend edition of the *Salinas Californian* tries to use a special story on the front page each week. This article about a notorious street in the city uses color photos. It jumps to a full ad-free page inside.

been talking to people in the city government who were really interested in cleaning up the area.

The story was brought up at one of our daily news meetings by the city editor, who had gotten it from the reporter. We decided to look at the city's plans to clean up the area, and we had the reporter and a photographer ride with the police one night.

Early on we knew that a map would be necessary. We wanted to show a closeup of the area as well. It's only a block long and it's an isolated street.

When did thoughts about the looks of the package begin? It pretty much came together right from the start. When we edited the color photos we decided the basic design of the front, with the day and night photos played the way you see them. I sized the color to fit the layout.

Why did you use a gray screen with the story? We used the gray screen to package the Soledad Street story, to pull the whole thing together on the page. We have the ability to run 5 percent screens for subtle tones. On the inside page, we devoted the entire page to the package, which included a jump, a map, a

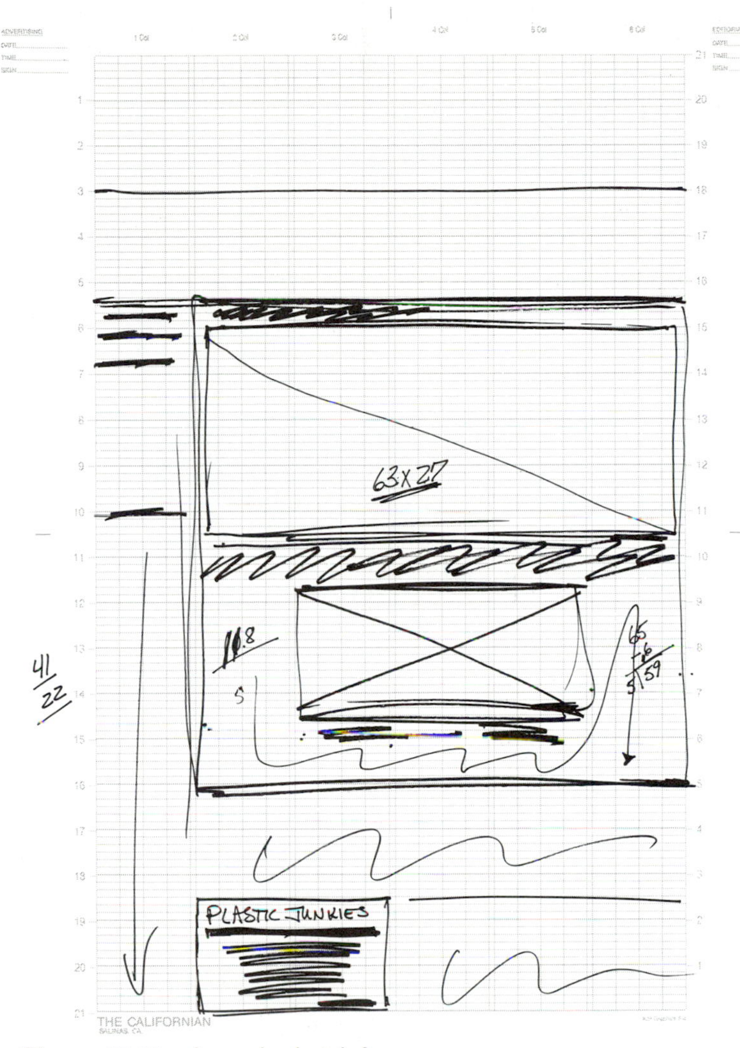

Figure 15-11 An early sketch for page one.

sidebar, and more photos. We used another gray screen to highlight the sidebar and to maintain continuity from the front page.

Why is the sidebar photo so large? The sidebar photo was played big in part because of the large amount of copy. And we just didn't think it should have a play any smaller.

The cutline in the bottom right corner leaves a lot of white space. Why did you position it there? My feeling is that white space at the top would have been trapped. If we had centered the cutline, the remaining white space would have no impact. A two-inch white space is better than two one-inch spaces.

When did the decision about the map occur, early or late in the process? We always knew we would use a map, with a larger map to locate the street. With this kind of story it is important to *show* readers the where, not merely tell them.

The jump page has a lot of copy with no breakers—subheads, initial letters, pullouts, etc. Why didn't you try to break up the gray? We decided not to use any of those for two reasons. First, we felt the story was good enough to keep readers interested without worrying about those typographical "extras." Second, we didn't want to take away from the dominant art.

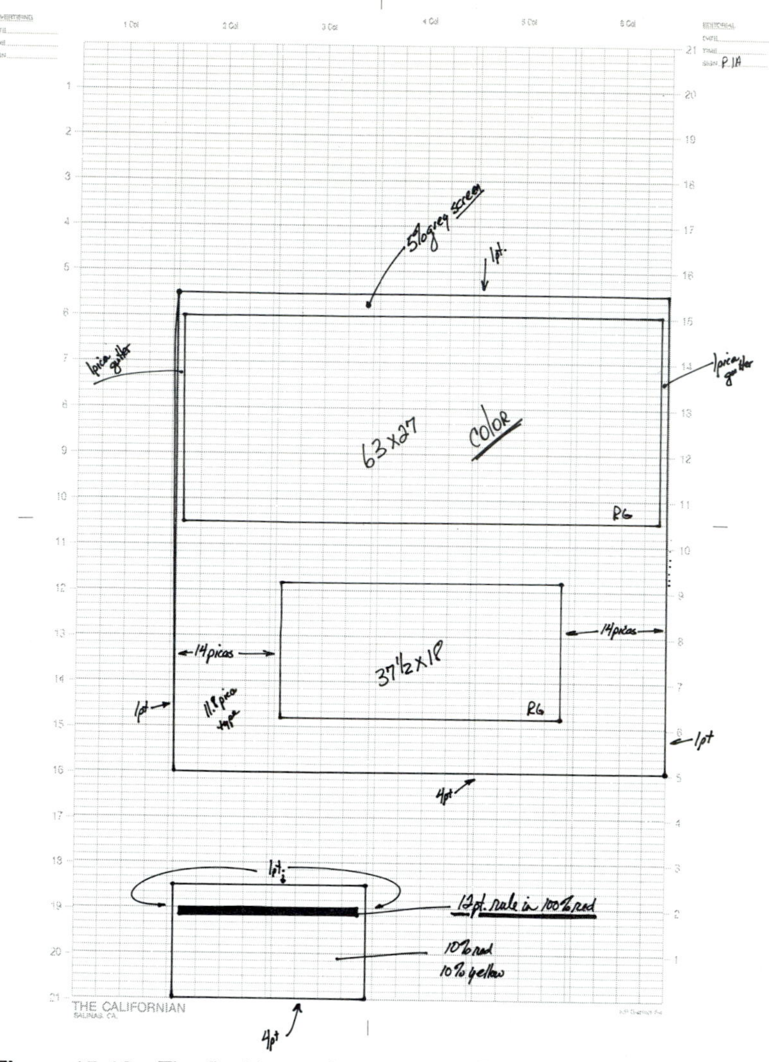

Figure 15-12 The final layout for page one. The exact dimensions are decided upon at this point so the color work, which must begin early, can be sized reliably for the final page.

My Analysis

The concept, the approach, and most of the results are basically good. The Soledad Street story is a terrific Saturday/(Sunday) story for the racks. The photos are good, as is the writing. I like the gray screen on the front-page package. The sidebar about a woman acting as a hooker decoy is good. I would have preferred a few changes, however.

First, I think the history of Soledad Street should have been outlined in some kind of sidebar or pullout; perhaps even an information graphic. Info graphics are a good way to inject context into a story. The lead mentions that Soledad Street has been a long-standing problem. Readers only can guess what that means. It's too easy sometimes to forget that many readers will not be aware of an event's history, though more in-touch editors are. Here was an opportunity to do something snappy visually with information, but it was missed.

The front page package is well-conceived, but I would like a few adjustments. First, although I understand the idea, I think the two photographs are too similar. They are meant to show a day-night contrast, but the contrast is not clear. Also, I think the legs of type under the smaller photo are simply too short.

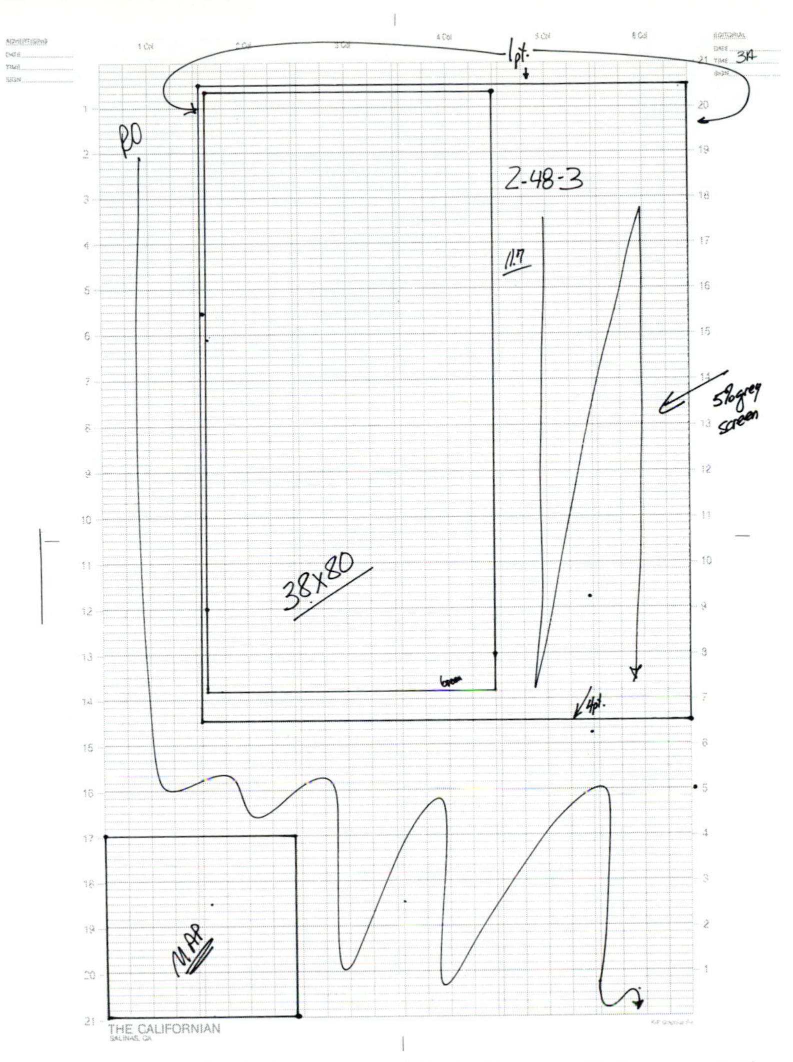

Figure 15-13 Original page layout for inside page. Notice on actual page that an additional photo appears in lower right. During last-minute editing, the story was shortened and the photo became necessary.

They get confused with the cutline type as well. As a baseline, try to get no fewer than six lines of type. If there were more lines of type here, the cutline would no doubt stand out better.

On the inside, the use of the gray screen to help visual continuation from the front is good. I would have preferred seeing it as a "wallpaper" effect to connect the entire package. It may be too easy at first glance to connect *only* the gray, which is the sidebar. Some overarching graphic element or logo might also have helped the reader see the entire page as the continuation.

I disagree with Dave's decision about the subheads. I would have liked them. They could have helped readers enter the story at different places. As it is, the body copy offers no visually appealing entry point.

Summary

This is exactly the kind of story and presentation that more small newspapers should be doing, but often are not. It's not that they can't, it's just that they *think*

Figure 15-14 Editor Dave Doucette, who laid out the spread, and photographer Richard Green work together in selecting photos.

Figure 15-15 Both the editor and photographer continue to monitor the progress of the spread as it goes through production. (All examples courtesy of the Salinas Californian, Salinas, Calif.)

they can't. That may be the difference between a good newspaper and a mediocre one. A good newspaper is willing to tackle big projects, to try new approaches, even if the result is not perfect. The *Salinas Californian* is a good small newspaper in large part because the editors and staff are willing to tackle projects such as this one.

CHECKLIST

1. Integrated editing provides you with a method to get information to readers fast. It can provide additional visual elements without the need for artists (through the use of typographical elements).
2. Integrated editing provides you with the best possible publication: the words honed to their sharpest, and attractive and information-packed visuals to tempt even the most recalcitrant reader.
3. Broadsheet newspaper pages are too large to be seen at a glance by a reader. Thus, creating full-page spreads may be counterproductive. Instead of informing the reader, the size and amount of information may turn readers away. Aim for one-half to two-thirds of a page for your largest packages.
4. Because of the speed at which newspapers are produced, the best place to get visual people involved is during the planning stage. Have the photo editor and the art editor involved in all planning and assigning sessions.
5. Design an **L**- or **U**-shaped format for a section front page. Then take some pages from a local newspaper that does not use this approach and redesign a few pages. Compare them. Ask some "average newspaper readers" what they think.
6. Take some particularly unattractive newspaper pages (they shouldn't be all that hard to find!) and do "blueprints" of them. A *blueprint* is a tracing of the outlines of the various modules on the page. Could you predict their final "ugliness" from the blueprint alone? Or are other factors involved? Redesign these pages and do blueprints again. Compare the blueprints. Decide which pages had the best "architects."

7. Take a particularly gray newspaper page and create some typographical visuals for it: quoteouts, at-a-glance boxes, etc. Carefully paste these in the proper places on a second copy of the same page. Is there a difference in the impact of the page? Have a disinterested other compare the two pages as well. Which one is preferred? Why?
8. Write to newspapers that you think are well-designed and ask them for a copy of their type and design style manual. These may be the best design reference materials you can get your hands on.

APPENDIX

A

Good editors, those who have mastered the "art of the second look," are hard to find. That is because good editors have to be specialist-generalists: They need to know a little about everything. They have to be able to correct misspellings and faulty grammar, spot weak logic, and fill gaps in stories that reporters didn't see. And they have to be able to do this quickly. It is a good thing they don't have to do all that with a smile on their faces as well!

As part of the word-editing portion of an editor's job, attention must be paid to the mechanics—spelling, punctuation, syntax, grammar, etc.—word choice, sentence length and order, story organization and length, style, and legal and ethical issues.

This appendix cannot attempt to address all the possible problems in the readers' knowledge of these subjects. But a quick review of the important points is in order.

SPELLING

Naturally, every word in your publication should be spelled correctly. Chances are, however, that the writers are not misspelling all those words on purpose: Somehow they believe they are correct. You don't look up words in the dictionary you (think you) know how to spell. . . . Good spellers may be born and not made, but if they are made, they're done so at an early age. Weak spellers must work hard to correct the problem.

The best action to take is to create a list of words you have problems with. Keep this list with you at all times for quick reference (this will be easy for some people—those whose list of troublesome words has already been compiled by Webster. . .). Add to it when a new one crops up. Go over the list frequently to imprint the proper spellings on your mind.

Many lists of commonly misspelled words are available. You could use one of these as a starting point, and add your personal problem words. For instance, I have trouble with *-ent* and *-ant* endings. I've gone around and around so many times that I no longer can tell right from wrong. So I no longer even try: I just look up every one.

If you are truly bad at spelling, you might get a "bad speller's dictionary." These books list words phonetically—for example, *phonetically* would be in the *Fs*. This is because sometimes bad spellers can't even find a word in the dictionary because their conception of its spelling is so far off base.

Some words that are often on these lists are (the incorrect version, and then the correct version are shown):

accomodate or accommadate instead of *accommodate*
innoculate instead of *inoculate*
lecturn instead of *lectern*
tenament instead of *tenement*
sacreligious instead of *sacrilegious*

Another common problem area lies with compound words. My advice to neophytes is that any time you see a word that could be (1) one word, (2) two words, or (3) a hyphenated word: *Look it up*. To make matters more complex, some journalistic style guides go against the spelling as suggested by a dictionary. In those cases, check the stylebook first and, if it's not there, the dictionary next.

For instance, *springtime:* one word, two, or hyphenated? (One word.) How about *merry-go-round?* (With hyphens.) Or *menswear?* (Associated Press Stylebook version; *Webster's New World Dictionary* says *men's wear* also is correct.)

If you watch out for problems such as these, and have a working list of troublesome words, your spelling is bound to get better.

PUNCTUATION

Nearly anyone who has pushed a blue pencil or a cursor around a story long enough to become an editor can handle most punctuation rules. Usually, the major problem is with commas.

Commas are not signals to readers to pause and inhale. The rules for their placement are based on meaning, not breathing.

The best book to turn to for punctuation—and for nearly anything else you want to know about good writing—is William Strunk, Jr. and E. B. White's *The Elements of Style*.

The biggest problems are:

Introductory Clauses or Phrases. Generally, use a comma if the introductory clause or phrase is longer than five words. Sometimes, depending on the sense, you may have to use a comma with fewer words.

If you find that the session is running longer than planned, send a message to the guard.
When the game ended he celebrated with a cigar.
If you call, the police will give you the address.

The first example is longer than five words, so a comma is called for. The second is shorter than five and creates no misunderstandings, so a comma is not needed. The last example is shorter than five words, but ambiguity could result, so the comma is necessary.

Nonrestrictive (also called nonessential) Clauses. Restrictive clauses, which usually begin with "who" or "that," *restrict* the meaning of the noun they modify.

> Students who are late will not be allowed to take the exam.

Here, "students" is restricted to *only those* who are late. "Who are late" is a *restrictive clause.* You could change that sentence to:

> Students, who are usually late, will not be allowed to take the exam.

Here, the clause ("who are usually late") merely adds information. It does not restrict the meaning of students to only a certain group. Therefore, it's *non-restrictive.* This sentence says that all students will not be allowed to take the exam. Nonrestrictive clauses usually begin with "who" or "which," and never "that."

Semicolon (here you go: one word, two, or hyphenated? These compound words are everywhere!). In long, complex sentences both major and minor breaks occur. For instance, you may have a series of independent clauses, each with commas within the clause. In this instance, the semicolons provide the major separations, the commas the minor.

> The U.S. flag is red, white, and blue; the Mexican flag is red, white, and green; and the Swiss flag is red and white.

Note that not all independent clauses must have commas for the sentence to need semicolons: Even only one requires the semicolon for all major breaks.

Agreement. Many common problems surround agreement of subjects and verbs and pronouns and their antecedents.

Most subject-verb problems occur with collective nouns and with indefinite pronouns. Collective nouns are words such as *team, committee, jury, board,* etc. In general, because the group of people act as a single body, these words take singular verbs: The jury has (not have) reached a verdict. Occasionally, because of meaning, the word will require a plural verb. When this occurs, a word such as "members" is often added: The team (members) *are* getting *their* uniforms cleaned.

Pronoun agreement problems often center around words known as indefinite pronouns: *everybody, nobody, no one, none, all,* etc. In general, these take *singular* verbs although, in a sense, the reference is to many people: Everybody should be sure to turn in his or her (not their) story on time.

The verb with *none* and *all* depends on the meaning: You would say "all of the money is gone," but you would say "all of the dollars are gone."

Word Choice. This is where the truly expert editor can shine. Any mechanic can fix fundamental problems, but when the errors get into the subtleties of choosing the proper word, only a true wordsmith can correct the error.

For instance, "expect" means simple assumption that something will occur: "anticipate," however, means that some action must be taken with the expectation. In other words, if you took an umbrella with you today, you did so anticipating rain, not expecting rain.

"Because" and "since" are two more words that have slightly different meanings. Because can be used with simple cause and effect. Since can be used in a causal sense, too, but the first action must directly and immediately precede the effect, and it must be an exact cause. Since is better when passage of time is involved.

For instance: Because I touched the paint before it had dried completely, the wall had to be done over. (Direct cause/effect). Since we had extra time when the concert ended early, we stopped for an ice cream cone. (Immediately preceding, and the time did not *cause* the ice cream stop).

Selecting the proper word in these situations is harder, but more important than it may seem. People who work with words must be able to use them as tools in even the most subtle ways. A surgeon doesn't use a machete when a scalpel is called for; a good editor shouldn't use "since" when "because" is needed.

Many good books have been published about the finer points of language. These are listed in the Bibliography. You would do well to read them all, buy several, and refer to them frequently.

Sentence Length and Order. A study by Professor Harry Stapler of the University of Florida found that the longest sentence in a sample of newspaper stories was the lead paragraph. The lead is supposed to be the pithiest and most compelling sentence of all, yet it turned out to be almost the opposite.

In general, sentences should be kept short. After 25 or 30 words, readers begin to get lost. Sentence length also should vary. Occasionally, long sentences are necessary, but they should be relieved by short sentences for emphasis. Think short. It will be hard to go wrong.

Style. The reasons behind adopting a "style guide" for a publication are widely known. Simply put, readers appreciate consistency in capitalization, abbreviation, punctuation, spelling, use of numerals, design and typography. A full discussion is not needed here. If you do not now use a style guide for both your writers and your designers and composition people, get one tomorrow. To wait longer is to cheat your readers.

APPROACH TO EDITING

If you nodded your head knowingly as you read through the above, most of your "tool" box as an editor should now be in order. Only a few tools are missing, and these will be discussed later. But now, let's look at how editors approach stories.

All editors must address certain issues and answer certain questions as they go over copy prior to publication. First, they must respect the writer's abilities and writing skills. The editor's job is to make the writer's story the best it can be, not change the story so it looks as if the editor wrote it.

Editors must also respect the readers. The readers are the reason for the communication in the first place. If their needs and desires are not kept in mind, then the communication may well fail.

Some of your readers will no doubt read nearly every word you print. Faithfully. Every issue. No matter how much or how it is displayed. Others are in too much of a hurry to do that, so they scan every issue, waiting for something to reach up from the page and grab them.

Or they tend to look for quick reads, for briefs and lists. They are information junkies, but they simply don't want to wade through a lot of words to get to the point. For them, you need to provide a different approach.

Ask yourself, "What do you want your readers to remember about this story a few hours after they have read it?" In other words, what's most important about the story? In mass communications writing, the reader's enjoyment of the writer's style is of secondary importance: The goal is *communication.* Be sure that the story clearly shows what is important.

This can be done in a number of ways, but the most obvious is to put the important information first, where even the quick scanner of the story will find it. The basic information also can be put into a summary box or "At A Glance" box of some sort. This is also popular with scanners.

Then be brief. The reporters' job is to tell stories as they see them. The editor's job is to double-check the reporters' judgment. Good reporters and editors see themselves as members of a team working for the reader. Good reporters don't complain about their writing being edited well; good editors don't butcher reporters' writing just to make it fit their personal style.

William Zinsser, in his book *On Writing Well,* notes that a good editor "brings to a piece of writing. . .an objective eye that the reporter has long since lost, and there is no end of ways in which an editor can improve a manuscript."

Let's look at a few of those ways. Ask of the story:

- Have all possible questions by readers been answered?
- Is the most important information highlighted?
- Is the story fair and accurate?
- Is it mechanically correct?
- Can the story be shorter and not lose necessary detail?

It is the editor's job to be critical. (And some seem born to the task.) Editors look over copy for both meaning and for length. Stories obviously have to be accurate in both fact and grammar, and they often have to be made shorter to fit in a particular issue.

A good way to do this is to make multiple reads of the story:

1. First, read the story through quickly, perhaps as a reader would read it. This gives you an overview before you start fixing the lead. Heck, the true lead for the story may be buried. Why spend time "fixing" the lead graf when 10 minutes later you will be cutting it and moving the 10th graf up to be the new lead?

2. Make sure all possible factual questions by readers have been answered. If not, get the reporter to clarify.

3. Is there a better way to tell this story, perhaps a visual one? Or, is there a visual aid that would help tell this story better? If so, your creative visual people will need to get started on it immediately.

4. Now reread the story more carefully. Check the lead. Does it accurately summarize the story? Or, if not a news-oriented story, does it grab readers and lead them into the body of the story?

Be skeptical. Look for errors of commission and of omission by the writer. What facts has the writer simply left out? What facts are in, but wrong or confusing? Did the writer miss an angle on the story that would make it more accurate, or even a better read? It is not yet necessary to fix every mechanical error at this point.

Get the *story* right first, then fix the writing.

5. How long is the story? Will it fit as is into this issue or does it need shortening?

If the tightening is minimal, you can probably take care of the excess by "boiling" the story—that is, by eliminating excess words. Even the best reporters sometimes use four words when three will do.

6. If minor trimming is needed, a good editor can remove certain portions of a story with the delicacy of a surgeon's scalpel. But let's face it: Sometimes only a chain saw can make the appropriate cuts.

Editors should not be afraid to make major cuts on a story, although a reporter should have a chance to look over the story once again. Perhaps it can be saved for a later issue if it indeed cannot be cut short enough to fit. Don't sacrifice meaning for length. A story should be as short as it can be and keep meaning intact. Nonetheless, most stories can be drastically shorter than they are written.

Keep the reader in mind. Reporters, and frequently editors, get so close to and excited about a story that they overestimate reader interest in the subject. Remember that it is the reader you are writing for, not yourself. Find that fine line between giving readers what *you* think they ought to be interested in and know, and what they actually would be interested in.

7. Now reread one more time and catch all the mechanical errors that the writer missed, that you may have missed earlier, or that you may have even edited in during earlier reads—something that happens embarrassingly often.

Carl Sessions Stepp of the University of Maryland lists six traps an editor can fall into (*Military Media Review,* July 1986). Avoid these:

- Editing without reading, instead of reading an article through before lifting a pencil or shifting a cursor.
- Going it alone, instead of working with the reporter as a team.
- Revising it yourself, instead of encouraging the reporter to make the necessary changes.
- Changing without consulting the reporter to find out why certain decisions were made or not made.
- Being tone deaf and missing the mood and rhythms of a story, instead of trying to work with the writer's style to make it better.
- Bogging down in the mechanics, instead of blending mechanical precision with an eye for larger issues like content and logic.

The best editors can—and should—improve every story they touch by making it clearer, more accurate, and tighter than the writer could. The best writers know this. Though they complain about the editing of their work—I think it's part of the job description to complain—good writers know that their work always can stand a little polishing.

SELECTED BIBLIOGRAPHY

BOOKS

ALLEN, WALLACE, and CARROLL, MICHAEL. *A Design for News.* Minneapolis: Minneapolis Tribune, 1981.

ARNOLD, EDMUND C. *Designing the Total Newspaper.* New York: Harper & Row, 1981.

BIEGELEISEN, J.I. *Handbook of Typefaces and Lettering for Artists Typographers, Letterers, Teachers and Students,* 4th ed. New York: Arco, 1982.

BOHLE, ROBERT. *From News to Newsprint: Producing a Student Newspaper.* New York: Prentice-Hall, 1984.

CARDAMONE, TOM. *Chart and Graph Preparation Skills.* New York: Van Nostrand Reinhold, 1981.

CRAIG, JAMES. *Designing with Type.* New York: Watson-Guptill, 1981.

———. *Phototypesetting: A Design Manual.* New York: Watson-Guptill, 1978.

———. *Production for the Graphic Designer.* New York: Watson-Guptill, 1974.

Creativity Illustrated: A Compendium of 1000 & 10 Sources and Resources for Illustration from Durer to Dover. Washington, D.C.: Council for Advancement and Support of Education, 1983.

DORN, RAYMOND, *Tabloid Design for the Organizational Press: A Compendium of Designs.* Chicago: Lawrence Ragan Communication, 1983.

EVANS, HAROLD. *Editing and Design: A Manual of English, Typography and Layout.* New York: Holt, Rinehart & Winston, 1972–1978.

———. *Pictures on a Page—Photojournalism and Picture Editing.* New York: Holt, Rinehart & Winston, 1978.

GARCHIK, MORTON. *Creative Visual Thinking: How to Think Up Ideas Fast.* New York: Art Direction, 1982.

GARCIA, MARIO. *Contemporary Newspaper Design: A Structural Approach* (2nd ed.) Englewood Cliffs, NJ: Prentice-Hall, 1987.

GRAY, BILL. *Studio Tips for Artists and Graphic Designers.* New York: Van Nostrand Reinhold, 1976.

———. *More Studio Tips for Artists and Graphic Designers.* New York: Van Nostrand Reinhold, 1978.

HOLMES, NIGEL. *Designer's Guide to Creating Charts and Diagrams.* New York: Watson-Guptill, 1984.

HURLBURT, ALLEN. *The Grid: A Modular System for the Design of Newspapers, Magazines and Books.* New York: Van Nostrand Reinhold, 1979.

———. *Layout: The Design of the Printed Page.* New York: Watson-Guptill, 1977.

HURLEY, GERALD D., and MCDOUGAL, ANGUS. *Visual Impact in Print.* Chicago: Visual Impact, 1975.

HUTT, ALLEN. *The Changing Newspaper: Typographic Trends in Britain and America, 1622–1972.* New York: Beil, 1973.

ITTEN, JOHANNES. *Design and Form: The Basic Course at the Bauhaus.* New York: Van Nostrand Reinhold, 1975.

———. *The Elements of Color.* New York: Van Nostrand Reinhold, 1986.

KERNS, ROBERT L. *Photojournalism: Photography with a Purpose.* Englewood Cliffs, NJ: Prentice-Hall, 1980.

MEGGS, PHILLIP. *History of Graphic Design.* New York: Van Nostrand Reinhold, 1983.

MOEN, DARYL. *Newspaper Layout and Design.* Ames: Iowa State University Press, 1984.

MORRISON, SEAN. *A Guide to Type.* Englewood Cliffs, NJ: Prentice-Hall, 1986.

NELSON, ROY PAUL. *Publication Design,* 4th ed. Dubuque, IA: Wm. C. Brown, 1983.

PATERSON, D.G., and TINKER, M.A. *How to Make Type Readable.* New York: Harper and Brothers, 1982.

Pocket Pal: A Graphic Arts Reproduction Handbook. New York: International Paper Co., 1985.

REHE, ROLF F. *Typography and Design for Newspapers.* IFRA. Indianapolis: Design Research International, 1985.

———. *Typography: How to Make it Most Legible.* Indianapolis: Design Research, 1974.

ROMANO, FRANK J. *The TypEncyclopedia.* New York: R.R. Bowker Co., 1984.

ROSEN, BEN. *Type and Typography: The Designer's Type Book,* rev. ed. New York: Van Nostrand Reinhold, 1976.

RUDER, EMIL. *Typographie.* New York: Hastings House, 1981.

SHARPE, DEBORAH T. *The Psychology of Color and Design.* Chicago: Nelson-Hall Co., 1974.

SOLOMON, MARTIN. *The Art of Typography.* New York: Watson-Guptill, 1986.

SOUTHWORTH, MILES. *Pocket Guide to Color Reproduction.* Livonia, NY: Graphic Arts Pub., 1979.

STEVENSON, GEORGE A. *Graphic Arts Encyclopedia.* New York: McGraw-Hill, 1979.

TINKER, M.A. *Legibility of Print.* Ames: Iowa State University Press

TUFTE, EDWARD R. *The Visual Display of Quantitative Information.* Cheshire, CT: Graphics Press, 1983.

WHITE, JAN V. *Editing by Design: Word and Picture Communication for Editors and Designers,* 2nd ed. New York: R.R. Bowker Co., 1982.

PERIODICALS

Advertising Age. 740 Rush St., Chicago, IL 60611.

Art Direction. 10 E. 39th St., New York, NY 10016.

Communication Arts. 410 Sherman Ave., Palo Alto, CA 94303.

Design: The Journal of the Society of Newspaper Design. The Newspaper Center, Box 17290, Dulles International Airport, Washington, D.C. 20041 (free with membership).

Folio. 125 Elm St., New Canaan, CT 06840

Graphic Arts Monthly. 666 Fifth Ave., New York, NY 10103.

Graphis. Graphis Press Corp., 107 Dufourstrasse, CH-8008. Zurich, Switzerland.

Print. 6400 Goldsboro Rd., Washington, D.C. 20034.

Step-By-Step Graphics, 6000 N. Forest Park Dr., P.O. Box 1901, Peoria, IL, 61656-1901.

Typeworld. 15 Oakridge Circle, Wilmington, MA 01887.

U&lc. 2 Hammarskjold Plaza, New York, NY 10017 (free from International Typeface Corp.).

GLOSSARY

accessory type: typeface different from body type style; used for all the "accessory" information items on the page, such as subheadlines, jump lines, refer lines, pullouts, etc.

ad: abbreviation for "advertisement."

add: an additional page after the first page of a story.

advance: a story written before an event takes place.

agate: five and one-half point type. Used in sports summaries and other tabular material.

alley: horizontal space between modules in a Swiss grid layout plan. Usually the same width as the vertical gutters. Space is a multiple of the line spacing figure for your body type.

all caps: headline or other editorial material in all uppercase letters.

armpit: unattractive layout pattern in which the story has both a long and a short column in the shape of upside-down L.

art: a photo, illustration, map, graph, chart, drawing.

ascender: portion of a letter that extends above the *x*-height, such as in *b, d, h.*

banner: headline, usually the largest on the page, that extends across the width of the page.

baseline: imaginary line along the base of capital letters in a line of type.

basement: bottom half of the front page.

blanket roller: in offset printing, the roller that takes the inked impression from the printing plate and transfers it to the paper.

body type: type used for stories in the newspaper.

boldface: a typeface with think strokes that make the letter darker in the paper. Occasionally used for typographical emphasis in a story or for an all-caps caption. Subheads are also usually set in boldface style.

box: a border around a story or photo.

broadsheet: full size, the size of standard newspapers, such as *The New York Times.*

budget: a listing of all editorial matter for a page (page budget) or an entire issue (master budget).

bullet: an oversized period that precedes items in a list, used for emphasis in design.

bumping heads: two heads that fall together on a page so that they may be read as one. Also called *tombstoning*.

by-line: the name of the writer of the story, usually at the top of the first column, but sometimes used elsewhere for design purposes.

camera ready: the final status of the flat when it is ready to be sent to the camera for a page negative to be made.

cap: short for "capital" letter.

caption: brief, descriptive information for a photo. Usually short and above, or leading into, the cutline.

catchline: larger type used with a cutline (also a *caption*). Catchlines can also be used above a photo, when it is an *overline.*

cathode ray tube (CRT): another term for a VDT.

classified advertising: ads run in small type in a separate section apart from the editorial content. Ads are *classified* into categories, such as homes for sale, autos, help wanted.

cold type: type set by a phototypesetter.

column inch: a measurement of advertisements and stories. A column inch is one column wide (whatever the column width) and one inch deep.

combination head: a headline that covers two related stories although each story has a drop or readout head.

composing room: area where a newspaper is pasted up.

contact sheet: *see* proof sheet.

copy: a story or article written for a newspaper.

copy block: a brief story accompanying a photo story or essay.

copy editor: a person whose primary job is to read copy for errors, write headlines, and lay out pages.

copy flow: the system in which a story moves from reporter through editor to the typesetter.

copy-read: another term for editing a story.

copyright: legal procedure for protecting a story or photo from use by others.

copy wrap: fitting lines of type around an irregular shape.

crop: eliminating unwanted areas from a photo or cutting a photo down to publication size.

cursive: type that has visually connecting lines, although lines do not actually touch.

cut: a hot-type term for a photo (thus *cut*lines).

cutline: explanatory material that runs with a photo, either beneath it or, in the case of some photo essays and stories, in a separate block.

cut-off rule: a border beneath a cutline to visually separate the photo from a story it does not illustrate.

CVI: center of visual impact, that place on the page that draws the first attention of the reader.

deck: a second, smaller headline beneath a larger main headline.

descender: portion of a letter that descends below the baseline, such as in *g, p, q*.

dingbat: a typographical gimmick, such as a bullet or a star. Often used before a jump headline.

display type: type larger than body type, usually 14 points and up, that is used to attract attention. Includes headlines.

double truck: the middle two pages of a paper, separated only by the fold. Often used for special spreads that display type or photos across the fold.

down style: a headline style that capitalizes only the first word in the headline and all proper nouns.

drop head: a smaller head beneath a combination head. Also called a *readout*.

drop out: a special effect on a photograph in which white letters of a head (or another second image) show in a black or dark area of the photo. The opposite of an *overprint,* in which black letters appear over a light area of the photo. *See also* reverse.

duotone: printing process in which a light and dark color are mixed to produce a third color. A "fake" duotone photo is one in which the colored ink is merely placed on top of the normal screened photo.

Dutch wrap: term used in newspaper design to describe a column of type that appears even with the top of a headline in an adjacent column, not underneath it. This practice used to be avoided, but modular layout often calls for just such a device to avoid bumping heads.

EDFAT: a photographer's system devised by Frank Hoy: acronym for *E*ntire (shoot some overall shots of scene), *D*etails (get some closeups, too), *F*rame (be sure to compose in the camera), *A*ngles (don't shoot everything from your own eye level), and *T*ime (vary shutter speeds as well as shoot at various times during the course of an event).

editorial page: page in paper that carries editorial comments, letters to the editor, the masthead, editorial cartoons, and so on.

em space: a space equal to the width of the letter M in a given alphabet, which is usually the same as the point size of the letter.

en space: one half an em space.

fit: an instruction to paste-up personnel to adjust the page as necessary to include the entire story.

flag: the name of the newspaper on page 1 (*see also* nameplate), and section names inside the paper. Also called logos.

flat: paste-up sheet.

flexography: a printing method using a resilient letterpress-type plate and water-borne ink (instead of the normal oil base). Very high quality method.

flush left: all material is aligned along the left margin.

flush right: all material is aligned along the right margin.

folio: small lines of type that include the page number and date of publication.

formal balance: balance achieved through duplication of design elements on both halves of a page; the halves are mirror-images of each other.

format: size and general design appearance of a newspaper.

four-color process: the process by which color photographs are reproduced in the paper. Four separate printing plates are used.

full frame: the photo print when the entire negative is reproduced.

full size: the size of standard newspapers, such as *The New York Times*. *See also* broadsheet.

galley: long column of type that is to be proofread.

gestalt: principles of visual perception or how the brain organizes visual stimulation into organized patterns. Important in cognitive psychology, but also important in design because the principles can guide the designer to coherent, *functional* patterns of information on a page.

golden mean or proportion: a ratio of .62 to 1 that represents the most pleasing visual proportion. It should be used whenever possible in page design and photo cropping.

graf: short for "paragraph."

gutter: the narrow strip of white space that separates columns of type on a page.

hairline: the narrowest size of border tape.

halftone: a continuous-tone photo that has been converted into a dot pattern to represent shades of gray in a printed photograph.

hammer head: the opposite of a kicker. A large head of only one or two words, with a longer and smaller headline underneath. Also called reverse kicker.

hanging indent: the indented lines following the flush-left first line of a multiline head.

headline: display type above or to the side of a story.

headline schedule: list of all heads used in the paper and the unit counts for various column widths.

horizontal layout: design technique that displays stories and story/photo combinations across the width of the page.

hot type: old typesetting method using hot lead and Linotype machines.

informal balance: a method of designing a page so that the two sides are balanced by means other than exact replication, as in *formal balance.*

information graphic: information presented largely as a picture or visual, rather than as words strung together in a sentence. Typical examples are bar and pie charts, tables, fever-line or time-series line, combinations of these, and even maps.

initial letter: a large display-type letter that starts off a paragraph. Initial letters may be set within the graf (usually taking up three lines of type), or they may stick up above the first line of type. Use them to break up long columns of type.

italic: true italics are different cuts of a roman typeface, a cut in which the letterforms "lean" to the right. Several of the letters themselves often take different shapes (e.g., a vs. *a*). Letters that are made simply to lean to the right, as with sans serif faces, are actually just "oblique" faces, not true italics.

kern: the removing of white space between letters to make them fit more tightly together, often even touching or overlapping. Many typefaces can be improved by kerning slightly.

kicker: a small headline used above a larger main headline.

label head: to be avoided—this is a head without a verb.

layout, lay out: (*n*) the design of a page; (*v*) the process of making a layout.

leading: the amount of white space between lines.

leading lines: lines within a photograph that force the eye to move in the direction the lines point. These lines should not lead the eye away from the story the photo illustrates or off the page. Also called *lines of force* or *gaze motion.*

letterpress: a method of printing in which the inked printing plate is literally pressed on the paper. The printing surface is raised.

light table: a paste-up table from which light shines. When a flat is placed over the translucent glass cover, the light shows whether a column of type has been pasted down properly.

line: one line of a multiline headline; 1/14 inch, a measurement used in place of column inches in national advertising.

line art, line shot: an illustration with no shades of gray, such as a cartoon. May be reproduced without screening.

line-spacing: same as *leading*.

lower-case: small, noncapital letters.

make-up: *layout* in hot-type printing method.

master budget: listing of all editorial material for an issue of the paper.

masthead: box listing the publisher, editors, and other staff members that appears nearly always on the editorial page. Sometimes called staff box. Some magazines call their flag a masthead.

measure: term referring to the horizontal length of a line of type.

modular layout: page-design system in which all elements on the page fit into rectangular modules.

mortice: area removed from a photograph so another photo or copy block can fit into the space.

mug: a face or a head-and-shoulders shot of a person.

nameplate: the name of the paper and other information that goes with it on page 1.

news hole: the space left in the paper after the ads have been dummied onto the pages.

news peg: a news event that an issue, feature story, or editorial is tied to.

offset: a printing method of higher quality than letterpress in which the printing plate transfers an image to a blanket roller and from the roller to the paper.

op-ed: means Opposite Editorial. A page opposite the editorial page devoted to opinions from staff members and members of the public.

optical weight: the relative ability of a design element to draw the reader's eye. Dark or unusually shaped elements have heavier optical weights than light or usual elements.

overlay: clear acetate or tracing tissue laid over the page on which material to be overprinted is pasted up or drawn in.

overline: a headline above a stand-alone or wild photo.

overprint: a second printing impression directly on top of the first.

page budget: listing of all editorial material on a page.

page dummy: a scaled-down "map" of a page used by an editor to lay out the paper.

page proof: a copy of the page used in checking the pasted-up flat for errors.

pagination: a computer-based system of laying out a page inside a computer terminal.

paste-up, paste up: (*n*) the page with all material positioned in place; (*v*) the process of positioning ads, copy, and such on the final page.

photo credit: name of the photographer who shot a photograph.

photo editor: person in charge of photo staff, photo flow, and photo-filing systems.

photo mechanical transfer: PMT for short, another term for producing a halftone.

photo release: form used by photographers for persons in photos not taken at a news event. It gives the photographer and publication the right to print the photo.

phototypesetting: sometimes called cold type, this method of setting type involves light and light-sensitive paper.

pica: 1/6-inch printing measurement.

play: prominence in either placement or size of a story or photo.

point: 1/72-inch printing measurement.

process color: standard ink colors used in four-color printing process (cyan, magenta, yellow, black).

proofread: make corrections on a galley of type.

proof sheet: unenlarged prints directly from negative. Also called *contact sheet.*

proportional scale: device used to calculate dimensions of a photo for enlargement or reduction.

pullout: generic term for information pulled from within a story and used in display type as a quote, checklist, etc.

quoteout: term sometimes used for a quote pullout. Sometimes called a *call quote.*

ragged right: unjustified type set flush left.

readout: second, smaller head beneath a combination head.

refer lines: pronounced "reefer," this means a reference, usually set in the accessory typeface and given a different graphic display, to a related story, photo, or graphic elsewhere in the publication.

registration marks: usually crosses within circles that line up multiple printings from different plates.

reverse: *see* drop out.

reverse kicker: *see* hammer head.

rim: outside of U-shaped copy desk where stories are edited and headlines written. Term not used much anymore because VDTs have made the shape of copy desk of no concern.

roman: type with thick-and-thin strokes and serifs.

rule: line that separates columns of type or surrounds a design element to make a *box.* Made with a roll of border tape in photocomposition.

rule of thirds: concept in photography that the center of interest should fall on one of the lines that divides a photo into thirds, not in the exact center.

sans serif: type with no serifs.

SAU: Standard Advertising Units. Standard sizes for ads to minimize problems advertisers have because of varying column widths of papers across the country.

screen: a process that makes shades of gray from black ink by using various dot patterns.

script: type with connecting lines between letters, like handwriting.

serif: small decorative finishing stroke off the main stroke of a letter.

set solid: type set with leading the same size as the point size of the type.

shotgun head: *see* combination.

sidebar: a story, usually with a feature approach, that accompanies another story.

size: to enlarge or reduce a photo for reproduction in the newspaper. Also called scale.

skyline: head at top of the page that runs the width of the page.

slot: person who sits inside U-shaped copy desk, edits, assigns heads to be written to rim persons, and lays out pages. Term not used much anymore.

spot color: one or more additional colors besides black used for special design effects.

square serif: type with rectangular serifs. Also called slab serif.

stand-alone photo: photo that does not illustrate or accompany a story. Also called a feature photo, wild photo.

standing head: used over or within a regular column in every issue.

stet: copy-editing instruction meaning "let it stand."

streamer: *see* banner.

strip in: printing process in which halftone negatives are taped into place on the page negative. *Windows* are used on the flat instead of *veloxes.*

subhead: a boldface line of type used to break up columns of gray and introduce subsections of a story.

Swiss grid: a highly structured and formal layout system using a grid divided into not only regular vertical columns but also into regular horizontal spaces. Elements are fitted into the modules on this grid following certain rigid rules. In the hands of a knowledgeable person it can lead to systematic and creative layouts.

tabloid: newspaper format that is half the size of a standard broadsheet page, as in *Rolling Stone, The Sporting News.*

tear sheet: a page cut out of the paper and mailed to an advertiser as proof of publication.

30: symbol meaning the end. Also, #.

tombstone heads: *see* bumping heads.

type font: the alphabet, numbers, and symbols in one typeface. Also used to mean an entire negative of alphabets for a phototypesetter.

typo: typographical error, either by reporter or typesetter.

typographical contrast: use of different characteristics of typefaces—e.g., bold vs. light, caps vs. U&lc, roman vs. italic, etc.—to differentiate content on a page. Adds visual interest while helping reader through the information.

unit count: method of counting headline length.

unjustified type: type with ragged edges, rather than automatic spacing to have each line of type end at the same place. See also *ragged right.*

up style: headline in which all words are capped.

velox: screened version of a photo that is pasted down on the page. Also called *PMT,* for photo mechanical transfer.

video display terminal (VDT): a keyboard and "television" screen hooked to a computer that reporters, editors, and designers use to put the paper together.

web press: a press that uses a continuous roll of paper rather than individual sheets.

weight: *see* optical weight.

widow: a short line of type at the top of a column.

wild photo: *see* stand-alone photo.

x-height: height of lower-case letters, excluding ascenders and descenders.

INDEX